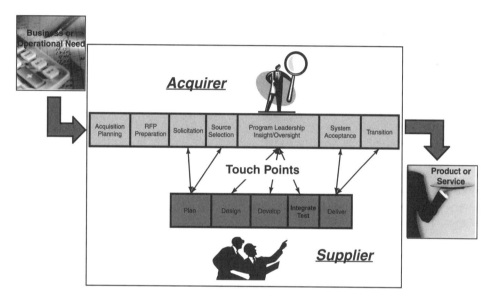

Source: Adapted from Software Engineering Institute, Acquisition Overview Course Material, 2004.

The acquisition process context

Praise for *CMMI® for Outsourcing*

General Motors has played a key role in driving the development of the CMMI® for Acquisition model [CMMI-ACQ], a detailed process improvement framework that helps organizations gain efficiency in their interactions with IT providers. *CMMI® for Outsourcing* provides practical, real-world examples that will help everyone from senior executives to front-line IT professionals work more effectively with the model and use it to deliver valuable benefits to their own organizations. IT providers also will benefit, by learning how to leverage the CMMI® model to provide more robust and efficient support to their customers.

> —*Ralph Szygenda, Group Vice President and Chief Information Officer,*
> *General Motors Corporation*

Strategic outsourcing is part of the new reality in many large enterprises. This book represents an essential guide to navigating the rapids of working with potential partners, understanding and managing your objectives, and quantifying the results in these most critical relationships.

> —*Rick Fricchione, Vice President, Enterprise Application Services,*
> *Hewlett-Packard Company*

After years of frenzied outsourcing, one fact is clear—low-maturity customers cannot take full advantage of high-maturity suppliers. The CMMI-ACQ offers the best guidance currently available for improving the client-side processes necessary to work effectively with high-maturity suppliers. Companies that integrate their acquisition processes seamlessly with the business processes of high-maturity suppliers will gain strong financial and performance advantages over their competitors.

> —*Dr. Bill Curtis, Chief Process Officer, McAfee Corporation*

CMMI® for Outsourcing focuses on a critical new component in the value equation for the outsourcing of software applications—the maturity of the target organization. By focusing on improvment, CMMI organizations can find savings and increase value by as much as 50% or more. The authors have done the industry a great service by illuminating this critical topic.

> —*Mark J. Bilger, Vice President and General Manager,*
> *EDS Global Applications Delivery*

The CMMI-ACQ offers the potential for intangible benefits that may be realized through efficiencies gained in applying engineering discipline and consistency to the acquisition process.

—Kristen Baldwin, Assistant Deputy Director for Software Engineering and System Assurance, U.S. Department of Defense

Everyone in business understands that outsourcing is the reality of today's global marketplace. But knowing what is required and knowing how to get it done are not synonymous. GM's efforts with Wipro, their other Tier-1 suppliers, and the SEI are groundbreaking in developing an approach to building high-quality software systems in the global multi-supplier reality that we live in. This book on CMMI outsourcing provides an excellent understanding of how to actually obtain the benefits of multi-supplier outsourcing while allowing each party to retain the benefits of their own individual standardized processes.

—Geoffrey Phillips, Vice President of Strategic Engagements, Wipro Technologies

The CMMI-ACQ delivers solid practices to those who manage and conduct product-based acquisition projects. Thank you GM and the SEI. You've forged an acquisition model that helps major programs and projects, in and out of Government, while remembering the small organizations.

—Charles Niles, Software Manager, NASA

As I've talked with companies about their outsourcing practices in the United States, Denmark, China, Japan, Australia, Singapore, and elsewhere, they've always wanted to know what other companies do and how those practices and measures work. Thanks to my work with GM, it's been possible to use GM's IS&S as an example, describing what worked well (as well as what didn't work). Now that the best practices have been gathered into the CMMI-ACQ, it's easy to refer those with questions to a more complete source than I can provide when handling the questions that immediately come to their minds. This will be an incredibly valuable resource to the industry, and we're all grateful to see it available.

—Dr. Joyce Statz, Vice President, Borland Software Corporation

CMMI® for Outsourcing

Carnegie Mellon
Software Engineering Institute

The SEI Series in Software Engineering represents a collaboration between the Software Engineering Institute of Carnegie Mellon University and Addison-Wesley to develop and publish a body of work on selected topics in software engineering. The common goal of the SEI and Addison-Wesley is to provide the most current software engineering information in a form that is easily usable by practitioners and students.

For more information point your browser to www.awprofessional.com/seiseries

Dennis M. Ahern, et al., *CMMI® SCAMPI Distilled.* ISBN: 0-321-22876-6

Dennis M. Ahern, et al., *CMMI® Distilled, Second Edition.* ISBN: 0-321-18613-3

Christopher Alberts and Audrey Dorofee, *Managing Information Security Risks.* ISBN: 0-321-11886-3

Len Bass, et al., *Software Architecture in Practice, Second Edition.* ISBN: 0-321-15495-9

Marilyn Bush and Donna Dunaway, *CMMI® Assessments.* ISBN: 0-321-17935-8

Carnegie Mellon University, Software Engineering Institute, *The Capability Maturity Model.* ISBN: 0-201-54664-7

Mary Beth Chrissis, et al., *CMMI®, Second Edition.* ISBN: 0-321-27967-0

Paul Clements, et al., *Documenting Software Architectures.* ISBN: 0-201-70372-6

Paul Clements, et al., *Evaluating Software Architectures.* ISBN: 0-201-70482-X

Paul Clements and Linda Northrop, *Software Product Lines.* ISBN: 0-201-70332-7

Bill Curtis, et al., *The People Capability Maturity Model®.* ISBN: 0-201-60445-0

William A. Florac and Anita D. Carleton, *Measuring the Software Process.* ISBN: 0-201-60444-2

Suzanne Garcia and Richard Turner, *CMMI® Survival Guide.* ISBN: 0-321-42277-5

Hassan Gomaa, *Software Design Methods for Concurrent and Real-Time Systems.* ISBN: 0-201-52577-1

Elaine M. Hall, *Managing Risk.* ISBN: 0-201-25592-8

Hubert F. Hofmann, et al., *CMMI® for Outsourcing.* ISBN: 0-321-47717-0

Watts S. Humphrey, *Managing Technical People.* ISBN: 0-201-54597-7

Watts S. Humphrey, *Introduction to the Personal Software Process^{SM}.* ISBN: 0-201-54809-7

Watts S. Humphrey, *Managing the Software Process.* ISBN: 0-201-18095-2

Watts S. Humphrey, *A Discipline for Software Engineering.* ISBN: 0-201-54610-8

Watts S. Humphrey, *Introduction to the Team Software Process^{SM}.* ISBN: 0-201-47719-X

Watts S. Humphrey, *Winning with Software.* ISBN: 0-201-77639-1

Watts S. Humphrey, *PSP^{SM}: A Self-Improvement Process for Software Engineers.* ISBN: 0-321-30549-3

Watts S. Humphrey, *TSP^{SM}—Leading a Development Team.* ISBN: 0-321-34962-8

Watts S. Humphrey, *TSP^{SM}—Coaching Development Teams.* ISBN: 0-201-73113-4

Daniel J. Paulish, *Architecture-Centric Software Project Management.* ISBN: 0-201-73409-5

Robert C. Seacord, *Secure Coding in C and C++.* ISBN: 0-321-33572-4

Richard D. Stutzke, *Estimating Software-Intensive Systems.* ISBN: 0-201-70312-2

Sami Zahran, *Software Process Improvement.* ISBN: 0-201-17782-X

CMMI® for Outsourcing

Guidelines for Software, Systems, and IT Acquisition

Hubert F. Hofmann
Deborah K. Yedlin
John W. Mishler
Susan Kushner

✦✦ Addison-Wesley

Upper Saddle River, NJ • Boston • Indianapolis • San Francisco
New York • Toronto • Montreal • London • Munich • Paris • Madrid
Capetown • Sydney • Tokyo • Singapore • Mexico City

This Book Is Safari Enabled

The Safari® Enabled icon on the cover of your favorite technology book means the book is available through Safari Bookshelf. When you buy this book, you get free access to the online edition for 45 days.

Safari Bookshelf is an electronic reference library that lets you easily search thousands of technical books, find code samples, download chapters, and access technical information whenever and wherever you need it.

To gain 45-day Safari Enabled access to this book:

• Go to http://www.awprofessional.com/safarienabled
• Complete the brief registration form
• Enter the coupon code VRG5-AD3I-BWKG-S5IJ-ELJZ

If you have difficulty registering on Safari Bookshelf or accessing the online edition, please e-mail customer-service@safaribooksonline.com.

Library of Congress Cataloging-in-Publication Data
   CMMI for outsourcing guidelines for software, systems, and IT acquisition / Hubert F. Hofmann.
      p. cm. — (The SEI series in software engineering)
   Includes bibliographical references and index.
   ISBN 0-321-47717-0 (hardback : alk. paper)
      1. apability maturity model (Computer software)   2. Software engineering.   3. Contracting out.
I. Hofmann, Hubert F.

   QA76.758.C558 2007
   005.1068'5—dc22   2006100749

ISBN 0-321-47717-0
Text printed in the United States on recycled paper at Courier in Westford, Massachusetts.
First printing, March 2007

"Make everything as simple as possible, but not simpler."

Albert Einstein

Contents

Foreword

Set the Scope, Focus the Team, and Deliver Value

When relying on outside suppliers to provide technology solutions, responsibility falls squarely on the acquiring party to define a reasonable set of project expectations, keep the development and operational stakeholders focused on the endgame, and successfully transition newly delivered systems and capabilities into operational use. Government and commercial organizations who depend on suppliers for critical systems continue to find themselves facing cost overruns, schedule breaches, depleted capability or worse, no capability delivered to their users. We must do better. Our obligation as acquisition or outsourcing professionals is to provide our customers with evolutionary (sometimes revolutionary), cutting-edge capabilities that are aligned with business and mission objectives—and to do it in a way that success is commonplace, not the exception. In addition to improving their own capability, acquirers play an important role in establishing incentives for good practice while working with their suppliers. The acquirer's leadership and vision are vital in ensuring the appropriate emphasis is placed on process and product quality within the value chain. This book, along with the CMMI-ACQ, was written to address these and many other acquisition issues. By following the guidance contained in each, you'll be able to build an organic acquisition capability that will position your organization to successfully set the scope of engagements with suppliers, keep suppliers and in-house users focused on a common picture of success, and deliver capabilities that will position your organization as a leader in your market or mission for years to come.

Brian Gallagher
Director, Acquisition Program
Software Engineering Institute
Carnegie Mellon University

Preface

What does it mean to successfully outsource software, systems, and information technology (IT)? Successful acquirer organizations use best practices to execute outsourcing projects that are completed on time and within budget, and these projects result in a product that meets the organization's business needs or mission. In addition, the product is of acceptable quality and meets the needs of customers or end users.

When you apply an outsourcing business strategy, it can improve your organization's operational efficiency by leveraging a supplier's capabilities to deliver quality solutions rapidly, at lower cost. With globalization, suppliers in developing countries can offer a highly skilled workforce at significantly lower labor rates, forcing organizations to leverage low-cost providers if they want to compete in the global marketplace. Companies also use outsourcing to gain a competitive advantage, creating value for the business customer and ultimately for the consumer.

Many organizations, both commercial and governmental, are becoming acquirers of software, systems, and IT. In both worlds, companies acquire systems, software, and IT that they cannot build or maintain themselves, especially within the required time frame. The constant pressure to deliver systems that meet cost, schedule, and quality objectives drives government program offices to contract with suppliers. Virtually all U.S. civil agencies and armed forces acquire systems. Often, the product to be delivered is unlike anything that has ever been built or even conceived of. In this case, acquiring the system externally allows the agency or company to evaluate various ideas about product design, implementation, and maintenance. Market forces require companies and government agencies to evaluate internal and external options for system development and make practical business decisions about whether to develop or acquire.

What factors are critical to these decisions? What processes should be followed? And once the decision is made to acquire, what are the necessary processes that help ensure a reasonable level of success in acquiring that system?

The Purpose of This Book

The purpose of this book is to help answer these questions and illustrate some of the processes and practices of successful acquirers. It is also intended to capture some of the challenges associated with acquisition projects. This book addresses acquiring organizations' need for information about how to effectively outsource software, systems, and IT in the current global marketplace.

Our intent in writing this book is to provide all organizations, whether in industry or in government, a pragmatic resource that captures some of the proven practices to make the acquisition of technology solutions successful and to guide process improvement efforts. By reading this book, those working in acquiring organizations will better understand the environment in which they are working, the challenges they face, and the processes, standards, and frameworks that can help them achieve success.

Who Should Read This Book?

This book is not intended to be simply an explanation of the initial draft CMMI for Acquisition (CMMI-ACQ). Rather, it is intended to help business leaders—from CEOs to project managers—tap in to the power of the "outsourcing movement" that has transformed the development of systems for some of the world's most successful companies. Reading this book will help decision makers become informed about the challenges of outsourcing technology solutions and will provide them with information about options available to guide their decisions and monitor their organizations' progress. It will help suppliers understand what is required of them to work well with acquiring organizations.

The Organization of This Book

This book contains five chapters, the order of which loosely corresponds to the phases of an acquisition life cycle for a project or program.

- Chapter 1, Introduction to the CMMI-ACQ, sets the stage with a series of "hidden truths" of successful acquisition projects. Some of these truths may not be hidden from you, depending on your acquisition experience.

But all are valuable to IT acquirers. This chapter also describes the characters that appear throughout the book. As you follow them through an IT acquisition project in the chapters that follow, you will experience the challenges and learn, along with them, the best practices and ideas for acquiring software, systems, and information technology solutions.

• Chapter 2, Getting Started, discusses how to formulate an acquisition strategy and align your strategy with your organization goals. This chapter also presents a framework for acquiring solutions. It describes outsourcing activities, with a focus on acquisition planning, writing requests for proposals (RFPs), handling supplier responses, negotiating, creating standard contracts, and collaborating with suppliers.

• Chapter 3, Engineering Solutions, explains how to get requirements right. It also describes how an acquirer translates requirements into practical design constraints that can be documented or referenced by the supplier agreement; in this way, the supplier can produce value-added technology solutions.

• Chapter 4, Delivering Solutions, outlines how to execute projects using integrated project plans and standards for measurement. You will learn how to manage uncertainty and risk, how to transition to operations, and how to implement ongoing maintenance and support.

• Chapter 5, Accelerating Acquisition Improvement, describes how to continuously improve acquisition processes and become a catalyst for change within an organization.

Finally, the Appendix, Overview of CMMI-ACQ, presents the six key process areas that are specific to acquisition organizations as well as the process areas common to all CMMI models.

Background and History

Capability Maturity Models (CMMs) were developed by the Carnegie Mellon Software Engineering Institute (SEI) to support a number of specific disciplines. The SEI acknowledged the need for organizations to leverage multiple models, so the government, industry, and the SEI embarked on an integration project to bring the various independent models into an integrated framework to support process improvement throughout the company or enterprise. The Capability Maturity Model Integration (CMMI) Framework that emerged from this integration initiative was designed to allow for future integration of other models, such as those covering development, acquisition, and services.

In 2005, General Motors Corporation teamed up with the SEI to help adapt CMMI to reflect the acquisition of technology solutions, and together the two organizations have published an initial draft version of the CMMI-ACQ. To develop this book and the CMMI-ACQ, we interviewed more than 250 executives, program managers, team members from government agencies, commercial companies, and their respective suppliers over the course of three years.

Acknowledgments

The research for this book started some five years ago. Hence, our gratitude has broad reach. Old friends and colleagues, along with new colleagues from various disciplines, have provided invaluable assistance through their constructive criticism and creative suggestions.

The central themes of this book have their roots in the practices of leading companies and government agencies that acquire systems, software, and IT, as well as leading suppliers of technology solutions. Although these organizations remain unnamed, we are deeply indebted to them for inspiring us to think in new and ever-evolving ways about acquiring technology solutions.

Many of the ideas and stories in this book have emerged from informal discussions. We would particularly like to thank Lloyd Anderson, Jon Bartol, Larry Casteel, Richard Cook, Frank DeArmas, Kathryn Dodson, Mike Edelman, Brian Gallagher, Corey Glickman, Theresa Hofmann, Kathy Keljo, Pam Kneeland, Jeff Liedel, Eric Litt, Earl Long, Bob Lowe, Nancy Malak, John Marano, Chris Mero, Tim McLachlan, Arne Moths, Chuck Niles, Paul Okoniewski, Mike Petit, Geoffrey Phillips, Vaughn Reid, Karen Richter, Roy Richter, Lynda Rosa, Bill Stout, Jeff Strohschein, Michael Terrett, and Mark Thompson.

Many talented people were involved in developing the initial draft CMMI for Acquisition (CMMI-ACQ); more than 150 individuals from more than 40 companies and government agencies helped collect the practices of the CMMI-ACQ and review it. We would like to especially thank Kathryn Dodson and Gowri Ramani for their dedication, perseverance, and insights as part of the author team to develop the CMMI-ACQ. We would also like to thank Roger Bate, the Software Engineering Institute's CMMI chief architect, for his leadership of the CMMI architecture group and for finding a way to a lean CMMI-ACQ. We would also like to thank Joe Elm of the SEI's Acquisition Support Program for insights shared from his development and teaching of the SEI's Software Acquisition Survival Skills Course and his early participation in and thoughtful critiques of this work. Brian Gallagher, SEI's director of the Acquisition Support Program, has also been very supportive of this work.

None of this would have been possible without the vision and support from Mark Schaeffer, Kristen Baldwin, and the NDIA, as sponsors for the CMMI-ACQ, and Ralph Szygenda, CIO of General Motors, who acted as the industry champion and made it possible to incorporate General Motors' innovative practices for outsourcing information technology.

A special thanks goes to Addison-Wesley publishing partner Peter Gordon for believing in this book from day one and his continued support and ideas that helped shape the content of this book. We would like to thank Betsy Hardinger for waving her magic wand over our manuscript to make our stories come to life and help our ideas shine through her insights, suggestions, and pragmatic approach. We would also like to thank the reviewers of earlier versions of this manuscript, especially Rich Turner for his idea to use a "chat" style to highlight the acquisition stories in this book.

Hubert Hofmann: Most importantly, I want to thank my family for their love and support during this book project. My deepest thanks go to my wife, Theresa, for arranging our lives to accommodate this whole project, for her countless ideas that have found their way into this book, and for the encouraging comments that have made this a better book.

Debbie Yedlin: Many thanks to my family, especially Andrew and Rebecca, who have never wavered in their support of my interests in the technology field, and in particular this project. I also want to thank Hubert Hofmann and John Mishler for their collaboration efforts and exchange of ideas, and Susan Kushner for her tireless dedication to make this a valuable reading experience for acquisition practitioners.

John Mishler: Thanks to my wife, Jullie and my daughter, Libby, for their support, love, and understanding and especially for the time they "shared" with this effort. I would like to dedicate my portion of this work to them and to the memory of my mother, Elizabeth Jane Hadfield Mishler.

Susan Kushner: Thank you to my family, who offered their support, consolation, and leftovers while I worked on this project. Thank you to my friends for understanding why I needed to spend weekends outside the social circle. Finally, many thanks to my colleagues at the SEI who offered their advice and guidance, especially Brian Gallagher, Mike Phillips, and Sandy Shrum.

Hubert F. Hofmann
Debbie Yedlin
John Mishler
Susan Kushner

Chapter 1

Introduction
to the CMMI-ACQ

A *model* is a representation of a complex entity or process. It can describe the details of a larger object, or it can be a schematic description of a system. A model can capture phenomena so that they can be analyzed and studied.

The value of a model is in its abstractions, and through these abstractions it simplifies what may be a complex reality. It is important, then, to be able to take a model, along with all its associated abstractions, and compare it to reality. In this way, you can use the model pragmatically to study phenomena and validate hypotheses. In the case of capability maturity models, you can compare your organization's acquisition processes to the standard model and determine how your practices differ from the model. You can also determine what you need to do in order to achieve a complete, executable, repeatable set of acquisition processes.

Many people find it difficult to apply CMMI (Capability Maturity Model Integration) efficiently and effectively in practice. The challenge of using CMMI, or any model, is in its interpretation. With CMMI you first define a process area, goal, or practice, and then you determine how to align these model components with processes, goals, and practices in your own acquisition environment. This book is written for those who are interested in improving their practices for acquiring technology solutions. If you have embarked on applying a model like CMMI to improve your project execution and organizational performance, you may be challenged because your organization still behaves like a developer of technology solutions rather than an acquirer.

It is not our intent to walk you though the CMMI for Acquisition (CMMI-ACQ) and explain what each goal, process, and practice might mean. (See the Appendix for a summary of the initial draft of CMMI-ACQ.) Rather, this book is intended to be a practical guide that gives you insights in applying the CMMI-ACQ. We describe the key areas of focus for an acquirer and address some of the challenges you will surely face.

1.1 What Is CMMI-ACQ?

CMMI is a collection of best practices that helps organizations improve their processes. It was initially developed by a team from industry, the U.S. government, and the Software Engineering Institute (SEI). CMMI is designed for application to process improvement in the development of products and services, covering the entire product life cycle from conceptualization through maintenance and disposal.

Following the success of the CMMI for development organizations, the group identified the need for a CMMI model to address the acquisition environment. This need was reinforced and gained further attention because of similar needs expressed by General Motors (GM), which acquires information technology (IT) solutions. In accord with GM's strategy, GM projects first develop requirements and design constraints and then oversee multiple suppliers, which develop IT solutions to be deployed in GM's business units. This approach parallels the acquisition processes used in many government organizations.

In both government and industry, acquirers must take overall accountability for solution delivery, allowing the supplier to perform the tasks necessary to develop and maintain the solution. Unfortunately, many organizations have not invested in the resources that are needed to effectively manage acquisition projects. Often, acquirers disengage from the project after the supplier is hired. Then they discover, too late, that the project is not on schedule, the selected technology is not viable, and the project has failed.

An acquirer has a focused set of major objectives. To deliver the requirements of the ultimate IT users and the acquisition sponsors, the acquirer must maintain relationships with them. In addition, the acquirer defines the needed scope and execution direction to deliver the technology solution through its relationship with the supplier (via the supplier agreement) and the acquirer's own supplier management activities. The acquirer owns the project, executes overall project management, and is accountable for delivering solutions.

You will find many maturity models, standards, methodologies, and guidelines that can help your organization improve the way it does business. However, most of these approaches focus on a specific part of the organization and do not offer a systemic approach to the problems that most organizations face. By focusing on improving one area of a business, these models unfortunately have perpetuated the stovepipes and barriers that exist in organizations.

The CMMI-ACQ contains 16 *core process areas* that cover project management, process management, and support processes. In addition, six process areas unique to acquisitions are included. These six process areas address unique acquisition practices, including development of solicitation and supplier agreements, acquisition management, development of acquisition requirements, development and verification of design constraints for technical solutions, acquisition validation, and acquisition verification.

The practices in all process areas focus on the activities of acquirers. Those activities include supplier sourcing, developing and awarding contracts (supplier agreements), and managing acquisition of solutions that include products and services. Supplier activities are not addressed in this document.

For suppliers, CMMI for Development (CMMI-DEV) can be treated as a reference model for developing technological solutions and products and services.

When your activities are focused either on the acquirer or on the interaction with the supplier, practices that are essential for executing acquisition processes are performed differently or with differing roles. These differences are apparent in monitoring, directing, or overseeing a supplier, which occur after you have selected a supplier or authorized a supplier to begin work.

1.2 The Structure of This Book

To bridge the gap between the CMMI-ACQ and its practical application, this book includes five characters who appear throughout the book. They are members of two fictitious acquirer and supplier organizations. Each chapter includes stories that engage these characters as they work through important areas of focus. The chapters are ordered to roughly reflect a project life cycle, and the stories describe the insights, pitfalls, and tips and tricks we've gathered over the past decade from commercial and government organizations that outsource work, as well as the suppliers that provide technology to these organizations.

We begin with the early phase of the acquisition life cycle—acquisition planning—and then proceed through subsequent phases as the acquisition project progresses. Along the way, you will meet the characters who make up the integrated team using outsourcing to work on a series of projects. The discussions are mainly focused on the acquirer.

This chapter introduces the characters and describes how the book is structured. Chapter 2, Getting Started, discusses how to formulate an acquisition strategy and align it with the organization's goals. That chapter presents a framework for acquiring solutions and describes outsourcing activities, with a focus on acquisition planning, writing requests for proposals (RFPs), handling supplier responses, conducting negotiation, creating standard contracts, and collaborating with suppliers.

Chapter 3, Engineering Solutions, explains how to get requirements right. It also shows how you translate requirements into practical design constraints that can be documented or referenced in the supplier agreement so that the supplier can produce value-added technology solutions. Chapter 4, Delivering Solutions, outlines how to execute projects that include integrated project plans, standards for measurement, uncertainty and risk, transition to operations, and maintenance and support.

Chapter 5, Accelerating Acquisition Improvement, describes how to continuously improve acquisition processes and become a catalyst for cultural change within an organization. The appendix, Overview of CMMI-ACQ, presents the six key process areas that are specific to acquisition organizations as well as the process areas common to all CMMI models. All these processes areas are vital to an acquirer's success.

1.3 Our Team: Recruiting the Project Manager

The characters that appear throughout this book are named Matt Vauban, Steve Reiter, George Taylor, Kristin Wells, and Paula Ressel. We created these character descriptions to capture the generic characteristics of individuals who typically apply CMMI-ACQ within an organization to improve the processes of their outsourcing engagements with suppliers.

As the story begins, Matt, a senior executive, has just been given what could be one of the most significant assignments of his career, from both a growth perspective and a career enhancement perspective. He has been asked by the executive board to salvage an outsourcing engagement that has not been successful for the organization. The first order of business is to assemble the acquisition team. Matt starts with a key position, the lead project manager. He is fortunate to have Steve Reiter, a superior candidate, in the organization. The only challenge is to persuade Steve that this is a viable initiative that can be turned around.

Matt also knows that he needs to have the best of the supplier's staff on board to make this partnership work. The organization has made it clear to the supplier that only their best, most qualified individuals will be acceptable if the engagement is to be salvaged. The supplier pulls its best troubleshooting individuals, Kristin Wells and George Taylor, for the project. Matt and Steve join forces to make sure that Kristin and George have the "right stuff." And finally, Matt needs to recruit a solid customer representative, and he finds that person in Paula Ressel.

As Matt drives to work, he sees the sun rising over Lake Michigan in the distance. He reflects on his career—where he's been and where he's going. Matt is the lead member of an elite team that has been hand-picked to troubleshoot a major assignment for his company: outsourcing a large portion of IT development to a group of suppliers. Matt has been preparing for this kind of opportunity his entire career. Right out of college, he worked as a programmer for a small software company. That was well before the dot-com boom. Even though he learned a great deal about developing software and he knew how many defects could be introduced when developers were tired and overworked, Matt found it difficult to survive on the unsatisfactory salary and the demanding hours. He soon realized that if he wanted to move up the corporate ladder in a high-tech organization on the management side of the house, he'd have to go back to school and get his MBA. The MBA was his ticket to bigger and better things, and Matt soon landed a job managing a development team and delivering software to the mass market.

Matt is a quiet guy who works and leads by example. If he asks a staff member to work beyond normal hours and spend time away from family, then he is right there with his sleeves rolled up, working alongside his staff to make sure that the job gets done and his employees go home.

As he turns the corner to drive into the parking lot, his only concern about his latest assignment is the team. Will he be in a position to assemble the "right" people so that he can get up to speed quickly to meet all the challenges? His boss has assured him that the composition of the team is the least of the challenges that lie ahead, but Matt knows that the team selection is key. He has scheduled interviews for the core team members, starting today.

Outsourcing has been attempted in this company in the recent past, an effort led by executives who had a short-term vision about cutting costs and a longer-term vision about using cost cutting to reach the next rung on the corporate ladder. Matt knows that he is walking into a highly visible situation. Others have failed or have conveniently moved on, and he doesn't want to become a casualty of a program that carries the stigma of failure. He knows instinctively that he needs to go back to basics. What are the key processes to execute with suppliers? How can he mitigate risk that he can't necessarily see or predict? Who will be his allies within the company? And how can he get his suppliers to a place where a true partnership is central to the development and deployment of systems using outsourcing?

Steve Reiter, a senior project manager, is Matt's first interview of the day. Steve has just completed a project management assignment that he really enjoyed. The project had to do with building self-service capability for the human resources department. The capabilities that he was able to deliver to the organization were, in a word, awesome. Everyone—from the senior executive of human resources to Steve's business counterparts in human resources—is congratulating Steve on a job well done, including requirements gathering, the design (which used a new Web technology), and a flawless launch. Steve has really showcased what a development team can do in a company.

Now Steve is between projects and looking for his next opportunity, and Matt hopes Steve will join him in this visible, high-potential initiative. Matt has already briefly explained to Steve what he is looking for: a strong project manager from within the company who will be vocal about and able to develop and implement key processes to partner with suppliers and effectively execute projects as an acquirer of technology solutions.

For his part, Steve is a six sigma black belt, experienced in process improvement, and he has 15 years of experience in project management. He knows he can take on this assignment, but he isn't sure that it is necessarily career-enhancing or desirable. The feedback in the organization indicates that this outsourcing activity might be the beginning of the end for any internal development teams and will usher in a management model that could make his teams' services obsolete. Steve doesn't like the idea of working on an initiative that has the potential of putting others out of a job. He is also concerned about the various development teams that he has worked with in the company. Are they at risk, or is the verbalized official position that was communicated around outsourcing real—that individuals who are involved in development internally have been given other opportunities to become part of the new order? Steve wants to ask Matt this question at the interview today. And with their positive professional relationship in the past, he is sure that he will get an honest answer.

As Steve walks into Matt's office, Matt congratulates him again on the success of the human resources project. After working with Matt on a number of initiatives, Steve knows that Matt's praise is sincere, because Matt is very careful to reinforce positive feedback and give praise for exceptional achievements. As Matt sits down and invites Steve to sit in an adjacent chair, he begins to describe the purpose of the meeting and what he is looking for from Steve.

> **Matt:** So, Steve, I asked you to come in today to talk very honestly about the new position I have open. I'm sure you want to know how it ties to our outsourcing model. I'd like to understand what you've heard about the company's experiences with outsourcing to date—because our experience has not been stellar, as you know. I'd also like to understand how you think you can help us make the right changes to our working model with suppliers to make this outsourcing approach work.

Matt stops at this point to give Steve the floor and let him share what he has heard about the job, outsourcing, and any other topics that might be on his mind.

> **Steve:** Well, to be honest, Matt, when you left me the voice mail inviting me to interview for this position, I have to say I had mixed feelings about it. I mean, there are rumors in the company that we're going to replace all of our software architects and developers with management folks who know nothing about building software, and hiring a bunch of suppliers who understand technology but know nothing about our business.

> **Matt:** Okay, that's good to know. Please go on.

> **Steve:** I've gotten mixed feedback about outsourcing. The suppliers like it because the contracts tend to be bigger, but the project managers who are trying to manage suppliers have run into some significant challenges. I know you've been asked to make this model work, but I'm concerned that success will be dependent on some serious efforts to define and implement the processes and practices that we need to perform versus what we are asking our suppliers to do. The last thing we

all want to do is to duplicate work with the supplier or lose control over the technology work that we ask the suppliers to do. This is really a paradigm shift for how we need to work!

Matt wants to make sure that he is very direct in responding to Steve's concerns.

Matt: Steve, as you know, management has every intention of repositioning staff and retraining for open positions if resources aren't needed in the development area. I have personally seen this under way, and I feel comfortable that this direction will continue. But I also want to make it clear that our ability to use suppliers has a direct impact on the bottom line and will help keep the company competitive. So our work with suppliers is not a part of a model that we can try as an experiment, and then, if it fails or is just too hard, toss it aside and go back to the way things used to be. This is an approach to systems development that we really have to figure out. And I'm looking to talent like you to step up and make this work for our organization.

Steve nods in agreement and feels comfortable that his reservations about the job have been addressed.

Matt then poses his next question. It's not only an interview question but also tests whether Steve has the "right stuff," the right insight into the course corrections that will be necessary to make outsourcing work. Matt looks directly at Steve as he continues.

Matt: Well, I know you've spent a great deal of time as a scholar of process, and from a very practical perspective, you've used this knowledge to be very successful in bringing projects in on time, on budget, and with quality. I know you're a black belt in six sigma and know a thing or two about process improvement. While I'm not as well versed as you in these areas, I have a general sense of what these two standards have done for us internally and how they have improved our processes through your hard work. The human resources project was just one example. So, if I asked you to apply your process knowledge to this outsourcing model, what would you focus on first, and how would you lead a supplier-acquirer team to develop functionality on time, within budget, and with quality?

Steve smiles.

Steve: Matt, when I got the call from you, the wheels started turning, and I did some research on this area. I think you knew I'd do that. So here's what I think. I believe we moved to an outsourcing model without the necessary planning to make it work. This doesn't mean we need to give up on the approach—I agree with you on that—but it does mean we have work to do. You know my favorite topics—process execution and process improvement. We need to identify the differences between an internal development process and an acquirer-supplier process, and we have to begin to develop everybody's skills and experience so they learn the core competencies of successful acquirers. And we must have process improvement that is driven by business goals. As I did my research on outsourcing and the acquirer-supplier model, I was also trying to answer the question of how to define those acquirer skills and processes. I was hoping to find something in the industry that would help us jump-start the work so we avoid making the same mistakes again.

Steve begins to draw a diagram on a nearby whiteboard.

> **Steve:** We have to start out with a strategy for acquisition, and it should drive everything else we do.

Steve writes "Acquisition Strategy" toward the top of the whiteboard.

> **Steve:** The acquisition strategy defines the answer to our key business question: What do we need to purchase to deliver technical capabilities to our organization and customers?

Matt looks at Steve and begins to give him additional points and positive feedback.

> **Matt:** I agree with you, Steve—this isn't just about technology. It must tie the business needs and goals to what we do, and then allow us to tie consistent processes to the execution of that work. As we move from an internal development organization and add acquisition, one of our new core competencies must be to pragmatically manage the acquisition. We need to learn how to develop accurate, minimum customer and technical requirements and craft solid, practical supplier agreements. Also, we have to verify that the solution not only works but also delights our customers.

Steve nods, because he is sure that he and Matt are absolutely on the same page. When that kind of alignment happens in a discussion, the direction outlined validates that the work is not only achievable but even interesting. Steve continues.

> **Steve:** Yes, we have to precisely focus our energy on developing the core competency necessary to be good acquirers. And let's not forget that all our development work is rooted in a set of practices that all successful

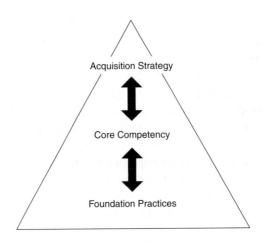

Figure 1-1 *Acquisition pyramid*

development organizations have to master, whether development happens internally with a development team or externally with suppliers.

Steve finishes his drawing on the whiteboard and contemplates it (see Figure 1-1).

> **Steve:**   It's like a Maslow's hierarchy for acquirers. If we forget to nurture the foundation practices, we trigger the need to readdress them. It's just like we, as humans, can't go too long without meeting our basic needs, like food and water. Let's see. The foundation practices cover activities like project planning and management, configuration management, training, managing requirements, and managing risk. These practices are the foundation of our core competency. All three levels—acquisition strategy, core competency, and foundation practices—are interrelated and feed into each other. If there are problems in any area, they permeate the entire system—our organization.

> **Matt:**   So, let me just play this all back to you. I want to be clear about this initial thinking. We know that whether we do development internally or externally, the work is the work. Someone still has to manage the project, gather requirements, design and code, and test the code before it's put into operation. Those are examples of the foundation practices in your pyramid picture. The difference in the acquirer-supplier model is around who performs the work and therefore how the work gets managed. Right?

> **Steve:**   Right. Let me draw another picture, because I think what you are describing looks something like this . . .

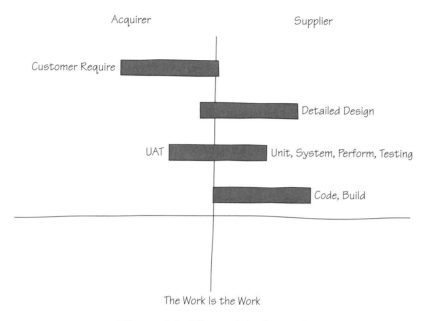

Figure 1-2 *The work is the work*

Steve draws a simple diagram on the whiteboard (see Figure 1-2). It has two columns—one labeled "Acquirer" and the other "Supplier." He draws several horizontal lines across the columns, each a different length.

> **Steve:** Each of these lines represents a process area from CMMI. The different lengths of the different lines reflect how much work should be performed by the acquirer or by the supplier. All the CMMI process areas, all the collections of best practices, are represented here. None of the work is eliminated. It's just allocated differently.

He then augments the drawing by adding a vital few process areas specific to an acquirer.

> **Steve:** What it boils down to is the work to deliver a technology solution. I mean, you are right on target—the work is the work. And we need to be clear about who does what and how we can perform as acquirers with suppliers to deliver the best solutions to our customers.

Matt is pleased that this interview has turned into a working session. As far as he is concerned, the interview is over and he has hooked Steve into the job through a lively discussion about Steve's ideas for solving this process challenge. He saw Steve's excitement as he whiteboarded the various pieces of the acquirer-supplier puzzle. Matt is now convinced that outsourcing has a really good chance to be successful. He and Steve can make it work.

Matt continues his line of thinking.

Matt: So the answer to our question, as simple as it seems, is that there are standard processes and best practices that all acquirers must follow to deliver technology solutions that improve the bottom line and give stakeholders what they need. If we can clearly determine who does what and eliminate duplicate work, we can better leverage the capabilities of our suppliers and create a win-win situation for both us and our suppliers. And I think we also need to avoid a bureaucratic process that creates a "micromanage the supplier" mentality. If we as acquirers focus too much on the suppliers' development work, we lose sight of the bigger picture—that we're the ones aligning technology solutions with business needs and user needs and holding the supplier accountable, but not doing the supplier's work. Our core competencies have to be things like strategy, requirements, program or project management, and supplier management. We have to figure out how to measure progress and enforce the delivery of value through effective processes as the supplier creates solutions to meet the specified requirements.

Steve nods in agreement.

Steve: That's exactly it. And it's feasible. During my research I found a new industry and government reference model for process improvement on the Software Engineering Institute's Web site—the initial draft CMMI for Acquisition. This model reflects all our discussion today and more. The CMMI-ACQ gives us an industry standard to help us determine whether or not our current processes are working. And then we can accelerate our improvement effort around acquisition because we will have a preexisting structure. Also, using the CMMI-ACQ will bring us closer to our suppliers. They apply a different model of the CMMI, the CMMI for Development, to do their development work, but we'll both be speaking the same process improvement language. For instance, the CMMI-ACQ clearly defines the touch points between acquirers and suppliers, effectively standardizing the acquirer-supplier interface for outsourcing transactions.

Matt is convinced that he has found the right person to lead the team in making acquisition work for the company, an individual who can help the organization move from an internal development model to a model that supports acquisition of technology solutions.

Steve and Matt are now feeding off of their mutual excitement about the potential for this project.

Matt: CMMI-ACQ addresses the key processes we need to focus on. Let's figure out the really important things we need to do to make outsourcing work for us, and then we can explain to the CEO how CMMI-ACQ is going to help us become a world-class acquirer. I have a meeting today with Kristin Wells and George Taylor, and we can just continue this discussion with them. They're the key supplier resources who have been newly assigned to our outsourcing initiatives by their company. The supplier says they're two of their most seasoned people, and together they have a wealth of experience in supporting companies outsourcing the development of systems. I'd like you to be at this meeting this afternoon. I'd like your feedback as to whether you think Kristin and George have the right skill set and experience. Steve, can you plan to be in that meeting?

Steve: Absolutely.

Matt: So, I take it you're willing to take on this assignment and work with me to ensure the company's success?

Steve smiles and responds.

Steve: After I started whiteboarding the solution, you knew I made the commitment!

1.4 Introducing the Supplier's Representatives

Kristin Wells is a seasoned executive who has moved up through her organization and has learned various aspects of the technology business through hands-on experience. She has actually performed many of the key jobs on a development team, so she is frequently called upon to troubleshoot an outsourced engagement that is "going into a ditch." Not only does she have the skills, but also she has a keen analytical mind that helps her zero in on areas that can be immediately triaged to put a project back on track.

Kristin also has an extensive process background. She has successfully completed every software development course offered by the Institute of Electrical and Electronics Engineers (IEEE), although she has never pursued formal certification. As far as she is concerned, what matters is the knowledge and how it can be applied from a practical perspective. And, given the renewed emphasis on outsourcing, Kristin finds herself in high demand as outsourcing engagements have proliferated.

George Taylor is one of those guys who live, eat, sleep, and breathe process improvement. Long before the industry understood the importance of standardized processes, George led all the outsourcing development teams in his organization through a series of exercises to develop an engineering process that all of them could use interchangeably. This initiative resulted in an invitation from the SEI for George to review the initial version of the SEI's software development process. He was thrilled to participate in that review, and he spent considerable time discussing aspects of development with his colleagues before he sent his feedback.

Now Kristin and George have just concluded a conference call with their company's senior executive in charge of outsourcing. He made it clear that the meeting with Matt is critical to both companies, because their continued partnership is at stake. Kristin turns to George to prepare for the meeting with Matt.

> **Kristin:** George, to make sure we don't miss anything in our discussion with Matt, let's outline the topics we want to touch on. I want to walk into the meeting this afternoon with both of our resumes in hand, so that Matt understands our backgrounds. I also want you to be prepared to discuss some of the troubleshooting you've done and the positive results. I want you to highlight your CMMI and ITIL [IT Infrastructure Library] experience as well. I'll focus on my breadth of knowledge in managing projects of all sizes, from large government contracts to smaller, early Web technology projects. I'll highlight what I believe has been an exemplary track record. Is there anything else we need to highlight?

> **George:** No, but based on my experience in these kinds of situations where I have been asked to come in and fix a bad engagement, we really need to be prepared to answer just about any type of question—from a company-specific question to an industry question about outsourcing.

1.5 The First Meeting with the Supplier's Reps

Matt invites Kristin, George, and Steve to sit around the small conference table in his office. He wants this to be an informal meeting, and he has erased the whiteboard with the pictures Steve drew earlier. Matt wants to use his mental notes from this morning to steer the conversation with the two supplier reps into a working session. It remains to be seen whether Kristin and George are up for the task.

Kristin starts the conversation by handing the two resumes to Matt.

> **Kristin:** Matt, George and I are prepared to talk about our past experiences with outsourcing engagements that have gotten off track and

what we have done specifically to get these initiatives righted. Or we can talk about our plans for your current outsourcing projects, or anything else you want to discuss. We had a conference call this morning with our executive in charge of all outsourcing engagements, and he wanted to assure you that we were recruited from other assignments within our company with the intent to do whatever it takes to make your outsourcing activities work. So we see this as a critical meeting for our company and our ongoing partnership.

Matt puts the resumes on the table and looks across the table at George and Kristin.

Matt: Your credentials preceded you, Kristin. If you weren't qualified on paper, we would not even be having this conversation. What I really want to focus on are the next steps. We have a number of things to accomplish, and we also have some lessons learned from previous supplier engagements. Where should we start, and which of these lessons should we apply?

George is the first to respond.

George: I've spent the last two weeks gathering data about the current situation from team members in your company as well as in ours, and with this data I've put together a root cause analysis as a first step. My analysis has surfaced two key facts. First, there was not enough clarity around the roles and responsibilities between supplier team members and your company team members. This resulted in confusion, lack of consistent management across the projects, and redundant work.

Matt: Okay. Can you give me an example?

George: Sure. You had an architect assigned to the project who was very enthusiastic about the technology. So not only did he create a high-level design, but he decided to start coding some of the functionality and demonstrate it to the business customer. Well, of course coding is not in the architect's job description, but, more important, all the functionality he coded was just for fun. Besides generating code that had to be rewritten, his demo changed the customer's expectations. That expanded the requirements, resulting in a significant delay and a less-than-satisfied customer.

Matt: So it's important that everyone understand their role.

George: That's right. The other key fact I uncovered had to do with process. It wasn't clear within the team who was supposed to execute what processes. As an example, some of the supplier team members were confused as to who should be doing detailed requirements for the project. Supplier team members waited for acquirer team members to complete the detailed requirements, when in fact it was a supplier responsibility to complete these based on the high-level business requirements. By the time our supplier lead finally realized what was happening and clarified the processes, we'd lost two weeks. To resolve these issues, I recommend that we quickly put together some team workshops, get the new teams together, and clarify the processes along with clearly defined roles and responsibilities. Then, with some expert project management skills, I believe we can execute and deliver to our commitments.

Steve speaks up.

> **Steve:**   George, are you a student of CMMI and process improvement?
>
> **George:**   Yes, I am. In fact, I've consulted with organizations to help them take their development groups to higher maturity and capability levels.
>
> **Steve:**   Sounds like you've been in the thick of CMMI for a while. Are you familiar with the CMMI-ACQ?
>
> **George:**   No, but I read something about it not too long ago. Isn't that being worked on? I think by one of the Big Three auto companies, the Department of Defense, several government agencies, and the SEI?
>
> **Steve:**   That's right. The initial draft of the model has been published, and I think we should use the CMMI-ACQ to help us accelerate these workshops and clarify what each of our groups on these joint teams needs to focus on. Matt, should I walk Kristin and George through our thought process from this morning?
>
> **Matt:**   Be my guest.

George and Kristin listen closely to Steve's descriptions of the CMMI-ACQ. Steve finishes the recap.

> **Steve:**   Let's see how quickly we can get the teams together. We want to reestablish the process partnership within our outsourced project teams and use the acquisition model to help standardize our processes. I'll ask my team to put together a slide documenting the division of work, and we can begin to reference this picture with the teams.

Kristin expands the discussion.

> **Kristin:**   It's my understanding that in the past your company struggled with interpreting how the CMMI for Development applies to acquirers.

Steve: Yes, and the more we used it, the more we understood that it fell short of what we needed as acquirers. We needed a more extensive collection of best practices for acquiring technology solutions. Then I found the CMMI-ACQ on the SEI Web site, and I thought, "Bingo! Somebody else must have had the same thought." The CMMI-ACQ has best practices that we can use right away.

Kristin: Can you give me an overview?

Steve: The CMMI-ACQ focuses on key acquirer activities—initiating and awarding supplier agreements, using a set of standard metrics to manage the acquisition of products and services, developing acceptance criteria, defining supplier deliverables, and so on. It's different from the CMMI for Development model, which focuses on development activities, including the supplier's activities to execute work.

Kristin: Makes sense. So, the CMMI for Development is the reference model that suppliers use for executing their systems engineering, hardware and design engineering, and software development work. In contrast, the CMMI-ACQ provides a road map for acquirers of the technology solutions that suppliers develop or configure.

Steve sets up a chart he has prepared for this meeting (see Figure 1-3).

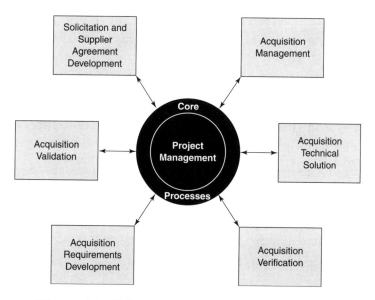

Figure 1-3 *CMMI-ACQ acquisition process areas*

Steve: Here are the six CMMI-ACQ process areas that are specific to acquirers. "Acquisition management" focuses on managing the supplier agreement—things like dispute resolution and change management. This includes managing payments and ongoing communications with suppliers. "Acquisition requirements development" defines processes for specifying measurable requirements that express customer value, which the supplier then translates into more specific, detailed requirements. "Acquisition technical solution" means you codify the role of the acquirer's architecture group in terms of high-level technology direction, nonnegotiable technology standards, and architecture reviews. We use the processes in the "acquisition validation" and "acquisition verification" process areas to ensure that the product or service received from the supplier fulfills its intended use and meets architectural technology constraints. The "solicitation and supplier agreement development" process area defines practices for preparing a solicitation package, selecting a capable supplier, and establishing the supplier agreement.

Matt nods as Steve continues.

Steve: The CMMI-ACQ also addresses the foundation practices that any organization must excel at if it wants to be successful. These are common to all CMMI models. They cover project management, support process areas, and process management. For project management, we're talking about planning, monitoring and control, and risk and requirements management, as well as measurement and analysis, configuration management, process and product quality assurance, causal analysis, and resolution. The foundation practices also cover activities that help us improve as an organization, not just project by project—organizational process definition, process performance, training, and innovation and deployment. These process areas essentially describe practices and capabilities that are our "required commodities." Each process area amplifies the nuances that successful acquirers master to implement these common practices and capabilities.

Kristin: If you apply the acquisition best practices to your work, and if we apply those practices in the development model that reflect the work that we need to do as a supplier, then together we can improve our results and achieve greater customer satisfaction.

Matt glances across the table at George and Steve, who are nodding in agreement.

Matt: I think we just defined our direction.

1.6 Recruiting the Internal Customer

Matt's last hurdle in recruiting the key players on his team is to effectively engage Paula Ressel, the internal customer for this product. Matt knows that Paula is going to be a challenge. By reputation, she is a demanding individual. Part of this attitude has to do with her background. She is by training an accountant who was chosen early in her career as a high-potential employee. She has taken this designation to heart and has tried to be assertive and exacting in every assignment.

Her director feels that Paula is perfect for this assignment—to use outsourcing to develop some of the financial business intelligence functionality—because Paula is a voracious reader. She reads everything that comes across her desk. She isn't shy about asking questions. She also has the uncanny ability to take the detail in any initiative and abstract it immediately to a high level, describing the salient deliverables and the overall business value. It is these two characteristics that Matt feels will be invaluable in keeping this integrated team moving forward and focused on the right things. Matt has arranged a luncheon meeting with Paula. He wants to make sure that she understands how he is going to proceed, and he wants to get her feedback from the business side of the company.

After describing for Paula some of the challenges uncovered in George and Kristin's two-week analysis, Matt focuses the discussion on workshops, getting all the teams on the same page from a roles and processes perspective, and then keeping a tight rein on oversight and management. Matt is trying to raise Paula's comfort level. He knows that the business intelligence functionality is directly tied to an important business case for the company. This functionality will be critical in the next 18 months to two years in giving the company information it needs to reposition its product line in an emerging global business. Paula asks the tough question that Matt anticipated.

> **Paula:**   How do you know you are making the right course corrections with outsourcing? How do you know that you're doing all the right things?

Up to this point in the conversation, Matt has avoided any discussion about the SEI, CMMI, IEEE, and process improvement—concepts that he knows he will have to put in a business context for Paula.

> **Matt:**   Paula, we have pulled in the best resources from within our organization and also within the supplier's ranks. We believe that we understand what went wrong, and it had to do with a lack of clarity

around roles and processes. To make sure that we're doing all the right things, we're also going to leverage some important industry standards. One in particular has been just recently published in response to the large number of companies who are now looking to outsourcing as a way to accelerate the development of systems. This is a set of best practices that will allow us to verify that we are doing all the necessary things to acquire solutions. We will also talk to suppliers who support outsourcing, other companies who are using outsourcing, and make sure that we do not repeat the same mistakes they've made.

Paula has worked with Matt in the past and has a great deal of respect for him. It has been her experience that, if Matt says he is going to make something work, he will do everything possible to follow through.

Paula: Matt, I believe that you will do everything to make outsourcing work for us. Now, what is it that I can do to help you?

Matt: I want you to do what you do so well. Make sure that we cover the details, that we include all your requirements, and that we deliver what you need for business intelligence. My door is always open, and I want your feedback as we build this functionality with our supplier. Let's schedule some brief checkpoint meetings so that we remain in alignment.

Paula agrees.

Matt has completed the work of building a team to work on improving the company's acquisitions processes.

1.7 Meeting with the Executive Board

Matt spends the next week synthesizing the information he has gleaned from his team members. He also references discussions he has held with project managers who were involved in some of the challenging projects that were part of the initial outsourcing activity. He has been told by the chief information officer that he will be invited to the next meeting of the executive board to discuss plans for getting the outsourcing initiative back on track.

Based on the interviews, the discussions with suppliers, and his contacts within other companies that have instituted outsourcing, Matt feels confident that he can put together a presentation for the board that will resonate with board members and give them confidence that the company can move forward with this approach and be successful.

Matt has hit upon the idea to characterize the key insights he has gained as "hidden truths." These are the main points about outsourcing that the company must understand and execute to be successful. Major analysis firms like Gartner and Forrester have echoed some of these concepts in their analyses, but no one has put together this list in exactly the way Matt intends to present it to the board.

The invitation comes from the CEO for Matt to appear at the next executive board meeting to discuss his plans for reversing the negative trends in using outsourcing to obtain technology solutions. The CEO wants to be convinced that the model can be workable, because the last thing that the executive board wants to do is to invest more funds with suppliers, with no guarantee that there will be any return on investment (ROI).

Matt begins his presentation to the board.

> **Matt:** Now more than ever, organizations are increasingly becoming acquirers of technology solutions by obtaining development and maintenance services from suppliers and developing fewer technology solutions in-house. Like many other organizations, we have adopted a business strategy to improve our operational efficiencies by leveraging suppliers' capabilities to deliver quality solutions rapidly, at lower cost, using the most appropriate technology.

Matt pauses, weighing his words carefully before he continues.

> **Matt:** Acquisition of technology solutions is challenging, because we must still hold overall accountability for solution delivery, while allowing the supplier to perform the activities necessary to develop and maintain the solution. According to some folks, 20 to 25 percent of large outsourcing projects fail within two years, and 50 percent fail within five years. And that's within the IT domain alone. A number of factors contribute to project failure: mismanagement, an inability to articulate customer needs, poor definition of requirements, inadequate processes for supplier selection and contracting, insufficient procedures for selecting technology, and uncontrolled changes to requirements. The onus for these disturbing statistics does not sit exclusively with the supplier, but also with us. Most project failures can be avoided if acquirers learn how to properly prepare for, engage with, and manage suppliers.

Matt glances around the room. He can tell that he has hit on points that matter to the board members.

> **Matt:** We've learned a lot about buying technology solutions over the years. Thinking back, it took a lot of perseverance and the collective

brain trust of all our customers, employees, suppliers, and partners to plainly see the hidden truths about acquiring technology solutions, and to decisively act on them. It boils down to six hidden truths.

1.7.1 Hidden Truth Number 1: Obtain and Maintain Executive Leadership

Matt explains that successful acquisition organizations don't engage in outsourcing without executive commitment.

> **Matt:** To implement the policies, processes, and activities that will drive our outsourcing efforts, we must have continued support from you and all the other members of the executive team. Deciding to use an outsourcing model is a strategic decision, and it is made by the executives at the highest levels of the organization. After we make this kind of commitment, the executive team is key in giving the organization and its suppliers consistent messages about the strategy and its importance to the company. This will include positive encouragement to support specific team initiatives, along with recognition of the successes of our project team members as well as supplier team members.

1.7.2 Hidden Truth Number 2: Strategic Partnering Is Essential

Coordination costs for outsourcing are incurred by both the acquirer and the supplier in this relationship; the acquirer largely assumes the risks of the supplier, Matt tells the board.

> **Matt:** Acquirers and suppliers must acknowledge these costs and risks and mitigate them through ongoing collaboration. One of the most important aspects of this partnership is to make risks and issues visible and manage them together. We've decided to immediately institute joint project reviews that are focused on early identification of risk and to make our managers, from our company and the supplier, squarely accountable for resolving these risks in the shortest time possible. And these risks and their mitigation are an important aspect of all of our outsourced projects that we measure on an ongoing basis.

1.7.3 Hidden Truth Number 3: Maintain Acquirer Core Competencies

Matt introduces the third hidden truth: In an outsourcing model, the acquirer must maintain and execute certain core competencies. As an example, he cites the role of IT broker as a core competency for acquirers.

Matt: We must solicit these high-level requirements and must clearly articulate the relationship between them and our business goals. Suppliers are not necessarily in a position to understand our business strategies. We must also develop expertise in maintaining architecture and standards in order to manage our solution costs and to drive selected technologies forward. Competing technologies are proliferating, and that drives cost; as an acquirer, we must drive the overall technology vision for our organization. We are also responsible for developing specific acceptance criteria for the functionality that is built. For this, we can adopt formal activities like user acceptance testing. As contractually specified deliverables are created and presented to us, we must have clear and complete acceptance criteria to ensure that our defined requirements have been met and that the right technology has been delivered.

1.7.4 Hidden Truth Number 4: Understand Conflicting Goals Between Suppliers and Between Suppliers and Acquirers

Organizations want to acquire solutions that benefit their bottom line and provide stakeholders with what they need. Suppliers want to fulfill their contracts, make a profit, and maintain their relationships with acquirers and with other suppliers.

Matt: Certain factors—such as lower costs versus higher profit margins, and fast delivery versus low deployment costs—may cause conflicts between the supplier and the acquirer, as well as among multiple suppliers. With all these different and occasionally conflicting goals in the mix, we must all agree on some balance to achieve success. We must build an environment of trust with our suppliers so that they can feel comfortable about sharing their ideas and work with us to leverage opportunities. If we approach them only from a cost-cutting perspective, we will miss the chance to jointly realize competitive opportunities that could make our relationship a true partnership and strengthen our company's position in the marketplace.

1.7.5 Hidden Truth Number 5: Understand the Difference Between Managing and Performing

Engaging in *active outsourcing* is one of the most difficult challenges for an organization that acquires rather than builds technology solutions, Matt explains.

Matt: We must manage our suppliers to achieve results and retain accountability for those results. We must plan, manage, motivate, and communicate with our suppliers but not participate in the detailed, technical development of the solution. This is why it's so important for us to have the right acquirer processes that are aligned with supplier processes. We can avoid confusion, redundant work, and nonstandard technologies, and we can seamlessly work together to deliver to our internal customers. The CMMI-ACQ model of best practices will help us create the clarity needed about roles, responsibilities, and processes.

1.7.6 Hidden Truth Number 6: Standardize Whenever Possible

Matt tells the board that processes, contracts, requirements, products, and product components are all viable candidates for standardization.

Matt: Don't buy in to the myth that standardization stifles creativity. On the contrary, teams have more freedom to be creative and productive when they are allowed to focus on a handful of requirements that are specific to the project and can leverage predefined requirements and reuse products and product components. The more we leverage standard contracts and reuse requirements, exploit products like standard reporting software, and take advantage of common capabilities like access controls or data warehousing, the more efficient our outsourcing activities can become. Our suppliers will become familiar with these standard requirements and components and can build them into their proposals. This should help our suppliers to more effectively leverage their skilled staffs and reduce overall development costs. Over time it should also have an impact on the cost and quality of application maintenance.

Table 1-1 shows the hidden truths and their alignment with the CMMI-ACQ processes.

Next, Matt summarizes the hidden truths.

Matt: These six hidden truths are the foundation of what our organization needs to do to become a successful acquirer of technology. Revealing these hidden truths is the first step, but making them a reality is an even bigger challenge. Based on our analysis, we firmly believe that it's critical for us to evolve our processes to make this happen. If we want to compete in a global marketplace, we need to get even more precise about what we focus on with technology, and how we bring together the right employees with the right suppliers to create the right

Table 1-1 *The Six Hidden Truths*

Hidden Truths	CMMI-ACQ Process Areas	Book Chapter
1. Obtain and maintain executive leadership. 2. Strategic partnering is essential.	• Acquisition management • Project planning • Risk management • Solicitation and supplier agreement development	Chapter 2
3. Maintain acquirer core competencies. 4. Understand conflicting goals between suppliers and acquirers.	• Acquisition requirements development • Acquisition technical solution • Decision analysis and resolution • Requirements management	Chapter 3
5. Understand the difference between managing and performing.	• Acquisition management (cont.) • Acquisition validation • Acquisition verification • Causal analysis and resolution • Configuration management • Integrated project management • Measurement and analysis • Project monitoring and control • Process and product quality assurance • Quantitative project management • Risk management (cont.)	Chapter 4
6. Standardize whenever possible.	• Organizational innovation and deployment • Organizational process definition • Organizational process focus • Organizational process performance • Organizational training	Chapter 5

technology solutions for our customers. We'll need to invest in the human capabilities necessary to effectively manage projects in an acquisition environment. Our teams must be engaged throughout the project life cycle. We can't afford any situations where the team disengages after the supplier is under contract. We can't afford to discover too late that a project is not on schedule, deadlines cannot be met, the selected technology isn't viable, and that the project has failed.

Matt concludes with the following remarks.

Matt: I am making a commitment to all of you today that we will work to effectively implement outsourcing for our company. I will come back on a quarterly basis and give you very detailed updates. In the interim, you will receive reports that will capture initiatives that are outsourced and their current status. Based on the commitment from our teams and the supplier teams, and the course corrections that we have identified, we believe that outsourcing can become an effective tool to deliver solutions to our organization. Any questions?

1.8 The Way Forward

In each chapter that follows, Matt, Steve, Paula, Kristin, and George—as well as Rosa Gonzales, a new hire joining the team in Chapter 5—will set the context for the CMMI-ACQ process areas by sharing their struggles, experiences, and ideas. In highlighted boxes within the text, you'll find tips to immediately direct you to some of the most important rules or tenets for improved acquisition practices. These tips include lessons learned, aspects of an acquisition that require special attention, or realities that may occur in your acquisition. We then explain the associated CMMI-ACQ elements as well as tie the tips to CMMI-ACQ process areas, goals, and practices.

Chapter 2

Getting Started

The general who wins a battle makes many calculations in his temple before the battle is fought. The general who loses a battle makes but few calculations beforehand.

Sun Tzu (6th century B.C.)

Individuals recognize leadership through observation—by watching the actions of the boss to see whether he or she exhibits certain characteristics. True leaders exhibit the attributes of their beliefs, values, ethics, character, knowledge, and skills. When followers share or admire these attributes, they want to achieve the goals set forth by the leaders of an organization. Therefore, hidden truth number 1, "Obtain and maintain executive leadership" (discussed in Chapter 1), is imperative to becoming a successful acquirer.

An engineering team cannot exclusively decide that the organization should outsource technology. The decision must come from executive managers, who must demonstrate their commitment to the decision. This commitment instills the trust and confidence necessary to empower individuals and teams to move forward as an organization. Obtaining and maintaining leadership is about setting and communicating the strategy, making it clear how teams can contribute, and giving the teams constructive feedback to demonstrate how their contributions move the organization toward its vision.

In this chapter we explore how to set the strategy for acquisition, how to put in motion the vision of sourcing technology solutions from suppliers, and how to execute the necessary policies, processes, and activities. This process requires continued support and encouragement from the executive team. Managers demonstrate their commitment through ongoing communications, making resources available to ensure success, removing roadblocks, and rewarding the teams' successes. Matt and his acquirer team, along with Kristin Wells and her supplier team, show how to execute decisions that are made in the context of an acquisition strategy. Along the way, we identify the tenets to put in place, the areas of particular focus, and some keys to success. As Kouzes and Posner explain in their book *The Leadership Challenge* (Jossey-Bass, San Francisco, 1987), there are a handful of things that leaders should focus on, and these can be directly applied to our hidden truth.

1. "Challenge the process." Define the set of processes that require internal technology development, and assess how a different approach might improve quality, reduce costs, and make new technologies available.
2. "Inspire a shared vision." Articulate your strategy of acquisition in enough detail to gain understanding.
3. "Enable others to act." Give the teams the resources and the decisions they need to execute the acquisition strategy.
4. "Model the way." Stay in touch with what is happening, clarify direction, and remove barriers.
5. "Encourage the heart." Share the successes with the combined team, and help them manage through the challenges.

It takes leadership to define your organization's acquisition strategy. Supplier agreements can be interpreted literally, or they can function as documents that create the basis for strategic opportunities for the supplier and acquirer. Hidden truth number 2, "Strategic partnering is essential," acknowledges that it is through ongoing collaboration that the acquirer and supplier manage risks and issues as they arise. In this chapter we discuss the reality and strategic importance of risk and risk management in an acquisition. As we explore how an acquirer finds the best supplier based on a set of defined criteria, we also discuss how a partnership between the acquirer and the supplier develops as communications lead to a shared understanding of the purpose of the acquisition.

As the acquisition strategy is formulated, the reasons for making certain decisions are solidified. The reasons might include the need to access new technologies, a lack of special technology skills, or merely the desire to gain economies of scale and ultimately reduce overall costs.

As the supplier selection process is completed and a formal agreement is signed, we look at the associated governance activities. We describe how integrated supplier-acquirer teams can move away from a formal, agree-ment-based set of activities to an ongoing focus on innovation, new opportunities, and continuous improvement—an environment that benefits both the acquirer and the supplier. This approach does not negate the need for a supplier agreement, but it expands the execution of the agreement into a collaborative partnership.

This chapter also discusses what happens after the ink dries on the formal agreement. For instance, how do integrated teams work together to share competencies and resources, establish active lines of communication, and promote trust and respect? You will learn that these competencies emanate from a clear purpose, executable processes, and a positive climate that sup-ports continuous improvement and communications.

2.1 Charting the Strategy

Although outsourcing as a management practice is gradually maturing, the practice is still prone to underachievement of expectations and, in some instances, outright failure. Mistakes are commonly made in supplier selec-tion, supplier agreements, and supplier management, and then they are repeated. To avoid these mistakes, organizations must clearly define out-comes and critical success factors as they engage in outsourcing and reduce operational costs, improve services, access new skills, and build a strategic partnership with suppliers. Partnerships can progress from contractually arranged resources to trusted relationships as integrated teams jointly resolve business issues and leverage innovation opportunities.

To be successful within any organization, a technologist must understand the strategic trade-offs between the potential benefit of using technologies and the inherent uncertainties. A similar understanding is critical to the suc-cess of acquirers of technology solutions. When your strategy is off the mark—when it is not consistent with business or mission needs—the stabil-ity of your organization is weakened because project planning is often built on quicksand. Projects or programs get caught between erratic changes in strategic direction. These shifts in direction are costly because they affect not only the organization but also supplier agreements, service level agreements (SLAs), and pricing, and ultimately these changes increase the risk of not delivering to the customer. Savvy acquirers avoid this scenario by adhering to a thoughtful, well-understood, well-documented, and feasible strategy that leverages the core competencies of the organization and targets well-understood business opportunities.

The process of developing an acquisition strategy clarifies the reasons your organization has decided to outsource the development of technology solutions. After you define your acquisition strategy, you can determine whether potential suppliers align with the strategy. You can also develop a proper solicitation package that documents all the work products to be supplied as well as the evaluation criteria for judging each competing supplier.

The acquisition strategy answers two fundamental questions: What technology solutions do I need to acquire? How do I acquire them? It establishes a road map that you follow throughout the life cycle of technology projects or programs. Strategy captures the decisions that direct the development of detailed plans, which in turn guide execution. Your acquisition strategy documents the ground rules and assumptions that precede and then lead to project or program initiation.

> **TIP** Establish a road map for acquiring technology solutions that is built on a sound rationale.

Developing a practical, executable acquisition strategy is daunting. As with many complex endeavors, often the best way to begin is to break the complex activity into simpler, more manageable tasks by defining the elements. It's useful to ask the question, "What acquisition choices can I make in structuring this project or program?"

Recall Matt Vauban, senior executive in the acquirer organization, who was introduced in Chapter 1. Matt has a strong opinion about the answers to this question.

Matt: We have to be true pioneers in providing technology solutions where we can get the biggest bang for the buck. Technology in and of itself doesn't create momentum. It can help or hinder it, but not create it in any sustainable fashion. We can't make good use of technologies until we can tell whether they're relevant to our business goals. If a technology doesn't fit squarely with the capabilities we need, we should ignore all the hype and move on. If something is relevant to the business, then we can become pioneers in applying the technology. We can allow nothing to distract us.

   Getting our focus right is critical, but a question remains: Who should be the supplier of the technology? Which supplier we choose is a crucial dimension of this strategy. We need to maintain and execute our core competencies flawlessly, and we need to improve them continuously by investing in people, equipment, facilities, and execution processes.

Another critical dimension is the roles played by external and internal stakeholders and the ways they collaborate to deliver technology solutions. We as acquirers must work hand-in-hand with suppliers to assess our project execution in terms of cost, schedule, productivity, and potential opportunities for improvement. We need to understand the maturity of our internal teams and our readiness to use external sources.

This move to outsourcing is really a transformation for our organization, and we'll be successful only if we are clear about what we want, understand how outsourcing supports business goals and objectives, and follow through with an operational model that allows us to manage the change within our organization while simultaneously managing the suppliers.

TIP   Strike the right balance between internal and external suppliers.

An acquisition strategy is the business and technical management framework for planning, directing, contracting for, and managing a project. It defines the objectives for the acquisition as well as the constraints, availability of resources and technology, decisions about acquisition methods, supplier agreement types, terms and conditions, business considerations (including risk), and decisions about support of the technology throughout its useful life, including its final disposal.

Those who define this strategy must understand both the target project and the general disposition of the target technology, along with the environment in which it will be deployed. You need to consider the value of each project in the light of potential risks, constraints, and available suppliers, as well as what you can manage in a supplier agreement. When you define a strategy, your overall intent is to streamline the acquisition process and ensure the best return on investment for the technology.

In your strategy document, you describe the capabilities you need from the supplier. It's a good idea to group these capabilities according to desired functionalities or interoperation between functionalities. In addition, the strategy identifies any dependencies this project has with planned or existing functionalities in other projects. For example, suppose you're outsourcing a project to provide a Web service that allows employees to view their compensation online. For this project, you would have to account for any dependencies on the Web technologies already in place.

Each project should have cost, schedule, and key performance objectives, including a description of your customers' expectations and a threshold for determining that the needed capability has been supplied. These thresholds should constitute the minimum number of performance parameters required for successful delivery of the capability. Your acquisition strategy defines required decision points, milestones, and deliverables for each project phase, and it identifies any business- or mission-critical deliverables.

Often, stakeholders have varying views of key business strategies and objectives. One popular acquisition strategy is to reduce and control costs while maintaining or improving quality. It's important for all organizations to implement cost containment and constantly look for cost-reduction opportunities, but organizations that have experienced a major organizational change (such as a merger or divestiture) may focus on cost cutting to the exclusion of other, equally important strategies. For these organizations, cost reduction is about freeing up funds to gain financial flexibility. But if they focus only on cost reduction, the risk is that they may cut too deeply, delaying programs that were intended to save money and failing to realize structural cost reductions. An acquisition strategy would uncover those programs that have true cost-reduction potential and keep them active.

> **TIP** Align your acquisition strategy with your overall business strategy and goals.

2.2 A Strategy Meeting with Senior Executives

Now let's return to the project introduced in Chapter 1. In the company where Matt Vauban works as a senior executive, the other senior executives have been directed to make themselves and their staffs available to participate in a series of workshops to extract and document short-term and long-term strategies, goals, and objectives. The goal of these workshops is not only to identify these strategies and objectives but also to put them in concrete terms, with priorities spanning multiple years. The idea is to align the priorities with the funding available to continue to support technology.

Matt knows that each element of the acquisition strategy offers a continuum of implementation approaches. Putting a stake in the ground and choosing a specific approach will support the project by allowing teams to focus on the functionality to be delivered, as opposed to focusing on the decisions about how the organization will relate to the supplier. Once made, these decisions will set a direction and eliminate certain options. Therefore, the company must consider its options carefully.

> **TIP** Carefully calibrate strategic choices for your acquisition strategy.

Matt sets up a meeting with the senior executives and invites Steve Reiter, the project lead, to participate. Matt begins by reminding everyone that the organization's acquisition strategy will define the approach that the project will use to deliver the acquired capabilities. This delivery can occur in one of two ways: providing the entire solution in one step, or providing the solution in increments—completed components that together constitute the total solution. The latter, called evolutionary acquisition, is necessitated by the company's strategy.

> **Matt:** We will continue to use an evolutionary acquisition approach. Given our business strategy, our projects must contribute a technology solution to at least some part of a strategic goal within a very short window, sometimes as short as six months. In some cases, the window is even shorter than that.
>
> So we'll contract for components to be delivered in several distinct, yet operational pieces, with each increment delivering a fully functioning subset of the total capabilities.

Evolutionary acquisition is used when single-step acquisition is not practical. The acquirer may need an early delivery of partial capability, or technologies needed for later increments are not sufficiently mature. Or perhaps the system is unprecedented and the requirements for the later phases of the project are not stable, or funding constraints may prevent using the single-step approach. Steve speaks up.

> **Steve:** Evolutionary acquisition has benefited us greatly. To make this work, however, we had to lay down the law—make some tough strategic decisions—to get everybody in line with executing to our core competencies efficiently and effectively. For instance, every acquisition project must have a project manager and a technology architect from our organization. The project manager provides the necessary oversight and interface to our customers. We cannot abdicate supplier management and just write the check when the supplier is ready to deliver. If our strategy is put together in the right way, it'll provide the necessary boundaries and focus for individual projects so they can succeed rapidly, instead of starting in the ditch.

> **TIP** Mandate an evolutionary approach when acquiring technology solutions, with single-step acquisition as the exception.

One of the executives asks how much competition among suppliers the company should seek when acquiring technology solutions. Steve smiles as he thinks about the answer.

Steve: In our organization, you can't get a project approved without competitively bidding it. Matt has made it abundantly clear to everybody that giving business to a supplier without allowing other suppliers to compete for a project isn't the way to go. If you want to single-source projects, you have to explain it to him personally. Guess how often that happens?

Everyone laughs. The same executive then asks, "So what if we need to select multiple suppliers for one project?"

Steve: Our strategy requires each project to have a prime supplier, who is responsible for subcontracting additional suppliers. This helps us stay focused on our core competencies and not get distracted in noncore activities. The key is to make sure we effectively manage all the prime contractor and subcontractor relationships. We should make sure that we have this visibility in project review meetings.

> **TIP** Structure competitive acquisitions to allow vendors to partner together on teams with prime and subcontractor relationships.

Another strategic decision involves the use of commercial off-the-shelf (COTS) products.

Steve: We work hard to make our technology solutions reusable. The strategic rule is, "Reuse before buying, buy before building." Why reinvent something, especially in an area where all we have to do is keep up with our competition?

Acquiring commercial products offers many advantages. Their initial cost is often less than that of developing a new product. COTS products are often available more quickly and can be more robust because extensive use by a broad customer base helps or forces the supplier to identify and repair defects.

But the use of commercial components in a project also introduces special challenges. When a system or component is built for a customer to meet a specified set of requirements, the development organization has extensive and often unlimited rights to the use of the component. The supplier has more detailed insight into its operation and can modify it if needed. With a COTS product, this is not the case. The system or component has been developed to meet a broader need defined by the larger market. If the market's needs do not fully align with a specific organization's needs, then an 80:20 solution (one that meets 80 percent of the organization's needs) might have to suffice.

Modifying a COTS product beyond the specified configuration options is not a good idea. When a product is changed and it diverges from the commercial product, it is no longer functioning to meet its defined purpose, and much of its original benefit is lost. Support of the product becomes complicated, if not impossible, and installing subsequent releases forces you to incorporate the changes into every new release. If your needs don't align fully with those of the commercial component, you should reconsider using COTS, or modify your needs to the capabilities of the COTS product.

> **TIP** When competitive parity or an 80:20 solution will suffice, incorporate COTS for technology solutions.

2.2.1 Deciding on the Type of Supplier Agreement

To gain significant potential for cost reduction and efficient management, one strategy is to identify a standard pricing model and associate it with agreement types. Some of these types include firm fixed-price contracts, fixed-price incentive contracts, cost-plus incentive-fee contracts, and cost-plus award-fee contracts. Each agreement type offers benefits and drawbacks. You should document your rationale for choosing an agreement type, including consideration of risk and risk distribution between the acquirer and the supplier. Matt comments on this topic in the executive meeting.

Matt: We've had lots of debates about which contract vehicles or supplier agreement types we should use. Every organization needs to decide this—just like the other strategic elements—for itself. In the early phases of a project, we cut time-and-material deals to quickly get the project's requirements and initial design, putting up with a certain amount of cost volatility in order to get the work going. Then for all subsequent phases, we require all projects to use fixed-price agreements. This gives us a defined deliverable in return for a defined price. For a firm fixed-price contract, the price is not subject to any adjustment. Other forms of fixed-price contracts allow for adjustment of the price under certain circumstances.

Your acquisition strategy describes any incentive structure for the project and outlines how the structure encourages the supplier to provide the technology solution at or below cost objectives while meeting schedule and quality objectives. Your strategy also defines how you approach the terms and conditions of the supplier agreement and any business decisions that deviate from your standard terms and conditions.

> **TIP** In incremental acquisitions, tailor the supplier agreement appropriately to the life cycle phase of the project.

Your acquisition strategy identifies how the technology solution will be supported during its projected life span, and who will support it. Defining these types of handoffs includes how you will transfer ownership to the customer after the product or service is delivered. Matt explains the need to look at how the system will be managed after deployment.

Matt: We can't afford not to take a comprehensive look at product support. We all know that the cost of initially acquiring a technology solution is only a fraction of the total cost that we have to pay over its useful life. Every project has to continuously attempt to reduce support costs to reduce our total cost of ownership. To support this, we've made the strategic decision to contract out the support and maintenance of our technology solutions. The supplier might be the original developer, or it might be a third-party supplier that specializes in maintaining technology solutions. The scope and the parameters of the support are defined in a support or maintain contract. This strategy reduces cost and lead time for support, especially when the supplier has already developed the know-how, technical data, and sources.

> **TIP** When you define your acquisition strategy, choose a strategy for operating and maintaining the solution.

2.2.2 Defining the Roles in the Project

The meeting agenda turns to personnel questions, and Steve speaks up to tell the team a story.

Steve: Let me share with you an example of one instance when we were unclear about our strategy. I mean, there seemed to be an unwritten set of strategies, goals, and objectives in the heads of our executives and acquisition officers, but they hadn't been consistently communicated to the teams building the solicitation packages. So, what did we do? We hired consultants and put them in charge of defining the scope of the outsourcing deal, via the solicitation package development activity.

Well, the consultants couldn't get anything in writing from us, so they tried to glean the objectives from discussions with various executive staff. They created this solicitation package that described the work needed and the supplier roles in enough detail for suppliers to bid. The package included specific supplier staffing requirements for necessary skills and experience.

Matt: That sounds pretty good.

Steve: But it was missing a key ingredient. There wasn't any clear definition of roles within our organization post-contract. We lost all sense of what roles we needed to fulfill to effectively work with the supplier. It was our own fault. We hadn't made clear decisions on an organizational level in the first place, so the consultants' hands were tied. It wasn't clear if we wanted the supplier to be accountable for a set of deliverables, but at the same time we wanted to use some of the supplier resources in the contract as supplemental staff to accomplish some of the assignments that weren't yet defined.

Matt: So what happened?

Steve: The suppliers who responded to the solicitation package merely inflated their cost estimates, anticipating that we would change our minds about the objectives or the strategy. So in the end, we missed out on our cost savings opportunities. The resulting contract was a mixed bag—some specific deliverables, some staff used to augment existing resources, and a confused supplier who continually tried to manage the project via SLAs that didn't cover the entire contract.

If we had more clearly thought through our objectives, we wouldn't have transferred that confusion into the contract language. This was also an opportunity missed from a transformation perspective. With more clarity about deliverables, we would have been in a position to look for ways to quickly replace obsolete technology with state-of-the-art, giving both the supplier and us expanded functionality for the same or even lower cost. And this is part of what the supplier wanted to achieve—to not only realize the cost reductions, but to quickly demonstrate their ability to partner with us and help us achieve our business goals. This is an example of what we do *not* want to do. Let's make sure we have the right individuals from the organization who can help us define the business objectives through the strategy.

> **TIP**   Make sure that your acquisition strategy is viewed as a core competency and is defined by your organization.

2.2.3 Evaluating Project Risk

Every acquisition project is subject to external and internal factors that create risks for the acquirer. Strategies and plans must account for and deal with these risks in a manner that maximizes the likelihood of success. Matt drives that point home.

Matt: What we're trying to manage is a specific risk: that the technical solution will not meet the customers' intent. In managing risks you have to get back to the basics of managing your program and your supplier. You have to face head-on the business and technical risks of every project, as well as the collective risk of your project portfolio. You need both categories—business and technical—for characterizing overall risk, because either one can prevent an initiative from being successful. Technological successes that have no business appeal, and business opportunities without feasible technology alternatives, add nothing to the bottom line.

Steve: Matt, can you explain the difference between business and technical risks so that we're all on the same page?

Matt: Sure. Technical risk characterizes the chances of developing or configuring a product or service in the available time-to-delivery, meeting the expected level of quality, and below or at cost. Business risk, on the other hand, deals with the uncertainty that customers are willing to pay for the product or service, the chances of realizing expected future returns of the business, the risk to equity that originates from the nature of our business or mission.

As engineers—and I can say this since I'm an engineer myself—we love to focus on technical risks. So we have to constantly remind ourselves that we must vigilantly address business risks. We must retain this focus even when we find abundant opportunities to better manage technical risk.

This is a very hard direction for a technical organization to understand, follow, and maintain in the heat of battle. It takes a lot of coaching to drive home the point that we can't spend millions of dollars verifying that the supplier's technical solution meets the contractual requirements and then, on the other hand, resist spending a couple thousand dollars to ensure that the contractual requirements actually meet the customers' intentions.

> **TIP** Account for business and technical risks at the project level and at the organizational level.

When establishing the acquisition strategy or when a project is just beginning, you need an easy way to systematically assess the business and technical risks that you can expect to encounter. One technique is to use a simple risk management scorecard to quickly and inexpensively determine whether there are any major technical or business risks that you need to manage. This scorecard can be as simple as a list of ten questions: five for technical risks and five for business risks. The idea is to assign a numerical value to each risk to arrive at a number that reflects the total risk for a project.

Technical risk is covered by five parameters:

- The novelty of the technology
- The complexity of the delivery process
- The severity of government regulations
- The level of acquisition expertise in the required technology
- The science that governs the project

The following parameters cover business risk:

- The innovative nature of product
- The level of business process transformation
- The stability of the targeted group or industry segment
- The familiarity of end users with the proposed product
- The extent of an established supplier network for delivering the product or service

> **TIP** Quantify risks early by using a simple, 5 × 5 risk scorecard.

To start, use a simple method to characterize risk; in the early stages of a project, you seldom have enough information to permit a comprehensive and detailed risk analysis. This basic risk management scorecard enables you to begin understanding your chances of achieving success.

You should also look for indicators of potential issues that might occur. Depending on how your acquisition team fills out the risk management scorecard, you may need to raise additional questions. For example, if you've selected a supplier that is strong in a particular technology but is only 18 months old, that should raise a red flag. You should stop and consider this a risk. Remember that you must assess and manage all risks, even those that are ultimately assigned to the supplier to manage.

In general, most project failures are caused by business risk. This is not because acquisition organizations are less competent than their suppliers, but rather because business risk is a much tougher problem than technical risk. Technical risk is governed by the laws of science, which do not change very often. In contrast, managing business risk means reflecting the uncertainties of what may be a diverse group of stakeholders. These people may have differing needs, they may have trouble expressing these needs, and their needs may change over time. This makes business risk a more formidable challenge than technical risk.

> **TIP** Set the direction for comprehensive risk avoidance and dispute resolution before the project starts.

The need for early and aggressive detection of risk is compounded by the inherent complexity of the acquirer-supplier relationship. Examples of such risks include the acquirer's capabilities, the supplier's experience of working with the acquirer, the supplier's financial stability, or the adoption of well-defined dispute resolution processes.

At our executive meeting, Steve clarifies how he has handled business risks in the past.

> **Steve:** You learn as you work with suppliers to get the job done. We have to constantly remind ourselves that the intrinsic incentives of our suppliers, such as maximizing profit, could lead them to exploit us as clients. This constitutes a major business risk. For instance, we had this supplier who figured out how to do less work than we had contracted for and still get paid in full. Part of this was caused by our lack of visibility into the supplier's work—and, even worse, our own. We now vigilantly guard against this risk by using standard measures and maintaining a staff with better technical skills.

Matt supports Steve and adds his own viewpoint.

> **Matt:** Another risk with suppliers is the supplier using our best practices and proprietary information to open up another revenue stream for themselves. You don't want somebody reverse-engineering critical proprietary business processes and reselling them to your closest competitor. So we've learned to manage that risk. We look into this carefully during supplier selection and management. For instance, we now make

sure that the suppliers make money, too, so they aren't motivated to look for alternative ways to generate revenue from the deal.

Renegotiation of agreements is another business risk that Steve wants to mention.

Steve: You get caught in a situation where you want to, or have to, redo the contract as soon as the ink is dry. Once that signature goes on the contract, you just lost bargaining power. You don't want to be that project. It feels like a holdup because the supplier now wants to behave a certain way and feels that it has the leverage. The problem is, if you don't have an alternative source, you're stuck. You're forced to accept the supplier's terms. So we seek and maintain a very collaborative environment with our suppliers, keep enough competition between suppliers alive, and at the same time give them an incentive to work together.

Matt nods in agreement.

Matt: Yes, getting all the suppliers to "play nice" was a struggle early on. Some of them took the stance that virtually everything they do is proprietary—their practices created a competitive advantage and therefore couldn't be shared with the other suppliers. They were very protective and suspicious of the other suppliers. You have to alleviate these fears by fostering a team environment and co-locating people from different suppliers with our people. We've also instituted a number of formal events, such as supplier conferences and supplier councils. We emphasize our joint goals and give everybody a voice in defining how we operate as one team. These various efforts eventually broke the ice. Everybody realized we're in this together, and nobody would be at a disadvantage if they shared information.

> **TIP** Encourage suppliers to work together by defining joint goals and operating principles for the integrated project team.

Additional risks associated with working with suppliers abound. For example, there are risks associated with geographic separation between acquirer personnel and supplier personnel. Other risks are the cultural gap between you and your suppliers' organizations, and the limitations of the communications and transmission systems between the two. Having remote suppliers can expose geopolitical risks, sovereignty risk, and exchange rate risk.

This by no means implies that technical risks are easy to address. Technical risks are rooted in the complexity of the solutions you need. In the past, for some IT solutions, all that was needed was a mainframe and a database; this limited the complexity and the number of components that could fail. With the proliferation of technology over the past 10 to 20 years, an application may have separate databases, a data warehouse, Web servers, customizable user interfaces, application code servers, wide area and local area networks, and routers, among other infrastructures. Now there are many more potential points of failure, and this risk becomes even more challenging as new technologies continue to proliferate.

> **TIP** Overly optimistic estimates are often at the core of a project's technical risks.

Many technical risks stem from inadequate resources to accomplish required tasks, sometimes fostered by imprecise estimates of the work required to complete the project.

Steve comments on the challenges of technical risks and obsolescence.

> **Steve:**   It's very difficult to predict and select the right technology, because it changes so fast. Most of the time you know that when you establish your design constraints, some significant part of the underlying technology will have changed by the time you attempt to deploy the product. We've had instances where we had to buy components off eBay, because you couldn't source the component through the suppliers any longer.

Matt knows exactly what Steve is talking about.

> **Matt:**   Thank goodness for eBay.

Steve laughs but then gets a somber look.

> **Steve:**   You'd be surprised how much work we do is actually supported that way.

Incorrect estimates can stem from poorly defined tasks, from excessive optimism, or from adjustments made by management. Some suppliers deliberately lowball their estimates to get the contract and then worry later how to execute it.

Your acquisition strategy initially identifies the risks associated with an acquisition. Then you plan your approach based on those risks. As the project progresses toward selecting a supplier, the risks specific to the supplier's technical and management approach become important. These risks particularly lie in the supplier's capability to meet contractual requirements, including schedules and cost targets.

2.2.4 Applying the CMMI-ACQ in Developing Your Strategy

The CMMI-ACQ provides specific recommendations on how to develop and maintain a business and technical management framework, a strategy for planning, directing, contracting for, and managing an acquisition project or program (see Table 2-1).

The acquisition strategy results from a thorough understanding of both the specific acquisition project and the general acquisition environment (Table 2-1, practice 1.1). You identify the capabilities and objectives that the acquisition is intended to meet. Typically, the capabilities documented in the acquisition strategy highlight the characteristics of the target technology solution. The strategy also identifies dependencies or interoperability requirements for planned or existing capabilities of other technology solutions in your intended environment.

The acquisition strategy also establishes planned milestone decision points and acquisition phases. It prescribes the accomplishments for each phase and identifies the critical events affecting project management. Schedule parameters include, at a minimum, the projected dates for project initiation, other major decision points, and initial operational capability.

Moreover, your acquisition strategy defines the acquisition approach that the project will use to achieve full capability: whether evolutionary or single-step. The strategy should include a rationale justifying the choice. When a project uses an evolutionary acquisition approach, the acquisition strategy describes the initial capability and how it will be funded, developed, tested, produced, and supported. The acquisition strategy previews similar planning for subsequent increments or spirals and identifies the approach used to integrate or retrofit earlier increments with later increments.

The acquisition strategy also describes how risk is to be handled, identifies major risks, and documents which risks are to be shared with the supplier and which risks are to be retained by the acquirer. Standardized procurement documents (for example, standard supplier agreements) are yet another ingredient of an acquisition strategy. The acquirer determines the type of supplier agreement planned for acquiring the technology solution (for example, firm fixed-price; fixed-price incentive; cost-plus incentive fee; and cost-plus award fee) and the reasons it is suitable, including considerations of risk assessment and reasonable risk sharing by the acquirer and the supplier.

The acquisition strategy also explains the planned incentive structure for the acquisition and describes how it gives the supplier an incentive to provide the product or services at or below the established cost objectives and to sat-

Table 2-1 *Solicitation and Supplier Agreement Development Goal 1: Practices and Tips*

CMMI-ACQ Process Area: Solicitation and Supplier Agreement Development	
1. Goal: Develop the acquisition strategy, qualify potential suppliers, and develop a solicitation package that includes the requirements and proposal evaluation criteria.	
Practice	**Tips**
1.1 Develop and maintain the overall acquisition strategy content.	• Establish a road map for technology solutions built on a sound rationale. • Strike the right balance between internal and external suppliers. • Align the acquisition strategy with the overall business strategy and your own goals. • Carefully calibrate strategic choices for the acquisition strategy. • Mandate an evolutionary approach when acquiring technology solutions, with single-step acquisition as the exception. • Structure competitive acquisitions to allow vendors to partner together on teams with prime and subcontractor relationships. • If an evolutionary or incremental approach is adopted, ensure that the supplier and acquirer life-cycle phases are aligned. • Incorporate COTS for technology solutions where competitive parity or an 80:20 solution will suffice. • In incremental acquisitions, tailor the agreement type appropriately to the life-cycle phase of the project. • When you define your acquisition strategy, choose the approach for operating and maintaining the solution. • Make sure that the acquisition strategy is viewed as a core competency and is defined by the organization. • Account for business and technical risks at the project and at the organizational level. • Quantify risks early with a simple, 5×5 scorecard. • Set the direction for a comprehensive risk avoidance and dispute resolution before the project starts. • Encourage suppliers to work together by defining joint operating principles for the team. • Overly optimistic estimates are often at the core of a project's technical risks.

isfy the schedule and key performance objectives. If more than one incentive is planned for a supplier agreement, the acquisition strategy explains how the incentives complement each other without overlapping. The acquisition strategy identifies any unusual terms and conditions of the planned supplier agreement and all existing or contemplated deviations to an organization's terms and conditions, if any.

Finally, the acquirer develops a strategy for supporting the acquired technology solution as part of the acquisition strategy. The support strategy addresses how the acquirer has planning to support the fielded technology solution throughout its life.

2.3 From Strategy to Plan

The primary objective of any strategy is to better focus, bound, and set the stage for planning and executing projects, because individual projects build on the organizational strategy as they start their own planning phase. At the beginning of planning for a project, you need a process to align and connect the project to your broader strategy and direction.

An important part of connecting strategy to plans is to establish clear, measurable goals that guide development of acquired technology solutions and ensure the project's contribution to your objectives. It is critical to carefully and pragmatically plan how to realize the acquisition strategy through budgeting, scheduling, supervision, and control of resources. Tightly integrated strategy and planning enable the organization to ensure that any engagement with technology suppliers matches these strategies and measurable objectives.

> **TIP** Tightly integrate acquisition strategy and acquisition project plans.

An acquirer depends on the collective capability of its suppliers to deliver technology solutions that meet contractual requirements and satisfy customers. Leveraging suppliers to obtain technology requires up-front planning. Plans may be for a single project or initiative, or for your entire technology portfolio. Nevertheless, planning is a key component of your success.

A project team must make choices: how tasks and activities should be sequenced, how work should be organized, how the effort should be led and managed, what milestones should be established, how senior management will interact with the project, and how problems should be framed and solved. Those choices are based on the acquisition strategy.

Let's return to the strategy meeting among the senior executives. Steve wants to speak about the importance of following the acquisition strategy.

Steve: One thing I hear all the time: "Well, let's get started, let's do something. We've got a strategy, let's get going." I hear this only too often—most of the time mixed with some battle cry to rally the troops. But then I say something like, "Let's define scope," or "Let's get a solid estimate," and all the air goes out of the balloon. Some folks will surely think, "What a waste of time. You're holding us up from getting real work done. Can't we figure this out as we go?" The sentiment seems to be, let's not waste any time visualizing the steps it takes to be successful, but let's charge ahead, all heroes in the first row, and the stars will align—somehow.

Steve looks around the room. Lots of wry smiles.

Steve: Not to give away my age, but this reminds me of the attitude that led to the spaghetti code of the 1960s: Let's code first and figure out the architecture of the technology solution later. Or, let's code first and get the requirements later. More often than not, we ended up with a tangled mess of missed expectations and an unmaintainable solution that didn't fit very well into the overall landscape. Now that we're acquiring technology solutions, turning everybody loose without an understanding of scope and without a thorough estimate virtually guarantees a new version of spaghetti code—but now it's spaghetti with collections of programs as well as individual programs. It's a much more potent mixture—more like the *spaghetti all'arrabbiata* of technology solutions.

Matt: Well, I don't know what *spaghetti whatchamacallit* means, but—

Everyone laughs.

Steve: It means "angry spaghetti."

Matt: Angry. I hear that.

Steve waits until the laughter subsides.

Steve: Yes, it's a real mess. The problem is that it puts the squeeze on the development budget. Even worse, we'll end up spending the monies earmarked for new capability and innovation on trying to maintain the mess we created together with our suppliers. There has to be a better way.

Matt: Yes, I agree. But how can we pragmatically address scope and estimates without ending up in analysis paralysis?

Steve: You have to know what you're talking about, both from a business and a technology perspective, to get a firm handle on the scope that needs to be addressed. You and your team have to have a deep understanding and experience in the area of the business that needs the technology solution. And I mean a group of folks that have lived the business process, the technology—not somebody that has read about it in the latest issue of *Technology Widget* magazine. You're always tempted to get a project off the ground immediately. We've learned the hard way that without the right people on the bus it is dangerous to start the engine and get going. More often than not, the project will end up in the ditch.

> **TIP**   To develop your acquisition plan, leverage competent individuals in the organization who understand both process and technology.

Steve shakes his head and continues.

Steve: To get a handle on this, we're becoming much more demand-driven, letting our customers pull technology rather than us pushing technology to them. With this customer-centric view, we're rethinking how we treat the definition of project scope. Traditionally, we attempted to lock in scope for a project and negotiated or varied the resources assigned and the schedule. Success was defined by delivering the scope that was originally promised, fully functional, on or before the delivery date. Getting a scope change was virtually impossible.

Matt: But isn't it a good idea to define the scope of a project early on?

Steve: Yes—in a world without uncertainty and with perfect estimates. To get the scope defined perfectly before any real work begins, we've added more and more analysis techniques over the years. But this has made the project durations even longer, making the estimates even less reliable—and we experienced a classic "loop of doom." Applying a customer-centric view has changed all that.

Matt: How does it work?

Steve: The scope is more of a variable rather than a constant. We treat scope as negotiable and build in an agreed-upon "scope buffer" in order to adjust during a project as necessary. It took some time to get to this point—to build trust between our team and the customers, who needed to see that we can commit and deliver. Building in this flexibility has actually stabilized our scope definition, because we've learned how to listen better to our customers, and we've drastically reduced our delivery time by executing projects for only the functionality needed according to the customer's schedule.

Matt: But this doesn't mean you start a project with a blank sheet of paper, right?

Steve: That's right. We start with an initial set of requirements and the project objectives. We use them to establish the WBS [work breakdown structure] or to select a standard WBS from our process assets. We're very clear about what type of work to give to a supplier. The only variable is how much work a supplier gets for a given project. We develop a WBS that clearly identifies what project work is performed by us and what project work is performed by the supplier. The supplier work identified in the WBS then becomes the foundation for the supplier's statement of work, which identifies those items being acquired—only the portion of the project scope that is included within the related supplier agreement.

> **TIP**   Listen to the voice of the customer to determine project scope.

2.3.1 Developing the Acquirer and Supplier Work Breakdown Structures

Typically, you develop two WBSs for an acquisition project: an acquirer overall project WBS and a supplier WBS. The scope of the acquirer WBS is the entire project or program, including work performed by your employees as well as the products and services acquired from the supplier. Your overall project WBS clearly identifies which elements are acquired, and which are the result of your internal efforts. This WBS includes activities performed by you as well as milestones and deliverables for the suppliers.

From an acquirer's point of view, the acquirer's WBS tends to be much more focused on the project life cycle, whereas the supplier WBS is typically structured around the deliverables. The supplier WBS defines the structure to be used by the supplier in reporting costs and progress. The supplier milestones and deliverables are typically associated with payments if the supplier meets the milestone or deliverable acceptance criteria. Usually, the acquirer defines the WBS only to two or three levels of detail, as depicted in Table 2-2. Suppliers often expand these WBS elements into deeper levels of detail to suit their project management and delivery processes and procedures.

> **TIP**   Cover all necessary work for an acquisition in the acquirer's WBS, indicating supplier work through deliverables only.

Table 2-2 *Acquirer and Supplier Work Breakdown Structures*

Acquirer WBS	Supplier WBS
1 Project	1 Product
1.1 Acquisition Planning	1.1 \<subsystem1\>
1.1.1 Stakeholder Data Collection	1.1.1 \<component11\>
1.1.2 Systems Engineering	1.1.2 \<component12\>
1.1.3 Acquisition Strategy Development	1.1.3 \<component13\>
1.1.4 Program Staffing	1.2 \<subsystem2\>
1.1.5 Program Training	1.2.1 \<component21\>
1.2 RFP	1.2.2 \<component22\>
1.2.1 Development	1.3 \<subsystem3\>
1.2.2 Review and Approval	1.4 Integration, Assembly, Test, and Checkout
1.3 Solicitation and Source Selection	1.5 Systems Engineering
1.3.1 Proposal Review	1.6 Program Management
1.3.2 Source Selection	1.7 Training
1.3.3 Contracting	1.8 Data
1.4 Procurement	1.9 System Test and Evaluation
1.4.1 System procurement	1.10 Peculiar Support Equipment
1.4.2 Training procurement	1.11 Common Support Equipment
1.4.3 Support procurement	1.12 Operational and Site Activation
1.5 Contract Monitoring	1.13 Industrial Facilities
1.5.1 Deliverable Evaluations	1.14 Initial Spares and Repair Parts
1.5.2 Metric Reviews	
1.5.3 Program Reviews	
1.5.4 Contractor Appraisals	
1.6 Training	
1.6.1 User Training	
1.6.2 Maintainer Training	
1.7 System Acceptance	
1.8 Installation	
1.8.1 System Installation	
1.8.2 Intersystem Integration	
1.9 System Validation	
1.10 Operational Switch-over	
1.11 Program Management	
1.12 Peculiar Support Equipment	
1.13 Common Support Equipment	
1.14 Initial Spares and Repair Parts	

Creating the WBS helps you in developing estimates for the project work, including high-level estimates of the work to be done by suppliers. If you don't have any estimates, you risk making the wrong decisions for the right reasons. In any case, the organization runs the risk of suboptimizing the project and any associated projects by removing the wrong items from the scope or looking only at the short term and sacrificing long-term opportunities.

2.3.2 Improving Your Project Estimates

Often when engineers look at quality, cost, and schedule for programs and projects, optimism takes over. There is a strong tendency to overcommit. As a result, every estimate covers only 50 percent of what is truly involved to meet the commitment. This is like "management by rebate"; everything is half-off.

When an organization understands and recognizes this tendency, it has taken the first step toward correcting the behavior. Acquirers are always eager to put technology in place, because they know it has the potential of making the organization more efficient and thus more profitable. A specific technology may be deployed only once in an organization, but the supplier may have packaged, implemented, and configured this particular solution a hundred times before, especially if it is a COTS product. As an acquirer, you must reenergize the supplier with your excitement about the pending technology solution as if the supplier were implementing it for the first time. You must work to form a cohesive team and at the same time leverage the fact that the supplier has done this a number of times.

TIP Improve the fidelity of project estimates through collaboration with your supplier.

Acquirers tend to use estimation models and tools that they are comfortable with—unfortunately, in some cases, whether or not the models and tools support the acquisition modus operandi. Most of the time, the models or tools in use are more appropriate for in-house work, and therefore they're not calibrated for outsourcing technology solutions. Historically, they tend to take a very "insourced" view of delivering technology solutions.

Matt recognizes this at both the project and the organizational level as the acquisition strategy for this latest project is being developed. To correct this, he requires the project managers to come together and build an estimation model that takes outsourcing into account.

TIP Augment estimation models available for suppliers to differentiate between your work and the supplier's work.

Matt also asks to see the operating model and requires that it include personnel and associated skills. And finally, he wants an overall risk assessment of the outsourcing engagement, including such elements as how the company's skills and maturity will help or hinder this approach, as well as recommendations for mitigating any organizational issues that might arise.

Although Steve believes that this is a "mission impossible" task, he is up for the challenge. By the time he is finished, he has talked to key leaders and collected their input through a series of workshops and personal interviews. One need he has identified is the need for global reach. Other needs include the following:

- To respond more rapidly to business change
- To estimate operating costs more accurately
- To reduce capital investments
- To focus on a set of core business capabilities
- To gain access to high-demand technology skills
- To achieve flexibility to grow or shrink as the business demands
- To bring together internal technology resources
- To standardize the technology environment

All the leadership team members agree that upon closer analysis it is shortsighted to move to outsourcing or change the mix of internal to external resources because it is in vogue, or simply because it might potentially reduce costs; instead, they have worked to make sure that outsourcing is a fit for the organization by ensuring that the organization can continue to meet its stated goals and objectives.

TIP To establish a practical estimation model for acquisition projects, involve all the affected functions of your organization.

Steve works with the finance staff to build an "as-is" cost and resource model, and for the first time he has a detailed handle on which expenditures are truly technology-related. He also has the first draft of an operating model in the anticipated outsourced environment. He calls a meeting, inviting Matt as well as Kristin Wells and George Taylor, executives for one of the company's key suppliers.

Steve: In all my years of consulting in this area before I joined our company, I've never seen an organization become so committed so quickly to try to do the right thing from a strategy and planning perspective. And our leadership team believes that as a result of our efforts, the business has a much better handle on strategy and technology alignment than ever before. We've set out a good path that we can now articulate to our potential suppliers so that they can come back with creative proposals to help us meet the needs of the business.

This estimation model lets us make better estimates. We'll use a combined top-down and bottom-up estimation approach. The supplier estimates are an important part in all this. For instance, initial estimates can be revised based on the suppliers' estimates in responses to the solicitation package.

Kristin elaborates on this point.

Kristin: We have established a working relationship with Matt and his team so that we can review our supplier estimates in detail. We do this as an "open book" review. We provide our underlying estimation parameters and models. In many cases, we hadn't calibrated our estimation models to account for the joint capabilities we've built with Matt and the team. This took some time, but now we can start up any project and get it off to a good start.

Understanding and estimating the total work are critical, and so are the decisions about which life-cycle approach best delivers a technology solution. When you're acquiring technology solutions, multiple life cycles are probably involved in a project. Your life cycle typically begins at the inception of the acquisition—a time when a need is recognized and a determination is made to address it. The life cycle extends at least until the delivery, acceptance, and commissioning of the acquired product. Sometimes, it is extended to cover acquisition of support and maintenance services after the product is fielded.

The supplier's life cycle, in contrast, begins with the issuance of the solicitation package by the acquirer. For the successful bidder, the life cycle extends until the delivery and acceptance of the technology solution. In some cases, the supplier is also responsible for training, support, and maintenance. In other cases, training and support may be provided by independent suppliers. In such cases, you negotiate separate agreements with these suppliers and they in turn establish their own life cycles.

> **TIP** Explicitly agree on how to align your project life cycle with the supplier's project life cycle. Review and maintain this mapping throughout the project.

Steve: It's key to explicitly agree on the linkages—the interfaces—between our project life cycle and the supplier's life cycle. We strongly believe in letting the suppliers use their own life-cycle models, because we want to ensure that they use tightly controlled, repeatable processes rather than doing a "one off" for us. At the same time, as acquirers of technology solutions, we establish stringent transition criteria for progressing from one stage to the next, including completion criteria for the current stage plus choice criteria and entrance criteria for the next stage.

Matt interjects a question.

Matt: So how do these fit our desire for maximum transparency and practical management oversight with, let's say, the supplier's desire to execute agile life cycles and processes?

Steve: Years ago I might have said, "Well, not my problem. The suppliers just need to figure out how to fit into our stage-gate process." But after 15 years of sourcing technologies from companies all over the globe, I know better now. We've converted our acquirer life-cycle options as a framework that allows us to match up and tailor our life cycle to different supplier life cycles. This way we can use the same level of management oversight with multiple suppliers and at the same time allow the supplier to use its own methodologies.

You have to lay down a path to success. The question is, what are the key elements that will allow the project to be successful? Even in the early stages, the plan gives us a template for thinking about all the elements we need to create a value-added technology solution. This plan isn't just about technology. It has to address all aspects of the project, including foundation and structure for the targeted business process and supplier management processes that are so necessary for project success.

2.3.3 Developing Your Project Plan

The project plan is an important communication tool, and it provides an overarching framework against which all work is accomplished. For that, the plan documents the tasks required to deliver a technology solution and to facilitate success throughout the project's life cycle. Developing an effective project plan is a challenge in itself, and it can be even more daunting if it's being done for the first time. Even those with advanced degrees may not have learned how to put together a comprehensive project plan for acquiring technology solutions.

It's important to think about all the relevant facets, but it is equally important not to get bogged down with unnecessary detail early in a project. Generating a large volume of paper is definitely not the best game plan early on. Acquirers do not want to find themselves in a situation where the maintenance of the project plan and the project paper flow become as crucial as accomplishing the tasks that the project needs to complete. George Taylor speaks up.

> **George:**   Often the problem is that our acquirer customers plan the minutest things, and we sometimes cannot even find the information we need to get started. We spend all our time looking for the basic information.

> **Steve:**   I know what you mean, George. We continuously take a hard look at the amount of paperwork we generate together with our suppliers. You don't want your project managers to say, "Well, out of the five-day week it takes me two days to just keep up with the paperwork. I get paperwork that doesn't even affect me, and I have to sort through it to find the stuff I need."

Project plans are living documents. They contain information that is needed to understand the scope of work required and the likely structure of the project, and to determine the risk of continuing to the next phase of the acquisition project, including having a good handle on the likelihood that you'll be able to hit the delivery date. The plan also identifies dependencies between various organizations within the acquirer and with the supplier.

> **TIP**   Keep plans current. Capture information when it is needed, but not earlier than absolutely necessary.

Information acquired before it is needed—or, even worse, information acquired and never used—is a waste of time and money. Steve emphasizes this point.

> **Steve:**   You need a level of detail that allows you to flawlessly execute the project with the current parameters such as business conditions, state of technology, or staffing. But you need to recognize that if the parameters change, the plan needs to be adjusted. The fact is, original plans often turn out to be wrong or at least need to be adjusted along the way. This doesn't mean we shouldn't create any plans to begin with. But it's a reminder to avoid treating plans as static. We'll have to plan in such a way that we can adjust. It's important to create plans that account for uncertainty and are flexible.

As the project is defined—and in many cases, throughout the project—the plan is updated several times, each time increasing the level of detail and confidence that all the essential work has been covered.

The specific format of a project plan isn't critical, but Matt highlights what is important about planning.

> **Matt:** Without any doubt, people who plan have a much higher chance of successfully delivering technology solutions. Project managers often find it harder than they expected to prepare their plans, thinking through the technical and business constraints, and building their joint acquirer-supplier teams. Before committing funds, my staff and I want to be certain that the plan has been carefully thought through and the project team has the appropriate skills and experience. They have to manage effectively, seize opportunities along the way, solve problems, and, at the end of the day, add money to the bottom line. The plan must be well prepared and persuasive in conveying the project's potential. It should cover all the major issues but not be so detailed that it puts the reader off. The emphasis must be on substance and not form.

Senior managers in the acquisition organization are not the only people who find project plans invaluable. For technology project managers, careful preparation of a plan is an opportunity to think through all facets of a project, to examine the consequences of various approaches to deployment, operations, and financing, and to determine what human, physical, and financial resources are required. The plan facilitates error-free delivery of technology solutions and avoids the crippling expense of trial-and-error operation.

The discipline of writing a project plan can cause program or project managers and their teams to realize that (using an engineering example) the major application of a technology is not to create efficiencies in the existing product development process but instead to allow customers to directly interact with the engineering staff during product development. Then a good project manager can change the focus of the project accordingly. The successful project manager finds that the plan helps in monitoring the project's performance. If the need arises to modify the project's direction, the project manager can do so rapidly by adjusting the plan, getting it approved, and using it to communicate effectively to all stakeholders.

> **TIP** Focus on substance over form when pulling together your project plans.

A plan typically starts with a summary, as shown in Table 2-3. For instance, it summarizes the technology solution briefly and describes the nature and current condition of the targeted business process and industry. In this way,

Table 2-3 *Sample Outline of a Project Plan*

Project Plan
• Project Summary
• Features and Advantages of the Technology Solution
• Business Process/User Analysis
• Deployment Plan
• Design and Development Plan
• Operations and Support Plan
• Project Team and Stakeholders
• Financial Plan
• Critical Issues and Risks
• Schedule

it shows where and how the technology fits in, along with potential customers and physical locations where the technology may reside.

A section in the plan usually contains detailed information about the technology solution and highlights its distinctive features and the needs it satisfies. Diagrams and sketches are useful to clarify the project's intent. Steve explains.

> **Steve:**   You want to know: What is the project team trying to build? What kind of special know-how or competitive advantage does the supplier bring to the table? What are the advantages and drawbacks of the proposed technology solution? Are there any opportunities for logically extending it to other business processes? All the answers to these questions are in the plan.

The plan also discusses in some detail the nature and size of the targeted business process and potential users. Furthermore, key financial characteristics, as well as recent trends and the growth potential of the targeted business processes, lead to initial demand estimates for the acquired product or service.

Program managers must develop enough facts to convince themselves and senior management that the business process for the acquired product or service is such that return on investment targets can be met despite competition and other factors. The business process analysis must home in on the area addressed by the technology solution. If the business process analysis lacks insight and information, the whole project plan will be vague and risky. A good business process analysis goes a long way toward creating a value-added technology solution and should be viewed as the plan's keystone. The choice of deployment strategies, the size of the project team and support organization, and facilities are all derived from the project team's understanding of the targeted business process.

> **TIP**   Structure project plans like business plans.

Deployment is part of a well-conceived project plan and a prerequisite for success. A comprehensive plan details the steps necessary to penetrate the targeted business process and includes a description of the solution's warranty as well as strategies for distribution and training. It is critical to work closely with your business partners to specify deployment objectives. These objectives should be quantifiable and measurable, and they should specify a time frame.

You set your initial deployment objectives early on when you capture ideas for transforming or improving a business process and tentatively allocate a budget for their exploration. These initial objectives are often an educated guess that you refine throughout the project's life cycle.

The plan deployment also discusses the kinds of users who will be targeted for an initial rollout and those who will be sought for later deployments. The plan specifies methods of identifying and contacting specific potential users and lists the features that will be emphasized to support adoption of the solution by the users.

The project plan covers the nature and extent of required design and development work by the supplier. This work might include the engineering necessary to convert a prototype to a finished product, the design of special interfaces to use the product in a business process, the effort of a user interface designer to make the product more usable, or the identification and organization of people, equipment, and special techniques to implement a service.

To make all this happen, you need people, facilities, and capital equipment. Acquisition personnel carefully weigh make-or-buy decisions in terms of which parts of the technology solution will be purchased and which operations will be performed by your workers. The acquisition strategy provides clear direction for this. Work should be allocated to your employees if it matches your organization's strategy and fits the identified core competencies. Often, it becomes a challenge for an organization when its skills and experience to support identified core competencies, such as requirements elicitation and program management, are inadequate. In this case, you might elect to contract for supplemental staff—temporary personnel who have the needed skills.

This approach allows you to move forward with a project while buying time to close the skill and experience gap with internal resources. No acquirer can afford to be exposed in one of its core competencies for too long a time. It is important that the supplemental staffing not come from the same suppliers that are providing the technology solution. Otherwise, your ability to execute might be eroded and a conflict of interest might arise.

> **TIP** Use supplemental staff to temporarily fill gaps in core competencies. These personnel should not come from the same supplier providing the technology solution.

The plan extends throughout the projected useful life of the technology solution in the acquirer's or customer's environment. This component of the plan is critical, because for most technology solutions the initial cost of acquiring the product is only a fraction of the total cost of ownership. The project plan shows the analysis of operations and support via cost-volume information at various levels of operation, with breakdowns of applicable material, labor, purchased components, and management overhead. It also describes the approach to quality, production, and inventory control. For example, the plan contains readiness criteria for the technology solution, the operations organization, and the support organization. Quality control and inspection procedures are important so that operations teams can minimize service problems and ensure customer satisfaction. In addition, it is important to plan how purchasing will operate during the steady use of the technology so that you have adequate materials on hand to ensure uninterrupted operations, that you have obtained the best price and payment terms, and that you have minimized in-process inventory.

> **TIP** Thoroughly understand the commitment of each stakeholder affected by the project.

The project team is the key to this success, as Matt explains.

> **Matt:**   You always look for a committed team, with a balance in skills and experience that match our core competencies.

Accordingly, every plan needs a description of the key members of the project team and their primary responsibilities.

Steve: As part of a project plan, we list all our stakeholders—everybody who has a significant impact, or is significantly impacted, by the project. Each stakeholder has a unique perspective of and specific interests in the project. Our plan calls for one or more people from each stakeholder group to periodically meet throughout the project—for instance, to review project status, project plans, and key project decisions. It's key that we understand the stakeholders' commitment to participate in the project.

The project plan also indicates the financial potential of the project, its return on investment, and its capital needs. The financial plan includes details of the financial commitment to operate the solution after transition from the supplier into the intended environment. When you seek funds for a project to acquire a technology solution, the organization should review the balance sheet and income statement of the affected area for the current and the two prior years. Together with the responsible business lead, you should make a financial projection for the next three years to show the impact of the proposed solution and to highlight the necessary operational financial commitments. You can then analyze this financial information to determine whether the described approach is the best use of resources, or whether there are other ways to improve customer service using the same amount of resources, to offer a new product to your customers, or to deliver more output with fewer resources. The financial analysis gives a clear understanding of the return on investment of a given project.

> **TIP**   Be sure to check the financial viability of suppliers.

Every project has issues and risks, and the project plan invariably contains some implicit assumptions about them. Any risks identified during creation of the acquisition strategy should be captured in the plan. It is important that you understand and communicate negative factors that affect projects. If these factors are not identified and communicated, the credibility of the project manager is at risk and it jeopardizes any future requests for funding. On the other hand, taking the initiative to identify and discuss risks helps demonstrate that risks and issues have been anticipated and can be managed.

Not all risks are created equal. Every project must determine which are most critical to success. The project then must attempt to minimize the impact of unfavorable developments in each risk area. Together with the acquisition strategy, the risks identified in project planning form the basis for some of the criteria used in evaluating suppliers. As the project evolves, risks may be revised based on changing conditions (e.g., new circumstances during execution of the supplier agreement).

> **TIP**   Identify the most critical risks and analyze them comprehensively.

A schedule that shows the timing and dependencies of the major tasks and events such as milestones is an essential part of a project plan. In addition to a planning aid that shows critical deadlines, a well-prepared schedule can be an effective communication and management tool. Such a schedule demonstrates the ability of the project manager and the team to plan for successful delivery of a technology solution in a way that recognizes obstacles and minimizes risk.

> **Steve:**   In a way, a good schedule is like a river where work flows smoothly from one task to the next to reach the customer at just the right time. The river—the main work flow—gets fed by secondary streams of work; those are tasks that have to get done in support of the main work flow. Unlike when a tributary meets a river, we often have to do some work to integrate the secondary stream of work into the main work flow. This is especially important since a large portion of the work comes from the supplier.
>
> So our schedule always has to consider how to best integrate our work with the supplier's work to get the solution to the customer as promised.

> **Matt:**   That's right, Steve. Each task requires different levels of effort, personnel, resources, and time, with some being more difficult than others. A meaningful, executable schedule clearly identifies the potential bottlenecks that could keep the work from flowing as planned. It is crucial to build control points into the schedule to provide visibility of changes to conditions or new situations. We integrate standard measures to get a handle on our progress according to schedule as well as the customer's perception. It's important that all this is actually reflected in the schedule rather than viewed as information that is ancillary to creating it.

The most elegant plan has no value without organizational commitment. Project plans should be circulated among the acquisition team members to ensure consistency, to stakeholders for review and comment, and to management for review and approval. Nevertheless, an executable plan evolves over time, as teams find alternative technologies or better ways to deliver functionality.

> **TIP**   Establish and maintain a resource-based schedule containing all acquirer tasks, supplier deliverables, and milestones.

2.3.4 Applying the CMMI-ACQ to Developing Your Project Plan

The CMMI-ACQ provides specific recommendations on project planning as it relates to estimation of the work for a given project, both for the work required by the acquirer and the work that is negotiated from the supplier. It also establishes the chosen life cycle, a top-level WBS, and project effort and cost (see Table 2-4).

Project planning involves developing the plan, interacting with stakeholders, obtaining commitment to the plan, and managing the plan (Table 2-4, practice 1.1). You build the acquisition plan on the acquisition strategy, which you develop by applying the processes in the Solicitation and Supplier Agreement Development process area. The plan must reflect the objectives of the acquisition as well as constraints, technologies, supplier agreement types, end user requirements, risk, and product support.

Planning focuses initially on estimates of project planning parameters. These include estimates for the work to be done by you and high-level estimates of the work to be done by the supplier.

Estimates used in putting together the initial plan will be revised later based on suppliers' estimates in response to the proposal (Table 2-4, practices 1.2–1.4). In

Table 2-4 *Project Planning Goal 1: Practices and Tips*

CMMI-ACQ Process Area: Project Planning	
1. Goal: Estimates of project planning parameters are established and maintained.	
Practices	**Tips**
1.1 Establish a top-level work breakdown structure (WBS) to estimate the scope of the project.	• Tightly integrate acquisition strategy and acquisition project plans. • To quickly develop the plan, leverage competent individuals in the organization who understand both process and technology.
1.2 Establish and maintain estimates of the attributes of the work products and tasks. 1.3 Define the project life-cycle phases on which to scope the planning effort. 1.4 Estimate the project effort and cost for the work products and tasks based on estimation rationale.	• Cover all necessary work for an acquisition with the acquirer's WBS, indicating supplier work through deliverables only. • Improve the fidelity of project estimates through collaboration between acquirer and supplier. • Augment estimation models available for suppliers to differentiate between your work and the supplier's work. • Involve all impacted functions of your organization to establish a practical estimation model for acquisition projects. • Keep plans current, capturing information when it is needed but not earlier than absolutely necessary.

formulating these estimates you should consider project requirements (including any specific products or technologies), organizational requirements, and any customer requirements. The scope of the project is also important. The scope can be managed in a project plan in a number of ways, including breaking the scope into manageable, deliverable pieces by using an incremental acquisition approach. The list of deliverables, along with their complexity, has a direct impact on the schedule. When you're converting project attributes into labor hours and costs, it's useful to study historical data from similar projects.

The WBS delineates the work that is given to the acquirer and the work that is given to the supplier based on the acquisition strategy. The supplier work becomes the basis for the statement of work as a part of the solicitation proposal from the acquirer.

The CMMI-ACQ also provides specific recommendations for project planning as it relates to the creation of an integrated plan that manages the work of the acquirer and supplier. It also acknowledges the use of project planning to manage the solicitation and management activities for a given effort (see Table 2-5).

After project estimates are completed, the project's budget and schedule can be finalized. The project's budget and schedule include the efforts of the acquirer, the efforts of the supplier, and those of any supporting organizations for the duration of the project (Table 2-5, practice 2.1).

You establish major milestones to ensure the completeness of one or more deliverables. Milestones can be either event-based or calendar-based. Many schedules include durations for activities for which little or no data is available. Identifying the extent and potential impact of these assumptions gives you some insight into an overall level of confidence for the project.

Constraints in the project need to be identified as early as possible because they limit the options you will have. This is of particular importance because some of these constraints are directly related to characteristics that are used to prequalify suppliers—characteristics such as technology capabilities, processes, domain knowledge, and production capability.

Risks to the project should be identified and analyzed (Table 2-5, practice 2.2). These risks come from multiple perspectives, including acquisition, technology, management, operations, supplier agreements, industry, support, and users. Statutory and regulatory requirements also must be analyzed from a risk perspective.

Together with the acquisition strategy, risks are used as part of the basis for evaluation criteria for supplier proposals. As the project evolves, you update the risks based on any changes. Risks should be documented and managed based on their potential downside to the project.

Table 2-5 *Project Planning Goal 2: Practices and Tips*

CMMI-ACQ Process Area: Project Planning	
2. Goal: A project plan is established and maintained as the basis for managing the project.	
Practices	**Tips**
2.1 Establish and maintain the project's budget and schedule.	• Build an "as-is" cost and resource model, including independent estimates of supplier proposals.
2.2 Identify and analyze project risks. 2.3 Plan for the management of project data. 2.4 Plan for necessary resources to perform the project. 2.5 Plan for knowledge and skills necessary to perform the project. 2.6 Plan for the involvement of identified stakeholders. 2.7 Establish and maintain the overall project plan content. 2.8 Plan for the transition and life-cycle operations and support for the project.	• Identify the most critical risks, and analyze them comprehensively. • Be sure to check the financial viability of suppliers. • Use supplemental staff to temporarily fill gaps in core competencies. These personnel should not come from the same supplier providing the technology solution. • Use supplemental staff if there is a gap in acquirer core competencies. • Use the voice of the customer to acquire only the functionality needed. • Focus on substance over form when pulling together your project plans. • Explicitly agree on how to align the acquirer's project life cycle with the supplier's project life cycle. Review and maintain this mapping throughout the project.

Data management includes all the forms of documentation required to support a project (Table 2-5, practice 2.3). Data requirements should be established based on a common set of standards for the organization. Standards for data management are important for consistent, efficient management. One of the most important aspects of data in an acquisition is to specify who creates what data and how data will be shared between the acquirer and the supplier. The supplier agreement should outline any uses of data and data access rights. It's crucial to the viability of a product's operation that you plan for data management as the product transitions to operations.

You use initial estimates to build required project resources for the plan (Table 2-5, practices 2.4–2.8). The expansion of the WBS allows you to create a resource plan that can be tracked and managed. The plan should identify the necessary skills to execute the project based on the defined roles. The plan also identifies any critical facilities or equipment.

In addition, the CMMI-ACQ provides recommendations on project planning as it relates to capturing the specific commitments that have been made, including resources, requirements, and stakeholders (see Table 2-6).

After the plans are developed, you should review them to understand the commitments based on the estimates and compare them to the available resources (Table 2-6, practice 3.1). Then you reconcile any differences by prioritizing technical requirements, obtaining more resources, finding ways to make the execution of the project more efficient, purchasing some of the technology components, or adjusting the mix of staff skills (Table 2-6, practice 3.2). During supplier selection and negotiation, you also reconcile the planned project work with supplier proposals. Following the completion of the supplier agreement, you incorporate the supplier's plans into the overall project plan in order to ensure alignment. This consolidation should include the agreed-to major milestones, deliverables, and reviews.

Stakeholder commitment is also obtained (Table 2-6, practice 3.3). The individual or group making the commitment should have a high level of

Table 2-6 *Project Planning Goal 3: Practices and Tips*

CMMI-ACQ Process Area: Project Planning	
3. Goal: Commitments to the project plan are established and maintained.	
Practices	**Tips**
3.1 Review all plans that affect the project to understand project commitments.	• Structure project plans like business plans.
3.2 Reconcile the project plan to reflect available and estimated resources. 3.3 Obtain commitment from relevant stakeholders responsible for performing and supporting plan execution.	• Establish and maintain a resource-based schedule containing all acquirer tasks, supplier deliverables, and milestones. • Thoroughly understand the commitment of each stakeholder affected by the project.

confidence that the work can be performed within the specified cost, schedule, and performance constraints. Occasionally, provisional commitments are adequate to support initial work. You can use the WBS to manage commitments throughout the plan. Internal and external commitments should be reviewed with management as appropriate.

2.4 Partnering with Suppliers

Deciding whom to partner with requires information validated through supplier responses, external sources of information about suppliers, due diligence, and team interactions. After the acquisition strategy is developed, you must first identify potential suppliers that have the capabilities and resources to meet the needs of the acquisition. Section 2.4.1 discusses how to find suppliers for the bidding supplier list, how to create the proposal, and how to communicate to potential suppliers that a proposal is in development.

After the bidding suppliers submit their responses, you must evaluate and rank them based on their ability to meet the proposal as described. Section 2.4.2 outlines the key activities in this evaluation, including giving suppliers the opportunity to further clarify and communicate their understanding of the work. Then negotiations are finalized and a final supplier selection is made.

After the supplier is selected, the supplier agreement is created, documented, reviewed, agreed to, and signed. Section 2.4.3 focuses on these activities.

2.4.1 Discovering What Fits

In a technology sourcing relationship, one of your most important decisions is which supplier to partner with, whether you are purchasing one capability or a portfolio of initiatives. It is critical to conduct research to determine the pool of capable suppliers. This may be as simple as leveraging technology research firms like Gartner or Forrester, surveying other organizations in the same industry to leverage their expertise, or submitting a request for information (RFI) to potential suppliers.

TIP Use multiple sources to identify potential supplier capabilities.

Consistent with the acquisition strategy and with the project being sourced, you develop a list of potential suppliers that can deliver the required capability. These suppliers are identified from a variety of sources, including past experience, industry analyses, and industry publications. This list should be kept to a manageable size to avoid excessive costs in managing the outsourcing efforts.

Even if you typically rely on the major companies in the field, you should include an adequate number of suppliers to foster a competitive environment.

A competitive environment is valuable not only from a pricing perspective but also because it allows you to review various technology solutions and look at alternatives from the competing suppliers. Another approach is to sole-source the project if it has characteristics that warrant this action. You might choose this option if you have worked with a supplier on this project and this supplier is the most efficient builder of certain additional functionality. Another reason might be that the supplier happens to have sole access to technology that is critical to the delivery of the specified functionality.

Before you consider a supplier, it should pass certain criteria: its experience with similar projects, whether it has the critical technical resources to execute the project, and the availability of these critical resources. In addition, the supplier's current financial status, credit status, financial stability, and access to capital need to be evaluated.

The pool of viable supplier candidates can be small. For example, if you decide to bundle products or services into one solicitation package, then there may not be a single supplier that can meet all your needs. In this case, you can identify a small group of suppliers that can work in various technology areas to deliver the desired capability. In addition, you must have the appropriate level of oversight in place to manage a multisupplier engagement, with clearly identified roles and responsibilities among the suppliers and your own personnel. You must clearly identify how the various suppliers will work with each other to deliver the solution.

Let's return to our fictitious acquisition project. It's time to narrow the number of suppliers for his solicitation proposals, and Matt has choices to make. He can use a "safe" set of suppliers that the company traditionally has used for the required technology solution. He can rely on these suppliers because they own the majority of the market share in this technology space and can leverage their remote development centers to get lower, blended rates for skilled labor. Another alternative is to go to the major suppliers in India and negotiate deals directly. The choice is not an easy one, because Matt has talked to people in other organizations who have gotten mixed results from using both models.

Matt: If we use a well-known, large supplier, I should have a higher expectation of success and reduce my risks. And yet, if there isn't good communication between the prime supplier and their offshore development centers, my risks increase. On the other hand, if I go directly to an offshore supplier—from, let's say, India—will I have other risks around communications? It seems that success rates working directly with an

Indian supplier are higher if the contract is well defined. So, for fixed-price contracts, I will include Indian suppliers in my solicitation package distribution. For those contracts that we will approach from a value-pricing perspective—contracts that call for thought leadership and transformation capabilities—I'll use well-established suppliers with a strong presence in our part of the world.

> **TIP** Use the collective capabilities of available suppliers as a key factor in determining the choice of single-source or multisourcing the technology.

Matt and Steve have had numerous discussions about the paradigm shift of moving to an outsourcing model for new areas of technology. They've talked about which technology areas should continue to be executed by their own organization.

Matt: Before we write this contract, we've got to be clear about what we've determined to be core—those activities that we see as our core competencies.

Steve: What's really clear to me is the need to maintain technology standards as a core competency for us, both from a capability perspective as well as standardizing the underlying infrastructure.

Matt: I agree. And of course we need to have program management oversight across the entire engagement.

Steve: And don't forget we're the customer-facing group. We're responsible for the customer requirements. So when we review and approve the high-level design, we have to make sure that it covers those requirements.

Matt: So it would be well worth it for us to go back to the CMMI-ACQ as a reference document. We can use it to make sure that the team is clear about what the work of an acquirer is, and we can use it to validate the solicitation package as we put it together.

> **TIP** Clearly understand your organization's core competencies, and let them guide the outsourcing approach.

Traditionally, outsourcing has focused on big deals—those that come from billion-dollar organizations and run for years. So if you're working in a medium-sized or small organization, you may question whether you can compete with larger companies for the same supplier resources. Do a supplier's best technology architects always go to the biggest contracts, leaving the medium-sized or small acquirers to work with whoever is left? How can such acquirers be sure that they are getting the best resources for their money? What is the industry saying about the treatment of medium-sized or small companies in the outsourcing market?

Matt has this discussion with Kristin Wells (recall that Kristin is a senior executive at one of the suppliers Matt has worked with for a number of years). Kristin tries to assure Matt that his fears are unfounded, but he knows he must be vigilant in verifying that the resources being put in place by suppliers and the quality of the deliverables they were producing are up to snuff.

Kristin: Smaller deals are now driving outsourcing growth, so the market has moved from larger deals to smaller ones. Suppliers understand that the days of the mega-deal are largely a thing of the past. As acquirers have become more selective about outsourcing, suppliers have had to become more nimble in their delivery and support smaller deals, whether from a smaller organization or from a specific segment that's carved out of a larger organization.

Matt: But is that true for IT?

Kristin: In IT, there seem to be two paths emerging. The first is focused on infrastructure transformation. One of the biggest challenges today for companies going global is the lack of a common infrastructure. The faster they can build a common infrastructure, the faster they can build truly common, global systems. Large suppliers are working this space aggressively. Suppliers are offering experts in specific technology areas who can make certain areas more efficient and effective—what I call "desktop in a box." They're approaching it as more of a commodity service. In the industry, we see this outsourcing approach as a reaction to some of the dissatisfaction with the mega-deals. So, many of the larger deals are being broken apart and reduced to the $10–15 million range in overall value. This fosters competition, spreads the risk across multiple suppliers, and challenges the suppliers to become much more focused on specific business needs.

Matt: What does that mean for us?

Kristin: It means you can more easily compare what it costs to perform a set of operations internally versus what it would cost to outsource them, given the internal data that you've collected. So as prices fall across specific service areas like infrastructure, suppliers can bundle specific services to gain scale and remain cost-effective. This will continue to put pressure on internal technology organizations like yours to move to outsourcing.

Your business leaders, if they are savvy, will use this information to force any internal technology activities to justify their existence and remain cost-competitive. Then the obvious business strategy becomes one of taking the noncore, but still required, services to a supplier, one who has demonstrated the best price performance for its customers.

Matt smiles.

Matt: Well, thanks for the sales pitch.

Kristin: Hey, you're not the only one. Suppliers like us are also looking at these changes in the market. We all understand that we need to capture the medium and small deals. Many suppliers have decided to partner with small companies that have very specific technology capabilities. Many times these are technology competencies that the larger suppliers do not possess. So by expanding or contracting this kind of structure, a larger supplier can be more cost-effective and continue to compete by including the smaller, "best of breed" specialty suppliers. Smaller suppliers have the opportunity to compete in a number of ways.

Matt: Again, though, what does that mean for us specifically?

Kristin: It means the size of supplier is not as important as being clear about what you're looking for from your bidding suppliers. You can then encourage them to be creative in forging alliances to get you the best capability in the industry. Smaller suppliers can now offer outsourcing services to any size organization, either directly or through another major supplier. You can use a number of different supplier structures to leverage a more effective best of breed group of suppliers who are highly motivated to keep your business.

Kristin pauses for a moment.

Matt: But won't more suppliers require additional oversight from my organization? Doesn't that drive up costs exponentially? Working with one or two suppliers is one thing . . . working with a group of suppliers sounds like it has the potential for disaster!

Kristin: Matt, that was going to be my next discussion point. You should expect each bidding supplier to address that issue in their proposed solution. There is an operational structure that takes the multisupplier environment into account. Put the option on the table with your bidding suppliers, and see what they come up with!

TIP   Where feasible, seek "commodity" transactions with suppliers in support of smaller, more flexible deals.

Acquirers often notify potential suppliers that a solicitation package will be coming soon. One of the reasons for the advance notice is to determine whether the suppliers you've identified are interested. Given the costs of preparing proposals, it is important to determine their interest and then put appropriate nondisclosure agreements in place. You need to communicate the scope and schedule of the project (and the proposal response), the processes to be used during the proposal process, your evaluation criteria, supplier qualifications, and a date for the supplier to respond.

Most organizations can access credible information about potential suppliers through business contacts and technology knowledge management organizations (for example, Gartner or Forrester). This reduces the need to spend months on RFIs, site visits, and initial due diligence. Nevertheless, you can use success factors available from industry analysts to rank potential suppliers, and you should consider them as part of your outsourcing strategy.

The size of the supplier, the availability of required skills, any past history with the customer, and a demonstrated understanding of the assignment are all major factors in selecting a potential supplier. How well the supplier will work with the internal team and with other partners in a multisourced environment are also important. These cultural factors are subjective and difficult to evaluate, but they must be considered. They require significant flexibility as you build relationships with your suppliers. The cultural factors include organizational structures, the predominant forms of communication (formal and informal), and ways that knowledge is transferred.

> **TIP** Consider multiple factors, including organizational culture, when evaluating potential suppliers.

In a work environment, culture translates into the ways individuals deal with people, processes, performance, values, and expectations. Measuring cultural alignment is one of the most difficult aspects of an acquirer-supplier relationship. Some indicators of cultural sophistication (or its lack) may be how a supplier handles human resources policies, how its organization is structured, and how it sets goals and executes to them—as well as how it deals with customers when goals cannot be met.

George Taylor, the supplier's program manager, has firsthand experience with a cultural mismatch that occurred in one of his outsourcing assignments. He relates this experience to Steve, who has encountered a similar situation.

George: One of our development centers is located in Asia. We had a female staff member who traveled there with me to explain to the development team what the customer wanted and how we were going to execute to plan. When the two of us arrived, I was immediately brought into the team structure and treated as an equal. But our female project lead wasn't included in the initial discussions, and it wasn't until I said something to the development center manager that the situation was fixed. The point I'm making here is that there are long-standing cultural differences not only in the business culture but in how we're brought up. In this instance, it had to do with gender, but it can be other things, too. These differences permeate the business environment, and we have to make sure that they are identified and managed. Otherwise we risk wasting team resources and not delivering with quality to our customers.

Steve nods.

Steve: We've seen these situations in other geographies, too—as well as right here at home. I'm glad you sensed the situation early and were able to fix it before it did any damage. We have to be concerned about culture, and we also need to make sure that the skills and competencies exist within our organization and within the supplier organization to support an outsourced environment.

George: We need to have people who've had experience with new technologies and are willing to listen, synthesize, and assume some risks to leverage supplier talent. And the supplier has to be sure that when they bring something to the table, it has value and can be put to use in our environment.

The solicitation package is a combination of form and function. Its structure should support an accurate and complete response from potential suppliers, which in turn supports an effective base on which to compare proposals. A typical solicitation package includes three basic things:

- A description of the form of the response
- A statement of work to be provided by the supplier
- Any required contractual provisions (for example, nondisclosure agreements and standard supplier terms and conditions)

In government agreements, some or all of the content and structure of the solicitation package may be dictated by regulation.

A solicitation package also includes the criteria that will be used to evaluate the proposals so that bidders understand where to focus their responses. It also includes documentation requirements, which can consist of specific forms and templates to capture information (such as staffing in a specific geography or a schedule that lists the various rates for specific resource skills). There are also provisions in the solicitation package to answer any questions or concerns on the part of the supplier and a schedule for completing the solicitation process.

> **TIP** The supplier response can be only as good as the acquirer's proposal.

The solicitation package must be comprehensive enough for the supplier to formulate an accurate and targeted response but flexible enough to allow the supplier to offer suggestions of other ways to satisfy the requirements. One way to approach this challenge is to offer the supplier an option to respond as provided but also submit an alternative solution in a separate proposal. You must be careful to write the solicitation package so that it is commensurate with the value and the risk associated with the proposed acquisition. It is inconsistent and unfair to ask a supplier to respond in great detail to a proposal that is of small monetary value. The detail required in the bid should match the supplier's expected return on investment.

Sample content of the statement of work in a solicitation proposal includes the following:

- Acquisition objectives
- Requirements (location of work, proposed schedule, any legal, statutory, or regulatory requirements)
- Any design constraints (e.g., technology standards)
- Required deliverables
- Supplier transition of product to operations
- Measures, service levels, reports required
- Collateral services required (e.g., studies, training)
- Acquirer-specific standards (e.g., configuration management, escalation, corrective action, actions for nonconformance)
- Required reviews and communications
- Product acceptance criteria
- Post-project support (e.g., warranties)

In its most basic form, an acquisition encompasses one supplier performing to a supplier agreement written to cover deliverables for one project, such as building a single specific system. Although this approach may be the simplest one, it doesn't take advantage of economies of scale that could be obtained if, for example, you apportioned to specific suppliers (with a plan for delivery) an overall technology portfolio for the year, or even an identified area of work such as an engineering program. Bundling projects means that you can better leverage the work of the supplier and generate an overall better return on investment. In contrast, if an organization is new to acquisition and hasn't yet established working relationships with any suppliers, the risks increase when an acquirer clusters a large portion of the overall work and awards the contract to only one supplier.

> **TIP** To realize lower costs and ensure rapid delivery of technology solutions, include the option to source multiple projects from one supplier.

Another aspect of structuring the outsourced work is to break it down so that you give suppliers an incentive to improve service and reduce costs. In one approach, you associate services that tie the work of the supplier to accountability for cost and service improvements. For example, suppose you outsource a technology solution—such as consolidating management of Web applications—to a single supplier. This gives the supplier an incentive to make repetitive administrative support tasks more efficient and thus cost-effective. The result is lower costs for the supplier and improved service for you.

You must also consider the number of supplier agreements that you have the capacity to oversee during a given period. This decision in turn drives the number of solicitation packages that you develop and send out. An organization might have a handful of suppliers it would like to work with, but if it distributes a large number of individual proposals it could end up with a significant number of supplier agreements to manage.

An alternative is to align the number of proposals with the natural segmentation of the work. For example, you could negotiate agreements with one supplier to perform all engineering services that cover the three major areas of engineering. These might segment into engineering around the desktop, engineering visualization, and engineering business systems. In this example, specific managers in your organization could efficiently oversee the supplier in a specific engineering area and deliver to specific customers in that engineering area, and you would thereby minimize the number of agreements and suppliers. Each major engineering area could ensure that its specific requirements were captured in its solicitation proposal.

Another consideration is that the larger the number of individual agreements, the greater the need for resources to manage their execution. Decisions about segmenting outsourcing work can be based on business domains or on other dimensions such as availability of acquirer resources to manage more granular segments.

A typical technology solicitation package contains a number of contracting documents, including a standard set of terms and conditions for supplier agreements. Typically the terms and conditions for one agreement are written so that they can be reused in other agreements. Using standard language for terms and conditions, bidding suppliers are asked to respond to this language as part of their formal response. Often the final agreement of the supplier to the acquirer's terms and conditions becomes the first step in determining whether the acquirer and supplier can work together.

The solicitation package may include a set of methods, standards, and tools that the acquirer expects the supplier to conform to and use. As part of its response, the supplier must describe the standards and methods it will use to complete the project. Key staff members should be identified, along with their qualifications. Pricing is also part of the supplier's response, and the supplier's technical portion describes how it will manage any necessary knowledge transfer.

The solicitation package should give bidders some latitude for describing areas of opportunity for transforming the use of technology in the acquirer or customer organization. This could be as simple as a supplier presenting a set of processes or tools for the integrated team to use, or as significant as identifying a new technology set to leverage. The more complete the solicitation package, the more complete the suppliers' responses should be.

TIP Leave flexibility in the proposal so that a supplier can demonstrate creative alternative solutions.

It is also important to create traceability between the project requirements and the solicitation package. The solicitation package is reviewed by stakeholders to ensure that the requirements are accurately and completely addressed. Often, for larger outsourcing agreements, peer review teams are asked to exchange packages and provide objective feedback to improve the solicitation package before it's distributed. It may be prudent to include suppliers in this review so that you can test the solicitation package for clarity by someone outside the organization. You also ensure that the solicitation package meets all legal requirements and includes all qualified suppliers.

After the solicitation package is distributed to potential bidders, it is critical to ensure that all potential suppliers have equal access to information that clarifies points of confusion in the requirements and any disconnects or concerns with the solicitation package. If questions arise that have implications for all bidders, you should formulate the answers and distribute them among all bidding suppliers.

> **TIP** Allow all bidding suppliers equal access to information concerning the solicitation package.

Steve evaluates options with Matt to handle acquirer-supplier interactions during the proposal process.

Steve: We can have a meeting with all the suppliers to answer their questions. We can also set up mechanisms for each supplier to submit formal questions to us, which we will then answer on an individual basis. Or we can do some combination of both.

Matt: What do you recommend?

Steve: I think a combination is the best approach, because face-to-face communication gives the suppliers a better overall understanding of each solicitation package. That is really important if you want to get quality supplier responses. It also allows us to answer any questions about the format of the response itself. Or we could use a more formal approach, such as asking them to submit questions in writing. That gives us immediate feedback to determine if there are any gaps in the package and also helps us identify any risks that we didn't pinpoint when we wrote the proposal.

Communication is critical as you and suppliers work together to answer all questions and resolve as many issues as possible before the supplier agreement is awarded. This means that part of your responsibility is to conduct formal, detailed reviews with each bidding supplier so that everyone involved has a clear understanding of all aspects of the solicitation package. This may require two or three rounds of documented feedback or face-to-face sessions. Any changes or errors identified in the solicitation package need to be communicated to all suppliers. This collaboration and exchange continues until the bidding suppliers submit their final proposals, which should include a plan for addressing all the aspects needed to meet business requirements, pricing that's in line with the solicitation package requirements, and a transformation road map for implementing the customer vision.

2.4.2 Applying the CMMI-ACQ to Partnering with Suppliers

The CMMI-ACQ provides specific recommendations on qualifying potential suppliers, creating and gaining stakeholder concurrence for the solicitation package, and distributing the package to qualified suppliers (see Table 2-7).

Consistent with the acquisition strategy and along with the project's scope and requirements, you indemnify potential suppliers who will receive the solicitation package (Table 2-7, practices 1.2 and 1.3). To reduce costs and effort, you limit the number of suppliers from which you solicit proposals, while at the same time making sure that you have included suppliers that can meet the requirements and ensuring that enough suppliers are included to provide a competitive environment.

You structure the solicitation package to facilitate an accurate and complete response from each potential bidder and to allow for an effective comparison and evaluation of proposals. The package is rigorous enough to ensure consistent, comparable responses but flexible enough to allow suppliers to suggest alternative ways to satisfy the requirements.

The solicitation package is reviewed with end users and other stakeholders to make sure that the requirements have been accurately and sufficiently stated so that the solicitation can lead to a manageable agreement (Table 2-7, practice 1.4). Then the solicitation package is distributed to the potential bidders that have been identified through research or other means (Table 2-7, practice 1.5). You use standard project planning, monitoring, and control practices to manage your activities during the solicitation process as necessary.

2.4.3 Evaluation and Negotiation

Solicitation packages and supplier responses are key documents supporting a series of activities that culminate in the selection of a supplier. The request for proposal is the initial requirements document for the supplier and serves as the base document against which the bidders' responses are measured. Responses are read in their entirety by acquirer team members. They use criteria based on the requirements to determine whether each response is complete, includes all the requested information, and is in the requested form.

You may invite bidding suppliers to present their proposals to your team, giving the bidders a chance to answer any questions from your review and to ensure that your team members fully understand the supplier's response. Any risks or assumptions in the response are validated through due diligence activities: reviews of the requirements with current suppliers that are performing similar work, reviews of any affected technology solutions, vali-

Table 2-7 *Solicitation and Supplier Agreement Development Goal 1: Practices and Tips*

CMMI-ACQ Area: Solicitation and Supplier Agreement Development	
1. Goal: Develop the acquisition strategy, qualify potential suppliers, and develop a solicitation package that includes the requirements and proposal evaluation criteria.	
Practices	**Tips**
1.2 Identify and qualify potential suppliers.	• Use multiple sources to verify supplier capabilities. • Use the collective capabilities of available suppliers as a key factor in determining the choice to single-source or multisource the technology solution. • Clearly understand the organization's core competencies, and let them guide the outsourcing approach. • When feasible, seek "commodity" transactions with suppliers in support of smaller, more flexible deals. • Consider multiple factors, including organizational culture, when evaluating potential suppliers.
1.3 Establish and maintain a solicitation package that includes the requirements and proposal evaluation criteria. 1.4 Review the solicitation package with stakeholders to make sure the approach is realistic and can reasonably lead to a usable product. 1.5 Distribute the solicitation package to potential suppliers for their response, and maintain its content throughout the solicitation.	• The supplier response can be only as good as the acquirer's proposal. • Compile the solicitation package commensurate with the value and risk of the capability to be acquired. • Leave flexibility in the proposal for a supplier to demonstrate creative alternative solutions. • To realize lower cost and rapid delivery of technology solutions, include the option to source multiple projects from one supplier. • Contractually establish how the acquirer and the supplier will jointly deal with the unknown. • Compensate and reward the supplier for innovation and its willingness to think creatively. • Service level agreements should reflect supplier performance. • Allow equal access for all bidding suppliers to information concerning the solicitation package.

dation of bidder references, reviews of any affected operating facilities and capabilities, and reviews of bidder capabilities.

Due diligence is a legal term that refers to how parties to an agreement ensure that they understand the work that is being contracted for and any associated risks. Suppliers as well as acquirers should perform due diligence. Initial supplier responses are built on the information presented in the solicitation package. A period of time should be spent on additional investigation so that each supplier can validate its assumptions, verify the information submitted by the acquirer in the solicitation package, and obtain additional information about the work. At this point, the acquirer expects that the supplier will adjust its response, especially in delivery solution, transformation, and costs. The acquiring organization ensures that all data is available to answer supplier questions, including metrics, reporting, and key personnel.

> **TIP** Due diligence may uncover additional work or risk for the supplier or acquirer that should be documented in the final supplier agreement.

You perform your own due diligence to ensure that the bidder can deliver as described in the response. In the case of technology development, you should visit supplier delivery sites to examine personnel and capacity and ultimately judge whether the supplier can fulfill the business objectives. You should ask a number of questions: Do the suppliers have significant experience in the delivery of the technology needed? Can they demonstrate a track record of success, including documented customer satisfaction results?

Steve and Matt review this issue in a discussion.

> **Matt:** We set up visits to the development centers of our bidding suppliers. Each supplier has been very cooperative and really wants us to make these visits. Before we go, we need to be clear as to what questions we need to ask, what observations we want to make, and what documentation we want to request.

Steve supports Matt's statements.

> **Steve:** It's a significant investment of time and resources to make these visits, and we want to make sure that we make good use of the time, both ours and the supplier's. To support due diligence for the suppliers, we gave them complete information about the technology we're looking at. We want to make sure we answer all their questions. We want to give them access to any information that does not give any one bidder a competitive advantage. Of course, all the suppliers are working under nondisclosure agreements.

Based on new information from due diligence, suppliers may update their proposed technology solutions, transformation plans, and even cost models. Why should you expect pricing changes after due diligence? The reason is that more recent data and an external view of the environment may result in a more current and comprehensive understanding of cost drivers, including newly identified risks and material deviations from the solicitation package. That said, all substantive changes should be justifiable by the supplier, and you should cast a wary eye toward any wide swings in the cost models at this point.

TIP   Anticipate changes to supplier responses based on due diligence.

Ideally, due diligence is a two-way street. In addition to responding to supplier inquiries, you should continue your own investigations by visiting delivery sites, checking with reference customers, and continuing to drive the solution and project planning. Organizations need to manage risk by confirming that bidding suppliers have successfully delivered technology solutions in the past.

> **Steve:**   Now is the time to kick the tires, to validate suppliers' claims about their capabilities.

After the proposals are evaluated, a negotiation plan is developed for each of the candidate suppliers. The size of the negotiation team depends on the size and complexity of the project and the overall outsourcing deal. The negotiation team is composed of individuals who have knowledge of the statement of work and the solicitation package. The team has the support of your legal staff, financial staff, and purchasing staff. The roles and responsibilities of the negotiation team include the following:

- Define the roles and responsibilities of team members.
- Identify the key issues to be negotiated.
- Know how and when to use negotiation "levers."
- Know the fallback or compromise positions and when to use them.
- Pinpoint any nonnegotiable items.
- Schedule the meetings.
- Understand the meeting objectives.
- Be aware of the risks, consequences, and mitigation thresholds and alternatives.

"Why should I choose you?" is the initial question that Matt asks as he begins each session with a bidding supplier. It's an important question, because as Matt talks to various groups sent from the same supplier, he gets various answers, and these answers allow him to formulate a clearer, more well-rounded picture.

Beyond this simple question, Matt has a set of solid criteria that is shared with each supplier. He and the negotiation team use these criteria to rank each bid. The criteria include identification of each major chunk of work, such as scope, SLAs, overall approach, tools and technology, process and methods, personnel skills, continuous improvement, and global support. His CIO wants to capture other considerations.

> **TIP** Look for "highlights" and "lowlights" in the proposal that differentiate suppliers.

Matt: In the past, as I evaluated suppliers for other parts of our organization, I tried to capture general impressions, financials, governance, delivery organization, solution, and tools. Now I'm also interested in exploring technical transformation, experience, service delivery, and service support. We can then synthesize this information into a technical summary and an "intangibles" summary. Other important areas are highlights—significant aspects of the proposal that differentiate one supplier from another. I also look for "lowlights," which are areas missed. I'm looking for new approaches proposed by the bidders and any issues that surface from the proposal.

At the end of the day, we also need to be concerned about how we will work together—the cultural fit. One way we determine this is through ongoing dialog with the bidding suppliers before we receive any proposal. If we maintain open discussions and a considerable level of visibility between ourselves and the suppliers as they build their responses, we can begin to see how the teams collaborate. Then cultural fit becomes much more obvious and easier to assess.

Steve also weighs in on the responses.

Steve: You can determine a great deal about a organization by reviewing how they demonstrate capabilities in offering a complete solution, and also in how they articulate the way to get the organization to the vision through a systematic series of steps and a logical, credible plan. If their response includes descriptions of implementation how-to's and the technical solution itself, then we know that they get it. There should also be ample explanations about how transitions and any major opportunities or transformations will take place.

Often, the supplier's sales team is the only group working with you until the response is submitted. It is important for your team to ask for a supplier pursuit team that will deliver the technology solution. This means that key individuals are identified and brought in early as part of the initial supplier pursuit team. You also need to understand the supplier's physical locations where the work will be done. As you continue to evaluate a specific supplier, technical and cultural differences should emerge. A working marriage is important, because recovering from a "divorce" from a supplier is painful and difficult.

Steve describes a situation he experienced when the delivery team did not show up until after the ink was dry on the agreement.

> **Steve:**   The proposal from this supplier was solid. The supplier pursuit team and the acquisition team worked extremely well together. For some reason, we had made an unspoken assumption that the individuals involved on the supplier's pursuit team would automatically become a part of the delivery team. After the contract was signed, we were informed that the delivery team would have a different lead and that a large portion of the supplier technical support team would be new. The new individuals came from the supplier's low-cost outsourcing subsidiary, along with some additional people from their offshore team.
>
>   Well, right way the new team was unclear and really confused about the contract language, which we'd already talked about with the first team. The new group began staffing the project very differently from what we'd agreed to. Although the staffing approach and detail had been captured in the contract, there was some flexibility in the language that allowed interpretation. It took an additional three months for us and the supplier teams to really get up to speed, because knowledge transfer had to begin all over again. I was so frustrated that I lodged numerous complaints with the supplier. Unfortunately for everyone involved, we were never able to reconstitute the delivery team as it had been originally intended. The loss was one of time, fit, and relationship building.

> **TIP**   To facilitate knowledge transfer, ensure that members of the supplier pursuit team are part of the delivery team.

Suppliers typically have numerous questions about organizational structures and processes as they put together their responses. Suppliers' proposals include details about the program management office, reporting structure, service level targets, benchmarking and auditing, and quality improvements to indicate to the customer organization how such a structure supports the inevitable changes in staffing that occur as the program evolves. Bidders want to give the acquirer visibility into the skills of their staffs. And because suppliers know that there is shared risk inherent in outsourcing, they want to surface the management structure they believe will mitigate risks, usually a structure that has been used in other engagements. Suppliers also identify dependencies on the acquisition organization that impact their ability to meet commitments.

Down-selecting—narrowing the field of bidders—is a significant activity that can occur several times during solicitation. Typically, the initial list of suppliers is larger than you can manage in final negotiations. The list is narrowed to one or two as the teams plan for and execute the negotiation process. Down-selecting can happen at the end of the first proposal review and again after due diligence. If down-selecting is part of your process, you should include each of these milestones in the supplier selection activities communicated in the solicitation package.

> **TIP** To simplify negotiations, reduce the number of suppliers through a down-select process.

Matt wants his team to clearly understand when they can down-select the suppliers who are submitting bids. He has a team of several staff members working full-time on these deals, and he wants to make sure that two down-select steps are completed at the appropriate time. He discusses the timing with his team.

Matt: We need to down-select to efficiently evaluate supplier bids. We've narrowed our original list to four prequalified suppliers, and we've had site visits at these four. Now we need to down-select to focus on the important aspects of the responses and to start making choices and focus our energy where it matters most. This is tough duty.

I've asked management to give you relief from your everyday job responsibilities, but I know that that hasn't happened in all cases.

Matt pauses to look around the table.

Matt: If we're going to pick the best supplier for this solicitation package, we have to be sure that we spend an adequate amount of time evaluating the bids. I know that it's a lot of work, and for some of the criteria, this evaluation will get tedious, but I need you to look at some criteria. It will save time and effort in the long run.

Matt distributes a handout and takes the group through a bullet list of criteria.

- Partnership and cultural fit
- Price
- Technical skills

- Demonstrated quality of service from other customers
- Professionalism throughout the solicitation process as well as other engagements
- Flexibility
- Innovativeness
- Customer references

Matt: I also want to see if the suppliers have put into their bids some discussion of knowledge transfer. If they didn't, they don't understand what they're undertaking in this engagement. There are costs to move from one supplier to another. When one supplier ramps down and a new one ramps up, you almost always have additional costs. We figure we'll have to pay additional costs for one to three months when we transfer a contract from one supplier to another. So, my point is that there are costs involved in knowledge transfer, whether this is the first supplier contract, or if we are moving from supplier to supplier. So we should see the knowledge transfer activity as a line item in all price estimates.

TIP Build evaluation criteria for proposals that link to business objectives.

A key element in evaluating the proposed solutions is directly tied to the delivery of quality within an agreed-upon budget. Can suppliers deliver with increasing quality at a lower cost?

Steve: A lot of suppliers have this as their business strategy, and usually the only way they can achieve it is to leverage their resources across multiple organizations or a large group of activities.

One of the drivers for the achievement of this goal is standardization in the technology industry.

Steve: I've done some research on this, and what I found is that as technology functionality becomes more commoditized, costs go down. This is not only important in estimating the cost of functionality, but it also relates to all the processes and measurements we use to manage the supplier to delivery. So, they can continue to deliver quality at a lower cost, but only to the extent that they can make the technology less of a "custom" offering and more of a standardized commodity. By the way, this is why emerging or new technology tends to cost more from a development and delivery perspective.

Another criterion to be considered is the supplier's domain expertise and its importance to the project. Some suppliers are stronger than others in a specific area such as product development or marketing domains. Finding a supplier that can combine domain expertise with technology prowess can offer tremendous value. Unfortunately, many suppliers are technologists first and domain experts second. The importance of domain expertise relates to strategic insight. The functionality required by the end customer can be enhanced by the supplier's knowledge and experience. Domain expertise also fosters mutual respect between you and your supplier. If the relationship is grounded on mutual respect within a certain domain, more partnering occurs, and the likelihood increases that the organizations can weather challenges in the relationship. Other considerations include the supplier's delivery approach (e.g., offshore versus onshore delivery) and the supplier's ability to manage certain aspects of technology, such as a secure hosting environment for IT solutions.

> **TIP**   Treat strategic insight of a supplier as a differentiator while under-standing technology prowess as a given.

Matt and his team are ready for their first down-select. Three candidates remain, and, of the three, two seem to have clearly understood the solicitation package and responded accordingly. The third seems to have put minimal effort into understanding the work, and its response reflects that level of effort. In addition, its pricing is way out of line compared with the other bidders. In the down-select meeting, the acquisition team looks at the three supplier scores side-by-side. Steve expresses his disappointment with the respondent that has put minimal effort into its proposal.

Steve: I really wanted to see what this supplier could do for us. After all, they are the market leader in this set of activities. I'm not sure why they submitted such a lousy proposal, but it's barely worth looking at. In fact, did you note areas in the document where they actually referenced the wrong organization? That tells me they just reworked a document that they used for another solicitation response. And they took up so much space promoting themselves that there wasn't much space left in the template to explain their approach. They just didn't seem to be serious about the bid.

Matt: That's right. And they only sent in one guy to explain the response. I anticipated that they'd send three of their senior domain experts to describe the three technical areas we're soliciting. Clearly, this is the proposal we should discard.

Matt looks around the table. Everyone is nodding in agreement.

Matt: Okay, before we dig into the pizza, let's look briefly at the two other proposals. They're really excellent. They spent some quality time putting their responses together, and it shows. They each have a different approach to managing the three areas of technology, but that's what we really wanted to see. I also received phone calls from all the leads in each one of the technology areas asking some very probing questions about our technology strategy. It made me feel good that they were looking at our needs and coming back with solid approaches to support our goals. The next down-select that we do just before negotiations will be the tough one. I want everyone on the team to begin to think about differentiators for the two remaining suppliers.

Negotiating the language of the final supplier agreement should be based on the final responses submitted by the suppliers. After comparing the final responses, you usually perform a down-select to one supplier. Negotiations—in-depth discussions with the selected supplier—focus on reaching compromises on any remaining issues such as outstanding contract terms, concerns about SLAs, or any of the details in the plans and deliverables. Usually, the suppliers not chosen for final negotiations are not informed immediately. If you cannot reach an agreement with the supplier in negotiations, then you may want to enter into negotiations with an alternative supplier.

One of the challenges in negotiation is the need to preserve cost visibility in the agreements as negotiations evolve. This element, along with flexibility, also can create issues with the supplier's future performance, especially when it assigns personnel with specific skill levels to the projects.

Before negotiations begin, you must establish the negotiation team members, their roles, and the rules of engagement. Team members begin by translating the supplier's motives into potential negotiation levers to realize the best deal.

> **TIP**   Negotiate with your chosen supplier, but don't tip your hand to your second choice until the deal is signed.

Matt brings his team together to discuss some of the rules of negotiation.

Matt: You've all spent considerable time working with these suppliers, and I want to commend you on the relationships that you've formed with the suppliers' pursuit teams. That's allowed us to do what I believe is an outstanding job of clarifying our needs and identifying the best supplier for the job. We have to negotiate with one supplier. Based on the evaluations I've seen, I think everyone is very comfortable with this supplier and their proposed solution, and I think they can get the job done together with our people. We'll get better technology than we have today and at a better price.

Matt pauses and consults his notes.

> **Matt:**   There are still some issues on the table about final pricing, the skills of some of the technical staff, and also about some of the "value-added" items that this supplier put in its proposal. This is where true negotiation begins. For us to be successful, we must now manage what we say to the supplier pursuit team. One of the rules I want to put in place is that now all communications with the supplier must come from the negotiation team. We need to project clarity in our messages until we close this deal. We've identified the key players on our negotiation team, and they include the director in charge of the area of the solicitation package, a finance staff member, and a procurement manager. Since I'm the executive manager, I'm the decision maker. End of story.

Steve, who has put in many hours evaluating proposals, is not happy about this edict and the ramifications of putting communications under such stringent controls.

> **Steve:**   But what about the rest of us? Are we supposed to just quit communicating with these guys?

> **Matt:**   Don't get me wrong, Steve. Everyone who has worked on this deal is important during negotiations. You're all going to be available in the sessions to help us answer questions. Here's how it will work. You'll be in the sessions, and if we need clarification from one of you, or if you have something to contribute, we'll do one of two things. We'll either let you stop the session and ask for five or ten minutes, whatever is needed to talk about a specific point privately with the team. In that case, the supplier leaves the room and our team will discuss the point. Or, you can add additional clarifying information to the discussion. What I want you to keep in mind, though, is that we need to err on the side of caution. If you have information that you believe will help us in the negotiations, until we all get comfortable with the process and format, I would prefer that you stop the discussions so that our team can have a private discussion. That way we have a chance to put together the best deal for our organization.

Matt looks at Steve, who nods.

> **Matt:**   We need to be aware that there are areas that the supplier will be willing to broaden to give us what is termed in the industry a "special deal" as a result of the way we structure other deals in conjunction with this one. Discussions will focus on volume discounts, value-added services, multiyear discounts, prepayment options, on-demand services,

or pay-per-use where appropriate. Oh, and I want to make sure again that everyone involved in the negotiations on both sides is aware that they have signed nondisclosure agreements.

Matt wants to talk about supplier motives before he lets the team walk through a mock session of how negotiations would go.

Matt: Supplier motives are important in creating the best deal for us. This means that we need to spend the next few days capturing what we think are their business drivers. For example, if we're willing to be a customer reference for them, this may translate into additional discounts. This requires that we put in writing what we're willing to do as a customer reference. What are some of the other hot buttons we could push?

Steve: We could offer to host other clients at our facilities and share some of the things that have happened with this supplier that make them exceptional. Or we could do joint presentations at conferences, interviews, case studies, those kinds of things.

Matt nods and looks at the team.

Matt: I want each of you to send me an e-mail with your thoughts on this topic. I want you to capture what you know about the supplier's revenue and sales targets. These often change from quarter to quarter, and it will be important for us to know what is motivating the supplier's team at the time of negotiations. Also, the bigger the deal for them, the bigger the discounts we expect. The more we can demonstrate total spend for the supplier, the higher our expectation of a significant discount. Steve, I want you to work on the numbers for me as you brainstorm these kinds of motivations, and give me some potential estimates of what it could mean to the overall deal.

It is important to set the supplier's expectations indicating what you believe the work is worth from a cost perspective. In some cases, you set cost targets as part of developing the solicitation package. Many acquirers set very aggressive cost targets and see how the suppliers respond. The upside of this technique is that it gives the supplier a sense of the value you place on the work. The overriding concern about targets is the potential impact on quality. For a supplier, cost can be reduced in a number of areas: process, testing, scope, staff, and more. You also need to be sure that your message is viewed by each bidding supplier as a challenge to stretch from a number of points of view. You want suppliers to stretch by looking at costs, margins, resource mix, and offshore versus onshore and come up with a solution that really meets your needs. That should not compromise quality. Each supplier should work the various cost components and determine the optimal mix to meet or exceed the targets you've set. You can then come back and revisit the targets to make sure that requirements are still being met.

It is important for an acquirer to understand who is willing to take a run at the target and how creative they can be. This also says a great deal about how that supplier can and will work with you and how flexible it is willing to be. These are characteristics that you would like to see translated into transformational activities as the supplier identifies opportunities for your organization. If a bidding supplier is not willing to try to meet the targets, this needs to be noted as you make your evaluations.

> **TIP** Communicate cost targets as stretch goals for suppliers.

2.4.4 Appling the CMMI-ACQ to Evaluation and Negotiation

The CMMI-ACQ provides specific recommendations on how to evaluate proposed solutions in accordance with the time line, the preliminary project plans, and the evaluation criteria. The recommendations include the formulation and execution of negotiations that culminate in the selection of a supplier (see Table 2-8).

Proposals submitted in response to solicitation packages are evaluated based on the proposal evaluation criteria, the established time line, and the project plan (Table 2-8, practice 2.1). Evaluation notes should be documented and maintained. You refine your negotiation strategy based on your evaluation of the suppliers' proposals and the evaluation of the suppliers. The proposal evaluation and the negotiations with the suppliers provide the basis for selecting a supplier that is best able to meet the requirements of the solicitation.

For each of the candidate suppliers, you develop a negotiation plan based on evaluation of the suppliers and their proposals (Table 2-8, practice 2.2). The size of the negotiation team depends on the size and complexity of the project. The negotiation team typically is supported by legal staff, a financial analyst, purchasing, and the project manager.

Proposal evaluation results are used to select a supplier based on the outcome of negotiations (Table 2-8, practice 2.3). The negotiation enables you to ensure that you are selecting the best supplier for the project. The evaluation results, along with the negotiation results, support the selection decision or cause you to take other action as appropriate.

Table 2-8 *Solicitation and Supplier Agreement Development Goal 2: Practices and Tips*

CMMI-ACQ Process Area: Solicitation and Supplier Agreement Development	
2. Goal: Select suppliers based on an evaluation of their ability to meet the specified requirements and established criteria.	
Practices	**Tips**
2.1 Evaluate proposed solutions according to the documented proposal evaluation plans and criteria.	• Due diligence may uncover additional work or risk for the supplier or acquirer that should be documented in the final supplier agreement. • Anticipate changes to the supplier responses based on due diligence. • Look for "highlights" and "lowlights" in the proposal that differentiate suppliers. • To ensure knowledge transfer, ensure that members of the supplier pursuit team are part of the delivery team. • To simplify negotiations, reduce the number of suppliers through a down-select process.
2.2 Develop negotiation plans to use in competing a supplier agreement. 2.3 Select suppliers based on an evaluation of their ability to meet the specified requirements and established criteria.	• Negotiation teams should have clear roles and responsibilities. • Practice negotiation sessions that specifically address the perceived motives of the suppliers. • Build evaluation criteria for proposals that link to business objectives. • Treat strategic insight of a supplier as a differentiator while understanding technology prowess as a given. • Negotiate with your chosen supplier, but don't tip your hand to your second choice until the deal is signed. • Communicate cost targets as stretch goals for the suppliers.

2.4.5 Signed and Sealed

After you negotiate the agreement, you and the supplier write a formal supplier agreement based on your acquisition needs and the supplier's proposed approach. It is important for you to ensure that all critical aspects of the supplier's final bid, especially the negotiated changes and the results of due diligence, are captured in the supplier agreement.

These agreements form the basis of the relationship between you and the supplier. They describe the technology solution or solutions to be built, the quality expected, and the timing of the delivery. Agreements define the service level credits to be given to you when supplier commitments are not met.

> **TIP** All changes to the final proposal, both verbal and written, should be incorporated into the final supplier agreement.

Supplier agreements can include incentive clauses to encourage performance. For you to realize the benefit of creativity and transformational activities, it's a good idea to include clauses that support sharing of the monetary value of any improvements or new business achieved by the delivered technology solution. This can happen when a supplier builds a technology solution that has applicability beyond your organization. For example, suppose you and the supplier agree to build a self-service timekeeping system. As the supplier develops this solution, it creates a unique Java component that supports time computation across all possible requirements of calendar management—including geography, language, religion, and culture—for resource scheduling. If the supplier has the freedom to provide this capability to other customers (if it does not relate to your core business or a competitive advantage), then the supplier has an incentive to look for additional opportunities in future projects.

> **TIP** Consider incentive clauses in the supplier agreement to encourage innovation.

The types of agreements and pricing mechanisms documented in the supplier agreement affect the products and services delivered. The type of agreement you choose depends on the quality of the supplier, your business goals, and the maturity of your processes. Projects that lack a clearly defined scope tend to fall into a time-and-materials type of agreement, because the risks center on effective management and cost overruns. Nevertheless, a time-and-materials agreement gives an organization some visibility into supplier costs and significant insight into how the supplier calculates the costs of an outsourcing engagement. With a time-and-materials agreement, you can see materials costs, rates for specific personnel, and time expended to complete specific tasks.

> **TIP** Compensate and reward the supplier for innovation and its willingness to think creatively.

Matt's fellow executives want all supplier agreements to be fixed-price. Fixed-price agreements work well for predictable activities that can be accurately scoped, such as maintenance services or network operations. They don't work well for many of the groundbreaking activities that Matt is looking for, such as transformation opportunities in the IT areas of Web services, reporting, or identity services. After some rather heated discussions, Matt and his staff begrudgingly authorize a combination of time-and-materials agreements and fixed-price agreements.

Matt still has concerns about the impact of fixed-price agreements, especially in the area of skilled workers.

> **Matt:** With a fixed-price contract you won't get the best people. When you talk about transformation, it's about creativity. To reward creativity, there must be tangible incentives—for example, opportunities for the supplier to leverage discoveries with other customers. These monetary benefits could be shared between us and the supplier. I'm talking about a value-priced contract. If we can clearly define the scope of the transformational activities we want, we can make these happen by using the best minds from our supplier, because we can compensate them for their creative efforts.

You can employ various types of agreements to reflect combinations of work, such as designing, coding, maintenance, and operation. A design-and-code agreement covers both designing a solution and generating the source code. These agreements are not complex, and they can speed the delivery of projects because they promote innovation and minimize the required knowledge transfer between the designers and the developers.

Agreements that cover designing, coding, maintenance, and operation mirror the life cycle of a technology solution. This approach offers the supplier a number of incentives to deliver quality. Because it must maintain or host the code that it has designed and developed, there is more incentive to deliver first-time quality and build for efficiency in maintenance and operations.

Another approach to the structure of agreements is to create a *master agreement*. The analogy in nonproductive materials procurement is a blanket order—for example, an open purchase agreement that is used to obtain office supplies on an as-needed basis. In this master agreement approach, you package requirements and select one or a small group of suppliers to meet specific project requests as *task orders* over a period of time. In this type of agreement, terms are set, but quantity is not. Master agreements can be used with or without competition and speed up the overall acquisition process.

In a master agreement structure, the terms and conditions of the agreement must be generic to support a long-term relationship with the supplier. These terms and conditions are not reviewed every time the project cost is estimated, thereby allowing an expedient project start-up. This structure also supports continuous improvement with the supplier, because a strategic partnership can be forged more easily. A challenge of the master agreement approach is that it requires clarity for overall requirements that are expected for all projects. Because these agreements are in place for extended periods—typically three to five years—they require understanding on your part and accurate documentation to support the strategic partnership.

Although the timing of any project is unknown at the time the master agreement is put into place, price competition becomes important. For pricing to remain fair and competitive, you need mechanisms in place over the period of the agreement to manage pricing. Examples are adjustments for rate cards of supplier services or for supplier resources based on cost of living adjustments. To manage costs and foster continuous improvement, you should use ongoing benchmarking to monitor performance standards and cost standards in the industry.

> **TIP** Consider a master agreement approach to speed delivery and build long-term relationships with suppliers.

In the master agreement, the payment mechanism is crucial. Although price certainty is relaxed, the supplier receives a constant revenue stream from the project assignments, which continue to roll in as long as the supplier maintains quality and value. Care must be taken to put in place a payment mechanism that results in the smallest risk premium from the supplier to reflect its estimate of overall uncertainty in the agreement. This structure also affords you an opportunity for cost visibility tied to continuous improvement. Efficiencies come from repeated execution of projects by the same small set of suppliers. If you adopt this approach, you must consider the need for some level of competition now and into the future, especially when the agreement expires. And finally, the mechanism to distribute the work must be clearly documented so that you can realize the flexibility, speed of delivery, quality, reliability, and value that this structure can offer.

In selecting an agreement type and executing against it, both the acquirer and the supplier understand that the basic principles of contract law apply. There are a number of areas to take into consideration to avoid problems and make the most of the acquirer-supplier relationship. If the agreement is not sound and basic tenets are absent, then uncertainty, disputes, and failure will result.

After a brief discussion about what should be in the agreement and what happens if something is missing, Matt looks at Steve and poses a question.

Matt: Are you saying that everything that I can think of needs to be in the contract? If I'm concerned about business interruptions, liability limitations, Sarbanes-Oxley compliance, privacy laws in Europe, extended outages, et cetera, et cetera? If so, I need to get my internal council of experts together to brainstorm and capture all this data as quickly as possible so that we can start writing the supplier agreement. It's going to be quite a document!

Steve: You can't put everything in the contract. Nor would you want to. The experts—the lawyers, purchasing staff, and contracts staff—will fill in the words for the things that are givens, like Sarbanes-Oxley. But not everything lends itself to contract language. That's why I highlighted the importance of the governance model in our earlier discussions. There will be things that come up because of a change in our business environment that neither we nor the supplier can predict. Those are the things that we will have to work through with them in a logical and rational fashion. What is important to us is that we touch on the major items. The other point I want to make is that you cannot shift all the risk to your supplier. If you do, the supplier will charge you for the privilege.

If the description of the desired capability is ambiguous, it leads to scope creep. Clarity is required for the products to be developed or the services to be performed, the timing of delivery, the specific acceptance criteria to be used, and when the supplier can expect to get paid.

> **TIP**   Contractually establish how the acquirer and supplier will jointly deal with the unknown.

Provisions for the ongoing update of technologies should also appear in the supplier agreement. You should outline how new technologies will be introduced, whether this agreement covers one project or many. There should be provisions and some flexibility to handle hidden costs; typically, these types of deviations are controlled through a change management process.

Applying standard agreements is a good practice whenever practical. You can build reusable, standard agreements for technology solutions that can be customized to match the need. For example, nonproductive material agreements used to order office supplies will not work for technology solutions. Even though this seems obvious, some acquirers try to shortcut the agreement development cycle by using something that, even when modified, just doesn't fit. Acquirers and suppliers should agree and document who owns the intellectual property that will be built, and the copyrights, database rights, and patent rights should be clearly spelled out in the agreement. This ensures that the party that should own the product does indeed own it.

Many organizations have a history of reusing contract language for commodity purchases. In more sophisticated agreement structures, this can be viewed as *modularity:* Modules of contract language and documents are put together in various combinations to reuse descriptions of how work is to be accomplished by a supplier for a specific customer. Modularity gives you the flexibility to manage variations in specific customer requirements. The variation in any agreement is then focused on the statement of work, which describes the work that needs to be done to develop the specific technology desired. The common agreement language remains the same.

Provisions for open source code should be specified. You and the supplier need to agree on whether it is excluded or included and, if included, who will manage it. The issue of indemnification should also be documented. Often, acquirers want suppliers to indemnify them against any third-party license infringements. Both parties will also want explicit limitations on liability by setting a cap on liability, especially failure to perform. You may ask your suppliers to sign nondisclosure agreements even before the supplier has had a chance to respond to a solicitation package. Nondisclosure agreements should cover the time before, during, and after the award of the agreement.

TIP Reuse standard contract language for all acquisition projects.

Required acceptance testing should be clearly defined. Any warranties should be part of the acceptance criteria and should include the requirements for things such as defect-free technology solutions and compatibility with the intended environment, especially infrastructure compatibility.

The management of supplier staff is an area that requires specific detail. The agreement should describe who will manage them, what their reporting structure is, and what processes should be executed for supplier employee performance. This is of particular concern to maintain compliance with labor laws in various jurisdictions. Information security and data protection should be outlined and should always be in compliance with local statutes. Audit trails for the development and deployment of the product should be specified as to the archival and access requirements. And finally, SLAs for responsiveness, availability, and performance should be captured.

Service level agreements—the methods used to measure supplier performance negotiated in agreements—can be effective in motivating suppliers to perform according to the terms of the agreement. As an important part of formulating a response to the solicitation package, bidding suppliers want to understand the methods and the risks associated with service levels. If used appropriately, SLAs work as the foundation for continuous improvement for the supplier and your relationship with the supplier.

SLAs are often based on what is known by you and what is easy to measure, rather than align performance measures with the key objectives and expectations of technology delivery. Not all measures are SLAs, nor should all measures be converted into SLAs. To be an acceptable SLA, the product or service to be measured should be described in the statement of work along with the assigned calculations and their timing. In addition, any applicable tools and processes should be defined, along with reporting frequency and content.

Matt wants to be sure that the team is aligned on SLAs, so he uses reports as his example.

> **Matt:** Let's say I have an SLA for reports, and it says that monthly reports need to be submitted by a certain calendar day each month. There could be a penalty if the supplier misses one month or a series of months. This might be a credit to our monthly invoice from the supplier. Or here's another example—service delivery risks, like the amount of time it takes to resolve a severity 1 incident of a system that's in production. We'll be compensated for poor performance by getting predetermined credits of services. But the point of SLAs is not to accumulate credits. The idea is to incentivize the supplier so that we can deliver the contracted products and services to customers.

Steve is concerned about the implications of service levels to the business objectives. After all, "on time, on budget, with quality" resonates with what he learned many years ago in his computer science classes. Capturing these measures is very simple. In fact, these are the internal measures that his teams are already using. Do they work in an outsourced model? How do they relate to business objectives? What about "real" quality measures? Are they direct or indirect? After the work is outsourced and performed at arm's length, how do we know that the quality of the staff is up to par, something that becomes a direct reflection of the quality delivered? In other words, what are the predictors of success? Steve discusses the implications of SLAs with the team.

Steve: There are some basics that we can start out with. We still want to include schedule and cost. We also need to think about aspects that are less obvious to us, things that we may want to know to begin to mitigate our risk. For example, we want to understand the technical skills and training and staff turnover of individuals who are going to be doing our development work. We will need to determine how these information needs translate into SLAs in the supplier agreement.

I want to know what product quality we are getting—so we want to really be able to assess this. I want to know how many projects delivered and put into production don't require rework. Before that, I want to know the same thing about supplier deliverables—how many deliverables do not require rework. And don't we need to take a cue from other products that are built for customer use, like washing machines or cars, and determine what the warranty periods should be and how they work? In other words, if I put a technology solution into production and I experience a severity 1 incident that shuts down the system, the warranty period should start over.

What Steve is really trying to do is to develop an SLA architecture that ties the business goals to the outsourcing goals and then to the services delivered. Operational performance can then be driven through the service requirements.

In general, the number of critical SLAs should be kept to a minimum for each technology solution. SLAs must use the right measures and must have enough influence for you to maintain control of the supplier and result in appropriate performance. The most important aspect of SLAs is tying them to the main objective of the agreement.

TIP Service level agreements should give suppliers an incentive for high performance.

After all the parties agree to the terms of the agreement, it needs to be approved by management and other approval staffs (e.g., legal, purchasing, finance). The agreement should take effect on the negotiated date. In addition, those suppliers who were not awarded the contract are notified and any communication between the organizations is completed.

> **TIP** Expand communications to the affected acquirer and supplier organizations as the contract is awarded.

2.4.6 Applying the CMMI-ACQ to Signing the Agreement

The CMMI-ACQ provides specific recommendations on how to establish an understanding with the supplier about the intent of the supplier agreement through formal documentation and approvals. You and the supplier continue to work together to maintain this mutual understanding through execution to the completion of the project (see Table 2-9).

Table 2-9 *Solicitation and Supplier Agreement Development Goal 3: Practices and Tips*

CMMI-ACQ Process Area: Solicitation and Supplier Agreement Development	
3. Goal: Establish and maintain formal agreements with selected suppliers.	
Practices	**Tips**
3.1 Establish and maintain a mutual understanding of the contract with selected suppliers and end users based on the acquisition needs and the suppliers' proposed approaches.	• Compensate and reward the supplier for innovations and its willingness to think creatively. • Expand communications to the affected acquirer and supplier organizations as the contract is awarded.
3.2 Document the approved supplier agreement.	• All changes to the final proposal, both verbal and written, should be incorporated into the final agreement. • Consider a master agreement approach to speed delivery and build longer-term relationships with suppliers. • Contractually establish how you and the supplier will jointly deal with the unknown. • Reuse standard contract language for all acquisition projects. • Service level agreements should give suppliers an incentive for high performance.

A formal agreement based on the sourcing decision of the acquirer is established. The acquirer and the supplier work together to gain a mutual understanding of the agreement based on the acquisition needs and the supplier's proposed solution (Table 2-9, practice 3.1). As points of clarification and ambiguities arise after the contract is awarded, you and the supplier ensure that this mutual understanding is maintained throughout the life of the project.

You and the supplier document the approved supplier agreement (Table 2-9, practice 3.2). This agreement may be a stand-alone agreement or part of a master agreement. When the supplier agreement is a master agreement, the project can be managed as an addendum, work order, or service request to the master agreement. All the standard elements should be in the supplier agreement, including the terms and conditions, which should include the following:

- Statement of work, list of deliverables, schedule, budget, and acceptance criteria
- Any required measurements and reports
- Who is authorized to approve changes to the agreement
- How requirements will be managed
- Standards, processes, and procedures to be followed
- Critical dependencies
- Acquirer-provided resources
- Project oversight processes and reviews
- Corrective action requirements and processes
- Nonhire, noncompete, nondisclosure, intellectual capital clauses
- Deployment, maintenance, and support requirements
- Warranty, ownership, and security provisions
- Legal penalties

2.4.7 Manage Your Suppliers Through Productive Alliances

Managing a well-run technology organization that engages in outsourcing doesn't happen simply because senior management signs the supplier agreement. In the same way that a technology organization should have a governance structure in place that reflects the business areas it supports, there must be a supplier management function to manage the various aspects of an outsourcing engagement. To ensure the success of outsourcing, you must establish a governance structure in cooperation with the supplier. The activities managed under this structure include maintaining ongoing communication and understanding, resolving issues and disputes in a timely fashion, managing any changes to agreements, accepting delivery of supplier-assigned products, and ensuring timely payments.

> **TIP** Start planning for the implementation of the supplier agreement long before the supplier is chosen.

Information about the awarded agreement and the chosen supplier should be communicated to all affected parties in both organizations. In many instances, these initial communications will be the first time that those outside the pursuit teams begin to learn about the project and its goals. It is important for both organizations to understand what has been negotiated and to have an initial sense of how it will affect them. Roles, responsibilities, and accountability are quickly defined so you and the supplier understand how you will work together to successfully implement the agreement. Planning for implementation should begin long before pen touches paper. After the final down-select occurs and before negotiations start, you should identify implementation leads and begin work on time lines and deliverables, dependencies, governance, and risks. After the agreement is in effect, you can move into the next phase of work by starting to transition knowledge to the supplier.

Steve is proud to have led the solicitation team, which has dedicated itself to hard work and long hours. He feels that it has really paid off in the end, because the team understands what it means to plan ahead and the importance of working in parallel. During the lull while the solicitation package is put together, especially during negotiations, the team members use the supplier operating models in their solicitation package responses to build a high-level view of how their organization and the supplier teams will integrate and work together.

They begin to build a list of deliverables as outlined in the solicitation package and then assign each deliverable a specific target date. They review the staffing model and begin to align their subject matter experts with the supplier's experts outlined in the proposals. They develop more detailed staffing requirements for each of the identified subject matter experts. They also look at the existing tools and discuss how they can be leveraged across the two groups to begin to share ideas, concepts, and general information. Matt is pleased that this work is coming together in parallel.

> **Matt:** I'm happy with our team's work. For example, Steve was assigned to collect orientation information that would be helpful for any of the new supplier staff, information about our general organizational struc-

ture, key individuals to know, physical locations, and so on. He was even able to start sharing some of this information with the individuals from the supplier team who have been identified as part of the initial transition.

Steve wants to make sure that the team understands two more aspects of supplier management: customer delivery and supplier success.

Steve: We need to step back periodically and look at the big picture. We're putting this contract in place to improve delivery to our customers, to get the best technology available, and to respond efficiently and effectively to our customers' needs. At the end of the day, we're always the group accountable for what's delivered to our customers.

The key is to translate that high-level goal into our day-to-day work with our suppliers. We need to understand their issues and challenges and help them resolve these. We also need to measure supplier performance, especially schedule and customer satisfaction. When changes occur, and they will, we must manage them with the supplier. And finally, in the worst case scenario, we must leverage legal remedies as a last resort if performance processes or products fail to meet our criteria. If we manage these things correctly, we can work effectively with our suppliers and develop any product or functionality requested by our customers. So when you think about it, a big part of our job is to make the suppliers successful.

> **TIP**   It is the acquirer's responsibility to help the supplier succeed.

Putting an outsourcing agreement in place is where the business dreams run headlong into the harsh reality of solutions delivery. Steve describes it this way.

Steve: The scenario goes something like this. The strategy is the vision, and the initial plan emerges from the vision. The supplier agreement is the blueprint. The blueprint now moves into the construction phase, and the only certainty at this point is that the plans will change.

Matt: That's right, Steve. Change management is critical. We know there will be business and technical problems during the life of the agreement, and we have to manage that. Getting these processes in place quickly is important to the deal, because it puts in place the steady-state structure that is so critical to delivering the work efficiently and effectively.

Steve: We need to be careful when we use the term "steady state." Even though it is often used in the outsourcing context, in reality outsourcing is a complex thing and nothing is ever totally steady. What it really means is that there's a point when the future state described in the agreement becomes implemented. This becomes a state of continuous quality improvement, cost reduction, and vigilant oversight. That's why it's so important for us and our supplier to get a structure in place in a matter of months, not years.

After the contract is awarded, the acquirer teams responsible for implementing the supplier agreement must move beyond negotiations and work diligently to build trust with the supplier. In some situations, acquirers who work on negotiation teams find that the style and approach used in the negotiation influences their ongoing relationship with the supplier. This holds true regardless of the type of supplier agreement. If the negotiations are ugly, the deal can get spoiled and the trust relationship never materializes. One way teams resolve this is to expand the integrated team, change team leadership, or otherwise change the team composition to force changes in attitudes formed during the pursuit process. One critical success factor is to transfer the knowledge about the final agreement to the new team.

> **TIP** Trust evolves as members of the integrated team understand they are working toward common goals.

When there is effective communication between you and the supplier, the relationship thrives; without it, it is at higher risk to wither and die. In outsourcing, both you and the supplier must feel free to discuss performance problems, technical challenges, and any other issues that surface. Communication builds the bridge between the two groups and is based on a foundation of trust.

Both you and the supplier need to be up to speed on available tools to support communications. You should select those that fit the relationship by taking into consideration characteristics like geography and technology, as well as organizational culture. For example, a certain individual might use e-mail for routine communications because she has limited time to access e-mail. But for urgent issues she might use voice mail, because it gives her better, more frequent access. Everyone needs to understand these types of preferences, because they directly affect the effectiveness of communication.

You can use collaboration tools to support your work with your suppliers. These tools allow suppliers to work directly with members of your team across organizational boundaries. You must establish ground rules about what information can be shared. Nondisclosure agreements should be in place, but for information that is considered sensitive—such as finances, documentation of internal escalation, or human resource information—access must be closely managed. Any costs for collaboration tools should be part of the overall contract budget.

> **TIP** Collaboration tools bridge organizational boundaries and foster teamwork.

Matt speaks to George Taylor, the supplier's project manager, about how the integrated team needs to leverage the tools that they have defined as a part of the agreement.

Matt: George, we use Lotus Notes for e-mail, and your organization uses a Microsoft product. Unfortunately, the calendar features aren't as compatible as we'd like. This makes it hard to schedule joint meetings and confirm appointments. In any case, we need to have some visibility to effectively manage our standing meetings and other work commitments. I think it's time to bring in that collaboration tool you demonstrated during due diligence so that we can really start to work as one integrated team.

George: I agree, Matt. I've been working behind the scenes with your support team to get that tool in house ASAP. You should see it up and running by the end of the week. Someone on my team has already built a combined calendar capability and a basic work flow for managing critical deliverables. I think you'll be very impressed.

Effective communications between you and the supplier must begin as early as the selection process, especially during due diligence. If a supplier believes that you are understating the work involved in the agreement, it will be much harder to build a trusted relationship and it may never happen. One way to manage communications early in the solicitation process is to use a trusted third-party adviser. A consultant can often play this role to explain differences between acquirer views and supplier views and clarify critical topics for both sides. The consultant can rapidly clear up misunderstandings and help align interests between you and the supplier.

Even an invoice is a method of communication. For example, are the charges accurate? Are the listed items clearly associated with the actual work? The need for clear and trusted communication requires that you and the supplier agree on a communication framework, or what has been termed *time management*, as a significant part of the overall governance structure. Committees, forums, frequency of meetings, roles and responsibilities, and escalation processes are all part of a communication framework that should be detailed in the supplier agreement.

Holding initial face-to-face meetings after the agreement is signed is one way to solidify the human aspects of the contractual relationship. It is beneficial to send your team members to meet with the supplier's development team members to solidify the integrated team, whether in a formal meeting, a workshop, or a set of team-building sessions.

You might define two or three categories of meetings that support communication for you and the supplier. For example, both leadership teams could get together in a strategic partnership meeting. This meeting would be structured to foster sharing between the two organizations at the executive level and to help resolve any major challenges or issues that arise about the agreement. It is a forum for the discussion of any major changes to programs or projects, especially those that affect cost and require executive approval.

> **TIP** Use a communication framework to execute ongoing communication and demonstrate its importance.

Another kind of meeting is for the people responsible for the processes and procedures related to the purchase of goods or services. This meeting is a forum for discussions about interpretation of contract language, dispute resolution processes, or any other topic that relates to how the organization performs business-to-business purchasing. Yet another set of meetings addresses project reviews, manages issues and risks, and assesses the ongoing progress of the project.

The nature of outsourcing requires that you and the supplier apply process discipline. This means that everyone is clear about who does what, how it is done, who measures what, and who owns what. Suppliers support this need for clarity by sharing with you what has worked in past engagements, viewing communication as a value-added feature rather than an afterthought, creating a climate of collaboration by removing defensiveness in communication, and approaching all communication from a position of mutual respect. These are all ways to facilitate good communication during an engagement. Mechanisms put in place to understand one another's perspectives build an environment of mutual trust and benefit.

> **TIP** For success in project execution, process discipline is required from both the acquirer and the supplier.

Matt's team demonstrates a commitment to making the deal work and, through word of mouth, also gets some of the "techies" in the organization interested in what the supplier has proposed. The team also offers feedback to the negotiation team and begins immediately to promote the value of the proposal. Matt didn't predict this excitement, and he sees it as a major win.

TIP Use key influencers in the organization to promote outsourcing.

Kristin Wells, the executive for the winning supplier, is intent on quickly getting the necessary supplier reporting systems in place. She speaks to George Taylor, the supplier's project manager, about what she wants.

Kristin: It's important to get all our business management systems in place quickly, and they should be kept simple. This includes SLA reporting, balanced scorecards, escalation management, project reporting, staffing policies and procedures, project initiation processes, and so on. I don't want any of these areas to be neglected, as has happened in some of our other deals. Some of our solution delivery staff believes that we need to bring in a large team, the back-office team, to manage the deal. I don't want a large group, because I don't believe that it's in our best interest or in the customer's best interest. The capabilities of Matt's team are pretty mature, because they've done outsourcing in the past. I want to be sure that we keep this agreement as cost-effective as possible. I want to prove to Matt and his team that we were the right supplier to choose. I want more business from this organization.

George: You read my mind, Kristin. We can't just relax because we won the contract. We have to continually prove that we can help this company move its technology to the next level. That's what makes these jobs fun. That's the challenge. We must have a lean management structure in place by the end of the week.

An escalation process as a governing principle is a specific form of communication and should be agreed upon and documented in the supplier agreement. It is a reflection of the rules of cooperation that should be executed by you and the supplier when necessary. To the extent possible, you and the supplier choose to resolve questions or concerns without triggering formal escalation processes or corrective action. The rule should require that any issues or conflicts be resolved as close to their origin as possible. If that fails, then all parties should agree to follow the documented escalation process. For significant issues that cannot be resolved through escalation, an alternative is having a negotiation team and strategy in place to resolve the disputed issues. After the issue is resolved, the terms of the resolution are documented and monitored to ensure compliance by both parties.

> **TIP**   Put rules in place to encourage the resolution of issues and disputes close to the source.

Disputes and differing interpretations of the supplier agreement are frequently the result of undercommunication. You and the supplier should make every effort to overcommunicate, especially during the initial stages of the project. George shares the industry statistics he has read that underscore the need for communication and describe what happens if communication doesn't happen.

George: We really need to focus on communication, and we need to work at overcommunicating. According to the experts, under the best of circumstances the technology project failure rate is somewhere around 40 to 80 percent, and the greatest contributory factor is communication. This means that a lack of communication in our outsourcing deal increases our risk of failure in any delivery activities.

Kristin: Yes, that tracks with my experience.

George: A big issue is managing expectations between our teams. Expectations that don't get communicated can't be met. Expectations not managed through communication will never be satisfied. And transformation visions that are not communicated are never met. If they don't appear in the contract, the deal doesn't get staffed to realize true technological innovations. The "thought leadership" that everyone talked about never happens. We need to be careful about this issue, because many outsourcers are disappointed about the thought leadership they get from contractors, even when the transformational opportunities are not documented in the agreement.

On one hand, acquirers want to tie their suppliers to very specific SLAs to assure themselves of a measurable level of performance. On the other hand, they also want their suppliers to be flexible, proactive, and thought leaders. These conflicting expectations can lead to concerns over the loss of control, questions about the cost-effectiveness of outsourcing, unmet expectations for transformation, and so on. Your suppliers may feel that they are required only to meet the SLAs, whereas you may be looking to expand your technology horizons. Because suppliers are accountable for SLAs and there are usually monetary penalties tied to not meeting them, suppliers feel an overriding need to mitigate their own risk by meeting the SLAs first and thinking about creativity and possible innovation second.

In one meeting, George speaks to Matt about what he sees as an unrealistic expectation.

George: Matt, as your supplier we have a contract to support your systems from a maintenance perspective, and you also know that we will be completing "in-flight" projects as we take over this contract. The contract also specifies an additional set of deliverables with target dates that you've set—like the one that asks us to look at the reporting of our activities and come up with suggestions to make it better and also describes the delivery of a balanced scorecard.

Matt: That's right.

George: Well, I think you have another, unstated requirement, which is to have us offer some of the more leading edge technologies in the projects we're supporting. This is where the challenge is. To do that, we need to bring in experts in those technology areas, especially in data management. We have these skills in our group, but the individuals are not readily available. They all have current assignments, they're scarce resources, and there isn't a provision in the contract to pay for them.

Matt: That sounds like something we need to look at.

George: Yes, I agree. If we're going to meet this requirement, we need to sit down and talk about this and any other unstated requirements to understand your needs. We also need to have a very real discussion about the additional costs to do this. I think your ideas are great. We just need to talk about priorities and impact on cost.

> **TIP** Suppliers will always be motivated to meet SLAs first and innovate later.

It is up to the acquiring organization and the supplier to determine what is significant enough to warrant a change to the agreement. Kristin runs into this dilemma when the structure of the customer's change management board is altered. She talks it over with her management team.

Kristin: We have an opportunity to consolidate the structure of the change control board with our customer. The idea is that when any change is made through new development, we're in control of the deployment of that change and have visibility into it. But this will require additional administrative support for two hours a week. We gave our customer the best overall deal possible, with a bare bones agreement, and we really don't have the flexibility built in to add any new work. If we decide to add this to the agreement, then we may have to submit a formal change to cover the additional cost.

Kristin knows that her managers are not pleased with the thought of adding new costs to the contract for this expanded visibility. But when Kristin runs the numbers in her head, she sees that the impact of the change is eight hours per month. If the task is performed offshore, it will cost around $400 per month, for an annualized cost of approximately $4800 per year. For a $10 million contract (annualized), it seems that this cost could be covered without a formal change. Kristin's management team is willing to cover this expense at no additional cost, but they're concerned that the accumulation of small items like this one might quickly become a large problem. They ask her to communicate to Matt the implications and cumulative effect of this change and all the changes to date in total.

When there is a change in the environment that affects a project, or when a new project requirement surfaces, requirements documented in the original supplier agreement may no longer be applicable. For example, a new technology may become available or the reporting requirements may be judged too burdensome. There may be changes to the agreement stemming from the supplier's inability to meet acceptance criteria or service levels. When these situations occur, it is important that the changes be formally documented and agreed to by both the acquirer and the supplier before they are implemented. Changes can have an impact on pricing, the product to be delivered, or the results required from the technology solution. Acquirers typically use their formal configuration management processes to manage these changes.

> **TIP** Acquirers and suppliers must work together to determine what changes are material enough to change the agreement.

How well the acquirer-supplier relationship works is driven mainly by how committed each organization is to building true partnerships. Teams must move away from ongoing discussions about "What's in the contract?" and "That's not how I read the contract" to "How can we work together to accomplish these goals for the project?" Often, short-term cost savings get in the way of a long-term potential partnership with a supplier. Many elements factor into whether an acquirer chooses to partner, and this also relates directly to what the acquirer wants from the supplier. Organizations understand the need for fixed-price agreements, aggressive price targets, and stringent SLAs to manage delivery, while still encouraging those behaviors that move toward a partnership that can work to the benefit of both acquirer and supplier.

> **TIP** Work beyond agreement terms to build a partnership with suppliers.

Over the course of the project, the supplier is compensated based on some measure of work completed. The agreement specifies when and under what conditions the supplier is paid. Often, acquirers link the payment of invoices to specific deliverables. This practice lets you manage nonperformance by using the remedies outlined in the agreement, such as withholding or reducing payments. You must ensure that the proper financial controls are in place for compliant invoicing and payment activities.

> **TIP** Link supplier payments to some tangible measure of progress.

After a supplier agreement is signed, it becomes expensive to make significant modifications or to change to another supplier. So a change control process is outlined in the agreement's terms and conditions. To ensure that the agreement remains viable over its intended life, many acquirers use benchmarking to determine whether the agreed system or service costs have changed. If there are significant changes in technology or cost based on this benchmarking data, then you have the option to open the agreement (based on its terms for renegotiation) and work with the supplier to modify any agreement requirements. Opening up an agreement costs time and money, especially if you have multiple agreements with various suppliers. Before an agreement is signed, you can easily make changes as you gain clarity about your needs. But after the deal is signed, risk and interdependency increase, and the acquirer and supplier must look for ways to work together without opening the agreement for renegotiation.

> **TIP** Use benchmarking and industry norms to validate price and terms of agreements.

Before the product is accepted, you must ensure that all acceptance criteria in the agreement have been met. If the supplier fails to perform as specified, you can exercise any and all remedies as outlined in the agreement. You provide the supplier with formal written notice that the supplier deliverables have been accepted or rejected. It is also at this point that you assume ownership of the specific deliverables, product, or service as partial or complete performance of the supplier agreement. For you to be assured that all aspects of the agreement are completed, you also need to verify that all specified customer and contractual requirements have been completed. Contractual requirements may include such things as license, warranty, ownership, usage, support, or maintenance agreements. You verify that the requirements are fulfilled and that all contracted deliverables and supporting documents are completed.

You also have the responsibility of communicating that the product is ready for transition to operations. Typically the supplier is responsible for integrating and packaging the product and preparing for the transition to operations and support, as outlined in the agreement. Often you outline a pilot activity during which the supplier maintains control of the product. This gives you the opportunity to validate that the product is usable and ready for full operation. To mitigate risks until the capability is proven to be operational, a pilot is typically deployed only to a subset of the intended user population.

> **TIP** To ensure supplier completion, use simple checklists of all the requirements and conditions in the supplier agreement.

You also must be assured by the supplier that the product can be backed out in the event of any failures before transitioning to the production environment. If there is a warranty period for the technology solution, you and the supplier work together to ensure that the product is operating as specified and that no corrective actions are required. The product is transitioned to the operating team when the team can demonstrate the capability to operate the product.

You are responsible for maintaining oversight until all transition activities are complete and the support of operations is in place. If you group functionality from multiple suppliers to create a release for your customers, then you designate one supplier to function as the *prime* supplier. The prime supplier is responsible for making sure that all the functionality is integrated so that the release can be successfully deployed.

> **TIP** If functionality from multiple suppliers is combined into a single release, designate a prime supplier.

After the product is transitioned, you are responsible for analyzing and reviewing the results of the transition to make sure that all corrective actions are completed before project close. In addition, you need to ensure that product storage, distribution, and use comply with the terms of the agreement or license.

When the project is completed, transitioned, and deployed successfully, the supplier agreement is formally closed. Closure means that all the supplier requirements in the agreement are complete. Other closure activities include ensuring that all project records are complete and managed for future use. A formal communication is sent to stakeholders to let them know that the supplier agreement has been closed.

> **TIP** The acquirer never abdicates the oversight role as transition activities are executed.

2.4.8 Applying the CMMI-ACQ to Managing Your Supplier Agreement

The CMMI-ACQ provides specific recommendations on how to manage the execution of the supplier agreement to ensure that you perform in accordance with the agreement (see Table 2-10).

Communication is the key to successfully completing the agreement. You manage the relationship with the supplier through effective communication and mutual understanding throughout the life of the project. It is of particular importance to you that these communications are documented when they affect issues such as a change in the business objectives or business processes

Table 2-10 *Acquisition Management Goal 1: Practices and Tips*

CMMI-ACQ Process Area: Acquisition Management	
1. Goal: Manage Supplier Agreements.	
Practices	**Tips**
1.1 Manage changes and revise the supplier agreement if necessary, and resolve supplier agreement issues or disputes.	• Start planning for the implementation of the supplier agreement before the final supplier decision is made. • It is your responsibility to help the supplier succeed. • Trust evolves as the integrated team members understand they are working toward common goals. • Build a governance structure that supports clear roles, responsibilities, and accountability. • Collaboration tools bridge organizational boundaries and foster collaboration. • Use a communication framework to execute ongoing communication and demonstrate its importance. • For successful project execution, process discipline is required from both the acquirer and the supplier. • Use key influencers in the organization to promote outsourcing. • Suppliers will always be motivated to meet SLAs first and innovate later.

Table 2-10 *Acquisition Management Goal 1: Practices and Tips (Continued)*

Practices	Tips
1.2 Resolve issues and disputes associated with the supplier agreement, and determine corrective actions necessary to address the issues and disputes. 1.3 Revise the supplier agreement to reflect changes in conditions where appropriate. 1.4 Close the supplier agreement after verifying completion of all supplier requirements.	• Put rules in place to encourage the resolution of issues and disputes close to the source. • Acquirers and suppliers must work together to determine what changes are material enough to change the agreement. • Work beyond agreement terms to build a partnership with suppliers. • Start to build trust as quickly as possible. • Organizational change activities should be executed at the same time as the supplier agreement, if not before.

that directly affects the project (Table 2-10, practice 1.1). Supplier management also supports the resolution of any issues or disputes between you and the supplier (Table 2-10, practice 1.2). And finally, communication covers information exchange that supports marketing or public relations.

The process of escalating unresolved issues has multiple phases before possible litigation. It is your responsibility to collect and manage issues until they are resolved. These issues can be identified from team communication or in milestone or progress reviews. If the supplier does not comply with corrective action, it is escalated and becomes a supplier agreement dispute.

Suppliers have the option to escalate issues about the agreement, especially those about the acquirer meeting its commitments as outlined in the agreement. Critical stakeholders such as senior managers, governance bodies, and legal counsel may participate.

Changes to the agreement that are deemed necessary by both parties should be captured in the supplier agreement, with the appropriate approvals from both parties (Table 2-10, practice 1.3). Changes can come from new requirements, new technologies, or changes in the SLAs. They can also occur when the supplier's processes or products do not meet agreed-upon criteria.

Closing a project requires that all the stipulations in the agreement be met, including specified customer requirements, regulation requirements, and specific contractual requirements as well as customer deliverables (Table 2-10, practice 1.4). It is your responsibility to go through the necessary verification and validation processes to ensure that all stipulations have been met.

2.4.9 Applying the CMMI-ACQ to Fostering Cooperation

The CMMI-ACQ provides specific recommendations on how to build the kind of collaborative environment that supports the execution of the agreement and completion of the project (see Table 2-11).

One of the goals of acquisition management is to set up the proper environment for the supplier to work with the acquirer. This includes adopting routines for reviewing and approving invoices as well as building standard acceptance criteria (Table 2-11, practices 2.1 and 2.2). Payments tied to deliverables or completed functionality are important milestones to indicate the readiness of the product to transition. Based on the acquisition strategy, the product is transitioned to the acquirer and placed in operation (Table 2-11, practice 2.3). Your final reviews of the product signal that the project is completed, and the appropriate steps are taken to ensure that all documentation for the technology solution is managed.

Table 2-11 *Acquisition Management Goal 2: Practices and Tips*

CMMI-ACQ Process Area: Acquisition Management	
2. Goal: Establish a productive and cooperative environment to meet the goals of the project.	
Practices	**Tips**
2.1 Receive, review, approve, and remit invoices provided by the supplier.	• Link supplier payments to some tangible measure of progress.
2.2 Ensure that the supplier agreement is satisfied before accepting the acquired product. 2.3 Transition the acquired product from the supplier to the acquirer.	• To ensure supplier completion, use simple checklists of all the requirements and conditions in the supplier agreement. • If functionality from multiple suppliers is combined into a single release, designate a prime supplier. • The acquirer never abdicates the oversight role as transition activities are executed.

2.5 Summary

Sound strategy and effective execution are the two necessary ingredients for success in a competitive business environment. Realizing one without the other causes organizations to perform below their potential. Strategy drives all activities, but a process that aligns business strategy with execution is essential to applying the strategy. Organizations need to define strategic activities or areas of activities, develop a clear action plan to achieve the goals, and then allocate resources (people, time, money) to accomplish the activities. For growth in profitability, development resources are crucial to the achievement of targets and must therefore be managed in accordance with the business strategy. Managers need tools for evaluating and controlling the development portfolio, and metrics must be in place to ensure that the project portfolio and the resources expended on various projects remain consistent with the business goals.

Acquiring organizations leverage acquisition strategies and up-front planning to formulate processes to help meet the challenges of getting the right technologies to their customers. Traditionally, the organizations that participate in outsourcing and offshoring have been large ones that make mega-deals. Now, it seems that everyone wants to leverage the benefits of outsourcing, even small to medium-sized organizations. One of the key issues that these smaller acquirers face is forming an outsourcing team that has the skills, knowledge, and experience to build high-quality solicitation packages, select optimal suppliers, and successfully manage their relationships with suppliers. Typically, few organizations automatically possess this special expertise, so they must take care to ensure that contract activities are worked by experienced, qualified personnel.

The first step is to ensure that everyone on your team is on the same page with regard to the acquisition strategy. All the members must understand why they are there and what they bring to the table. The team must understand not only the acquisition project but also the general acquisition environment.

When it comes to building solicitation packages and agreements, the saying "Garbage in, garbage out," applies, but it's more like "Garbage out, garbage in." If you don't release a solid RFP, the proposals will not likely be of the caliber required for a complex undertaking such as outsourcing technology. If you don't clearly articulate your objectives, the suppliers who respond will merely add risk to the project or program, negating any cost savings promised by outsourcing.

A poorly developed solicitation package also makes it more difficult to compare suppliers' bids on an apples-to-apples basis. To this end, the acquirer

team can work more efficiently if it uses templates or other tools to standardize the parts of RFIs and RFPs that apply across the organization. Starting
from scratch for each request consumes resources on all sides and injects
variability and risk into the process.

Another key to ensuring that the solicitation package isn't "garbage out" is
to have it reviewed by as many senior personnel and other stakeholders as
possible before it is let. Like many other acquisition efforts, developing information and making assumptions in isolation usually lead to problems. Get
others involved, and do so early on.

After the solicitation package is released, you face the monumental task of
choosing one or more suppliers. It's important to consider whether a single
supplier or several suppliers, each performing part of the development,
works best and yields the highest return and lowest risk. On one hand, a single supplier may not have all the capabilities or resources needed to fulfill the
agreement within budget, on time, and with quality. On the other hand, managing multiple suppliers can drive your complexity, risks, and costs skyward.
Balancing economies of scale and diminishing returns is a challenge indeed.

Several tools are available to help you evaluate potential suppliers. It's
important to employ these foundational tools before you invest resources in
conducting on-site interviews and visits with a long list of potential suppliers. The first line of defense is evaluating the bids themselves. A bid that
doesn't seem to correspond directly to the information outlined in the proposal may mean that the supplier didn't invest much effort, perhaps
indicating that it may not be responsive to your needs in the future. It's akin
to advertising an open position and receiving a resume from someone whose
skills and background don't match the job description. It makes interviewers
wonder, "Why is he applying for this job? Not only is he not in the ballpark,
he's not even sure what team he plays for." And just as you would research a
potential new employee, you should use business contacts to learn what you
can about potential suppliers. Never underestimate the power of learning
from others' past mistakes (or successes, for that matter).

Another resource for reliable information about candidates is outside
sources such as industry analyst groups like Gartner or Forrester. Evaluations using common success factors from these organizations can be
especially helpful in narrowing the field. Of course, don't forget to assess the
basic characteristics of the pool of suppliers to see how they align with the
acquisition. These are the traditional characteristics used to evaluate any
supplier, whether you're purchasing a new appliance or any other commodity: the size of the supplier, redundancy, its skills, its history, and a

demonstrated understanding of customer needs. How well the supplier will work with your team and with other partners in a multisourced environment is also important.

It's difficult to evaluate one of the most important aspects of a potential sourcing relationship: how the culture of a supplier aligns with yours. Candidates should demonstrate an understanding of organizational structures: what their predominant forms of communication are and how to perform knowledge transfer. Some indicators of cultural alignment are how the supplier handles personnel and policies, its organizational structure, and how it sets and executes goals. Bidders should demonstrate to your stakeholders how they plan to perform knowledge transfer.

Next is the challenge of negotiating a supplier agreement based on the final bids. You use all the available information to narrow the field, gradually down-selecting until you identify the best supplier, or group of suppliers, for the project. The negotiation process is an in-depth discussion with a supplier that focuses on reaching compromises on any outstanding issues for both parties. Your negotiation team focuses the discussion on outstanding contract terms, SLAs, and details in the plans and deliverables that need to be worked through. It's also critical to ensure that cost visibility is built into the agreements. During the negotiation sessions, it's important for the negotiation team to understand the factors motivating the supplier team. Also, negotiators should be controlled in their communication with others on their team and should not reveal too much to the supplier team. To get the best deal, your team members should don their poker faces and not show their cards.

Usually, you encourage competition between potential suppliers by challenging them to meet aggressive cost targets and other constraints. The suppliers must show their creative abilities in how they plan to meet these goals, whether it's by rearranging staff or subcontracting with an offshore supplier to complete a discrete chunk of the work. The agreement should present a win-win endeavor that adds value and profit for all parties.

To that end, the agreement should not contain every possible facet for which the supplier is responsible, only the givens that are standard parts of a supplier agreement and a well-defined statement of work for the technology or service being acquired. In this way, you ensure that the supplier doesn't assume all the risk and the extra costs of addressing these risks as they see fit, a practice that eats into your profit. The supplier must also stand to earn a profit by not throwing all available resources at fulfilling a single contract.

The types of agreements and pricing mechanisms you use affects the products and services delivered. The type of agreement depends on the quality of the supplier as well as your business goals and the maturity of your processes. For example, projects without a clearly defined scope—such as those that develop an unprecedented technology—often employ a time-and-materials type of agreement. For products or services that are well defined and of limited scope, a fixed-price agreement might work best.

Value-priced contracts are the most complex because they require the most up-front details, such as roles and responsibilities, measurement of results, measurement of overall gain, and methods of ongoing measurement and payments. This type of agreement can best be used when there is a high level of trust between you and the supplier, perhaps when you have a history of successfully working together on other projects or programs.

Any SLAs built into an agreement help you measure the performance of the supplier and give the supplier an incentive to meet the terms of the agreement on time and within budget. To determine performance levels, you must define an appropriate measurement and reporting plan as part of the SLA. After all the parties agree to the terms, the agreement needs to be approved by management and other approval staffs (e.g., legal, purchasing, finance) and signed to become a legal document.

Long before the agreement is signed, however, you should formulate an operating model—a high-level view of how the acquirer and supplier teams will integrate and work together. The operating model might include a list of deliverables and target dates, staffing requirements for special domain areas, and key background information about your organization that will help new supplier staff ramp up quickly. Also, working together in an outsourcing model requires a governance structure under which both you and the supplier can work. Governance determines how to make decisions about applying the organization's resources. Key elements of a technology governance model include delivery, management of risk, accountability, and measurement. Without strong governance, any outsourcing or services contracts will fail.

After negotiations have been completed, the teams responsible for implementing the agreement must work diligently to build a trust relationship. Fostering a long-term relationship, mutual well-being, discipline, continuous improvement, and learning doesn't happen overnight, nor do these things happen just because a contract was signed. Techniques to start building this relationship can include a workshop where acquirers and suppliers meet to discuss the aspects of partnership that both parties want to emulate and talk about how to start building that type of relationship. Sessions to work through solving common problems can also strengthen bonds between the teams. Over time, acquirers can progress from a contractual relationship to a partnership with their suppliers by taking small steps to build an overall environment that supports trust, innovation, and capability. The key to success in supplier partnering is a commitment to partner through strong leadership, ongoing support to make the partnership work, and the desire to continuously improve. And as with many other aspects of successful business practices, communication is the key.

After an agreement is signed and technology development is under way, it's expensive to make changes. This is another reason the supplier agreement should not be an airtight, inflexible plan. There must be room to move. Status changes in the supplier's progress and issues such as organizational shifts can increase the risk in a project, and risk always carries the potential of throwing the schedule or, worse, driving up the cost. The integrated team must carefully weigh the benefits and risks of changing the terms of an agreement, the processes being followed, the technologies used, reengineering, and so on. Any organizational change should be built into the agreement, with clarifications about ownership, scope, and resources.

This chapter outlined the importance of formulating an acquisition strategy, manifesting that strategy in the acquisition plan, building a solid solicitation package, choosing the best supplier, and developing and approving a supplier agreement. In Chapter 3, Engineering Solutions, we take a deeper look at the activities that take place during execution of the supplier agreement, such as clarifying the value of the technology solution for the customer, developing accurate customer requirements, and obtaining and understanding feedback from customers.

Chapter 3

Engineering Solutions

None of my inventions came by accident. I see a worthwhile need to be met and I make trial after trial until it comes. What it boils down to is one per cent inspiration and ninety-nine percent perspiration.
Thomas Edison (1929)

The success of any project depends on delighting the customer, and that requires understanding the customer. Poor understanding of customer intentions—needs, expectations, and constraints—accounts for most project failures. This chapter highlights the vital importance of eliciting high-level requirements and maintaining the relationship between these and your business goals (see hidden truth number 3, "Maintain acquirer core competencies," in Chapter 1).

We focus first on developing requirements, explaining how to successfully develop customer requirements and contractual requirements to guide the supplier's work. The first step in developing good customer requirements is to elicit customer needs. We cover this important practice in depth by focusing on how to clarify the value of the technology solution for the customer through requirements, why it's important to involve the customer early, and how to manage the gaps that naturally occur between stakeholders. You will learn that there is no substitute for direct interaction with the customer.

These interactions take a spiral pattern of repeated steps and increasing mutual understanding. You build a relationship in which each party continually increases its realization of what each can contribute. The process begins with the germ of an idea—a few words or a sketch—and eventually matures into a fully developed, operational technology solution.

The first step is to present the idea to the prospective customer immediately. Promote the idea. Help the customer understand what you have in mind. With truly novel solutions to problems, the customer may initially have difficulty seeing what you are offering. The second step is to listen to the customers' views carefully, thoroughly, and in enough detail and context that you can understand what is really being described. The third step is to develop or modify the product or service in creative response to what you've heard from the customer. Then you return for further rounds of promotion, customer feedback, and development.

We then turn our attention to writing contractual requirements by describing how to capture minimum, accurate requirements and translate these into practical design constraints for the supplier. In this process, you must be cognizant of the conflicting goals between suppliers and acquirers and often between different suppliers (see hidden truth number 4, "Understand conflicting goals between suppliers and between suppliers and acquirers," in Chapter 1). Acquirers want to obtain solutions that benefit their bottom line and provide stakeholders with what they need. Suppliers want to fulfill their contracts, make a profit, and maintain their relationships with you and with other suppliers.

Certain factors—such as lower costs versus higher profit margins, and fast delivery versus low deployment costs—may cause conflicts between you and the supplier as well as among multiple suppliers. We cover your role in designing the technology solution and in managing requirements throughout the project to discuss remedies for conflicting goals between various stakeholders and to achieve value-added technology solutions.

3.1 Focus on Value

The essence of engineering successful solutions is to understand which solutions will add value for your customer. Eliciting needs goes beyond the initial collecting of requirements to proactively identifying additional requirements not explicitly provided by the stakeholders. You consult relevant stakeholders representing all phases of the product's life cycle in the intended environment and ask them to describe business as well as technical functions. In this way, needs for all product-related life-cycle processes are considered concurrently with the concepts of the products you seek to acquire.

Frequently, the needs or requirements of stakeholders such as customers, end users, and suppliers are poorly identified or conflicting. Because you need to clearly identify and understand the stakeholders' intentions throughout the project life cycle, you use an iterative process. You involve the relevant stakeholders to communicate their needs, expectations, and constraints and to help resolve conflicts. For that, successful project teams engage the customers from the beginning and proactively deal with the sometimes conflicting viewpoints of different stakeholders.

3.1.1 Involve Customers from the Beginning

All projects begin with the customer, and you need a deep understanding of the customer's business model (or mission) and processes. Matt Vauban, an executive in our fictitious acquisition organization, ponders this seemingly simple statement as he looks out his office window to the other side of the river. Then he turns to Steve Reiter, the project manager for the project, which is aimed at improving the company's acquisition processes.

> **Matt:** Steve, we always have to keep our business model in mind. We can't afford to buy into some new technology just to make us feel good and look better. When I listen to our CEO, I get a clear message: We need to carefully look at everything we're doing as a business and eliminate activities and technologies that don't add value.

Also meeting with Matt and Steve is Paula Ressel, the internal customer for our acquisition project.

> **Paula:** You're right, Matt. I don't think we've done that very well.

> **Steve:** I agree. Whenever we invest money in the future, we better have a promising business model of what the future will look like.

This exchange is similar to an anecdote that John Marano Jr., now CEO and president of the start-up Vascular Insights, told nearly a decade ago:

> The company laboratory invents a device with a wire frame and cocking spring on a nice piece of wood. When the wire frame is cocked, a small disturbance causes the frame to slap onto the wood with a great deal of force. The device is taken to a customer with the plea, "I don't know what to use this device for, but if you tell me, I'll be happy to sell it to you." A highly negative cus-

tomer response is common. On the other hand, if discussions with a customer result in, "I need a better mousetrap," it is much easier to invent and sell a wire frame with a spring on a nice piece of wood.

Undertaking a development effort with a true understanding of customer requirements leads to easier and more frequent success.

> **TIP** Carefully assess how much value the proposed solution adds to your customer.

Although it's crucial to satisfy the customer, this satisfaction must emanate from a specific business need; this need may leverage new technology and create new products, but it must always add to the bottom line.

George Taylor, an executive from the supplier hired for this project, joins the meeting. Matt continues the discussion.

> **Matt:** You can almost always develop a system to solve a business problem, but the cost might be horrendous. The question is, Is it okay with the customer? We go back to them and say, "I know you have these problems. However, for these reasons it will cost this much money. Are you willing to live with the current situation, or are we going to move forward and add this functionality?" We have to be honest about how much money we're willing to spend to resolve a specific business problem.

You need deep organizational and business process knowledge to build value-added solutions. Yet gaining access to this knowledge is one of the most critical problems in acquiring technology solutions. For many project teams, the required breadth of skill and experience for engineering large, complex systems is a scarce attribute. One business-savvy technology leader lamented,

> I ask projects to show me the business model that implementing this system will enable. The response I get is, "That's probably something that needs to be created." And you then wonder, "How many tens of millions of dollars have we spent developing a system to go global where we don't have a global business model that my business partners can look at and agree with?" How can we build a system if we haven't agreed to the business model? I don't get that.

> **TIP** Affirm the business model before you specify the technology solution.

> **TIP** Communicate with your customers directly. Never outsource this critical connection.

An organization might be tempted to bring in additional resources from suppliers to attempt to quickly fill this gap. Paula doesn't buy that approach.

Paula: We've had limited success in using suppliers' requirements analysts. They tend to be entry-level people, so there is a lot of turnover. When we go from project to project, even with the same supplier, rarely do we get the same requirements team assigned. We often get a person who needs to get up to speed, and that can be painful. They may understand technical best practices or they may have some helpful industry best practice knowledge, but they tend to lack business process knowledge.

Matt: How do you mitigate this risk?

Paula: We provide our own requirements team to support the supplier from a coaching and mentoring standpoint, and we leverage the supplier's technical knowledge and best practices.

To focus on delivering value when buying and implementing technology throughout an organization, Matt, a seasoned executive, calls for a new role for acquirers.

Matt: It's helpful for us to see ourselves as technology brokers. I'm not alone in this viewpoint. Senior executives in several companies like ours have publicly said this. I measure everybody who works for me on business transformation—not technology transformation, not the technical elegance of a solution.

Steve: Being an engineer by training, I find it sometimes hard for techies not to fall in love with the elegance of their designs.

Matt: I know, Steve. But we're measured on achieving six sigma-type improvements, on world-class quality, efficiency, and effectiveness. Every dollar that goes into technology must benefit the business and our customers. It's a different mentality. The technology broker's only job is to transform the business—to get business results.

Key individuals in an acquisition organization must step up to the challenge of functioning as businesspeople first and then technologists. They must learn not only to use the language of the customer's business but also to think like the business—understand business issues and propose business solutions. By combining deep business savvy with keen technology insight, acquisition organizations can more effectively conceive, develop, and support ideas for improving organizational performance, as Steve describes.

Steve: I think the key to any project is involving the right people who have business knowledge. It's important that the project team understands the system delivery and acquisition management process, but that's probably 25 percent. It's more about somebody that the customer will respect when they talk to them. When you have someone who comes in and talks to the business in their own language, the team instantly gets respect.

George: When I've worked to gather requirements either for or with an acquisition organization, finding the right people to gather requirements is a challenge. We tend to look for what you might call "Sherpas" and "Yodas." Remember *Star Wars?* You know Yoda, the Jedi master?

Everyone smiles and nods.

George: Well, of course Yoda is the wisest and most powerful Jedi of his time. That's who we need—somebody who has the most knowledge and experience, somebody who has a really good context of the work that's going on in their organization.

Someone in the back of the room is heard to say, "Yes, but talk funny Yoda does," and everyone laughs. George continues the analogy.

George: Then you have the Sherpas—you know, the guys who guide the mountain climbers in the Himalayas. They're the experts, they know the territory, they have endurance and resilience. Sherpas have all the effective job aids, and they often point you to best practices for actually getting the work done.

> **TIP**   Identify and engage those individuals who have deep business knowledge and are well respected by their peers.

Before the integrated project team starts interviewing customers to elicit their requirements, it needs to conduct due diligence to find the Sherpas and Yodas. The team also needs to keep its eyes and ears open to identify potential Sherpas and Yodas during requirements gathering sessions.

> **TIP**   Employ a standardized, hierarchical decomposition of business processes.

Even if you have well-understood as-is and to-be business models and processes, it's critical to have ongoing communication with stakeholders, especially the customer. Matt wants to review this issue with Steve.

Matt: How do you establish effective communication with other business functions? We need to make sure they don't think we're out there developing fancy technology solutions and wasting scarce resources instead of delivering value.

Steve: To get everybody on the same page, we use what we call a "bill of process." This is a way to document a business process and help us maintain a common language with the business. It's kind of like a bill of materials, which manufacturers use to describe a product in terms of its assemblies, subassemblies, and basic parts.

Matt: A bill of materials?

Steve: Let me explain. A BOM hierarchically decomposes a product until it reaches some constituent part or module that is out of the scope of the BOM. So we took the business processes and broke them down globally into subprocesses and activities. We augmented that with flow diagrams that show relationships and who is responsible for what.

Steve laughs.

Steve: As we went through this exercise some people discovered processes they didn't know they had in their own areas.

> **TIP** Regularly benchmark your business model and processes against your competition and best-in-class organizations.

Methods like decomposing business processes and maintaining accurate process descriptions are ingredients for achieving common processes that are, in turn, the foundation for consistent execution of work. Matt reiterates this point from a global perspective.

Matt: Today, people focus much more on standardized processes and globalization—the ability to develop, manufacture, sell, and distribute products anywhere in the world at the lowest price. If you're expanding into new regions or new product lines, you have to leverage common processes to keep your costs down and drive efficiency into every part of your business. The best product with the lowest cost structure wins.

Steve: Yes, the world is getting flatter every day.

Matt: And to survive, you have to do all this through seamless expansion or contraction. If you disrupt your business doing this, your competitors will eat you for breakfast.

Steve: In fact, focusing on value is why we're looking outside ourselves in the first place.

Matt: We do frequent competitive analyses of business processes and the application of IT. We have numbers that go back more than a decade. Our business process leaders and my staff have process reviews with our CEO every year. Every process officer and information officer has to present a competitive assessment—where they are in their business processes relative to their competition and versus the theoretical limit of a particular business process or technology.

The joint leadership of business functions and the acquisition organization—in other words, the shared governance—is at the heart of effectively harmonizing business processes and technology solutions and thereby enabling the acquisition organization to add value to the endeavor. Steve illustrates.

Steve: The way global projects used to work was we built it at our headquarters and then called it "global" and deployed it everywhere else. But on this project we made a concerted effort to define the global requirements and the global process as a group. The initial phase wasn't so much IT-related; it was more like defining how they currently did work and then defining what the new business process would be. To achieve this we put together a steering committee with equal representation from each region. So instead of having a heavy influence from headquarters, we were very conscious of the number of people from each region and created a team that represented IT and business equally.

Various techniques are available to interact with customers and stakeholders.

Paula: We use a variety of techniques to gather requirements. It depends on the type of project and the type of stakeholder. We like to give everybody a way to get heard. Sometimes this is easier said than done in a workshop environment. We do use workshops quite a bit, along with interviews or brainstorming. We don't use questionnaires very much. They tend to be more impersonal and used for data collection. It's often hard to interpret what's written on a piece of paper, and the return rates tend to be very poor. Interactive sessions are much better.

TIP   Form a joint leadership team of your business customer and your acquisition team.

In virtually all projects, you need to adopt a mix of requirements gathering techniques. This flexibility is even more important in an outsourced environment. Suppliers need to be involved early, and the combination of techniques must compensate for the additional handoffs from you to the supplier and, in many cases, from the supplier's account manager or on-site team to a (perhaps offshore) development center.

> **TIP**   Use a variety of techniques to elicit requirements from all likely sources.

The environment you select is an important aspect of eliciting requirements.

> **Paula:**   If you're interviewing people to gather requirements, the best place is in the work environment. Working directly in the users' environment is critical to our success.

> **Steve:**   We like to use a supplier team together with folks from our organization who understand the business process inside-out. They ask questions like, "How do you do this task or that activity?" while sitting next to the users or customers. The information we get that way is priceless.

> **Paula:**   How do you record the info?

> **Steve:**   Videotape. It's extremely helpful. It's really interesting when you look at these videos later and notice all those "job aids" people use that you completely missed during the interview—for instance, sticky notes on their computers with a list of quick commands and passwords. People don't mention these things, because they're so used to them they forget they're even there.

Steve laughs as he remembers.

> **Steve:**   Sometimes when they tell you about a task or a sequence it sounds trivial. Then when you watch the video later you realize that they've described a very involved process. For instance, they might have to log on to three systems simultaneously to perform a seemingly simple task. They use a myriad of tools around their desk to work around a broken process, but they don't realize the complexity anymore because the process has become second nature.

Sometimes observations are useful for eliciting needs. In conducting an observation, project teams watch individuals for an extended time and produce detailed records of work practices. The rationale for these studies is that actual work practices differ from prescribed practices as documented in procedures, policies, and handbooks. You can partially uncover these processes by studying videotapes, as Steve mentions. Observations, however, are a more thorough investigation to discover tacit requirements. Steve recalls the use of observation on a recent project.

Steve: We did visits of two to four weeks at each site, just as fact finding. We sat with the users to understand what they did. We did their job with them.

> **TIP**   Instead of relying only on people's stories about how work is performed, observe how work gets done.

Matt: Looks like you immersed yourself in the users' work environment and business process.

Steve: Exactly. And we discussed with them how they perform a particular activity and really focused on getting to know the people and building that team. So everybody in every region felt part of the project. They didn't always feel they needed it, because everybody thinks their own process is good enough. But they were proud of what they did, they showed it, and we understood it.

Another approach is to install a camera to videotape a work environment to quietly observe what's going on. In this way, you can record work patterns in an unobtrusive way.

> **TIP**   Immerse yourself in the users' environment.

> **TIP**   Always probe for the rationale of business processes, tasks, and deliverables.

Observations provide additional insight into how practitioners perform their activities. They emphasize the importance of social interaction rather than data, data structure, or processing. By analyzing social interactions, you gain a better understanding of what people do and how or why they do it. Analysis of recordings and results from field studies reveal the practices through which information is communicated and tasks accomplished. Even apparently individual tasks such as reading, writing, or typing into a computer are embedded in interactions with others and are designed in relation to others' activities.

However, records from observations are inherently unstructured. For example, observation records contain significant duplication, and the collected information ranges from specific observations of particular activities to anecdotes and war stories told by customers and users. With this kind of information, there is seldom a clear and simple correspondence between an observational record and a requirements document, model, or prototype. To bridge this gap, it is critical to move the customer and users from "How do I perform a particular process or function?" to "Why am I performing this process or function?"

Steve: People get so tied up in their day-to-day tasks, sometimes they can't step back and understand why they're doing a particular step. When we're analyzing the business process to identify technology opportunities, it's important to move away from the actual task, such as entering the data into a specific spreadsheet, and focus on why they're doing that step.

Matt: How do you do that?

Steve: We try to get the process into flowcharts or process maps. This lets us break the process into subsets and get agreement on the individual components. Everyone thinks that their own job is very complex and no one else can do it. In fact, after you break it into pieces you can identify the few complex pieces and focus on them.

After stakeholder intentions have been made explicit, they must be prioritized for effective realization as a technology solution.

Paula: We basically had 16 high-level requirements, and then we asked the team to prioritize them based on their business value. We took a vote of all the stakeholders to get a forced ranking. We wanted to understand what was more important so we'd be ready to work through issues as they came up.

Prioritized requirements drive the process of successful project teams. Customers and users establish priorities for requirements, and this allows the project team to decide which requirements to investigate when and to what degree of detail.

To specify prioritized requirements, you need to take into account that requirements fall into several groups. In the 1980s, Noriaki Kano discovered that some requirements are not one-dimensional, where customer satisfaction is simply proportional to how functional the technology solution is (*Center for Quality Management Journal*, vol. 2, no. 4, 1993). In the so-called Kano diagram shown in Figure 3-1, the line going through the origin at 45 degrees depicts the situation in which customer satisfaction is simply proportional to how functional the technology solution is: the situation in which the customer is more satisfied (up) with a more fully functional technology solution (right), and less satisfied (down) with a less functional technology solution (left).

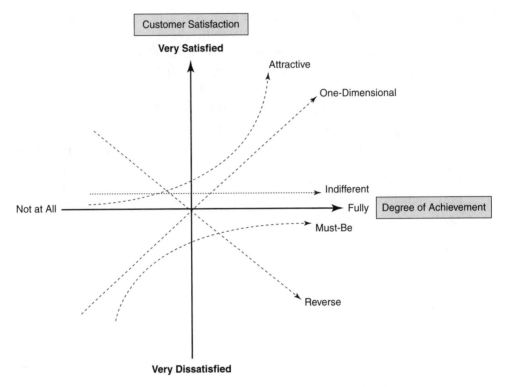

Figure 3-1 *Sample Kano diagram*

Often we can distinguish between "must-be" and "attractive" requirements. The must-be curve in Figure 3-1 indicates aspects with which the customer is more dissatisfied when the technology solution is less functional; but the customer's satisfaction never rises above neutral no matter how functional the technology solution becomes. For instance, having a lack of security in an online banking system causes the customer to be dissatisfied; having airtight security, however, doesn't raise the level of satisfaction. Good security is expected. It is a must-have requirement.

The curve labeled "Attractive" indicates areas in which the customer is more satisfied when the technology solution is more functional but is not dissatisfied when the technology solution is less functional. For instance, a customer may be more satisfied when word processing software can automatically hide menu items that haven't been used for a while, but may not be dissatisfied if this feature isn't available.

Understanding the Kano diagram has important implications for the way you specify solutions. Matt emphasizes this point.

Matt: I would much rather focus on solving the problems of my business customers than worry about some of the run-of-the-mill, technology-driven requirements. I want to focus on the business issue and be able to come back to the customer and say, "You want to go with some of these, and I want to put them together in record time."

3.1.2 Applying the CMMI-ACQ to Involving Customers

The CMMI-ACQ provides specific practices for eliciting customer needs, expectations, and constraints to obtain customer requirements that constitute an understanding of what will satisfy stakeholders (see Table 3-1).

Table 3-1 *Acquisition Requirements Development Goal 1: Practices and Tips*

CMMI-ACQ Process Area: Acquisition Requirements Development	
1. Goal: Stakeholder needs, expectations, constraints, and interfaces are collected and translated into customer requirements.	
Practices	**Tips**
1.1 Elicit stakeholder needs, expectations, constraints, and interfaces for all phases of the product life cycle.	• Affirm the business model before you specify the technology solution. • Communicate with your customers directly. Never outsource this critical connection. • Identify and engage those individuals who have deep business knowledge and are well respected by their peers. • Form a joint leadership team of your business customer and your acquisition team. • Use a variety of techniques to elicit requirements from all likely sources. • Immerse yourself in the users' environment. • Always probe for the rationale of business processes, tasks, and deliverables.
1.2 Transform stakeholder needs, expectations, constraints, and interfaces into customer requirements.	• Carefully assess how much value the proposed solution adds to your customer. • Instead of relying only on people's stories about how work is performed, observe how work gets done. • Employ a standardized, hierarchical decomposition of business processes. • Regularly benchmark your business model and processes against your competition and best-in-class organizations.

The intentions of stakeholders such as customers and users are the basis for determining requirements. The stakeholders' needs, expectations, constraints, interfaces, operational concepts, and product concepts are analyzed, harmonized, refined, and elaborated for translation into a set of customer requirements.

Eliciting needs, however, goes beyond collecting requirements from stakeholders to proactively identifying additional requirements not explicitly stated (Table 3-1, practice 1.1). Various techniques are available to elicit needs from current and potential customers and other stakeholders. For example, the following tools are all useful in eliciting needs:

- Questionnaires, interviews, and operational scenarios obtained from end users
- Technology demonstrations, operational walkthroughs, and end user task analysis
- Prototypes and models
- Observation of existing products, environments, and workflow patterns
- Quality function deployment (QFD), which employs a series of matrices to translate qualitative customer requirements into quantitative technical requirements

The customer typically describes requirements as capabilities expressed in broad operational terms concerned with achieving a desired effect under specified standards and regulations (Table 3-1, practice 1.2). The various inputs from the customer and other stakeholders must be aligned with your strategy. As you document the customer requirements, you must obtain any missing information and resolve any conflicts (e.g., customer requirements that exist as an output of another project's activities, such as a previous project that delivered the initial capability).

Here are examples of considerations you should keep in mind for expressing customer requirements:

- Key characteristics (attributes) of the desired capability, with appropriate parameters and measures
- Obstacles to overcome to achieve the capability
- Competitive gap between existing and desired capability

3.1.3 Significant Differentiators

The customer's requirements establish the basis for what an acquisition must deliver, why the technology solution is needed, and how it must function to be of value to the acquirer. Making customer requirements explicit early in the acquisition process reduces the need for later redesign, rebuilding, and retesting.

For you as an acquirer, simply defining customer requirements isn't enough. Customer requirements must be clearly and concisely translated into a set of supplier agreements that will guide the supplier in developing or configuring a technology solution that fits its intended use. In other words, you further specify the customer requirements so that they can guide the supplier's technical work, considering other constraining factors such as safety and regulatory requirements.

In addition, you augment your customer requirements with technical specifications to ensure that the technology solution will fit well into the intended environment.

All this results in so-called *contractual requirements:* precise requirements contained or referenced by the supplier agreement that serve as the baseline for controlling the acquisition's scope. In other words, subsequent changes to these requirements are permitted only upon formal approval and, in many cases, necessitate a change in the supplier agreement. In addition, contractual requirements provide a realistic basis for estimating project parameters such as cost and schedule and can be used as a reference point from which to measure the performance of the solution. Contractual requirements included in the RFP form the basis for evaluating alternative solutions and support negotiations with the potential suppliers.

> **TIP** When you're documenting contractual requirements, focus on what's new and different.

Sound easy enough? Not quite. The dilemma faced by every acquirer is how to best translate customer requirements into contractual requirements. Time and again, acquirers and suppliers alike find it exceedingly difficult to arrive at an accurate, minimal set of contractual requirements.

> **Paula:** Writing contractual requirements is hard. It gets easier if you focus on communicating and documenting those aspects of the solution that most clearly demand attention and seem most likely to create problems.

Requirements that are already common knowledge communicate little new information to a project team. This suggests that acquirers want to be particularly good at communicating a limited number of nonobvious or counterintuitive requirements. The contractual requirements should therefore focus on communicating the significant differentiators and avoid arbitrary requirements that make the technology solution do more than necessary to accomplish its purpose.

Unfortunately, many acquisition organizations and suppliers consider it desirable to create a highly detailed specification of contractual requirements. There is a long tradition in software engineering of making the specification document the sole body of knowledge about the solution. Many people think the only good specification is a highly detailed or "complete" one. Often we hear, "If only you had written a more detailed specification of the requirements, you wouldn't be having these problems." In other words, this myth is at the heart of the belief that you can eliminate risk by including more detail, if not mathematical precision, in specifying technology solutions.

> **TIP**   To support tailored communication to the customer and supplier, tag requirements by audience.

Steve highlights an important lesson he has learned: In some cases, overly detailed standard templates used to document requirements can lead project managers to the conclusion that more detailed specifications are better.

Steve: A standard work product of our process is a requirements document that can be several hundred pages long. It has all the system requirements that are already well known to the supplier and the traceability data that is relevant only to the project team. It also has a lot of white space. This document was just indigestible.

Matt: What happened?

Steve: The supplier sent us a note: "Please don't subject me to such torture."

Everyone at the table laughs, and then Steve continues quoting the harried supplier.

Steve: "The requirements we need are in here somewhere, but I can't find them. I shouldn't have to read 300 pages to figure out the 30 functions that are critical to your business process." The sad part was that virtually every project was using this format. So it took us a while to turn off the spigot. We organized an improvement workshop to change the template so that we only present relevant requirements to the supplier.

Steve smiles and continues.

Steve: We even applied the same approach to communicate requirements to our customer. During the workshop we found that one group had a custom-coded query tool that went into their requirements database and pulled out only the specific requirements that a customer would be interested in and formatted them into an output that was more readable than the standard template. We now use this tool to do the same for our suppliers.

A razor-sharp focus on the significant differentiators will result in a successful exchange with customers. In contrast, a full definition of all requirements can do more harm than good. Each requirement is a constraint for the supplier and can complicate the design task. These constraints can be arbitrary and can result in compromising a significant customer differentiator. In reality, a specification that contains too many constraints only draws the attention of the project team away from the things that really need to be optimized.

> **TIP**   Let the business situation determine the technology solution.

Surprisingly, it is much harder to produce an accurate, minimum specification than it is to create a detailed one. This situation is the perfect manifestation of something Blaise Pascal wrote: "I apologize for the length of this letter, but I didn't have time to make it shorter." It's easy to create detailed specifications because, in many cases, we can simply copy every feature offered by the technology solution in use or by available technology solutions in the marketplace. In contrast, to arrive at an accurate minimum specification, you need to make choices—such as what to focus on and at what level of granularity—and to do that, you must know which requirements are truly important to the customer. This takes a much more profound knowledge of the customer. Paula confirms this observation.

Paula: It totally depends on whether the project manager is just a technology guru or whether he is, for instance, a business process expert as well as a great technologist. That combination of skills is hard to find. Some of the project managers are very deep into the business. They can tell you not only the key differentiators of what they're changing in the application to improve the business, but also what the application does and how it fits into the business process. Other project managers just understand basic requirements. It could be an application that makes doughnuts versus compiling insurance reports. Their attitude is, "Give me the requirements and let's code and deliver." What we're trying to evolve to is a state where a project manager is not only a great technologist but also has a feel for the business and understands what we're trying to achieve as a business.

Matt: That's right. Ideally, a project manager needs to understand why a customer should buy the technology solution we're offering. In other words, what is the value proposition of this project?

Paula: Often people don't understand the business process, and then they have a hard time answering these questions—expressing the significant differentiators. Engineers try to invent the perfect solution rather than a solution that will work based on the business strategy we have or the business reality we're faced with. So rather than the perfect set of requirements down to the nth decimal point, I want a set of requirements that meets my needs within my business reality. Don't give me a perfect solution, but give me a solution I can afford. We have a huge chasm between technical purists and the business realities we face.

The bottom line is that a project manager should be able to explain the significant differentiators in a compelling way. In many cases, the time span of an elevator ride (say, 30 seconds) should be enough time to get these differentiators across to someone. Many executives—just like venture capitalists—judge the quality of a project on the basis of the quality of its "elevator pitch."

> **TIP**   Quantify the market and competitive position for the significant characteristics of your technology solution.

You should document the advantages and disadvantages of each significant differentiator—those requirements that identify a solution as adding high value for the acquirer. Emphasize the distinctive features by highlighting the differences between what competitors currently have in use or on the market and what will be delivered by the project team. In addition, you should be aware of any patents, trade secrets, or other proprietary features, as well as any opportunities for the logical extension of the solution in use or the development of related IT products or services.

The project team can then quantify the significant differentiators as a way of quantifying the value of the opportunity to solve a customer problem. This allows acquirers to answer the question, How good is the idea in satisfying a customer need compared with how that need is satisfied today? Each differentiator has a quantitatively defined goal, and that allows the project team to quantitatively track progress toward achieving the goals over time. Additionally, the values of the same differentiators are established for any known competitive process or product and the best that is theoretically or practically achievable. The latter value is also a measure of the difficulty of the project objective.

Functional requirements traditionally dominate the quest for significant differentiators, but you cannot ignore *nonfunctional requirements,* or *quality attributes,* which are concerned with things like usability, reliability, safety, security, and performance. These may be significant differentiators for the customer.

Nonfunctional requirements stem from organizational policies, budget constraints, standardized processes, and external factors such as safety and security regulations. They define the behavioral characteristics or physical attributes of the technology solution—for example, "The software must respond to the user's request within five seconds of a card being inserted in the ATM." Nonfunctional requirements such as portability also relate to, for instance, the source code of software.

Frequently, nonfunctional requirements are mutually conflicting, at least initially. Required response time may be contradicted by, for instance, security and safety requirements. The process you use to arrive at a trade-off of these conflicts depends on the level of importance attached to the requirements and the consequences of the changes on other requirements and your goals.

> **TIP** Specify how the technology solution fits in your environment, from legal and performance requirements to security requirements.

You often see an overemphasis on functional requirements when the supplier has a dominant role in engineering solutions. When suppliers drive the process, they specify requirements from their point of view. Typically, suppliers formalize the functions of the technology solution to translate them directly into code and hardware. Requirements then address aspects of functionality, interface, and structure, insofar as they are important to the supplier but not necessarily to the customer. In other words, requirements discovery for the supplier revolves around the premise that the supplier has already selected the "right" solution and its functions simply need to be mapped to the customer's and acquisition organization's needs.

However, acquisition organizations must choose technology solutions with nonfunctional requirements in mind. Nonfunctional requirements address things such as country-specific regulations, skill level of the end users, and ways the product will be used. In many instances, nonfunctional requirements determine functional requirements and can be the deciding criteria for a technology solution. As the project team develops the specification, nonfunctional requirements are also likely to become functional ones for some part of the technology solution. For example, a reliability requirement can be translated into a function for error reporting.

> **TIP** Identify common (standard) requirements for your technology solutions, and make them available to all projects.

Often, many functional and nonfunctional requirements of one technology solution turn out to be the same for your other technology solutions. This in turn means that any new technology solution must account for those common or standard requirements. When standard requirements are documented and shared across projects, they allow a project team to stay focused on the significant differentiators, in part because they don't allow the team to succumb to the "clean slate" myth.

When you're engineering a technology solution, the clean slate myth postulates that project teams do not need to consider existing technology solutions and business processes that are in use. By throwing away these "troublesome" assets and building new technology solutions from scratch, organizations expect to find less expensive and more effective solutions. In practice, however, this situation rarely occurs, because very few technology solutions are built from scratch. Instead, many projects extend operational solutions. Thus, the project team must understand any deployed technology solutions, which usually integrate components from multiple suppliers.

Matt: How can we get to a state where our projects consistently acquire technology solutions that fully address the significant differentiators and satisfy all other requirements necessary to operate the technology solution in the intended environment?

Paula: We need to write requirements up front and make them available to the project team before the project starts. This gives us standard requirements that every project can use.

Acquirers and suppliers hear this straightforward answer time and again. Can it be that the solution to this problem has been right here all these years?

Paula: If you don't start with standard requirements, every project manager looks at the customer requirements and delivers precisely those requirements. Unfortunately, often this solution won't be extensible or won't operate well with other solutions in our business processes.

Standard requirements are a key ingredient for advancing the project's focus on what matters: the significant differentiators required to deliver the needed capabilities to the customer. In addition to the supplier agreement containing the core terms and conditions, service level agreements, and pricing, this allows you to standardize requirements for all acquisition projects (see Figure 3-2). Making clearly defined, concise requirements available to

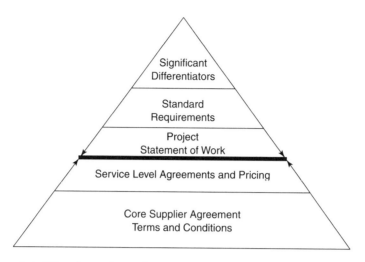

Figure 3-2 *The place of standard requirements in the supplier agreement*

projects up front reduces project start-up time and improves your consistency in implementing common requirements across the organization.

What goes into standard requirements?

Matt: In virtually any organization, you have different layers of management decisions with different reach—some global, some local—as well as policies. We want our projects to remember these decisions and policies when they specify a solution.

Steve: Why not just reference decisions and policies in the contracts?

Matt: We went down that path and found that it results in missed requirements. Projects would focus on the more prominent functional requirements rather than going through the published decisions and policies to translate them into requirements. Since we want projects to focus on the significant differentiators, why not translate the decisions and policies into standard requirements and associated test cases one time and then reuse them many times on every project in the corporation? The idea was to start simple with standard requirements—for instance, basic security, operational, and data management requirements. And we gradually added the more sophisticated stuff, let's say testing and architecture requirements. The standard requirements are an open-book test for the suppliers—no surprises for them. The suppliers will get used to the standard requirements over time, and they will become a standard way of doing business.

Predefining those requirements that matter across all projects or across the organization, making them visible to the acquisition organization and to the supplier, is a win-win situation for everyone involved.

> **TIP**   Use standard requirements as an open-book test for suppliers.

> **TIP**   Translate policies and standards into clear, concise, and testable requirements.

Steve: This is a great idea. It avoids the situation where the project blindly refers to a set of standards or includes a laundry list of standards in a contract. These projects eventually find out that half the standards have no value. They're outdated, or they don't work with the given technology. Projects get in trouble that way. We want to be very cautious about people not listing reams and reams of standards just because they can. We want people to think about standards and explicitly say what part of the standard applies and whether the standard needs to be tailored for the application. We try to get people to think about that.

You need to carefully weigh your options before elevating a requirement to a standard requirement. Matt recalls an attempt to standardize the functionality of supporting different languages.

> **TIP**   Thoroughly evaluate a requirement before elevating it to a standard requirement.

Matt: I remember a proposal that contained all the different systems and what languages they would use. For the Swiss group, we went through the proposal and checkmarked English, French, and German wherever appropriate. Then I called the originator of the request and said, "Look, you got English, French, and German in all the right places." I'm sure the originator—a global IT architecture director—was thinking, "Great, we did something good." Then through a business partner I sent the originator a follow-up message: "Remember that Swiss French and Canadian French are different." Then we waited a day or two and sent another message: "Don't forget that we need to use English, French, and German together in some instances rather than assuming that those are exclusive choices."

Well, *c'est la vie* ("such is life"). Acquirers must carefully choose between establishing a standard requirement that, on one hand, specifies that systems need to support multiple languages concurrently and, on the other hand, requires systems to support one language. In Matt's example, such a requirement would force customers to add a translator function to the standard solution to support their business units in French, German, and English.

Steve: We carefully design standard requirements so that they don't overconstrain projects. For each standard requirement, you have to decide to what degree you specify it, based on the risk; otherwise, we run the risk of turning a $25,000 project into a $1,000,000 project.

3.1.4 Applying the CMMI-ACQ to Writing Contractual Requirements

The CMMI-ACQ provides specific recommendations for deriving more detailed and precise sets of requirements, called contractual requirements, from customer requirements (see Table 3-2). Contractual requirements are

Table 3-2 *Acquisition Requirements Development Goal 2: Practices and Tips*

CMMI-ACQ Process Area: Acquisition Requirements Development	
2. Goal: Customer requirements are refined and elaborated to develop contractual requirements.	
Practices	**Tips**
2.1 Establish and maintain contractual requirements, which are based on the stakeholder requirements.	• Let the business situation determine the technology solution. • When you're documenting contractual requirements, focus on what's new and different. • Specify how the technology solution fits into your environment, from legal and performance requirements to security requirements. • Quantify the market and competitive position for the significant characteristics of the technology solution. • Translate policies and standards into clear, concise, and testable requirements. • Identify common (standard) requirements for your technology solutions, and make them available to all projects. • Thoroughly evaluate a requirement before elevating it to a standard requirement.
2.2 Allocate the requirements for each supplier deliverable.	• To support tailored communication to the customer and supplier, tag requirements by audience. • Use standard requirements as an open-book test with suppliers.

included in the solicitation package for potential suppliers and eventually in the supplier agreement.

Contractual requirements arise from constraints, from consideration of issues implied but not explicitly stated in the customer requirements baseline, and from factors introduced by the design constraints and the supplier's capabilities (Table 3-2, practice 2.1). In other words, contractual requirements express customer requirements in technical terms that can be used to make design decisions. In addition to technical requirements (e.g., requirements specifying interfaces with other products or applications, functional requirements and their validation, and verification requirements such as product acceptance criteria), contractual requirements cover nontechnical stakeholder needs, expectations, and constraints.

Examples of considerations for nontechnical requirements include the following:

- Frequency and format of supplier reviews
- Standard measures and service levels for the technology solution
- Supplier reports and other communications
- Availability of support to meet levels of business processes or product performance
- Warranty of products provided by the supplier
- Logistics support that sustains both short- and long-term readiness
- Minimum total life-cycle cost to own and operate (i.e., minimum total ownership cost)
- Maintenance concepts that optimize readiness while drawing on both acquirer and supplier sources
- Data management and configuration management that facilitate cost-effective product support throughout the product's use by the acquirer

The level of detail of contractual requirements is based on the acquisition strategy and project characteristics.

The contractual requirements are allocated to supplier deliverables (Table 3-2, practice 2.2). When multiple suppliers are developing the technology solution, different products or product components may be allocated to different suppliers. In addition, you may allocate technical requirements to third-party products that must be used by the supplier (e.g., commercial off-the-shelf products).

3.2 Specify Realistic Design Constraints

As an acquirer of technology solutions, you must make sure that all your solutions fit together, but you must also remember that you do not build these solutions yourself. Because many acquirers grew up as part of an insourced organization or have worked for a technology supplier, their first reaction, as acquirers of technology solutions, is to spell out all the gory technical detail and overly constrain the solution. Steve answers the question, "What's wrong with this picture?"

> **Steve:**   Well, you won't leverage the technical capabilities of your suppliers, for one thing. What's worse, you lose your focus on laying down realistic design constraints so that everything fits in your landscape of stakeholders, business processes, and technology solutions. I had to work hard on myself and with my team to transition to the mind-set of my new role as an architect for an acquirer. It made it easier to know that we weren't alone out there.

Steve laughs as he recalls one incident.

> **Steve:**   One of my team members brought in a reference from a Roman architect, Marcus Vitruvius, who figured this out in the context of building design back in the day. We're talking about 80–70 B.C. This guy claimed that well-designed buildings exhibited three virtues: firmness, commodity, and delight. If you're an architect, you start with commodity and delight, what we'd call the look-and-feel end of the problem. The prime contractor and suppliers, on the other hand, they're more concerned with the firmness: economy, safety, constructability. If you look at modern building practice, this is pretty much the division of labor among the architect, the builder (or prime contractor), and the individual laborers or suppliers.

As the design of technology solutions continues to mature, perhaps we will see a similar evolution in an environment that includes acquirers of technology solutions that have architects on staff. Perhaps someday there will be firms specializing in technology architecture that vie for work by demonstrating originality, elegance, and affordability in their architectures but are not responsible for implementing or configuring the architectures. To support this journey, the next two sections cover the practices you apply to develop design constraints and to verify the designs of the supplier.

3.2.1 Underlying Principles and Common Design Constraints

Design constraints are a type of technical requirement. They express the qualities and performance points that are critical to the success of the product or service in the operational environment. Design constraints can include standards and design rules governing development and configuration of technology solutions, such as cost per component, the required database, the required type of application servers, and criteria for interfaces. The latter are often associated with safety, security, durability, and mission-critical characteristics.

> **TIP**   Define the core of the solution first, and then gradually add connections to other solutions and the environment.

Why is it difficult to find the right balance between leveraging the supplier's ability to deliver cutting-edge technology solutions and your desire for seamless, flawless technology integration and use? Steve contemplates this challenge.

Steve: As an acquirer of technology solutions, you're given a problem in the real world and it's typically really messy. When you develop design constraints you initially spend your time cutting yourself off from connections—trying to simplify things, trying to make sense out of often conflicting requirements. You eventually say, "Well, let's assume it's a sphere," and you start adding connections, and first-, second-, third-, and fourth-order effects, to come up with a viable set of design constraints.

I'm not talking about a trivial system. You're creating a technology solution that has significant economic value, that involves some degree of integration with other systems, interplay between software and hardware. It's only when you start adding these other approximations that you start seeing what goes on—how tough it will be to either configure or develop a new solution or application thereof. You start to realize how big it is, and you either get scared and you don't do anything—that happens to a large number of projects—or you're naïve and proceed.

Matt: Well, you can't get scared into doing nothing. You won't get paid.

Everyone laughs.

Steve: In our team, we remind ourselves to think about Thomas Edison, who created the light bulb because he didn't realize he couldn't. Common wisdom thought it was impossible. So Edison went ahead and did it anyway.

You codify the design intent in the form of design constraints. Design constraints drive the design processes of the supplier and are your means for judging the supplier's feedback on the current state of the design. You must stay focused to determine the design constraints that matter, use those constraints to drive the design, and then analyze the design to determine whether the constraints were met (or could be met).

Paula: A lot of effort goes into arriving at design constraints that are unambiguous and easy to understand. Without this clarity it's excruciating to verify designs.

The design verification process is usually repeated several times until a workable design is achieved. The decisions that result in the design constraints must be made manifest and visible throughout the life cycle of the system.

Paula: There are always trade-offs. I mean you have to keep your options open. Most architects or designers would love to develop these technically elegant, complicated systems that are intriguing and professionally groundbreaking—but very expensive. I have to remind my project teams, including the suppliers, that we're here to add value to the business, we're here to enable our businesses to grow and move forward and deliver within the agreed-upon schedule. So that has to be the top priority for us. And when we look at it, my teams are also responsible for keeping our cost down, meeting the cost design constraint so to speak. So one of the things we have institutionalized is taking a hard look at cost.

Steve: How do you do that?

Paula: We ask questions like, "What will this design constraint do to my operational cost going forward?" Most of the time, this question stomps the project team, because they're focused on the development cost and don't consider the maintenance cost, which often is higher. We roll up our sleeves and work with the team to get a design that won't add any operational cost and meets the return on investment long-term. In doing this, we take a hard line against suboptimization. We obliterate any fine-tuning of an individual technology solution, if it doesn't optimize the set of technology solutions that support a particular business process or the organization overall.

TIP   Judge a solution's elegance by its value to the business, and not by how technically sophisticated or professionally intriguing it is.

For example, you must carefully analyze the implications for maintenance when you use off-the-shelf or nondevelopmental items (for example, COTS products, government off-the-shelf products, and open source software). Consider the compatibility of the proposed technology solution with future releases of COTS products, and assess known defects in reused or off-the-shelf products and the status of their resolution.

> **TIP** Take into account the total cost impact of a design constraint for a technology solution before levying it on the supplier.

> **TIP** Always look for ways to optimize the business process before constraining the technology solution.

Your principal choice is often a trade-off between efficiency and flexibility. The goal is to avoid premature commitment to a particular technology solution—that is, to not make a binding decision before all the required information is known. Often, the decision is made in favor of an efficiency that is not worth the cost. Steve emphasizes this point.

Steve: Nine out of ten times, the customer will say we need to make our systems more flexible, because we need to be making changes to either business rules or processes or something on a weekly basis, bimonthly basis, and so on. So it's critical to figure out what things in the system don't change very often, what things should be allowed to change often, and how we establish design constraints that provide parameters for the supplier to meet these objectives.

Establishing practical design constraints takes work.

Steve: Some of the first systems we built had pretty sloppy constraints and were too aggressive. The key is to make sure the constraints you give the suppliers are real. You can't just throw a bunch of design constraints over the wall to suppliers down the street, let alone if your supplier is in China or India and you're on the other side of the globe. With outsourcing, you're entering into a close partnership that will require ongoing interaction, supervision, and quality control.

It's important to have clear criteria for addressing design issues for the life of the product in the operational environment. Such criteria tend to focus on provisions for more easily inserting new technologies or the ability to better exploit commercial products. Examples include criteria related to open design or open architecture concepts for the alternatives being evaluated. To make this happen requires close partnership between acquirer and supplier.

> **TIP** Craft clear and concise design constraints covering the entire product life cycle.

Matt: The notion of handoff has become obsolete. We're engaged with suppliers from the beginning, and we work very closely with them throughout the delivery process.

However, he adds a word of caution.

Matt: It's hard work to get from a handoff-based environment to a thought-process-based environment. So it's really about taking ownership of the technology solution from beginning to end and making sure suppliers are bringing in the right skills to make it all work. It's like taking accountability for the whole solution even though they may not own some things. It requires a supplier to take the responsibility of making sure all the right things are done to have the appropriate level of engagement and oversight around a third party doing work for the same project.

> **TIP** Instill in your suppliers an end-to-end accountability for the technology solution.

> **TIP** Identify design constraints that apply to all technology solutions that enable a business process.

Designing a technology solution is an iterative process.

Steve: Everybody involved in designing technology solutions has to recognize that there's constant evolution. After that prototype or next system is out there, customers start realizing all the additional benefits and then start adding more things on your plate. That's a good thing. The problem with many projects at this stage is that they're only looking at solving their immediate problem and don't account for the fact that their solutions will be part of a whole landscape of technology solutions. They're not looking at what are or could be common business processes and their solutions holistically. You need to create a solid to-be picture and thoroughly understand that your project is one puzzle piece in a system of systems.

Matt: The question is, of course, how do you get that comprehensive view of a process and what should be common so that you can try to build one solution once? If we do that, we have more money to spend on meeting more business needs. And then the customer would look at something and say, "Well, it took you nine months to put this solution in place, and you're telling me I can't get this change in for another six months?" You'll try to explain—but it's based on priority. You'll have no way to accelerate your solutions engineering, because you don't have the ability to apply solutions or at least pieces of your solutions to different business problems. It's very important that you extract as many of the critical design constraints early on, preferably as implemented in the first increment or version of your solution.

To achieve high levels of reuse and interoperability in technology solutions, you typically establish common design constraints for products or product families that can be deployed in one or more domains. Common design constraints (also called *reference architectures* or *product line architectures*) provide a proven bundling of products, applications, and configurations. They give you a base for creating technology solutions that use design constraints reliably and cost-effectively. For example, some acquirers encapsulate functionality in the form of services that can be leveraged by multiple, if not all, technology solutions. Common design constraints are then organized in the form of service-oriented architectures.

To make all this happen, even large, global suppliers often use supplemental third-party resources, and suppliers may subcontract with one another, depending on areas of expertise and available business opportunities.

> **Kristin Wells:**   There are many suppliers in the world of acquired technology solutions. We may compete one day and partner the next.

Engagement models are varied and complex. Some companies require only a set of high-level standards and outsource everything else; others outsource a specific portion of the design, such as a high-level architecture or physical design. Up-front planning and realistic constraints help you avoid unnecessary iterations when you build the system. To minimize rework, some suppliers have a well-defined flow to verify the acquirer's technology standards, standard requirements, and constraint quality.

TIP   Hold firm on common design constraints—no exceptions.

> **Matt:**   You're right, Kristin—there are many suppliers out there. That's why the governance of the technical design is so important for us as an acquirer of technology solutions. You have to stay within common design constraints, such as standards first of all, and those standards have to be current and they have to be rigorously enforced.

Steve adds his thoughts.

Steve: I couldn't agree more. All this makes a difference. It's easy to say this doesn't matter and let our supplier run off and do what they want and we just accept what they do. The problem is when you do that, you don't get any synergy from system to system, from one project to the next. You die the death of a thousand cuts. We finish one system and we're all happy about it. Then we start another project, only to realize that we have to go back to the drawing board and don't have any money.

We can avoid this scenario. We just have to define early on what the common constraints are for the project and the supplier. And then we have to put our foot down and hold firm in our discussions with the suppliers.

Matt: How does that usually go?

Steve: Well, you always have one project or supplier that says, "For what I'm doing, software X is better." Then another project or supplier says, "I can increase performance if I use software Y." You always have this tension back and forth where there is no piece of software that's better for everybody, there is no data model that's better for everybody. But there is a single piece of software or a single data model that falls into a strategic category that is better for the acquisition organization as a whole.

Apparently this topic has hit a nerve. Steve continues passionately.

Steve: Let me just tell you about this one project we're working on. It's a broad project across all groups. The supplier has a real difficult time understanding why we wanted to use a certain server from one supplier as a common design constraint for all our application servers, why we wanted to use a particular Web server from another supplier, and why we wanted to use one type of database. There were reasons why those common design constraints where picked across the organization. Performance, reliability, availability—the whole nine yards. We took all this into account. We have one set of hardware—different sizing, but one hardware platform that we actually run our software on. Every Web application is targeting that common design constraint.

Matt: I'm with you so far.

Steve: So the supplier came back and said, "We support the application server and the Web server, but not the mix-and-match approach your design constraints require. As a matter of fact, our product most likely won't even work in this configuration." We actually had to tell the project team of the supplier, "Look, we wrote in the contract you signed that you have to fully implement our design constraints and support our target environment." The problem was that nobody on the supplier team had bothered to analyze the common design constraints.

> **TIP** Establish and maintain technical design constraints jointly with your supplier.

The best way to avoid such a situation is to include suppliers in the creation of common design constraints as appropriate, and thoroughly educate them on the intent of the constraints.

Matt: Now my architecture group invites the supplier's chief architects to be part of the technical discussion when we debate the best way to build common design constraints. They are essentially considered part of my staff. So we're all in it together. It doesn't make sense for them to have a myopic view of what they're delivering.

However, simply compiling a list of technology standards as your common design constraints isn't enough to effectively guide the design of technology solutions.

Matt: We used to say to a supplier, "Here are the technology standards we use"—in most cases, a list of standard products. And a supplier will come in and, for instance, say, "I'm going to use this standard from a work flow standpoint, and that one from an integration standpoint. And these other two standards over here, we're going to plug in together." We would all walk away happy, expecting a perfect solution to arrive at our doorstep. Then when the suppliers are configuring or developing the solution, they're convinced that's all the effort they really need to put into meeting our design constraints. As long as the technology standards are met one at a time they would say, "Oh, that's an acquirer-approved implementation."

But when you look at it from a total solutions viewpoint, you have to go back to the requirements and figure out, "Okay, with all these standards fitted together in a particular way, are we looking at a proposed solution that is beneficial to us?" So you have to dive into what is happening at different layers of the proposed solution. What are the performance expectations across the solution? What is its total cost of ownership? It isn't enough to simply stay within a list of standard products. You have to come up with an integrated set of common design constraints.

Providing a list of technology standards is a good start in helping suppliers understand the technical constraints that are important to you. However, it leaves the question of how to mix and match your technology standards to arrive at an appropriate technology solution.

> **TIP** Create an integrated set of design constraints to serve as a reference architecture.

Steve: A list of technology standards is only a first step, because the standards can be mixed and matched many different ways. So as an integrated set of design constraints, we hand a reference or product line architecture to the supplier that defines a set of technology standards— for instance, standardized IT applications, infrastructure elements, and implementation and support methods—for a particular business process. This creates a mapping from the business process to the technology architecture, and that's critical for reducing technological uncertainties by standardizing on common design constraints. These get the project and supplier on track to understanding what the solution should look like.

Getting common design constraints right is a learning process in and of itself.

Matt: On one hand, you have to be incredibly firm in establishing and enforcing what will be identical across technology solutions in the intended environment. You have to communicate both internally and externally: "Now that's fixed. If you don't agree with that, then that's your prerogative. This is how we will run the business." On the other hand, you have to make it very clear what other parts are up for discussion. You have to say, "Within this reference architecture, in this area down here, you have an option." You can say, for instance, "If performance is required, then you're allowed to use these types of interoperable capabilities versus Web services." That's a discussion that is captured in the common design constraints.

Steve: Part of the learning in getting the design constraints right is to neither overspecify nor underspecify. For example, let's say a supplier embeds a certain database, which isn't our preferred database, in their standard solution. This database is completely encapsulated in the solution. In this case, we never have to interface with this database directly. Our common design constraint would allow for that. We would let the supplier use a database of their choosing because we follow a "black box" approach for system components we don't own and that we don't directly interface with.

But let's say we're hiring a supplier to develop a system that we will own, and we intend to store the system's data in a database shared by other technology solutions in the intended environment. In this case, we want to enforce a more stringent set of design constraints. For instance, the supplier will have to satisfy the common design constraint for databases.

> **TIP** Build alternative approaches or variations of design constraints into the reference architecture.

> **TIP** Carefully weigh the trade-offs of using packaged functionality or services with the impact of their failure on the business process.

Commercial off-the-shelf products are both a blessing and a curse for acquirers. Using COTS components in a true plug-and-play fashion can be exhilarating. However, COTS products make the world very complicated because COTS suppliers are not under the same time constraints as acquirers are—for instance, to upgrade a solution to keep pace with the changing business environment. And not all COTS suppliers can accommodate your desired time frame for upgrades and modifications. You must therefore look at common design constraints for COTS products that isolate those risks but still allow you to use COTS products effectively.

That's why many organizations are attempting to isolate their technical environment from this downside of COTS products. For instance, some organizations have outsourced the care and feeding of these technology solutions to suppliers, paying for it as a service from a technology company or service provider. Unfortunately, this isn't always possible. You might need certain functionality to gain a competitive advantage, and there's only one supplier with 15 employees who can provide this solution. How many times have we heard this story? This scenario keeps acquirers up at night. Acquiring organizations mitigate this risk by protecting and minimizing the risk to the rest of the infrastructure. This practice becomes increasingly important every day as environments become more integrated than ever before.

Steve: People say, "You know, it's great that we have moved into the distributed world—ubiquitous computing and all that." I'm afraid the talent we have in place to manage those types of environments is not sufficient. What's even harder is that given the unique design constraints that we settle on based on our business model, it is not something your employees can learn in college and come out after four years and know all the "gotchas" relevant to your environment. We have seriously accelerated our technical training to combat this trend.

Establishing common design constraints is not just a technology decision.

> **TIP** Keep score of how your technology solutions meet your design
> constraints.

Matt: The leadership of an organization must decide together what systems must be common. For instance, if you're a car company you might say, "We don't care if you are in Canada or South Africa; you will order cars this way." Now, from a Canadian perspective, I have to go to the standard vehicle order management system—that's it. However, I have to handle French if that's not covered in the standard system, so I have to funnel data through a translator—whatever I have to do locally to stay within that standard. Getting to this state is a bumpy journey, because when you first create a scorecard of your existing technology solutions against your common design constraints, most likely you'll be faced with a plethora of red, if red is your color of choice for discrepancies.

Steve: It gets to where you can't read the specs for all the red everywhere.

Matt: Sometimes it's frustrating trying to figure out how you can close the gap and how you can get there fast enough. What a change in attitude and delivery speed if you stick with it. Instead of grappling with, "I only want to pay for the solution that works with my project," you end up with an organization and a set of suppliers that sees the power of flexibility and drives to implement with more shared cost across processes and applications. The suppliers want to be successful, and they know they have to do certain things in order to integrate into this bigger environment they're working on. You can't just have your teams and the different suppliers doing things their way and at the end of the day be able to integrate into a larger organization.

3.2.2 Applying the CMMI-ACQ to Developing Design Constraints

The CMMI-ACQ provides specific recommendations on how to develop design constraints for the supplier's technical solution that potentially satisfy an appropriate set of allocated requirements (see Table 3-3).

Design constraints express the qualities and performance points that are critical to the success of the product in your operational environment (Table 3-3, practice 1.1). They may include standards and design rules governing the development of products and their interfaces. The criteria for interfaces

Table 3-3 *Acquisition Technical Solution Goal 1: Practices and Tips*

CMMI-ACQ Process Area: Acquisition Technical Solution	
1. Goal: Constraints for the technical solution are developed and satisfied by the supplier's design.	
Practices	**Tips**
1.1 Determine the design constraints for a technical solution.	• Always look for ways to optimize the business process before constraining the technology solution. • Define the core of the solution first, and then gradually add connections to other solutions and the environment. • Establish and maintain technical design constraints jointly with your supplier. • Craft clear and concise design constraints covering the entire product life cycle. • Create an integrated set of design constraints to serve as a reference architecture. • Build alternative approaches or variations of design constraints into the reference architecture. • Carefully weigh the trade-offs of using packaged functionality or services with the impact of their failure on the business process. • Take into account the total cost impact of a design constraint for a technology solution before levying it on the supplier. • Identify design constraints that apply to all technology solutions enabling a business process.
1.2 Verify the design to ensure that the resulting product will perform as intended in the acquirer's environment.	• Instill in your suppliers an end-to-end accountability for the technology solution. • Keep score of how technology solutions meet design constraints. • Hold firm on common design constraints—no exceptions. • Judge a solution's elegance by its value to the business, and not by how technically sophisticated or professionally intriguing it is.

are often associated with safety, security, durability, and mission-critical characteristics.

Tasks for identifying common design criteria may include the following:

- Establishing the structural relations of products and rules regarding interfaces between products
- Identifying external interfaces of the technology solution
- Identifying common products and common interfaces for all technology solutions
- Developing reference architectures or frameworks
- Establishing design rules and authority for making decisions
- Defining criteria for the physical deployment of software to hardware
- Identifying major reuse approaches and sources, including legacy and COTS products

The CMMI-ACQ includes a collection of practices under the label "Decision Analysis and Resolution" to support acquirers that are using a formal evaluation process to analyze identified alternatives against established criteria. These practices cover how to establish guidelines to determine which issues should be formally evaluated and then apply a structured approach to determine a recommended solution.

A repeatable criteria-based decision-making process is especially important, both when you're making the critical decisions that define and guide the acquisition process and later when you're making critical decisions with the selected supplier. Establishing a formal process for decision-making gives you documentation of the decision rationale. Such documentation lets you revisit the criteria for decisions when you're considering changes or technology insertion decisions that affect requirements or other critical project parameters. A formal process also supports the communication of decisions between you and the supplier.

You perform *design verification* (or *technical review* or *architectural evaluation*) throughout the project life cycle to gain confidence that the requirements are capable of guiding a development that results in a satisfactory technical solution (Table 3-3, practice 1.2). This practice should be integrated with risk management. Mature organizations typically perform design verification in a sophisticated way by using multiple techniques and broadening the verification to include other stakeholder needs and expectations.

3.2.3 Goodness of Fit

Technology becomes more ubiquitous every day and is rapidly expanding into every facet of our lives. This means the early days of "green field" solutions, when you could begin totally anew, are virtually gone. It is somewhat analogous to how the frontier of the American West began to fill up around 1870. In the early days of the Wild West, a great deal of land was open to open-range livestock and for homesteading. There was little or no local law enforcement, and the military had a concentrated presence only at specific locations. It was common to witness shootings, where gunmen died "with their boots on."

Matt picks up on this analogy.

> **Matt:** In the technology space you still need Wyatt Earp, and there are still a lot of renegades out there who can get you in trouble.

Staying with the Western theme for a moment, we can't resist replaying a scene from the movie *Tombstone*. As Wyatt Earp runs a card table in a crowded saloon, with an inebriated Doc Holliday standing by, a group of cowboys enters noisily, led by Curly Bill and Johnny Ringo. Introductions are made (so to speak), and Doc Holliday makes a comment about Ringo. Ringo pats his gun before addressing Holliday with the words, *"Eventus stultorum magister"* ("Fools must be taught by experience"). Doc Holliday gives Ringo a smile and responds, *"In pace requiescat"* ("May he rest in peace"). Tombstone Marshal Fred White defuses the scene: "Come on now. We don't want any trouble in here. Not in any language." Matt can relate to this scenario.

> **Matt:** I've seen projects deployed where somebody says, "Oh, *this* just happened," and the project manager doesn't realize that this is a problem, and he mentions it to some folks, and eventually it goes all the way back to the architect. And the architect gets this look of horror on his face and says, "I never thought of that." Those are absolutely the worst moments. That's a system doomed to failure if it gets deployed.

How can you avoid a situation where the project has to "die" so that you can learn a valuable lesson, and the sheriff has to mitigate between acquirer and supplier?

The goodness of fit for a technology solution denotes the fulfillment of its requirements and the conformity of the solution with its specification. The easiest way to establish the goodness of fit is to know all the parameters of a solution. In the real world, this scenario is the least likely to occur.

Steve: What we mostly like are projects that don't make any changes—projects that come up and say, "Well, we're implementing this system and it has already been done. It works. It's put together exactly the same." But projects never work like that. There's always some "secret sauce" that somebody adds.

> **TIP** Mandate and enforce standards for representing the technical design constraints and for the supplier's design deliverables.

This is why technical reviews are critical. They formally establish the consistency of the proposed technology solution or between the technical design and its contractual requirements and design constraints. George Taylor, who represents our supplier, speaks to this.

George: Sophisticated acquirers mandate "drawing" standards that we have to deliver to for the technical design. There are no good drawing standards on the market for, let's say, distributed systems, so the acquirer requires us to show them the technical design in their specific format, which typically is pretty descriptive.

Steve: We need to understand what our suppliers are doing. When we started to do this we found that our suppliers didn't understand the implementations of their project decisions in the intended environment. For instance, they designed a single-threaded application for use in a distributed infrastructure. Suppliers didn't understand why the code they wrote didn't work in that environment. So when they had to actually draw it out as a technical design diagram following the standard notation, we would get into discussions with them. For instance, they would say, "I didn't know I had to have a load-balancing application for this distributed system." Clearly one of the benefits was that the supplier got educated through this process.

Technical reviews hold the supplier accountable for meeting the technical design constraints throughout the project. To be effective, such reviews involve, for instance, operations and maintenance personnel in addition to the integrated project team.

> **TIP** Contractually ensure that your prime supplier and its suppliers certify the technical design and the technology solution.

Steve: To get maximum benefit, all reviews need to be conducted the same way. You have to have clear entry criteria. We insist that the suppliers have done their homework before they show up for a review. The supplier's technical design and the resulting technology solution must be peer-reviewed by the supplier and the involved subcontractors and product suppliers. We contractually mandate that the prime supplier goes out to the product vendors and says, "Hey, give me your best engineers to come in and ratify our technical design." This also helps the supplier produce meaningful trade-off analyses to flush out performance versus flexibility versus availability versus all the other "-ilities." Then they rank them and come up with scenarios and really drill into it and figure out, from a design and technology perspective, how all this fits together. If you don't get the best people from your supplier engaged up front, you'll pay for it when you fix your systems over and over again.

Matt: How do these reviews work, Steve?

Steve: We conduct early design reviews with lots of very intelligent people in the room, on the phone, on the other side of the globe smiling from the video screen. We noticed a tremendous spike in successful projects after we mandated that operations people be part of technical reviews. This stopped the historical disconnect between applications teams and operations groups. Anyway, all these folks are trying to guide the project and the suppliers to be successful. Our project teams and the suppliers that come through once will always remember their first technical review with us.

Steve laughs.

Steve: Once in a while, you get the naïve project and they're bloodied every step of the way. These projects would get a rude shock when they go through the first review, because they get hit with the product standards and the other common design constraints. The project didn't bother with that. They would say, "We picked the best solution." This might be true if the system was running all by itself. You can count on the fact that they will have the right answers when they come through again.

George: I remember some of those. You have to make sure you and your team can clearly articulate what they have on paper. So you can pull in all the pretty diagrams from other projects or some Web site or whatever, but if you can't communicate what the solution is and how it meets the need, you're toast. I'd say the architecture really needs to be communicated on how it's going to meet the requirements and how it fits in. If you can't do that, the architecture's not worth anything.

> **TIP** Involve your operations and maintenance personnel in the technical reviews throughout the project.

Staying on top of the evolving technical design is critical for any acquirer of technology solutions. Throughout the project you probe for how "real" the proposed design is; for instance, does it live up to your requirements for performance, scalability, and availability?

George: The acquirer sits down with the project team and says, "You're proposing this technical design. Now show me how it will meet availability, how it's going to meet scalability, performance, and flexibility." They ask us to walk through some scenarios. Let's say a transaction comes back 90 percent of the time within 5 seconds. We would show how that transaction flows through the different layers of design and put some approximate timings on what we think it is, based on experience and proof of concepts and other things like that. So, it's really trying to tie back the nonfunctional requirements and showing evidence of meeting them.

Steve tends to apply the test of "reasonableness" with many suppliers.

Steve: I meet with the supplier and say, "I want to see the following performance and scalability graph," and I draw the graph and tell them what the axis is, and explain what the general performance and scalability curve should look like. The expected performance of a technology solution increases first. The curve in the chart goes up. And then depending on the workload—such as number of users, number of transactions—the curve eventually turns over and then the performance comes, in most cases, to a grinding halt.

George: As a supplier, I have to say we hate it when that happens.

Steve: Yes, but it's the nature of the beast. Suppliers tend to come in with performance and scalability graphs that show how the performance of the proposed solution increases. The charts basically tend to go up. And you say, "No, no, no. I want to see where the chart turns over and where it dies." And the supplier says, "Oh, don't worry about it, we'll never get to that point." So you insist: "Okay, but show me where that point is." That's a typical conversation that goes on in the technical review meetings with the supplier. We want to know what the practical and theoretical limits of the technology solution are.

Matt: Steve, can you give us an example?

George: Wait. Not us—somebody else.

Steve smiles.

Steve: Okay, let's say a supplier—not George, somebody else—wants to demonstrate to you that a piece of software will work up to the currently anticipated 5000 users. So you have to ask, "Okay, are there any components in the system that will not work with up to 5000 users?" After a little bit of back and forth you might get the following response: "Well, there is this component that tends to top out at 200 users when certain conditions are true. Anyway, all you have to do is buy 25 servers and you'll be fine." Okay, that's an answer I've heard—but is that a *reasonable* thing to do? You have to carefully look at the total cost of a solution. Otherwise you end up with a minimum initial investment and you lose your shirt in the long term. In the example I just gave, you would be stuck with an unreasonable number of servers that would tank even the most optimistic return on investment.

> **TIP** During development, continuously explore the performance limits of the proposed solution.

To get everybody in tune with the evolving technical design, acquirers typically conduct several design reviews. Projects are required to come in with key design goals and explain how the technical design maps back to requirements, what the operational costs associated with the alternatives are, and what the suggested trade-offs are to successfully implement the solution.

Steve: We have enough people review something that we rarely miss anything. When somebody does miss something, it's a white-knuckle moment—it's a horrible situation. It can get worse when senior management leans on you to turn this situation into a risk as opposed to an issue. I don't know if you're familiar with that little game. Instead of saying, "This is bad and we can't let it go through," somebody says, "Well, couldn't it *possibly* work?" Yeah, with the wind blowing behind you 100 mph and if everybody is working on it like the pit crew of a Formula 1 team and you set up some extra monitoring and yadda, yadda, yadda.

Matt: I've been in on some of those discussions.

Steve: So we eventually get to a "yes," but now you've set the precedent. You've triggered an avalanche, and suddenly you're looking at a long list of risks and your issue log is cleaned out. These are the projects that turn into a death march, because eventually somebody forgets to close the loop on one of those "risks" and the project never solves the problem. Those projects are the ones that go into production and the performance turns out to be horrible. We've learned the hard way that it's much better to bite the bullet early, but it can be a big cultural change to admit failure and do it quickly.

> **TIP** When the status of technical parameters indicates trouble for the project, act decisively.

The reviews are not only for the acquirer team but also require the active participation of the supplier's project team.

Steve: All the different suppliers are involved in the technical reviews. We make sure that everybody is there and participates. When I ask for technical approval, any supplier that has a problem in their area speaks up. And they will, because they need to protect themselves. The supplier is responsible for making sure the product works in the intended environment. If there's an issue, the supplier has to fix it. This is much cheaper to do during design than in production—everybody knows that. These joint reviews and rigorous supplier agreements establish clear accountability.

For some new suppliers, this is a learning curve. When something goes wrong in production, we have to bring them back and say, "You signed off during this technical review that this would work. Your supplier architect was there to sign off. He was there to review—remember, we take attendance. He was there. He listened. He signed off, and you need to stand behind that decision."

> **TIP** Actively involve suppliers in technical reviews, and record their approval of the proposed solutions.

With all the technical reviews and individual accountability, it is important to work hard to foster teamwork and constantly emphasize the fact that all parties are in this together.

Steve: When you put together the technical design, especially for a complex system, then it gets very testy and interesting. In the heat of the battle, there is a tendency for suppliers to want to point fingers at each other if, for example, a solution doesn't go right. One of the biggest challenges we face is to make sure that there is no finger-pointing. We have very little tolerance for a supplier to come into, let's say, a corrective action meeting and say, "Well, it was really the other supplier's fault." We really want to go in there with a team and say, "This is what went wrong, and this is how we will correct it as a team."

It helps to have a pool of technical experts—for instance, IT architects—who evaluate many projects throughout the year. Project managers can leverage this knowledge to expedite technical reviews and the design of the technology solution overall.

> **George:**   A lot of times people come to the architecture team not for approval, but long before that, just to bounce ideas off the team. There's only so much process guidance and design constraints that a project team can read. If we get a three-foot thick list of requirements, constraints, how-to, and lessons learned, then people can't read it all. Even if they had enough time to read it all, they couldn't comprehend it all. So they come to us and ask questions: "This is what I'm thinking about doing, here is my idea, here is what the business requirements are. What would you do?" "Oh, we would do this, this, and this." They run off and come back three weeks later with their actual plan. This saves months and months of delay for a project team trying to get up to speed independently.

3.2.4 Applying the CMMI-ACQ to Technical Reviews

The CMMI-ACQ provides specific recommendations on how to verify the implementation to ensure that it meets allocated requirements and that the product is ready to be brought into your environment for further integration and user acceptance testing (see Table 3-4).

The design implemented by the supplier includes development of product components, integration of the components, unit and integration testing of the product, and development of end user documentation. You verify the supplier's implementation to ensure that it meets allocated requirements and that the product is ready to be brought into your environment for further integration and user acceptance testing.

You examine a technology solution to determine whether it is ready for production and whether the supplier has adequately planned production (Table 3-4, practice 2.1). The verification process also examines risk; the process determines whether production or preparations incur unacceptable risks that might breach the objectives of schedule, performance, cost, or other established criteria. You evaluate the full, production-configured product to determine whether it correctly and completely implements all contractual requirements. You also determine whether traceability exists between the final contractual requirements and the final production-configured product.

Table 3-4 *Acquisition Technical Solution Goal 2: Practices and Tips*

CMMI-ACQ Process Area: Acquisition Technical Solution	
2. Goal: Analyze and verify the development and implementation of the technical solution by supplier.	
Practices	**Tips**
2.1 Verify the technical solution implementation by the supplier to ensure that contractual requirements continue to be met. 2.2 Analyze the product interface descriptions to ensure that they are complete and in alignment with the intended environment.	• Mandate and enforce standards for representing the technical design constraints and for the supplier's design deliverables. • During development, continuously explore the performance limits of the proposed solution. • Actively involve suppliers in technical reviews, and record their approval of the proposed solutions. • Foster an environment where project managers seek out the advice of technical experts throughout the projects. • Involve your operations and maintenance personnel in the technical reviews throughout the project. • When the status of technical parameters indicates trouble for the project, act decisively. • Contractually ensure that your prime supplier and its suppliers certify the technical design and the technology solution.

For this verification to be successful, you must determine that the requirements are fully met in the final production configuration and that production capability forms a satisfactory basis for proceeding into pilots or full production.

Rarely is an acquired product a stand-alone technology solution. Therefore, you must carefully analyze the descriptions of the product interface to ensure that they are complete and aligned with the intended environment (Table 3-4, practice 2.2). Here are typical criteria:

- The interface spans organizational boundaries.
- The interface is mission critical.
- The interface is not difficult or complex to manage.

- Capability, interoperability, or efficiency issues are not associated with the interface.
- The interface affects multiple acquisition projects or programs.

3.3 Practice Agility

To specify technology solutions, requirements and design constraints typically need to be discovered incrementally. This practice gives you additional opportunities to improve the conceived solution. Engineering a solution is therefore an evolutionary activity that investigates what the stakeholders are concerned with, what is important, and what they're trying to achieve. In other words, engineering continues in recurrent cycles of exploring the perceived problem and proposing, validating, and verifying improved specifications.

Most acquirers deliver technology solutions in a dynamic environment. This requires flexible requirements and pragmatic design constraints that can be clarified and changed as the project progresses. In other words, you must account for the learning of stakeholders and the negotiation of requirements and design constraints throughout the project. On most projects this causes the classic problems of rapidly fluctuating requirements and disjointed design constraints. Early on, some projects lament the lack of detailed design constraints to adequately express technical requirements, whereas others freeze their requirements prematurely and then face the wrath of unhappy customers who keep changing requirements and mistake acceptance meetings for prototyping sessions. The following sections propose some remedies and review practices to better practice agility.

3.3.1 Mind the Gap

Stakeholder feedback, especially from customers and users, plays a decisive role from the beginning to the end of successful projects.

Paula: It's not always easy to get somebody to raise their hand and say, "I will take responsibility and champion this initiative." The organization will say, "I want you to provide this capability," but trying to get an individual to raise their hand and say, "I'm willing to drive this to successful conclusion" is more of a challenge. One of our big development rules states that the acquisition organization will stop a project if the business resources are not committed to support it. We need to make sure that the business champion is committed, that he or she is willing to drive that project if the business really wants it, and that we have the appropriate stakeholders that are willing to go down that path with us. If they don't, then stay with the current process until the business is ready to redesign it. Without that, the project team will just end up chasing its tail.

> **TIP** Validate the business champion's and customer's commitment to the project. If there is no commitment, stop.

It's critical to have ongoing face-to-face discussions with a representative number of customers and stakeholders from the earliest conceptual phase through final delivery. This is the only reliable way to establish, continuously modify, and validate the idea's value proposition. Large numbers of contacts are not necessary, but it is important to hear the broad perspective of views within the affected business processes. For many projects, the number of customers and stakeholders is large, and it is important to make enough individual contacts to get a representative view of the customer requirements.

Matt adds a word of caution.

> **Matt:** A lot of ideas come from smart individuals who mean well and want their business unit to succeed. They go over to the acquisition organization, tap on their shoulders, and say, "I need X." No one ever asks these well-meaning individuals, "How does this help sell more products or deploy better capability in the field?" In addition to being good technologists, we need to ask why. We need to apply our limited technical wherewithal in the right places.

As a successful acquisition organization, you must identify your customers and keep them engaged throughout the project. In addition to having a project team that is well versed in the business process and technology, successful teams seem to identify a "partner" or a business liaison who keeps his eyes and ears open to help ensure the success of the project. This liaison—your Yoda, as discussed earlier in this chapter—knows the business or mission intimately, understands current requirements, and can anticipate future needs.

> **TIP** Invest in on-site, face-to-face requirements reviews.

It's difficult to maintain effective communication channels throughout the project. In particular, lengthy requirements documents hinder your communication with customers and suppliers, because they do not provide the interaction necessary to resolve misunderstandings about requirements. Rather, forging a common understanding of the proposed solution requires frequent interaction among stakeholders. Because documentation alone doesn't provide sufficient communication, reviews are often the most effective channels.

Suppliers and acquirers seem to agree that communicating the requirements by using prototypes helps prevent misunderstandings, but to be successful you must do more. For instance, you must insist that all the involved parties have access to the latest deliverables, and you need to find ways to bridge language barriers and cultural differences across extended teams. It's also important to avoid passing information through too many hands before it reaches the recipient. This is especially important for acquirers that work with offshore suppliers. This situation is often compounded if the supplier isn't involved in requirements development.

Paula feels she has a best remedy for this situation.

> **Paula:**   Let's host a validation workshop to walk through the requirements and ensure clear understanding, identify issues, and fill any gaps. The alternative to spending this time up front is to have the new supplier design and deliver a system without having an opportunity to clarify any issues. This means you end up with another problem, rather than a solution that eliminates the problem you started out with!
>   We often have stakeholders with a variety of backgrounds and different levels of expertise on our projects, and we need to leverage their knowledge and understanding of the business process. This can lead to conflicts among stakeholders. Both of these aspects of managing stakeholders are a challenge.

Stakeholders represent a diverse community, whether you are procuring or developing business application software or you are managing a program to deliver the next military fighter plane.

To increase the probability that the proposed solution will perform as intended in your environment, you validate requirements in frequent exchanges with the customer. Requirements validation should be integrated with risk management. Mature organizations typically validate requirements in a sophisticated way by using multiple techniques, and they broaden the basis of the validation to include other stakeholder needs and expectations. These organizations typically perform analyses, conduct simulations, or build prototypes to ensure that requirements satisfy stakeholder needs and expectations. Successful projects validate requirements with multiple stakeholders.

Paula: The intent behind our review process is to get commitment from all the stakeholders. We conduct functional requirements reviews with the customers and users, as well as with the technical team. We also hold frequent review meetings about the nonfunctional requirements or quality attributes. These meetings involve the business customer—we definitely focus on a deep dive with our technology people to get the input and feedback from our architecture team, operational team, suppliers, and security team. To streamline things, we highlight those requirements most pertinent to their area of expertise. That type of "involved" review process with all stakeholders helps us end up with a solid agreement on the right requirements.

> **TIP** Review requirements frequently with the affected stakeholders.

Successful projects also involve stakeholders who have a variety of technical knowledge about the business process, including operational specialists like security experts as well as maintenance suppliers. Including all these stakeholders creates an environment of early and open communication. It also ensures that the project team members, users, and customers pool their knowledge and help validate all ideas.

Steve: Team building is so important. It focuses on getting the business team to really get involved. Successful team building can make the difference between the business champion and users being your enemies or your allies—and a positive voice out to the customer. Before, when we started to build the trust relationship with our customer, there would be a lot of "You don't understand" from the customer, as well as "You can't make this work!" In these initial sessions, I would talk to my customer, and my business champion would say to me, "We've been with you for three hours, and you still don't understand."

Everyone around the table groans.

Steve: I'm happy to say that this relationship has changed dramatically. Today the business person is saying to the end user, "We just spent three hours with Steve Reiter and his team, so why can't you explain what you're doing?" The business champion has become more of a spokesperson and has taken ownership of the project. That's a key part of our success.

Even within a tightly knit group of stakeholders, however, the stakeholders establish different priorities and attach different importance to the requirements. For example, one group of stakeholders may emphasize the economic aspects of a problem (will we make money in the future?). Another stakeholder may be concerned about status and responsibility (will the software give managers more control?). Still others may worry about job satisfaction (will we get the opportunity for personal development?).

How can stakeholders cope with these differences? If you take into account these different and potentially conflicting views, you avoid a narrow frame of reference and help build an appropriate picture of the problem. Comparing different viewpoints helps you investigate the advantages and limitations of different solutions. In an outsourced environment, the consolidation of different viewpoints becomes the specification of the solution that is captured in an RFP and eventually in the contract that is executed by the supplier. Of course, it isn't easy to resolve conflicting stakeholder viewpoints.

> **Paula:** You have different layers of stakeholders and different regional or local groups, and there is definitely a certain amount of turf protection and politics.

> **Matt:** One thing we tend to overlook is how much time it takes to get everybody on the same page. If our deadlines don't leave us adequate time to align stakeholders, projects increase their risk of failure.

> **Paula:** That's right, Matt. One other thing. My team tries to take the input and feedback from all stakeholders without judgment—more from a brainstorming standpoint—and make it visible so that we can talk through the pros and cons. We then try to make the business responsible for resolving a lot of the inconsistencies. Where we have seen problems in the past is when the technology team is trying to meet the needs of multiple stakeholders that don't agree.

In this case, it's particularly important to have a governance structure in place, perhaps in the form of a steering committee in which the business and acquisition organizations are represented. This body can intervene and bring those issues to resolution.

However, pushing for a unified set of requirements, seeking a common solution where there is none, can be detrimental to a project or program.

> **Kristin:** Sometimes there is simply no common solution that will work across areas. The requirements are so different that I can't get an optimal system that does all of them. For example, in one of our government contracts the Air Force and the Navy are both looking at air superiority in their airspace. There are some very basic capabilities that are common between them. For instance, they might want planes that have two engines, radar, carry this type of payload, are supersonic or subsonic, and so on. So somebody might conclude, "A fighter plane is a fighter plane."

Well, it's not, because the environment that the Air Force deals with is very different than what the Navy deals with. The biggest difference is that the Navy lands on aircraft carriers, which is a moving airbase.

Matt: Sounds like a classic dilemma.

Kristin: That's right. We have a program called Joint Strike Fighter. The pain of this program is that it has tried to incorporate everybody's needs. This makes the price tag for each airplane a lot higher when you're trying to satisfy a set of disparate requirements. Overall, logic says, "Yeah, it's cheaper than buying two types of airplanes. I pay 1.5 times the price of a single airplane if I can do the job of two." So it will be interesting to see how the Joint Strike Fighter performs in the field in different environments.

The proof is in the final result. Projects must be extremely careful when combining disparate requirements into a single solution. Such an approach not only may represent a formidable engineering challenge but also might easily end up as a financial disaster.

As if understanding stakeholders' viewpoints isn't difficult enough, their viewpoints frequently change as the process of engineering a solution evolves. Careful project teams continuously validate their concepts with the stakeholders and involve them throughout the project.

Steve: It's kind of funny. On one of the main points of a global systems project, the North American group wasn't willing to budge on something where we thought Europe really had the best practice. So we agreed to create a regional solution for North America and a regional solution for Europe. Halfway through the project, North America realized that the European method was better, and we ended up redoing the system and bringing it together as a global, common solution.

Sometimes you find yourself in a variant of this situation caused by organizational inertia.

Steve: Part of this is driven by organizational culture. You have projects that start but never finish. Based on their knowledge and experience, people find themselves in situations where they conclude that this will not come together. So let's not talk about the difficult pieces of the problem because this project will never finish. It's not until people see something—maybe a prototype—that they realize this solution might have some validity. This happens quite a bit with big projects.

While exploring how projects "mind the gap" between stakeholder communications, acquirers often encounter a situation dubbed "the elephant in the room." The gray fellow is an idiom for a problem that obviously exists but is ignored for the convenience of one or more stakeholders. According to Wikipedia, it derives its symbolic meaning from the fact that an elephant would indeed be conspicuous and remarkable in a small room; thus the idiom also implies a value judgment that the issue should be discussed openly. Steve tells us how he has survived several encounters with the elephant.

> **Steve:**   We agreed with our organization in Mexico that they would start using the common global system to allocate their actual spending to their acquisition programs. During development of this financial system, we discussed how they allocated their actual spending and everybody felt this was a shoo-in—smooth sailing, no problems expected, since their processes matched how the common system was used in other parts of the company. But then after we deployed the system in Mexico, nothing was allocated to the acquisition programs. So we went back and said, "What's wrong? It looks like all your actual spending has been allocated to a financial holding account rather than to individual acquisition programs." And they said, "Well, it always goes into a holding account first. You don't need to worry about that."
>
> That's when I realized I was staring right at the elephant. They were using the system consistently but with a twist. Everything was parked in a holding account until month end, which caused interim reports to come up blank. Nobody discussed during development that they parked funds in this holding account rather than directly allocating it to acquisition programs. So nobody did anything about it.

> **TIP**   To represent requirements, develop prototypes together with complementary models such as business process flows.

There are some gaps in stakeholder interactions that cannot be resolved by communication alone. Customers and users often do not know what they need until they see it. Multiple representations of requirements (e.g., prototypes, simulations, models, scenarios, and storyboards) have proven extremely beneficial for identifying issues and exposing unstated needs and customer requirements. Steve couldn't agree more.

> **Steve:**   We had all the requirements written down in a Microsoft Word document. This was mostly because that's what we were told to do. However, the primary value was in the working models and the prototypes that we used in the sessions with the customer. It was more important that they saw a prototype compared to reading a requirements document. If it wasn't for the interactive sessions that we had with them, they wouldn't have signed off on the documents.

A few times we actually had to go back to the requirements document, and they would say, "Well, this is not what we decided in the meeting." And we would say, "Well this is how it is written." But then we would realize that how it was written was not how we actually did the prototype. So we agreed to use the prototype as the source of truth.

The use of prototypes early in the project increases the likelihood that customers, suppliers, and the acquisition team will have a better understanding of the real stakeholder needs. Thus, prototyping increases the useful functionality provided by the technology solution at delivery. The prototype needs to be based on a thorough understanding of the business processes. Paula illustrates this.

Paula: We do a lot of process modeling and prototyping to show how the process would be enabled by the proposed solution. We instruct the supplier to build some pieces so that the customer can see and understand what we're talking about. Frequently, we work with our hosting supplier to stand up one of the COTS packages we're considering and then use the COTS package as part of our prototype. With the help of the supplier, we build some of the computer screens and apply some of the business rules.

Steve: Can you give us an example?

Paula: Sure. My most recent project was a financial system. In our prototype we just did a small number of relevant transactions. We didn't create a lot of the fancy logic. But we let the customers and users see how they would input, for instance, their forecast, how they would then report back the variances and forecasts versus actuals. When we first presented our ideas to the customers we used business process flows and a simple slide show, but when we went to get sign off on the requirements we included this prototype.

> **TIP** Use commercial off-the-shelf products as ready-made prototypes for your technology solution.

Steve is also enthusiastic about prototyping.

Steve: Customers love prototypes. It also strengthens our communication with the suppliers. For instance, there can be major disconnects between the supplier's on-site team and their offshore development center. In many cases, we now give the supplier a prototype along with the requirements document. This has tremendously improved communication and reduced the amount of rework. In this case, it's true that a picture is worth a thousand words.

Matt: I understand you've taken this a step further. Tell us about that.

Steve: Well, it works so well that we've contracted with a supplier to establish an integrated prototyping environment that contains prototypes of all our technology solutions and associated scenarios of their application to a particular business process. So now we can show our customers not only the technology per se, but more importantly illustrate how it fits into the context of the business process.

Matt: So it's like having a library of prototypes.

Steve: That's right. And it has changed the way we work. Since the prototypes allow us much better communication with the business customer, we can adjust to a shared governance structure between the technology group and the business. We use this new structure to prioritize the requirements in the best interest of a business process overall, and not just for a particular project or single stakeholder. All this was enabled by this tight link between groups of prototypes and their associated business processes.

> **TIP**   To prioritize requirements for a technology solution, establish a collection of prototypes that optimize the entire business process.

Walkthroughs also encourage discussion of the functions and behavior of a technology solution. Walkthroughs present a series of scenarios that might occur during the use of the product and that make explicit some stakeholder intentions. Typically, operational scenarios are derived from business process descriptions and operational concepts.

Paula: We start out with the business process and derive customer requirements, which are really the value proposition—the stakeholder intentions—and then we walk through user scenarios. We work with the customers and users. They tend to say, "Let's take a particular business process or subprocess and start talking about how a user might be working with the business process to achieve a goal." What are all the scenarios and challenges that we can come up with to help us build and elaborate those with prototypes and wireframes so that the stakeholders see multiple views of requirements? We try not to go back to the business with just a requirements document but with prototypes, wireframes, summary business requirements, and rules. That way, we create an overall process on how we might document each of their different processes.

> **TIP** Jointly with the customer, develop and walk through scenarios that demonstrate how the technology solution will be used.

As solution decisions are made and more detailed requirements are developed, you refine the prototypes and scenarios. Requirements also evolve to facilitate the validation of the technology solutions delivered by the supplier.

Scenarios can represent historical records of executing software or a thought experiment of executing a proposed system. Intuit's innovative gathering of scenarios highlights this point. Intuit's "Follow Me Home" program started when software designers realized that testing in the usability laboratories could not accurately reflect the experiences of users who tried to install and use the software in their own environments. Customer surveys were not timely enough or detailed enough to expose potential problems. So staff from Intuit went to local stores and asked software buyers for permission to observe them as they first tried to use it. Watching people in their own homes with their own computers revealed subtle problems, such as the user who was confused by the "Register" item on the main menu, thinking that it had something to do with the product-registration card (De Young 1996, p. 263).

As you create and use prototypes and scenarios, engage in intensive dialog with your customers. This practice ensures that customers contribute to the requirements, and that immediately affects the technology solution. Scenarios serve as a means of discussing alternative solutions, grounding discussions and negotiations in real examples, and supporting trade-offs among design alternatives. Misunderstandings between stakeholders become apparent, and through prototypes the supplier's understanding of the problem to be solved can be validated quickly. Scenarios serve as a common basis for communication to help resolve such misunderstandings.

> **TIP** Use various techniques to drive out unnecessary functionality.

Equally important, validating requirements via a scenario lets stakeholders detect missing functionality, overspecification, errors, or unintended side effects. Teams frequently use prototypes or mock-ups to enact scenarios. This allows for a hands-on experience of the proposed system, making it easier for stakeholders to discover problems and suggest how the specification can be improved. Prototypes and mock-ups are therefore popular methods for validating requirements. When done correctly, both techniques are cost-effective. When done poorly, however, they can be expensive and sometimes even disastrous in misguiding stakeholder expectations.

3.3.2 Applying the CMMI-ACQ to Analyzing and Validating Requirements

The CMMI-ACQ provides specific recommendations on how to perform analyses to determine candidate requirements for product concepts that will satisfy stakeholder needs, expectations, and constraints. It also covers recommendations on how to validate requirements to increase the probability that the resulting product will perform as intended in your environment (see Table 3-5).

Operational concepts provide an overall description of the way in which the technology solution is intended to be used or operated, deployed, supported, and disposed of (Table 3-5, practice 3.1). For that, you take design constraints explicitly into account. In contrast, a scenario is a sequence of events that might occur during the use of the acquired product that makes explicit some stakeholder intentions.

As contractual requirements are defined, their relationship to customer requirements must be understood. In light of the operational concept and scenarios, the contractual requirements are analyzed to determine whether they are necessary and sufficient to meet the customer requirements (Table 3-5, practice 3.2). The analyzed requirements then provide the basis for more detailed and precise requirements throughout the project life cycle. You also need to determine which key requirements will be used to track technical progress. For instance, the weight of a product or the size of a software code base may be monitored throughout development to assess its risk.

Stakeholder needs and constraints can address cost, schedule, performance, functionality, reusable components, maintainability, or risk. Acquirers use proven models, simulations, and prototyping to analyze and balance stakeholder needs and constraints (Table 3-5, practice 3.3). You also perform a risk assessment on the requirements and design constraints and examine product life-cycle concepts for effects that requirements might have on risks.

You analyze the requirements to determine the risk that the resulting technology solution will not perform appropriately in its intended environment (Table 3-5, practice 3.4). For that, you explore the adequacy and completeness of requirements by developing product representations (e.g., prototypes, simulations, models, scenarios, and storyboards) and obtain feedback about them from relevant stakeholders. To gain adequate insight into how the technology solution progresses and to ensure that it meets customer expectations, you assess the technology solution as it is developed by the supplier in the context of the validation environment to identify issues and expose unstated needs and customer requirements.

Table 3-5 *Acquisition Requirements Development Goal 3: Practices and Tips*

CMMI-ACQ Process Area: Acquisition Requirements Development	
3. Goal: The requirements are analyzed and validated.	
Practices	**Tips**
3.1 Establish and maintain operational concepts and associated scenarios. 3.2 Analyze requirements to ensure that they are necessary and sufficient. 3.3 Analyze requirements to balance stakeholder needs and constraints. 3.4 Validate requirements to ensure that the resulting product will perform as intended in the user's environment using multiple techniques as appropriate.	• Validate the business champion's and customer's commitment to the project. If there is no commitment, stop. • Jointly with the customer, develop and walk through scenarios that reflect how the technology solution will be used. • Use various techniques to drive out unnecessary functionality. • To prioritize requirements for a technology solution, establish a collection of prototypes that optimize the entire business process. • Use commercial off-the-shelf products as ready-made prototypes for your technology solution. • Develop prototypes together with complementary models such as business process flows to represent requirements. • Frequently review requirements with the affected stakeholders. • Invest in on-site, face-to-face requirements reviews.

3.3.3 Controlled Requirements Changes

The many sentences beginning with "After the requirements are frozen . . ." embody a favorite myth of many acquirers and their contracting officers. Although the thought of "frozen" requirements is comforting, in reality this state never comes true, at least not for most technology solutions. In fact, many people argue that change is an inherent property of any technology project. Discovering requirements for a technology solution is a process of learning, communication, and negotiation. To specify technology solutions successfully, then, you must discover the requirements progressively. Stakeholders have an interest in transforming a situation from what it is to something they like better. They progressively relate a situation to technological artifacts as perceived solutions. Their understanding of the current situation serves as a springboard to a new cycle of improvement.

> **TIP** To maximize the value of the resulting technology solution, contractually allow for changing requirements.

This necessary learning is one reason for the cyclic characteristic of technology projects. Acquisition projects are in a constant dialog with the customer to generate requirements and negotiate design constraints, which in turn generate new possibilities for the customer and other stakeholders. As customers learn more about the desired capabilities and better understand their application, they envision many features they wish they had included in the original requirements.

Many customers and suppliers therefore argue that requirements should not be frozen while they learn about the application domain or the capabilities of the proposed solution. In other words, you should not formalize requirements any faster than you can reduce the rate of uncertainty about technical decisions.

However, this leaves the unresolved issue of finding an economical balance between supporting changes in requirements and delivering operational solutions. Such a balance is of utmost importance; otherwise, last-minute changes to the specification will keep delaying the deployment of the technology solution.

> **TIP** To account for customer and supplier learning, freeze requirements incrementally.

Stakeholders constantly struggle with getting the requirements right and getting them stable. Change may come from various sources, causing significant uncertainty in a project because of conflicting and missing information. For example, the enabled business processes often change, thus requiring the original specification to change, before even the best supplier can deliver the solution. Hence, it seems virtually impossible to produce defect-free specifications before building the technology solution or, at minimum, a prototype.

Paula: One side of it is, "We didn't do a good job up front, and our requirements baseline was bad." That's the risk of rushing through the requirements gathering—you end up with a highly inaccurate specification up front, and you end up in change control hell. And then you also have to cope with business change. In a project I'm working on right now, we just got a new business champion. That's very painful. From a project perspective it's not something I can really control, as much as we try to manage as best as we can. We have to be very diligent in how we manage change and traceability.

> **TIP**   Allow for different viewpoints of different stakeholders involved in different phases of the project.

No stakeholder can come up with a complete list of requirements at the start of requirements gathering. Rather, they evolve during the project as stakeholders increase their understanding. Moreover, requirements emerge from new stakeholders who were not originally consulted. The people consulted at some stage in the process may change jobs and thus are no longer available for consultation.

If a specification fails to integrate these changes, it becomes obsolete. It hinders people's communication and learning process and leads to inferior software. In other words, a static specification prohibits stakeholders from formulating their insights to improve the proposed solution.

> **TIP**   Negotiate with the customer and the supplier the deadline for stakeholders to change requirements.

The central question is this: How much of the specification do you need before the supplier can start the design and you and the supplier can establish the supplier agreement? In terms of the specification, some people would say you can never get it complete no matter how hard you try. But then the question is this: How can you tell that the specification is good enough?

Steve: You stop working on the initial requirements when you run out of time. That's it—we had to have this system up by the end of the year. So the business customer has to trust that you understand the problem to be solved. What we said to the business champion was, "We get the gist of the overall problem. We guarantee you as we build it, we will iterate. We will not hold you to every word that was said in the initial requirements session." That was the thing. They had to trust that we were not going to come back and say, "You signed the requirements specification, and see?

On line two on page seven, it says that we'll do it that way and now you're stuck with it." We were very clear to them that the process will be iterative. They're completely open to making changes, and we will just go through it and prioritize based on business value.

By starting without a complete specification you can overlap requirements discovery and the supplier's development of the technology solution, reducing everyone's overall time to delivery. Such a reduction is not free. It leaves you vulnerable to expensive rework, because the supplier may have completed detailed design work that changes later in the process. Thus, you face a trade-off between delivery speed and delivery expenses.

> **TIP** When the cost of potential rework is lower than the cost of reduced cycle time, overlap your specification with the supplier's design and development activities.

When the cost of potential rework is lower than the cost of increased cycle time, you should overlap your specification with the supplier's design and development activities. Steve is convinced that this is the way to go.

Steve: We struggled when we had contracts that forced us into a waterfall methodology. Everything was strictly sequential, locked in through firm fixed-price contracts. You were forced to get to a low level of detail in the plan so that the vendor could make a qualified bid. This caused analysis paralysis and a lot of angst. Sometimes you had to make decisions that you knew you were stuck with, even though you knew you'd want to change them when the supplier actually built the system or the business actually started to see the solution.

So you find yourself in a catch-22. To survive, some of us got together and decided to trick the system.

Steve laughs.

Steve: Well, sometimes you have to ask for forgiveness later, and in this case the workaround became the new way of doing things. So we decided to break our projects into smaller chunks. For instance, one of my projects turned into nine projects, one of Paula's ended up as five projects, and so on. We then used the related projects to institute a progressive freeze of the requirements.

Matt: A progressive freeze? How does that work?

Steve: We defined a schedule for freezing different requirements. For example, we might decide to freeze the number of screens in the financial services application 30 days after the start of the project, but we might determine some of its more detailed attributes—such as color, width, position on the screen—90 days later. The point is, we don't have to freeze all requirements at the same time. We can freeze them in increments, depending on when the information is needed. So we were still able to use firm fixed-price contracts for the smaller projects, and we learned more about our requirements faster, delivered workable solutions more rapidly, and made everybody happy along the way. How's that for a workaround?

> **TIP** Stay engaged with the supplier's design team as requirements are translated into detailed design decisions.

Stakeholders iteratively negotiate trade-offs between requested functions, the capabilities of the technology, the delivery schedule, and cost. In the case of conflicting requirements, an effective technique is to prioritize them and include as many as possible in the contractual requirements in order of importance. Even so, it's difficult to achieve a consensus on the requirements among the stakeholders that have to accept and abide by the rankings. Even after priorities are negotiated, it's hard to maintain consensus without strong leadership to oversee adherence to priorities. In addition to shifting priorities, Steve identifies two other reasons for fluctuating requirements.

> **Steve:** We're often faced with a loosely integrated technical design. Requirements occasionally fluctuate because the technical designs for different components aren't tightly coordinated. In making a detailed design decision, suppliers often make incorrect assumptions about how we intend a contractual requirement to be met. A requirement then becomes unstable across different components of the design. Without tight coordination of design decisions, inconsistencies become apparent only at integration time.
>
> And then there's the "creeping elegance" syndrome, or what some people call "gold-plating." Suppliers go beyond the contractual requirements by adding features we haven't requested. This also destabilizes the requirements. Often project managers recognize the impact of this on schedule and performance, but only after resources have been expended unnecessarily or when schedules have slipped irreversibly.

> **TIP** Always stay on the lookout to avoid "gold-plating" of the technology solution.

3.3.4 Applying the CMMI-ACQ to Managing Requirements

The CMMI-ACQ provides specific recommendations on how to manage the requirements of a technology solution and how to identify inconsistencies between the project's requirements and the plans and work products (see Table 3-6).

To avoid requirements creep, you establish criteria to designate appropriate channels or official sources of requirements. When a project receives requirements from an approved requirements provider, you review the requirements with the source to resolve issues and prevent misunderstanding before the requirements are incorporated into the project's plans (Table 3-6, practice 1.1).

The project maintains a current and approved set of requirements over the life of the project. This typically includes directly managing changes to customer and contractual requirements developed by the acquirer and oversight of the supplier's requirements management process (Table 3-6, practices 1.2 and 1.3). Changes to requirements may lead to changes in supplier agreements; these changes need to be agreed upon between the project and the supplier after appropriate negotiations. To effectively analyze the impact of the changes, you must know the source of each requirement and document the rationale for any change. The project manager, however, may want to track appropriate measures of requirements volatility to judge whether new or revised controls are necessary.

When the requirements are managed well, traceability can be established from the source requirement to its lower-level requirements and from the lower-level requirements back to their source (Table 3-6, practice 1.4). Such bidirectional traceability helps you determine whether all source requirements have been completely addressed and whether all lower-level requirements can be traced to a valid source. As the acquirer, you trace the contractual requirements to the customer requirements; the supplier maintains comprehensive bidirectional traceability to the requirements defined in the supplier agreement, and you verify that traceability.

You also need to identify inconsistencies between the requirements and the project plans and work products, if any, and initiate corrective action to fix them (Table 3-6, practice 1.5). Your corrective actions can also result in changes to project plans and supplier agreements.

Table 3-6 *Requirements Management Goal 1: Practices and Tips*

CMMI-ACQ Process Area: Requirements Management	
1. Goal: Requirements are managed, and inconsistencies with project plans and work products are identified.	
Practices	**Tips**
1.1 Develop an understanding with the requirements providers on the meaning of the requirements. 1.2 Obtain commitment to the requirements from the project participants. 1.3 Manage changes to the requirements as they evolve during the project. 1.4 Maintain bidirectional traceability among the requirements and work products. 1.5 Identify inconsistencies between the requirements and the project plans and work products.	• To account for customer and supplier learning, freeze requirements incrementally. • To maximize the value of the resulting technology solution, contractually allow for changing requirements. • Allow for different viewpoints of different stakeholders involved in different phases of the project. • Negotiate with the customer and the supplier the deadline for stakeholders to change requirements. • Stay engaged with the supplier's design team as requirements are translated into detailed design decisions. • Always stay on the lookout to avoid gold-plating of the technology solution. • When the cost of potential rework is lower than the cost of reduced cycle time, overlap the acquirer's specification and the supplier's design and development activities.

3.4 Summary

The single hardest part of building systems, software, and technology solutions is deciding what to build to address the stakeholders' needs. Getting the requirements right may be the most important and difficult part of a project. No other part of the work so cripples the resulting system if done wrong. No other part is more difficult to rectify later (Frederick P. Brooks Jr., *The Mythical Man-Month*, Addison-Wesley, 1995).

The requirements development effort comprises three information-gathering components:

- Gathering qualitative information through a continuous dialog with prospective stakeholders
- Getting quantitative information about stakeholders' business processes or operations, requirements, and competitive attributes to set the value of the opportunity, determine its size, and estimate the eventual rate of penetration and final level of acceptance into the business
- Addressing communication, distribution, and support strategies

The interactions between acquirers and stakeholders should form a spiral pattern of repeated steps and increasing mutual understanding. Through this iterative process, a relationship evolves in which each party continually increases its realization of what the other party has to offer. Engineering a solution begins with understanding the stakeholder's needs, expectations, and constraints for building the system, software, or technology solution.

The stakeholders' main focus, and therefore also that of the acquirer, is acquiring a solution that adds value to stakeholders' business or operations. The idea for this solution may start by being described in a few words or in a hand-drawn sketch, long before it matures into a fully developed product concept.

It is critical to foster an ongoing dialog with customers and stakeholders from the earliest phase of the acquisition life cycle through final delivery of a product. Clear communication and mutual understanding are the only reliable ways to establish requirements, continuously modify concepts, and verify the value of the deliverable. For many projects the number of customers and stakeholders is large, and it is vital to interact with a representative critical mass to form an accurate view of the requirements.

Your first step in developing your acquisition requirements is to present the idea to the prospective customer and promote it by helping the customer understand it and see how it will add value to the business or operations. With truly groundbreaking solutions to complex problems, the customer may initially have difficulty envisioning what you have to offer. Documents, diagrams, models, and prototypes are all ways to help stakeholders understand what the proposed idea will look like. By showing them something concrete, you ground discussions in reality and can begin to talk about what works and what needs to change in very specific terms. This is an opportunity for stakeholders to identify needs or requirements that may have been misunderstood or misinterpreted and reconcile those differences.

The second step in requirements development is for you to listen to the customer's perspective, carefully and in enough detail and context to understand the real needs that the stakeholders communicate through their words and actions. For this step, you can employ a combination of techniques to make these interactions successful and productive. By conducting brainstorming sessions, workshops, moderated focus groups, interviews, and observations, you can draw requirements out of the stakeholders, perhaps even requirements that they haven't thought of. All these techniques are important tools. It may also be beneficial for you to use a "formatted tool for hearing," such as quality function deployment, to ensure that the customers' views are documented and thoughtfully translated into terms that you, the stakeholders, and the suppliers can understand.

The third step in requirements gathering is to creatively modify or develop the idea to reflect a deeper understanding of requirements that fulfill stakeholders' needs. The spiral continues as you return to the stakeholders with further rounds of communication and development. As the process continues, the stakeholders' requirements become more refined and eventually you can translate them into documented customer requirements that are accurate, high-level, and easy to digest.

It's widely believed that a more detailed specification is better, but that is a myth. This myth is often perpetuated by project and program managers who feel obligated or are even mandated to use highly detailed standard templates for documenting specifications. Instead, the requirements should be accurate, minimal, and understandable. Remember that each requirement represents a constraint and a risk for the customer. The requirements must focus on the significant differentiators—the specific foundational characteristics that enable the system to achieve its purpose.

To maintain focus on significant differentiators, you, the customer, and the supplier must make choices about which requirements meet these criteria. This process of sorting and quantifying the criticality of a requirement—determining whether it is a must-be or an attractive requirement—is the first step in prioritizing customer requirements. Prioritizing is a tricky task, especially when you're evaluating nonfunctional requirements like reliability, scalability, safety, security, and performance, which often seem to conflict with other requirements. Standard requirements—such as those specifying architecture, data management, basic security, operational details, and testing—reflect the policies that projects adhere to across the organization. Clearly, developing acquisition requirements is more than just a balancing act; it's a balancing act that takes place on a tightrope, and one misstep can have disastrous results.

After the significant differentiators and standard requirements have been established, they're translated from customer requirements into contractual requirements. The contractual requirements specify the criteria that suppliers must meet to build a successful deliverable—one that is of high quality, within budget, and delivered on time. To ensure that contractual requirements leverage the supplier's capabilities, it is important to develop design constraints that must be satisfied by the supplier's design. Design constraints express the qualities and performance points that are critical to the success of the product in the acquirer's operational environment. They document the interfaces, product reuse, use of COTS components, criteria for evaluating the supplier's design, and criteria for screening and selecting possible alternative solutions.

Verifying the supplier's design to determine goodness of fit with the requirements is a critical, ongoing activity. You must ensure not only that the requirements have been met as promised but also that the design has not been "enhanced" to include features that were not requested. These features, which are said to "creep" into a system, add unnecessary complexity and potential risk. In determining goodness of fit, technical reviews are key practices for acquirers as well as suppliers. Reviews formally evaluate the consistency of the proposed technical design or the consistency between the technical design and its contractual requirements and design constraints.

Stakeholders and acquirers constantly struggle with two opposing forces: getting the requirements right and getting them stable. To support these goals, you use prototypes, models, and walkthroughs to encourage discussion of the system's functions and behavior and help keep the communication channels alive.

Like strands in a double helix, the requirements are continuously analyzed, validated, and adjusted as the technical design spirals in parallel. To keep these strands from becoming disconnected and frayed, you must continue fostering and mediating relationships with and between customers and suppliers; at the same time, you bear the responsibility of ensuring that the delivered solution will not only operate but also meet expectations in the deployed environment. Technical development involves addressing the project's technological uncertainties, and it can easily wander astray if it becomes isolated from customer needs. Development should be based on stakeholder targets for the system or service, including its cost, plus the specific plans and actions to achieve those targets.

In this chapter, we focused primarily on how to elicit requirements from stakeholders, translate them into contractual requirements, and validate that the supplier starts on the right path. In Chapter 4, we examine the acquirer-supplier relationship in more depth by discussing how to apply integrated project management, use configuration management, establish the right metrics, and, finally, live with the technology solution.

Chapter 4

Delivering Solutions

The best way to predict the future is to invent it.
Alan Kay (1971)

Delivery of technology solutions is where the rubber meets the road. In industry and in government, technology solutions exist only to enhance organizational processes to better meet the acquirer's strategies and objectives. This requires a persistent focus on measuring the critical dimensions of your work, the supplier's delivery capability, and the deliverables. You manage the overall delivery by keeping a keen eye on handling business and technical risks throughout any project or program. You must coordinate all the stakeholders while addressing all the facets of your acquisition projects. Only a well-orchestrated team of acquirer and supplier personnel can deliver the desired value-added solution without disrupting the acquirer's business or mission.

This chapter looks at the challenges of managing suppliers compared with performing the technical development yourself (recall hidden truth number 5, "Understand the difference between managing and performing," as discussed in Chapter 1). To do that, we describe the struggles, ideas, and discoveries of Matt Vauban, a seasoned executive within an acquisition organization, along with Steve Reiter, who has managed acquisition projects for years, and Paula Ressel, the internal customer. The supplier's perspectives are represented by Kristin Wells and George Taylor, who work for a key supplier. These fictitious characters are engaged in active outsourcing. The goal of the acquirer is to manage the supplier to achieve results while retaining accountability for the overall outcome of the acquisition projects.

This chapter focuses first on integrated project management. Our goal is to set the foundation for the things that acquirers, even when they are just starting out on the improvement journey toward excellence, should keep in mind when managing delivery of solutions. We highlight how to involve the relevant stakeholders according to an executable delivery process. Although integrated project management has its greatest impact when an acquirer has reached a certain level of process maturity, the practices and ideas help guide all acquirers.

We then turn our attention to the critical, but underappreciated, craft of configuration management. It takes numerous people to make outsourced projects successful, so it is critical to know where all the assets that make up a technology solution are stored. In addition, successful acquirers carefully monitor and control their projects by making targeted, concise, and actionable measurements. We cover such a set of measures and offer ideas about applying them. The chapter concludes with a discussion of going live with acquired products and services.

4.1 Treat Each Project as a Whole Endeavor

Successful projects are usually planned very carefully. Delayed or canceled projects, however, almost always exhibit planning failures. The most common planning failures include (1) not dealing effectively with changing requirements, (2) not anticipating staff hiring and turnover, (3) not allotting time for detailed requirements analysis, and (4) not allotting sufficient time for design and code inspections, testing, integration, and defect correction.

You need to involve all the relevant acquisition, technical, support, and operational stakeholders throughout the project. It's your task to ensure that all the stakeholders coordinate and cooperate to the maximum extent possible. Depending on the scope and risk of the project, coordination efforts with the supplier organization can be significant.

4.1.1 Work on All Aspects Concurrently

TIP Working with the customer and supplier, tie plans to business or mission objectives.

When Matt briefed the hidden truths to the board of directors and other senior managers, he was surprised that it created such a stir. "They all want us to get moving fast, delivering solutions like clockwork," he says to Paula. He pauses and then continues.

Matt: How can we get all our ducks in a row? We always agree to a plan with the stakeholders and suppliers, but then we seem to make a new plan every other week because "something happened."

Paula: I think I know what you mean.

Matt: We forget about this, that, and the other—we don't get the supplier agreement signed, or we forget about that cost or this task. So the replanning—or worse, rebaselining of the plan—continues on and on. I remember one project that we had to replan five times.

Paula: Five times? That's a lot.

Matt: What happens is, we don't recognize that a particular plan is in jeopardy. So then the suppliers just respond to that confusion and sometimes add to it. It throws us for a loop, and we end up in a vicious cycle of planning and replanning.

But I've seen planning work, too. It takes a lot of preparation. We have to hammer out clear business objectives and agree to them up front, so everyone knows how they will be measured. You have the business participation, buy-in, and agreement on the team, including our suppliers. As a team, we gather around and build an integrated plan and process and give it the chance to execute flawlessly.

Acquirers of technology solutions must keep in mind the overall picture and then continuously reinforce and improve the integration of acquirer, supplier, and stakeholder activities. Paula describes what it's like when a team hasn't achieved the desired level of integration.

> **TIP**   Synchronize early, and adjust the technical constraints along with the capability of the supply base.

> **TIP**   Establish frequent, reinforcing feedback loops with customers and suppliers.

Paula: The problem seems to be that we adopt a throw-it-over-the-wall mentality. For instance, sometimes we have fairly detailed design constraints, and we lock them down before the suppliers are even on board. When the suppliers come along, they're focused on design, development, or configuration. But this is after we've tried to freeze our requirements through ironclad supplier agreements.

Matt: I see what you mean. We establish the requirements and design constraints somewhat in isolation, so the supplier's delivery processes are slow and require a lot of rework. And that eats up a significant amount of our resources.

Paula: I just attended a review of one of our key projects, where we didn't even start looking for a supplier until many months into the project.

Another problem is that our technical experts make assumptions about COTS components and new technologies, and then it turns out they're not available. So anything they've done based on those assumptions is now dead.

And of course, our suppliers are experiencing an upheaval in their business environment, so they've been consolidating like mad, which has eliminated some delivery centers and components from the supply base. And the design assumed a certain level of process capability that the suppliers didn't possess. So we have a real mismatch between our requirements and what the suppliers can deliver.

Steve is also sitting in on the meeting.

Steve: Do you have any ideas for dealing with all this?

Paula: The only hope we have is truly integrated project management. Instead of executing all the work sequentially, we need to establish a set of standard processes that rely on early action by the suppliers. It will take precise and intense communication between our teams and the supplier teams. Plus, our relationship with suppliers must support and reinforce the early and frequent exchange of ideas, requirements, and constraints.

Achieving integrated project management requires an approach that is new to most organizations. You must make certain that your preferred technologies and your choices about your overall technology environment are aligned with the supplier's system processes and delivery capabilities, and you must do this early enough in the overall process that the two parties can influence and shape one another in a timely and effective way. You can examine suppliers' qualifications early in the process as requirements and technical constraints emerge. The suppliers can begin to participate in early discussions aimed at obtaining firsthand information about potential problems and opportunities inherent in the design trade-offs you present.

TIP   Find out what works, and then repeat—always.

However, people who work on technology projects don't have to reinvent the wheel. After you have documented some processes, procedures, templates, or guidelines, projects can leverage your organizational process and tailor it to their specific needs. A defined process not only covers the technical aspects of system delivery but also addresses organizational acquisition guidance, regulations, instructions, and practices that are established for use across projects. The project's processes logically sequence acquirer activities and supplier deliverables (as identified in the supplier agreement) to deliver a product that meets the requirements. Examples of integrated project activities include proposal evaluation, supplier selection, development and management of supplier agreements, and acceptance of supplier deliverables.

Although all processes must be aligned with the acquisition strategy, this alignment is particularly important if you plan to make processes available for projects so that they can tailor them. Markets and technologies are dynamic, and time is a critical element of competition. Therefore, deeper, more intensive acquirer-supplier integration is crucial for effectively delivering solutions.

> **TIP** Include your suppliers when establishing the project's work environment.

Steve picks up the dialog about integrated project management.

> **Steve:** You're right, Paula. It will require decisive actions to break up our functional silos and seamlessly integrate with our suppliers. Look at the systems engineering group, for example. Integrated project management would let us define design constraints that take the supplier's capabilities into account, and at the same time work with our acquisition strategy. This also means that the supplier's delivery processes must consistently live up to the capability and performance we need.

An integrated work environment fosters careful and practical planning.

> **Steve:** We really need to think through how to put together an integrated plan. For instance, one problem I see is that we don't put enough time and thought into how to deploy a technical solution. We put a lot of thought and design into the product, but not into the deployment. But when you think about it, what good is a so-called solution if it only sits on the shelf?

> **Paula:** What we need is to not get distracted. It's easy to fall into the trap of excessive multitasking and convince ourselves that working really hard on a bunch of things means it's all good. We end up working on everything and not getting anything done.

> **TIP**   Stay focused on deploying the solution, and not just on developing it.

Developing an integrated project plan requires an in-depth understanding of your and the supplier's capabilities. For instance, projects are often asked to accelerate the delivery schedule. If you can't accelerate work on your side, the relationship with the supplier comes into play. In a long-term acquirer-supplier relationship, the supplier might provide additional short-term capability without adding cost to help the acquirer out of a difficult situation.

Steve: A couple years back, we had many different suppliers who didn't necessarily want to accommodate our schedule changes. Often the squeaky wheel gets the grease. If our suppliers had another customer with a bigger contract or a more prestigious project, they got the most high-powered resources. So our suppliers weren't very flexible. They wouldn't just say, "Oh, yeah, you can change this activity or deliverable by a week. No problem. We don't care." We corrected this situation by establishing more mutually beneficial, medium- to long-term relationships with our suppliers.

> **TIP**   To achieve flexible, high-performance processes, maintain clearly defined, positive relationships with your suppliers.

Kristin confirms Steve's observation.

Kristin: If you have a one-shot relationship, you go in with the attitude, "What's the project? What's the margin I have to hit to make the acquirer happy enough that we get the next project?" This results in a very short-term focus, with minimum synergy. But when you have a strategic relationship, things change drastically. The analogy I like to use is going out to dinner with a bunch of friends. Sometimes you buy at a fast food restaurant, and sometimes they buy at the high-end steak house, but sometimes it's the opposite. It balances out. If there's trust between you and everyone understands that it's a strategic relationship, suppliers can put the date on the table without worrying that the acquirer's purchasing group is going to say, "I can squeeze out another 1 percent."

Steve: I'm not sure I follow you.

Kristin: For us, integrated planning is in the program domain, not the purchasing domain. We'd be happy to have your program or project managers discuss the size of the management reserve. Our concern is always that the purchasing person is going to say, "I've been advised to cut another 3 percent, and I'm going to do that no matter how if affects execution." Then we get concerned about putting the date on the table.

Steve: Can you give me an example?

Kristin: Well, let's look at a fixed-price contract. We're basically exposing our programming buffer for things that can go wrong. If we have a program that costs $1 million, we put in a 15 percent margin, because we know we need that. That's the first line item that'll disappear when purchasing gets involved. When that's gone, what do we do? We try to factor all of that gray area into the detailed project plan. So we can look at that project plan and say, "Okay, if it really explodes, this is the worst case scenario." To a certain extent, we can use that built-in buffer to manage our risk.

> **TIP**   Size project buffers according to the risk of the project.

Many acquirers (especially their purchasing departments) are tempted to dip into the project's management reserve or buffer and suggest that reducing the buffer is a painless way of reducing the planned project cost and delivery time. But this is a myth. Project buffers protect critical tasks from the project's inherent risk. Project buffers can consist of, for instance, additional resources that become available when you need to protect a critical task, or they may provide additional monies to buy capacity or capability to keep the project on track. Reducing the project buffer has no impact on project execution time; all it reduces are the chances that the promised delivery date will be missed, and potentially it causes excessive replanning.

Therefore, you should not cut the project buffer. Instead, clearly identify the risk associated with every project activity, and then size the project buffer according to the aggregate project risk. This practice not only makes the project risk visible but also provides a single convenient indicator for the impact of the risk on the project.

> **TIP**   Establish and frequently convene acquirer-supplier forums or councils at all levels of the organization.

In an integrated project environment, acquirers communicate with suppliers on a variety of issues common to both organizations throughout the project. This communication requires that you establish forums and create a context in which two-way communication is effective: You must comprehend issues of "manufacturability" or system delivery processes, foster skills in developing robust design constraints that exploit manufacturing capability, and be prepared to trim designs accordingly. Similarly, suppliers must be oriented toward customer satisfaction: They must comprehend issues of product performance and total cost of ownership and must be prepared to deliver and develop a solution that allows the design to achieve its objectives in the intended environment.

> **Kristin:** As suppliers, we really have to step beyond our traditional organizational boundaries. We have to make a concentrated effort to solve the problem from the acquirer's business perspective. The challenge is that sometimes it's easier for a supplier to look at it only from a technology perspective. But we can't become complacent. And that's where we need help from the acquirer to understand the parameters we can apply to a particular solution.

> **Matt:** We'll all be winners, or we'll all be losers. My people and the suppliers' people must form a high-performance team.

Matt's incisive statement brings home the point. Successful acquirers attempt to maximize cooperation among stakeholders. In other words, the acquirer involves and integrates all relevant stakeholders, and the supplier agreement provides the basis for managing the supplier's involvement. Kristin agrees.

> **Kristin:** You'd like everyone to get on board at the beginning of a project and agree. "Here's what we're doing, and here's the road map we're following." It's like when you get on an airplane and they announce, "This is the plane going to Spokane." Every once in a while you hear somebody say, "Spokane!? That's not where I'm headed." And they grab their stuff and get out of there. If they have any sense, they're glad the airline makes this announcement on every flight.

> **Matt:** I hear you. We spend our time discussing why a project exploded rather than spend a fraction of that time up front to ensure that it doesn't explode!

> **Kristin:** The problem we run into all the time is that acquirers focus on "Let's get going" and don't spend a day or an hour to establish an integrated plan that gets us closer to successfully executing the project. This situation is aggravated when we start a project and the acquirer's program manager says, "I didn't know the supplier agreement said that." Um, have you ever read the agreement? I'll tell you, the worst is when they say, "Well no, I don't even have a copy of it. Why would I? That's what purchasing is for." Yikes! That's when you know you're in trouble.

Involving all stakeholders throughout the project is critical.

> **TIP** Be persistent when it comes to ensuring that all the right stakeholders are engaged and accountable.

Paula: The stakeholders need to be involved. If they're not, we need to stop a project until we get them involved across the board. Otherwise, they'll show up when it's time to go live with the technical solution. Then you'll get their ideas, intentions, and requirements.

Steve laughs.

Steve: And then you get to start the project over—believe me, you don't want to be that project manager.

This gets tricky in a large organization where lots of tasks are delegated. For instance, some of our systems are fairly complex. They require big changes in business processes at the site where the system will be installed. If you don't engage the right stakeholders from that specific site, you get to the end of your project and then find out this is not what they wanted.

Depending on the scope and risk of the project, your coordination effort among stakeholders and with the supplier can be significant. To integrate the effort across functions and suppliers, you need to add specific activities that support cross-functional work. For example, a supplier might build prototypes to support your desire to develop richer customer understanding early in the process. To complete the loop, the supplier participates with your personnel when interacting with customers to strengthen and deepen their understanding of the experience that the product will create.

The supplier aligns its system delivery processes with your acquisition processes early in the project and, if necessary, collaborates with you to tailor processes. Moreover, prototype testing and evaluation are conducted jointly by all the functions involved in development.

All these interactions happen only when an integrated plan is in place that establishes clear accountability. George offers a comment.

George: What finally made it work was when Steve came on the scene and demanded the accountability of all players—his project team and all the suppliers. He insisted on everybody understanding their role and accountabilities, along with the accountability of every other role on the project. That's what Steve does so well.

Kristin: At every meeting, Steve went around the room and everyone had to give their yes or no on the decisions and their level of confidence that the decision would be carried out successfully. People don't like to do that. In any case, Steve's message was clear: If you didn't feel accountable, you'd be gone.

4.1.2 Applying the CMMI-ACQ to Integrated Project Management

The CMMI-ACQ provides specific processes for handling difficulties you might have with integrated project work. It attacks problems at their root and starts you on a path to improving your project execution. The Integrated Project Management process area focuses on establishing and managing projects and involving the relevant stakeholders according to an integrated and defined process that is tailored from your organization's set of standard processes (see Table 4-1).

According to the CMMI-ACQ, a project's defined process addresses all activities, tasks, templates, procedures, and guidelines that a project needs to execute to acquire and maintain the technology solution (Table 4-1, practice 1.1). The product-related life-cycle processes—for instance, support processes—are developed concurrently with the product. The project's defined process must satisfy the project's contractual and operational needs, opportunities, and constraints. A project's defined process is designed to provide a best fit for the project's needs and is based on the following factors:

1. Customer requirements
2. Product and component requirements
3. Commitments
4. Organizational process needs and objectives
5. Operational environment
6. Business environment

Project managers usually select a life-cycle model from those available in the organization's library of process assets. One approach is to contact another project manager who has executed a similar acquisition and who can help you select a subset of standard processes that best fit the needs of the project.

Some activities, templates, checklists, and guidelines might apply to a project only to some degree or in a modified form. Modifying the standard processes to fit a specific project is what we mean by tailoring. Typically, you provide tailoring guidelines to support the project when defining its processes. Some acquirers even provide "pretailored" versions to simplify and expedite tailoring.

Table 4-1 *Integrated Project Management Goal 1: Practices and Tips*

CMMI-ACQ Process Area: Integrated Project Management	
1. Goal: The project is conducted using a defined process that is tailored from the organization's set of standard processes.	
Practices	**Tips**
1.1 Establish and maintain the project's defined process.	• Working with the customer and supplier, tie plans to business or mission objectives. • Find out what works and then repeat—always.
1.2 Use the organizational process assets and measurement repository for estimating and planning the project's activities. 1.3 Establish and maintain the project's work environment based on the organization's work environment standards. 1.4 Integrate the project plan and the other plans that affect the project to describe the project's defined process. 1.5 Manage the project using the project plan, the other plans that affect the project, and the project's defined process. 1.6 Contribute work products, measures, and documented experiences to the organizational process assets.	• Size project buffers according to the risk of the project. • Synchronize early, and evolve technical constraints with the capability of the supply base. • Include your suppliers when you establish the project's work environment. • Stay focused on deploying the solution, and not just on developing it.

To develop a realistic plan, you must understand the relationships among the various tasks and work products of the defined process and the roles fulfilled by the stakeholders (Table 4-1, practice 1.2). When the results of previous planning and execution are available, use them as predictors of the relative scope and risk of the effort you're estimating. To arrive at accurate estimates during project planning, successful acquirers typically do the following:

- Use appropriate historical data from the current project or similar projects.
- Account for and record similarities and differences between the current project and the historical projects.
- Independently validate the historical data.
- Record the reasoning, assumptions, and rationale used to select the historical data.

To support the desired level of performance and reliability, it is critical to establish an appropriate work environment for the project (Table 4-1, practice 1.3). An appropriate work environment comprises the facilities, tools, and equipment people need to perform their jobs effectively. As with any other product, the critical aspects of the work environment are driven by requirements. You should explore the work environment's functionality and operations with the same rigor as you do for any other product development.

Depending on the scope of the outsourcing endeavor and the type of the technology solution, you might maintain your own environments for integrating, verifying, and validating the delivered technology solutions. Acquirers that productize and sell technology to their customers, or those that develop technology solutions in-house in addition to acquiring them, often prefer to establish their own integration and test environments. In contrast, organizations that rely solely on suppliers to provide (and maintain) technology solutions tend to hold their suppliers responsible for creating and maintaining integration and testing environments. This situation more closely resembles the purchase of commodities, where buyers pay to use the product but don't expend their own resources to ensure the product's quality.

Your integrated plan addresses additional planning activities such as incorporating the project's defined process, coordinating with relevant stakeholders, using organizational process assets, incorporating plans for peer reviews, and establishing objective entry and exit criteria for tasks (Table 4-1, practices 1.4–1.6). For you to continuously improve, projects must contribute to your process asset library, which documents lessons learned on projects and programs. Your process asset library is also a repository for storing process and product measures.

You manage and coordinate stakeholder involvement according to the project's integrated and defined process (see Table 4-2, practice 2.1). You manage the supplier's involvement according to the supplier agreement.

Acquirers conduct frequent reviews with stakeholders (Table 4-2, practice 2.2) and typically establish milestones for each critical dependency in the project schedule. Tracking the critical dependencies typically includes the following activities:

- Evaluating the impact of late and early completion on future activities and milestones
- Resolving actual and potential problems with the responsible parties whenever possible
- Escalating to the appropriate level the actual and potential problems not resolvable by the responsible individual or group

Inevitably, communication issues arise that require you to work even more closely with the stakeholders (Table 4-2, practice 2.3). In some cases, it might be necessary to escalate to the appropriate stakeholder managers any issues that cannot be resolved. You should anticipate this scenario and define clear, concise escalation procedures that are well understood by all stakeholders.

Table 4-2 *Integrated Project Management Goal 2: Practices and Tips*

CMMI-ACQ Process Area: Integrated Project Management	
2. Goal: Coordination and collaboration of the project with relevant stakeholders is conducted.	
Practices	**Tips**
2.1 Manage the involvement of the relevant stakeholders in the project.	• Be persistent when it comes to ensuring that all the right stakeholders are engaged and accountable.
2.2 Participate with relevant stakeholders to identify, negotiate, and track critical dependencies. 2.3 Resolve issues with relevant stakeholders.	• Size project buffers according to the risk of the project. • To achieve flexible, high-performance processes, maintain clearly defined, positive relationships with your suppliers. • Establish frequent, reinforcing feedback loops with customers and suppliers. • Establish and frequently convene acquirer-supplier forums or councils at all levels of the organization.

4.1.3 Where's Waldo?

Most people take configuration management (CM) for granted, but you will suffer great misery if your acquisition artifacts, products, and services aren't version controlled, stored, and easily accessible so that you can get to them when you need them. Only too quickly you will find yourself looking for the famous needle in the haystack.

> **Paula:** We're ready to kick off an enhancement project for the financial system. Where are all the artifacts we created for the last release? Where are the requirements specification, the release plans, the detailed design, the test cases and test results? Where is everything?

Steve, the project manager, wishes he hadn't picked up the phone. Now he's scrambling to answer Paula's piercing questions.

> **TIP** Treat configuration items as organizational assets, and tag them to the technical solution throughout its use.

> **Steve:** Give me a couple of hours, Paula, and I'll e-mail them to you.

After Steve snaps his cell phone shut, his face brightens. He thinks, "I'll call George Taylor." As the supplier's project manager, George delivered the first release of the financial system. Steve places the call.

> **Steve:** George, I need all the artifacts from the first release of the new financial system. Can you send them PDQ?

Silence greets Steve on the other end of the line. "Did I lose the connection?" he wonders. Finally George speaks.

> **George:** Well, as far as I can remember you kept the master copies. We have a policy to scrap all deliverables after the customer approves them.

Steve's heart sinks. He thinks, "I should've told Paula weeks, not hours. We'll have to conduct an archeological dig or, worse, re-create almost everything." He's determined to never let this happen again. He pulls together his team along with representatives from supplier organizations to discuss configuration management.

> **Steve:** Thanks for coming, everyone. We all know the purpose of configuration management. We want to establish and maintain the integrity of our acquirer work products and the solution. For every project, for every technical solution, we have to do some CM to maintain our documentation, and you suppliers have to do some to develop and operate

the technical solution. Let's define who's responsible for keeping what, and how we can store and retrieve project artifacts.

Your approach to configuration management depends on acquisition-specific factors such as the acquisition approach, the number of suppliers, the design responsibility, the support concept, and associated costs and risks. Configuration items can vary widely in complexity, size, and type, from COTS software to a test metric or project plan.

Steve: When we first tried to designate items for CM, we ended up with a long, long list. We all looked at each other. "What do we do now?" We didn't have the funds to apply rigorous CM to everything, nor does it make sense to carry this overhead for each program. In the end, the solution we came up with was simple and pragmatic—a kind of Occam's razor for CM. We designate only the minimum number of items we need to sustain a technical solution in the intended environment as configuration items. This resulted in very few acquirer-created items, and a well-defined list of supplier deliverables. For instance, on our side we concentrate on the requirements, design constraints, acceptance tests, and supplier agreement.

> **TIP**   Designate artifacts as configuration items only if they are necessary to maintain the technical solution.

Typically, any item required for product support and designated for separate procurement is a configuration item, along with acquirer work products provided to suppliers (for example, solicitation packages and technical standards). Paula, the internal customer for the current acquisition project, speaks up.

Paula: This approach to CM also made us rethink how we deal with information and data throughout the project life cycle. We used to be very document-centric. Our drive to minimize and reuse configuration items requires us to carefully examine whether a document is necessary or whether its content wouldn't be better stored in a database so that we can run a report to retrieve it. In other words, we now pursue a more data-centered approach.

> **TIP**   Control data at the source.

To avoid unexpected costs to procure, reformat, and receive configuration items from the supplier, you need to identify configuration items early and incorporate them into the integrated project plan. For acquirers, this includes considering how configuration items are shared between the acquirer and supplier and among relevant stakeholders. If you allow a supplier to use its CM system, you are responsible for implementing security and access control procedures. In many cases, an alternative solution is for the acquirer to grant physical possession of acquirer-created configuration items. In turn, the supplier gives the acquirer access to supplier deliverables.

> **TIP** Store configuration items with the responsible party and as close as possible to their primary use.

Steve: We heavily debated where to store our configuration items. Some folks started out with the belief that all items must be in our physical possession. Well, after we analyzed this, it turned out to be very costly and a bureaucratic nightmare. It would have created countless hand-offs, a complicated system of oversight, and multiple approvals for even the simplest transaction. In our multisupplier environment, this would have seriously impeded direct supplier-to-supplier interaction. Every transaction would have required us as the acquirer to serve as a middle layer to physically take possession of a supplier deliverable before it could be transferred from one supplier to the next.

Paula: That would have been a headache.

Steve: That's right. For instance, in my group we use one supplier to develop the technical solution and another set of suppliers to host and maintain it. The development supplier would have to work with a designated person on my staff to provide them with, let's say, the source code. That person would then have to provide the code to the hosting supplier. Any questions, issues, and interactions always required each supplier to interface with my acquisition team, who in turn would have to negotiate a set of action items on behalf of one supplier with another supplier.

Paula: A big hunk of time and resources.

Steve: So we said, "Why not encourage direct supplier-to-supplier interaction and only require acquirer approval when appropriate?" This way, my team could focus on more value-added activities. Eventually, all the acquisition teams agreed on an answer. First, no item is stored in more than one place. Keeping with the principle of storing a configuration item with the responsible party and as close as possible to its primary use, we also decided to keep many items with the suppliers, since they perform all development and maintenance work in our outsourced model. So in our own CM, we only store acquirer-created work-in-progress and sensitive deliverables. It's more of a document management system.

Paula: Yes, and suppliers are contractually required to maintain their work-in-progress documents, code, and supplier deliverables in their CM systems. The hosting and maintenance suppliers store the production version and required prior versions of the code and associated documents.

If a CM system is shared between acquirer and supplier, then the supplier agreement must specify the clear responsibility for managing the configuration items, baselines, security, access restrictions, and backup and restore processes. You must ensure that the supplier agreement specifies the CM requirements for the supplier (e.g., status reporting and providing configuration audit results).

The supplier agreement should also specify appropriate acquirer rights to the supplier deliverables, in addition to the requirements for delivery or access. For instance, you typically maintain the right to access configuration data at any level to implement planned or potential design changes and support options. Configuration management of legacy systems should be addressed on a case-by-case basis as design changes are contemplated.

> **TIP**   In the supplier agreement, clearly specify access and required security of the configuration management system.

When do you create a baseline for the configuration items? Steve ponders this question for a while.

> **TIP**   Tie baselines to project milestones and supplier payments.

Steve: You have to carefully decide when to lock down a set of items, because after you declare a baseline you can only adjust it through change control. You don't want to end up in change control hell, but you also don't want to baseline too late and lose all visibility into project activities and how artifacts develop and change.

Paula: How do you strike a happy medium?

Steve: Over the years, I've found it useful to tie baselines to major approvals or milestones in a project. For example, we create baselines for our own work products to mark agreement on the description of the project, requirements, funding, schedule, and performance parameters and to make a commitment to manage the program to those baselines. I'm talking about work products such as contractual requirements and acceptance criteria that are related to the product baseline managed by the supplier. We also review and approve the product baselines created by the supplier and contractually tie them to supplier payments.

With regard to the technical solution, you maintain configuration control of your requirements, and the supplier performs configuration management of the technical solution (e.g., establishing and maintaining the product baseline). In this way, you retain the authority and responsibility for approving any design changes that affect the product's ability to meet contractual requirements. The supplier manages other design changes.

> **TIP**   Use an artifact's value and its risk to the project to determine its required level of change control.

The level of control is typically selected based on project objectives, risk, and the value of the configuration item to the project. Levels of control can range from informal control (simply tracking changes made when you are developing the configuration items or when supplier work products are delivered or made accessible to you) to formal configuration control using baselines that can be changed only as part of a formal CM process. Although the supplier may manage configuration items on your behalf, you are responsible for approval and control of changes to such configuration items.

> **TIP**   Contractually institute change control for the supplier and acquirer.

Change requests can be initiated either by you or by the supplier. Changes that affect your work products and supplier deliverables as defined in the supplier agreement are typically handled through your CM process. You analyze the impact of submitted change requests on the supplier agreements.

> **Steve:**   All of our acquisition project teams and all of our suppliers have to follow the same change control process. The intent is to ensure smooth changes. The suppliers implement any requested changes, so we require them to log and track all changes in their area of responsibility. However, before work on a change request can begin, the change request must be approved by the relevant change control board. Each CCB consists of members from our organization, customers, and suppliers. The CCB ensures that all important viewpoints are considered when evaluating and prioritizing a change request.

4.1.4 Applying the CMMI-ACQ to Configuration Management

The CMMI-ACQ provides specific recommendations on how you can optimize configuration management as an acquirer of technology solutions. Configuration management specifically focuses on establishing and maintaining the integrity of work products using configuration identification, control, status accounting, and audits (see Table 4-3).

Table 4-3 *Configuration Management Goal 1: Practices and Tips*

CMMI-ACQ Process Area: Configuration Management	
1. Goal: Baselines of identified work products are established.	
Practices	**Tips**
1.1 Identify the configuration items, components, and related work products that will be placed under configuration management.	• Designate artifacts as configuration items only if they are necessary to maintain the technical solution. • Control data at the source.
1.2 Establish and maintain a configuration management and change management system for controlling work products.	• Store configuration items with the responsible party and as close as possible to their primary use. • In the supplier agreement, clearly specify access and required security of the configuration management system.
1.3 Create or release baselines for internal use and for delivery to the customer.	• Tie baselines to project milestones and supplier payments.

An acquirer typically designates work products or supplier deliverables as configuration items when they're critical to the project, are used by two or more groups, or are expected to change over time either because of errors or changes in requirements (Table 4-3, practice 1.1). Each configuration item has a responsible owner. In addition, each item has a unique identifier. Frequently, projects also specify important characteristics of each item for easier classification and retrieval.

To avoid unexpected costs to procure, reformat, and deliver configuration items from the supplier, you conduct your planning for managing configuration items—including during transition to operations and support—as part of project planning. Include plans and the infrastructure for managing these items within the project teams and between the acquirer, supplier, operational users, and other relevant stakeholders. You need to clearly define when each configuration item is placed under CM. Sample criteria include the following:

- Stage of the project life cycle
- Time when the acquirer work product is ready for review and approval

- Desired degree of control of the work product
- Cost and schedule limitations
- Customer requirements

To store configuration items with the responsible party and as close as possible to their primary use, you need to designate a CM system (Table 4-3, practice 1.2). Such a system describes the storage media, the procedures, and the tools for accessing the system. Sometimes this system also includes the tools for recording and accessing change requests. In addition to storing and retrieving configuration items, you include contractual provisions to ensure the necessary sharing and transfer of configuration items between you and the supplier.

You review and approve the release of the product baselines created by the supplier (Table 4-3, practice 1.3). A *baseline* is a set of specifications or work products that has been formally reviewed and agreed on. Thereafter it serves as the basis for further development or delivery and can be changed only through change control procedures. You also create baselines for acquirer work products to mark the agreement on the description of the project, requirements, funding, schedule, and performance parameters and to make a commitment to manage the program to those baselines. To create or release baselines of configuration items, a project must obtain authorization from the change control board.

Consistently tracking changes to baselined configuration items is critical for acquirer and supplier (see Table 4-4, practice 2.1). Change requests address not only new or changed requirements but also failures and defects in the work products. You analyze the impact that submitted change requests will have on the supplier agreements. You also determine the impact that the change will have on the work product, related work products, and schedule and cost.

Frequently, stakeholders request more changes than can be accommodated within a project. In this case, the change control board consults the relevant stakeholders and decides whether such change requests can be addressed in the next release of the solution; the stakeholders then agree to defer some the proposed changes. This negotiation includes keeping records of the disposition of each change request and the rationale for the decision, including success criteria, a brief action plan if appropriate, and needs met or not met by the change.

You maintain overall control of the configuration of the work product baseline (Table 4-4, practice 2.2). It's important to control changes to

Table 4-4 *Configuration Management Goal 2: Practices and Tips*

CMMI-ACQ Process Area: Configuration Management	
2. Goal: Changes to the work products under configuration management are tracked and controlled.	
Practices	**Tips**
2.1 Track change requests for the configuration items.	• Contractually institute change control for the supplier and acquirer.
2.2 Control changes to the configuration items.	• Use an artifact's value and its risk to the project to determine its required level of change control.

configuration items throughout the life of the product. This control includes tracking the version of each item, approving a new configuration of the solution if necessary, and updating the baseline. For example, authorization to access configuration items may come from the change control board, the project manager, or the customer. Only with the proper authorization are configuration items checked in or checked out of the CM system for review or modification. Changes must be incorporated in a manner that maintains the correctness and integrity of the items. In many cases, this requires reviews to ensure that changes do not cause unintended effects on the baselines (e.g., ensure that the changes have not compromised the safety or security of the system).

To establish and maintain the integrity of baselines, you record CM actions in sufficient detail that the content and status of each item is known and previous versions can be recovered (see Table 4-5, practice 3.1). In addition, projects can ensure the integrity of baselines by following these practices:

- Ensuring that relevant stakeholders have access to and knowledge of the configuration status of the items
- Specifying the latest version of the baselines
- Identifying the version of the configuration items that constitute a particular baseline
- Describing the differences between successive baselines
- Revising the status and history (i.e., changes and other actions) of each configuration item as necessary

Periodically, you perform configuration audits to confirm that the resulting baselines and documentation conform to a specified standard or require-

Table 4-5 *Configuration Management Goal 1: Practices and Tips*

CMMI-ACQ Process Area: Configuration Management	
3. Goal: Changes to the work products under configuration management are tracked and controlled.	
Practices	**Tips**
3.1 Establish and maintain records describing configuration items. 3.2 Perform configuration audits to maintain the integrity of the configuration baselines.	• Treat configuration items as organizational assets, and tag them to a technical solution throughout its use.

ment (Table 4-5, practice 3.2). The completeness and correctness of the content are based on the requirements as stated in the plan and the disposition of approved change requests.

4.2 Manage Project Risks

As an acquirer of technology solutions, you are still subject to the same business and technical risks that you had before the outsourcing deal. A supplier does not (and really cannot) take over liability for consequential damages. So the risk exists one way or another. To successfully execute a project, you must be able to accurately identify and proactively manage risks.

Throughout the life cycle of the project, you continue to manage the risks related to the supplier and the overall project risks. Both you and the supplier must understand the project risks and know how to modify the risk management strategy and plans as the project progresses. Managing a project's risks requires a close partnership between you and the supplier. Both organizations need to share risk management documentation and develop and execute risk management efforts.

4.2.1 Leave No Stone Unturned

Considering the track record of organizations that implement technology solutions, it is risky business. A variety of sources contributes to the risks that every acquirer must manage.

Steve: In my consulting days, I saw this all the time. The closer you get to the top of an organization—acquirer and supplier alike—the less likely people are to see a risk or its severity. They don't want to see it. It's the Icarus effect. When someone bears news of a potential risk, the leaders let them crash and burn. This kind of organization rewards fire-fighting, daily crisis management, and heroics to complete projects; it punishes people who try to explain why a project is at risk and try to prevent problems. So everybody learns that talking about risks is not condoned, and nobody will sound an alarm when they see a risk. Then bam! The company gets blindsided by critical problems they could have prevented.

Acquirers can't afford to possess this kind of attitude toward risk. To survive, you must be able to take rational risks. This means accepting the downside of a decision if the payoff is high enough.

> **TIP**   To avoid risk management blind spots, account for your organization's culture.

Steve: We have very strong support from our leadership team to bring risks forward and then use a structured risk management process to deal with them. We apply this process very early, rigorously, and continuously. It gives us a disciplined environment for decision making and for using resources efficiently.

> **TIP**   Carefully examine the acquirer-supplier relationship to detect risks.

By employing a disciplined process, acquirers can uncover risks before they occur so that risk-handling activities can be planned and invoked to mitigate adverse impacts on program objectives. The need for early and aggressive risk detection is compounded by the complexity of projects due to the acquirer-supplier relationship. For example, the supplier's experience of working with the acquirer, the supplier's financial stability, or the availability of well-defined dispute resolution processes all influence the risk of a project.

> **TIP**   Always document risks, and keep them visible to the project stakeholders.

Because of the inherent risks of projects attempting to produce a technology solution, especially in an outsourcing environment, it is paramount for any acquirer to document the risks and make them visible. It's much harder to ignore a risk if it's documented. Unfortunately, this task is fraught with peril. Your mind can play tricks on you when it comes to admitting risks. Steve explains.

> **Steve:**   We've built special provisions into our process to make suppliers, projects, and senior managers aware of risks and to compensate for any mind traps. For example, all employees and suppliers are encouraged to always view a project from different perspectives. We never accept the initial definition of a project or program.

> **Matt:**   Can you give an example?

> **Steve:**   We always try to reframe the problem in various ways. For instance, we pose problems in a neutral, redundant way that combines possible gains and losses, and then we elicit and embrace viewpoints from different stakeholders. The goal is to think about the full context of the project so that we're less likely to disregard important data. This also helps us in creating recommendations that don't have contradictory data or hidden risks. We train our employees as well as our suppliers to play devil's advocate. What if our approach is wrong? How would we know?
>
>   For important projects, the teams must bring in an outsider. This person must help the team dispel the disproportionate weight they tend to give to their own biases and the initial impressions formed about the nature of the risk. All this helps us to better judge our risks.

A simple risk assessment works well when a project possesses little data. Typically this is the case when an organization initially establishes an acquisition strategy. As a project or program progresses, however, greater knowledge justifies more detailed risk analysis.

TIP   Continuously probe for risks throughout the project's life cycle.

> **Steve:**   We use a risk scorecard and update it regularly based on lessons learned over time. If a project goes into the ditch, you do a post-mortem and ask questions: Why did this happen? What could we have done differently to avoid this? And then you incorporate the findings into your risk scorecard.

As you gain experience with the simple risk assessment, you can develop a risk scorecard based on the ten-question risk analysis presented in Chapter 2. This extended question set (see Figure 4-1) has weights or level of impact for each parameter.

Degree of Established Supplier Network for Delivering the Product or Service	Rating		Impact		Score
Rating Guidelines: 1 = Strongly Agree, 10 = Strongly Disagree					
Impact Guidelines: 1 = Negligible, 10 = Vital					
Does the supplier have experience working with our organization?		×		=	
Does the supplier have significant experience with the technology?		×		=	
Does the supplier have a well-defined and institutionalized development process?		×		=	
Do all vendors have qualified resources to handle the project?		×		=	
Is the supplier financially stable?		×		=	
• • •	• • •		• • •		• • •
Risk Score					

Figure 4-1 *Sample risk assessment*

Instead of intuitively assigning a score for each risk parameter, the project team can formulate and answer a series of detailed questions that produce a score. Additionally, the project team may know that some parameters affect overall risk more than others.

TIP Use structured ways to quantify risks.

Steve: With a risk scorecard, your objective is to quantify the risks you identify. This gives us a deeper, common understanding of the risks and their severity.

The questions, their ratings, and the level of impact reflect an organization's current capabilities and areas of emphasis. These data will change as the acquisition strategy and core capabilities change. George agrees.

TIP Standardize documentation of risks to support quantitative analysis.

George: We keep a risk log or database, too. We've even established a standard format for risk statements: the underlying premise of a condition, and then the predicted consequence. For example, let's say you have the statement, "If the code base grows in size, we won't have enough memory." Well, that isn't a valid risk statement, because the precursor, which is code growth, isn't justified. To meet our format, it has to be something like, "On the last three projects executed by our department, final code size was an average of 147 percent above initial estimates; similar results on this project will exceed memory capacity." See the difference?

4.2.2 Applying the CMMI-ACQ to Risk Management

The CMMI-ACQ provides specific recommendations on how to identify and analyze risks. Risk management identifies potential problems before they occur so that you can plan and invoke risk-handling activities as needed throughout the life of the product to mitigate adverse impacts on achieving objectives (see Table 4-6).

Analyzing risks entails identifying risks from internal and external sources and then evaluating each risk to determine its likelihood and consequences. Identifying potential issues, hazards, threats, and vulnerabilities that could negatively affect work efforts or plans is the basis for sound and successful

Table 4-6 *Risk Management Goal 2: Practices and Tips*

CMMI-ACQ Process Area: Risk Management	
2. Goal: Risks are identified and analyzed to determine their relative importance.	
Practices	**Tips**
2.1 Identify and document the risks.	• To avoid risk management blind spots, account for your organization's culture. • Carefully examine the acquirer-supplier relationship to detect risks. • Always document risks, and keep them visible to the project stakeholders. • Continuously probe for risks throughout the project's life cycle.
2.2 Evaluate and categorize each identified risk using the defined risk categories and parameters, and determine its relative priority.	• Use structured ways to quantify risks. • Standardize documentation of risks to support quantitative analysis.

risk management (Table 4-6, practice 2.1). Risks must be identified and described in an understandable, consistent way before they can be analyzed and managed properly. Risks are documented in a concise statement that includes the context, conditions, and consequences if the risk occurs.

You should follow an organized, thorough approach to seek out probable or realistic risks that might affect your achieving your objectives. To be effective, risk identification should not be an attempt to address every possible event no matter how improbable it may be. Instead, you should follow a disciplined, streamlined approach that uses the categories and parameters developed in your risk management strategy, along with the identified sources of risk. The identified risks form a baseline on which to initiate risk management activities. You should periodically review the list of risks to reexamine possible sources of risk and changing conditions and thereby uncover sources and risks previously overlooked or nonexistent when the risk management strategy was last updated.

Typical methods for identifying risks include the following:

- Examine each element of the project work breakdown structure to uncover risks.
- Conduct an informal risk assessment using, for instance, a risk taxonomy.
- Interview subject matter experts.
- Review risk management efforts from similar projects or programs.
- Examine lessons-learned documents or databases.
- Examine design specifications and agreement requirements.

You can identify some risks by using the categories and parameters developed in your risk management strategy to examine the supplier's work breakdown structure, product, and processes. You can identify risks in many areas (e.g., requirements, technology, design, testing, vulnerability to threats, life-cycle costs). Examining the project or program in each of these areas can help you develop or refine the acquisition strategy and the risk-sharing structure between you and the supplier.

You should also consider the risks associated with a supplier's capability (e.g., meeting schedule and cost requirements), including the potential risks to your intellectual capital or security vulnerabilities introduced by using a supplier.

Certain kinds of risks are often missed. These include risks thought to be outside the scope of the project; in fact, even though the project does not control whether they occur, you can mitigate their impact. Examples include the weather, natural or manmade disasters that affect the continuity of operations, political changes, and telecommunications failures.

To the extent that they affect project objectives, cost, schedule, and performance, risks should be examined during all phases of the product life cycle in the intended environment. You may discover potential risks that are outside the scope of the project's objectives but are vital to customer interests. For example, the risks in development costs, product acquisition costs, cost of spare (or replacement) products, and product disposition (or disposal) costs have design implications. The customer may not have provided requirements for the cost of supporting the fielded product. The customer should be informed of such risks, but it may not be necessary to actively manage those risks. The mechanisms for making such decisions should be examined at project and organization levels and put in place if deemed appropriate, especially for risks that affect the ability to verify and validate the product.

Risk statements are typically documented in a standard format that contains the risk context, conditions, and consequences. The risk context provides additional information so that the intent of the risk can be easily understood. In documenting the context of the risk, you should consider the relative time frame, the circumstances or conditions, and any doubt or uncertainty.

You need to evaluate risks so that you can assign relative importance to each identified risk and determine when appropriate management attention is required (Table 4-6, practice 2.2). Each risk is evaluated and assigned values in accordance with the defined risk parameters, which may include likelihood, consequence (severity of impact), and thresholds. You can integrate the assigned risk parameter values to produce additional measures, such as risk exposure, which can be used to prioritize risks. Often it is useful to aggregate risks based on their interrelationships and then develop options at an aggregate level. When you form an aggregate risk by rolling up lower-level risks, take care that important lower-level risks are not ignored.

You categorize risks into defined risk categories, providing a means to view risks according to their source, taxonomy, or project component. Related or equivalent risks can be grouped for efficient handling. You should document the cause-and-effect relationships between related risks. Your risk categories might include sourcing, contract management, and supplier execution in addition to project management, technology, and requirements.

Acquirers prioritize risks for mitigation. You use clear criteria to determine a relative priority for each risk based on the assigned risk parameters. Your goal is to determine the areas to which risk mitigation resources can be applied with the greatest positive impact to the project or program.

4.2.3 Keep Close Tabs on Risks

Risks are handled and mitigated, when appropriate, to reduce adverse effects on achieving your objectives.

> **TIP** Focus on the few critical risks that significantly affect the project or program.

> **Steve:** You can't fix everything! You have to ask as objectively as possible, "Which risks are truly important?" You must identify critical risks and watch them for significant changes.

You first identify the most important risks and then decide how many of them you have the resources to mitigate.

> **Steve:** When we decided to get serious about risk management, we started small. I guess you could say this is a risk mitigation approach of sorts. We had already learned that teams new to risk management have trouble dealing with more than ten risks. So we helped each project identify and handle their top ten risks. They periodically reorder their risks by voting or through forced ranking. It's based on the team's consensus about the most important parameter at the time, like quality or cost.

You must identify which risks can be accepted (that is, you can live with them if they do become problematic) and which risks can be assigned to someone who is better able to manage them.

> **Steve:** We look at this throughout the project. Most projects use a quick-and-dirty estimate to classify each risk as high, medium, and low impact. Unless the risk has a big impact, such as doubling the budget to deliver this solution, we make it clear to all projects that they really don't need to quantify impact and probability early. For example, one group filtered out the top five risks for precise analysis during risk planning, and they managed the other risks without further analysis.

> **Matt:** We should emphasize, though, that this doesn't negate a project's responsibility to perform risk management as a continuous activity throughout the project life cycle. It's really helpful to review risks at every regular project meeting. You may get to retire some risks, or you identify new risks that make it onto your top-ten risk list.

Paula adds an important point.

> **TIP** To establish comprehensive risk mitigation plans, involve suppliers.

Paula: I'm big on risk reporting—throughout the project, up the chain of command, down the chain of command, and any which way you can go on the org chart. I've seen many projects put together a 5×5 risk matrix color-coded in red, yellow, and green. This is a great practice, but only if the content is up-to-date. It's a warning sign—I guess you could say it's a risk in itself—if a project only updates the risk matrix at the last minute once every three or six months, and coincidentally right before a major program review. That's just nuts. You can be assured that we've developed an arsenal of probing questions about risks to encourage projects to adjust their behavior if necessary and treat risk management as a continuous activity.

The ultimate responsibility for risk management rests with you, but a close partnership between you and your suppliers is crucial if you are to effectively identify and mitigate risks. Both you and the supplier need to share risk information, understand each other's risk assessments, and develop and execute risk mitigation efforts. You must involve the supplier as early as possible so that you can establish effective risk assessment and reduction. For instance, the supplier has often much deeper insight into the technical risks than you have.

Kristin: Forming a joint acquirer-supplier risk evaluation team is a good way of fostering an effective partnership. This is especially true in the early days of a program, when uncertainty is high and both parties must frequently assess risks. Together with you guys, we form a joint team of subject matter experts who can evaluate the proposed program in detail to identify risks and propose strategies when necessary.

You need to include specific risk assessment and risk-handling tasks in the RFP and subsequent supplier agreement.

> **TIP**   Mitigate risks to reduce uncertainty and to increase the likelihood of success.

The progress of project activities should lower the project's perceived risk. In fact, when an organization pursues any new technical solution, it must deliberately acquire competencies to reduce risk and ensure success. If successive reviews demonstrate steady or rising project risk, it sends a strong signal that you need to reexamine the project's viability. In contrast, steadily decreasing risk increases your confidence of a successful outcome. A properly designed and executed risk management process lets you make decisions about the fate of a project, thereby enabling you to make intelligent bets. In general, acquirers are better off receiving risk information early, because it gives them an opportunity to decrease the downside and raise the upside.

> **TIP**   Reduce risks through prototyping and reuse of technology solutions.

Matt: You want to increase your odds. Smart risk mitigation puts you in a position to place your bets anew after projects clear a common milestone. As uncertainties decrease, expenditures can rise and risk is managed.

Steve: We've identified a couple of techniques to get a leg up on mitigating risks. One of the most breathtaking successes also turned out to be the simplest. You don't have to have a new technical solution to effectively resolve business or mission risk. You can use a competitor's product or a modified version of the product to gauge the customer's intent. This will teach you quickly if you're solving the right problem. When we pursue a COTS solution, we take it one step further and use the COTS product as the prototype. Given that we stand the COTS solution up in our hosting environment, this also doubles as an early technical evaluation of the supplier's product. Prototyping also lets you pick a particularly risky aspect or attribute of the technical solution and expose it to the customers to find out what they really want.

Moving fast is an additional risk mitigation technique commonly used by successful acquirers.

> **TIP**   Size projects small enough to avoid delivery of outdated solutions.

George: One of the difficulties we ran into with an acquirer was the program manager. She really wanted a big-bang approach—delivering a large chunk of new technology after it was in development for years. We spent a lot of time in highly emotional debates. Of course, we wanted a more phased approach to minimize risk to the business. All this changed when we started working with Steve. He understood exactly what we were saying, and actually drove us toward a more evolutionary, iterative approach. So, you really have to understand the risk to the business, and you have to look at your solution and how you could possibly roll it out and manage the change that's going to happen. I think this is a critical part of any project.

Controlling the technical risk of integration should be at the forefront of any acquirer's mind: How do you ensure that the suppliers integrate the various components into a value-added solution and then integrate the technical solution into your environment? Steve has a couple of ideas.

> **TIP**   Standardize the riskiest interfaces of technology solutions.

Steve: Like I always say, the more you can make the technology plug-and-play, the better off you'll be. We work hard on standardizing interfaces between systems so we can reuse them over and over again. We've also learned the hard way that you have to focus your energy on those pieces of the solution that really matter. So we specify tighter design constraints for the riskiest interfaces or parts, and give the supplier more leeway on lower-impact components. We also work with our suppliers to integrate solutions as early as possible. As soon as the suppliers have more than one component, the prime supplier forges them into a system weekly, if not daily.

When you close a risk, you document the rationale for closing it, along with successful and unsuccessful actions, assumptions that were proven wrong, mitigation costs, and project savings or return on investment.

> **TIP** Store project risk data in an organizational database.

Steve: We retain risk information in a database after the risks are closed. This information is a tremendous benefit to the organization on future projects.

4.2.4 Applying the CMMI-ACQ to Handling Risks

The CMMI-ACQ provides specific recommendations on how to handle risks, including developing risk-handling options, monitoring risks, and performing risk-handling activities when defined thresholds are exceeded (see Table 4-7).

You develop and implement risk mitigation plans for selected risks to proactively reduce their potential impact. A critical component of a risk mitigation plan is to develop alternative courses of action, workarounds, and fallback positions, with a recommended course of action for each critical risk (Table 4-7, practice 3.1). The risk mitigation plan for a given risk includes techniques and methods to avoid, reduce, and control the probability of occurrence, the extent of damage incurred should the risk occur (sometimes called a *contingency plan*), or both. You monitor risks, and when they exceed the established thresholds, you deploy the risk mitigation plans to return the affected effort to an acceptable risk level. If the risk cannot be mitigated, a contingency plan can be invoked. Both risk mitigation and contingency plans are often generated only for selected risks whose consequences are determined to be high or unacceptable; other risks may be accepted and simply monitored.

Options for handling risks typically include alternatives such as the following:

Table 4-7 *Risk Management Goal 3: Practices and Tips*

CMMI-ACQ Process Area: Risk Management	
3. Goal: Risks are handled and mitigated, where appropriate, to reduce adverse impacts on achieving objectives.	
Practices	**Tips**
3.1 Develop a risk mitigation plan for the most important risks to the project, as defined by the risk management strategy.	• To establish comprehensive risk mitigation plans, involve suppliers. • Focus on the few critical risks that significantly affect the project or program. • Mitigate risks to reduce uncertainty and to increase the likelihood of success.
3.2 Monitor the status of each risk periodically, and implement the risk mitigation plan as appropriate.	• Reduce risks through prototyping and reuse of technology solutions. • Size projects small enough to avoid delivery of outdated solutions. • Standardize the riskiest interfaces of technology solutions. • Store project risk data in an organizational database.

- Risk avoidance: changing or lowering requirements while still meeting the customer's needs
- Risk control: taking active steps to minimize risks
- Risk transfer: reallocating requirements to lower the risks
- Risk monitoring: watching and periodically reevaluating the risk for changes to the assigned risk parameters
- Risk acceptance: acknowledging risk but taking no action

Often, especially for high risks, you should generate more than one approach.

In many cases, risks are accepted or watched. Usually you accept a risk when you judge it too unimportant for formal mitigation, or when there appears to be no viable way to reduce it. If a risk is accepted, the rationale for this decision should be documented. Risks are watched when there is an objectively defined, verifiable, and documented threshold of performance, time, or risk exposure (the combination of likelihood and consequence) that will trigger risk mitigation planning or invoke a contingency plan if it is needed. Thresholds for supplier risks that affect the project (e.g., schedule, quality, or risk exposure due to supplier risks) are specified in the supplier agreement, along with escalation actions if the thresholds are exceeded.

Examine risk mitigation activities and assess the benefits they provide versus the resources they will expend. As with any other project activity, you may need to develop alternative plans and assess the costs and benefits of each alternative. You then select the most appropriate plan for implementation. At times the risk activity may be significant and the benefit small, but the risk must be mitigated to reduce the probability of incurring unacceptable consequences.

To effectively control and manage risks during the work effort, follow a proactive program to regularly monitor risks and the status and results of risk-handling actions (Table 4-7, practice 3.2). For that purpose, you establish a schedule or period of performance for each risk-handling activity that includes the start date and anticipated completion date. This requires continued commitment of resources for each plan.

The risk management strategy defines the intervals at which the risk status should be revisited. This activity may result in the discovery of new risks or new risk-handling options that can require replanning and reassessment. In either event, you should compare the acceptability thresholds associated with the risk against the status to determine the need for implementing a risk mitigation plan.

You share selected risks with the supplier. Risks associated specifically with the acquisition process are tracked and then resolved or controlled until mitigated. This monitoring includes risks that may be escalated by the supplier.

4.3 Measure for Success

Every acquirer uses measures; at a minimum, acquirers of technology solutions count their money. Measures provide data for making decisions and describe the results of those decisions. Measurement is the process that tells an organization how well it is doing what it wants to do. Commonly used measures are geared toward measuring current performance. When you are delivering projects, however, the concern is future performance. Decisions made today are tomorrow's results.

You need measurement systems that can indicate the expected future results so that you can make appropriate interventions in the present. An effective measurement system monitors individual projects, a program or portfolio of projects, and the process by which they are managed.

As you become more familiar with the concepts that are developed and illustrated in the pages that follow, you need to understand that the perfect process for measuring the success of technology solutions is as yet unknown.

The remainder of this chapter describes in detail a current best practice for an acquirer to develop and maintain a measurement capability that enables it to determine the status of its progress and output, the supplier's progress and output per contractual requirements, and the status of the evolving acquired products. It also covers monitoring and control of your own activities and overseeing the progress and performance of the supplier's execution according to the project plans.

4.3.1 The House of Measures

To effectively manage projects, you must have the necessary data or information at your fingertips when you need it. For many organizations, reaching this goal proves elusive. Matt, however, no longer worries about the usual disconnect between the data an acquirer needs to run its business and the data an acquirer has available to make decisions. Matt has what he calls the "House of Measures." Like an instrument panel in a car, the House of Measures provides critical information in easy-to-read graphics, assembled from data extracted in real time from the acquirer's measurement databases and, in some instances, directly from the suppliers' measurement repositories. Let's see how the House of Measures is built.

> **Matt:**   Before we had the House of Measures, taking our pulse was sort of ridiculous. To get the latest project delivery numbers, I would call several people and wait for days—sometimes weeks—for them to compile reports that were out of date by the time they hit my desk. Sometimes it was even worse. We didn't even have the data collected to answer a basic question about our business. You had to work on guesswork alone, with no real-time data to put you in touch with your business.

Before you can decide what the right measures are, you need to decide what to measure.

> **Matt:**   You have to be perfectly clear about the purpose of your endeavor. We're interested in achieving our economic goals. Our goal is to make money in the end. We acquire software, systems, and IT for this purpose and for this purpose only. We can never forget that. Every action every day is subordinated to achieving our purpose. To keep on track, we have to have measures that let us judge the impact of our decisions. We need to know what levers we need to pull to stay the course or to get back in the fast lane.

Without the right measures, you can start pulling the wrong levers—to use Matt's analogy—and you go out of business even though all indicators show green, full steam ahead into the abyss.

> **TIP** Specify measures that drive actions that allow you to achieve your goals.

Creating a good, precise set of measures to predict your success is difficult. It is often difficult to get consensus on how to measure the achievement of acquisition goals and the authoritative source for the measure. Yet getting buy in of key stakeholders and constituents is critical in obtaining a meaningful measurement of project execution. It is equally important to manage this process so that you end up with the few critical measures that truly matter.

> **TIP** Assemble a minimal set of integrated measures.

Steve: Don't make too many measures, or you'll cause what I call "metrics saturation." You can't just sprinkle measures like fairy dust over your processes. You have to get your hands on what makes a difference in the overall objective. If projects have to deal with a handful of measures they tend to do very well. If they have to deal with—let's say—110 metrics, they lose focus. Everything becomes critical, but nothing is important. At best, projects will probably rate "mediocre" in every one of those 110 metrics. So metrics saturation obscures your vision. The project manager loses his focus on the project itself. He starts to worry more about how the metrics are reported and interpreted by management.

So how do you arrive at the few critical measures? Acquiring software, systems, and IT, like any other business activity, works best with timely feedback. Such feedback indicates how a process is functioning and signals the need for intervention. Short-duration, repetitive processes, which are common in manufacturing environments, provide ample opportunities for measuring their efficacy through demonstrated results. But acquisition projects have comparatively long lead times and unrepetitive tasks, and that poses difficulties for acquirers that manage with results data only. You cannot afford to receive status reports only at the completion of a project or significant milestone; you need interim feedback. You must manage the acquisition process itself through results or output measures and progress measures.

Outcome metrics characterize activities' results by describing how well objectives are accomplished. *Progress metrics,* in contrast, characterize the current status of activities that are not yet complete. Outcome metrics allow you to look in the rearview mirror. They describe after-the-fact results, whereas progress metrics enable intervention that can affect results.

> **TIP** Require a balanced mix of outcome and progress measures.

To get a balanced mix of outcome and progress measures, you need to get a handle on how to use supplier measures. To manage projects, you use supplier-reported measures in addition to your own measures of progress and output. The addition of supplier measures allows you to comprehensively address the measurement objectives and determine the progress and output of the project. Supplier measures are the foundation of the House of Measures (see Figure 4-2).

To build a solid foundation for the House of Measures, you should use accepted standards within the industry when defining measures that the supplier reports to you.

TIP Use standards for defining and selecting supplier measures.

Kristin: It's frustrating to me—and I believe to every supplier or acquirer—that there is so much variance in the definition and interpretation of measures. Here's an analogy. Let's say you take a business trip and want to work out at the hotel's gym, but first you want to weigh

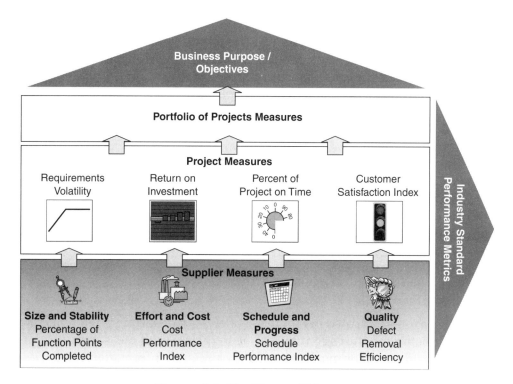

Figure 4-2 *The House of Measures*

yourself. "Not so fast," the gym manager says. "First you have to attend our three-day workshop to define the right measure for your needs. Pounds? Grams? Furlongs per fortnight?"

Nobody would accept this in today's world. Yet, here we are in the technology space redefining the same measures over and over again. Different organizations set up different ways of calculating what "on time" means, what "on budget" means, what "quality" means. One might determine their on-time metric by taking all the projects that have been performed and all the dates and hours that have been allocated. Then they'll roll up the data and take it and divide one into another to say that we're actually within 5 percent, or we're not. Another company will use a completely different calculation.

Steve: How do you deal with that?

Kristin: We actually show acquirers our measurement framework. We share with them the calculations, the terminology, the way they can roll them up. We're trying to get them to move to a more standard set of measures.

> **TIP**   Carefully specify supplier measures in the supplier agreement.

Let's hope that enough acquirers and suppliers adopt a common set of measurement definitions to increase the efficiency of acquiring technology solutions. However, standard or not, supplier measures must be defined in the supplier agreement. The agreement specifies which measurement data the supplier must provide, in what format, how the data will be collected and stored by the supplier (e.g., a retention period for data), how and how often it will be transferred to the acquirer, and who will have access to the data. Some suppliers may consider some of their data proprietary, so you may need to protect it. Also consider that some of your measurement data (e.g., total project cost data) may be proprietary and should not be shared with suppliers. You need to plan for the collection, storage, and access control of these types of sensitive data.

> **TIP**   Specify measures for project schedule and progress, effort and cost, size and stability, and quality.

Several measures indicated in Figure 4-2 offer a good starting point while the search for better measures continues. The regularly used measures can typically be traced to one or more of these measurement information categories: schedule and progress, effort and cost, size and stability, and quality.

Kristin: There's a lot of dissent—or lack of credibility, one could say—about how to measure output. Let me give you an analogy. Let's say you measure your progress over three years. You need to produce 5 tomatoes this year, 10 next year, and 15 the year after that. So now you're in year 3, and it looks like you've tripled your output. That's terrific. But wait a minute. You also need to look at your units of energy in producing those tomatoes. If your—let's call it—"effort measure" stayed consistent for those three years, then you have indeed tripled your output. But both measures are useless if you don't have a quality metric to verify that the tomatoes produced in year 3 are just as good or better than those from year 1, or at least approaching the same levels of quality. All four of those measures—schedule or progress, quality, effort to deliver, and size—have to be there.

It's frustrating when there is no accepted measure of size.

Kristin: In our organization, we don't have a good and commonly agreed-upon size measure. We use function points, and I'm very function-point biased, but purely because it's the only measure we've got that has a widely adopted industry standard, an active community, and a credible following. Even if you don't use formal function-point counters, you're better off. For instance, we use an informal tool that collects the basic parameters for function-point counting. It's a way for us to say to the team, "When you're working with an acquirer, you run this Web-based tool and understand the approximate size of what you're delivering." In the next release you use it again, and in the release after that you do the same thing. Over a year, you can go back to a customer and say, "Look, each request that you've done has averaged out to be this size, and we've improved in these ways as we've gone forward," as opposed to having no idea about size.

TIP Insist on a size measure.

Measures can be either base or derived. Data for *base* measures are obtained by direct measurement. Data for *derived* measures come from combining the results of two or more base measures. Derived measures are typically expressed as ratios, composite indices, or other aggregate summaries. Often, summary measures are more quantitatively reliable and meaningful than the base measures from which they're derived. A direct relationship exists between measurement objectives, measurement categories, base measures, and derived measures, as depicted in Table 4-8.

Table 4-8 *Measurement Examples*

Sample Measurement Objectives	Measurement Information Categories	Sample Base Measures	Sample Derived Measures
Shorter time to delivery	Schedule and Progress	• Estimated and Actual Start and End Dates by Task • Estimated and Actual Start and End Dates of Acquisition Tasks	• Percentage of Project on Time • Schedule Performance Index • Schedule Estimation Accuracy
Reduced total life-cycle cost	Effort and Cost	• Estimated and Actual Effort Hours • Estimated and Actual Cost	• Return on Investment • Cost Performance Index
Deliver specified functionality completely	Size and Stability	• Function-Points Count • Lines of Code Count • Requirements Count	• Requirements Volatility • Percentage of Function Points Completed • Size Estimation Accuracy • Amount of New, Modified, and Reused Code
Improve levels of quality	Quality	• Product Defects Count • Customer Satisfaction Survey Scores • Supplier Performance and Relationship Scores	• Customer Satisfaction Index • Defect Removal Efficiency • Number of Defects Per Phase • Total Unresolved Defects • Supplier Performance and Relationship Trends

In some cases, you augment your measures with supplier measures. For instance, your return on investment metric can incorporate the supplier's cost performance index. In most cases, however, the suppliers' measures are the primary source of data, especially with regard to the development of the acquired product or service. For instance, for effective management of the project's quality, size, cost, and schedule, it's essential to measure and analyze the supplier-provided product or components by using technical performance measures (e.g., amount of new, modified, reused code; percentage of function points completed; defect removal efficiency).

> **TIP** Thoroughly define how supplier measures, as a key source of data, fit with acquirer measures.

Steve: For each of our significant differentiators [see Chapter 3], we quantitatively define targeted goals, identify the units and methods of measurement, and quantitatively track progress in achieving those goals over time. This also shows us how good a product or service is in satisfying the customer's needs relative to how those needs are being satisfied today.

Matt: That's a meaningful number. How do you arrive at it?

Steve: We quantify the differentiators in 5 to 15 parameters. The parameters depend on the differentiators, with one exception: All projects have cost as one of the parameters. We get the cost from those elements that make up the cost of the product rather than relying on its "accounting" value.

So for each parameter, our starting point is established, quantified, and compared to the target. Where possible, we also determine the relative rating of any competitive product and the best value that is theoretically or practically achievable. The gap between the theoretical value and our starting point also give us an indication of a project's technical risk. This gap analysis is not a one-time deal. You need to report the progress toward meeting the targets at each status report and project review.

Because you receive a significant amount of measurement data from the supplier, it is important that you periodically audit how the supplier collects and analyzes this data. The supplier agreement defines the required data analysis and the definition and examples of the measures the supplier must provide.

> **TIP** Establish practically achievable and theoretically possible (or stretch) targets for each measure.

TIP Periodically audit how data for measures is collected and analyzed.

Having pristine measurement data and project measures is a prerequisite, but it isn't sufficient for achieving long-term success. You must also consolidate project measures into a portfolio of project measures—program and organizational measures—that help illuminate to what degree you're accomplishing your purpose through your collection of projects.

TIP Ensure seamless roll-up of project to portfolio measures.

4.3.2 Applying the CMMI-ACQ to Measuring Your Projects

The CMMI-ACQ provides specific recommendations on how to develop and sustain a measurement capability to support management information needs (see Table 4-9).

To tightly integrate measurement and analysis into your processes, you specify the objectives of measurement and analysis so that they are aligned with identified information needs and project objectives (Table 4-9, practice 1.1).

Table 4-9 *Measurement and Analysis Goal 1: Practices and Tips*

CMMI-ACQ Process Area: Measurement and Analysis	
1. Goal: Measurement objectives and activities are aligned with identified information needs and objectives.	
Practices	**Tips**
1.1 Establish and maintain measurement objectives that are derived from identified information needs and objectives. 1.2 Specify measures to address the measurement objectives. 1.3 Specify how measurement data will be obtained and stored. 1.4 Specify how measurement data will be analyzed and reported.	• Specify measures that drive actions that allow you to achieve your goals. • Assemble a minimal set of integrated measures. • Specify measures for project schedule and progress, effort and cost, size and stability, and quality. • Use standards for defining and selecting supplier measures. • Carefully specify supplier measures in the supplier agreement.

Measurement objectives document the purposes of measurements and analyses and specify the kinds of actions that may be taken based on the results. You establish measurement objectives for your activities and work products as well as for supplier deliverables and milestones. Measurement objectives can range from "reduce time to delivery" to "reduce total life-cycle cost of the acquired technology solution" to "improve customer satisfaction." They must be documented, reviewed by management and other relevant stakeholders, and updated as necessary.

The measurement objectives are refined into specific measures. Candidate measures are categorized and specified by name and unit of measure. To manage projects, you use supplier data (base measures) and supplier-reported derived measures, in addition to measures of your own progress and output (Table 4-9, practice 1.2). Supplier measures must be defined in the supplier agreement, including requirements for the supplier's measurement collection and the measurement reports to be provided to you. When you specify supplier measures, it is particularly important to specify acceptance criteria for the data to ensure that the intended use of the supplier measures, such as aggregation and analysis by the acquirer, is feasible. To that end, you state measurement specifications in precise and unambiguous terms. They address the following two important criteria:

- Communication: What has been measured, how was it measured, what are the units of measure, and what has been included or excluded?
- Repeatability: Can the measurement be repeated, given the same definition, to get the same results?

It is equally important to clearly specify how measurement data will be obtained and stored (Table 4-9, practice 1.3). In other words, explicit specifications are made for how, where, and when the data will be collected and retained. You must ensure that appropriate mechanisms are in place to obtain measurement data from the supplier in a consistent way—for instance, how data is to be transferred from the supplier to you. It is critical for you to insist in the supplier agreement on accurate data collection by the supplier. This includes requiring the use of applicable standard report formats and tools for reporting by the supplier.

It's also critical to clearly define in advance how the measures will be used (Table 4-9, practice 1.4). The analyses must explicitly address the documented measurement objectives, and the results of the measurement analyses must be clearly understandable by its intended audiences. Just as the need for measurement drives data analysis, clarification of analysis criteria can affect the measures in use. Specifications for some measures may be refined further based on the data analysis procedures.

4.3.3 Applying the CMMI-ACQ to Developing Project Measures

The CMMI-ACQ provides specific recommendations on how to develop and sustain a measurement capability that is tied to information needs and the objectives of the project or program (see Table 4-10).

The proof is in the pudding. You must be able to obtain specified measurement data (Table 4-10, practice 2.1). This requires the use of checks and balances to verify the completeness and integrity of acquirer and supplier measurement data. Checks can include scans for missing data, out-of-bounds data values, and unusual patterns and correlation across measures. Follow up with suppliers if data is not available or data checks indicate potential errors.

Rarely are the results of analyzing measurement data self-evident. For this reason, you use explicitly stated criteria for interpreting the results and drawing conclusions (Table 4-10, practice 2.2). Because suppliers provide important measurement data, it is paramount to discuss the results and preliminary conclusions with them. The results of planned analyses may suggest (or require) additional, unanticipated analyses. In addition, they may identify the need to refine existing measures, to calculate additional derived measures, or even to collect data for additional base measures to properly complete the planned analyses. Similarly, preparing the initial results for presentation may identify the need for additional analyses.

Storing measurement-related data enables the timely and cost-effective future use of historical data and results (Table 4-10, practice 2.3). You protect measurement data provided by the supplier according to the terms outlined in the supplier agreement. The agreement might specify that you must restrict access of a supplier's measurement data to your employees only. Typically, you store the following measurement data:

- Measurement plans
- Specifications of measures
- Sets of data that have been collected
- Analysis reports and presentations
- Retention period for data stored
- Data acceptance criteria for supplier data

Data sets for derived measures can typically be recalculated and need not be stored. However, it may be appropriate to store summaries based on derived measures (e.g., charts, tables of results, or report prose). Results of interim analyses need not be stored separately if they can be efficiently reconstructed.

Table 4.10 *Measurement and Analysis Goal 2: Practices and Tips*

CMMI-ACQ Process Area: Measurement and Analysis	
2. Goal: Measurement results that address identified information needs and objectives are provided.	
Practices	**Tips**
2.1 Obtain specified measurement data. 2.2 Analyze and interpret measurement data. 2.3 Manage and store measurement data, measurement specifications, and analysis results. 2.4 Report results of measurement and analysis activities to all relevant stakeholders.	• Require a balanced mix of outcome and progress measures. • Ensure seamless roll-up of project to portfolio measures. • Periodically audit how data for measures is collected and analyzed.

Results are reported in a clear and concise manner so that they are understandable, easily interpretable, and clearly tied to identified information needs and objectives. For that purpose, you establish and maintain a standard format for communicating measurement data to stakeholders, including suppliers (Table 4-10, practice 2.4).

4.3.4 Applying the CMMI-ACQ to Using Data in Managing Processes

The CMMI-ACQ provides specific recommendations on how to quantitatively manage the project's defined process to achieve the project's established objectives for quality and process performance (see Table 4-11).

You establish the project's quantitative objectives for quality and process performance based on the objectives of the organization and the project's objectives (Table 4-11, practice 1.1). The quantitative quality and process performance objectives for the supplier are documented in the supplier agreement. You typically expect the supplier to execute its processes and apply its performance models to meet your quality performance objectives.

Table 4-11 *Quantitative Project Management Goal 1: Practices and Tips*

CMMI-ACQ Process Area: Quantitative Project Management	
1. Goal: The project is quantitatively managed using quality and process-performance objectives.	
Practices	**Tips**
1.1 Establish and maintain the project's quality and process-performance objectives. 1.2 Select the subprocesses that compose the project's defined process based on historical stability and capability data. 1.3 Select the subprocesses of the project's defined process that will be statistically managed. 1.4 Monitor the project to determine whether the project's objectives for quality and process performance will be satisfied, and identify corrective action as appropriate.	• Establish practically achievable and theoretically possible (or stretch) targets for each measure. • Eliminate measures that are not connected to your business objectives.

It's critical for you to statistically manage those processes that are most critical to the overall process (Table 4-11, practices 1.2 and 1.3). You should pay particular attention to the subprocesses for interacting with a supplier—for example, negotiating a supplier agreement and conducting supplier reviews.

You monitor the performance of selected subprocesses, including those that involve interaction with a supplier, as well as the quality and performance of the supplier deliverables, for adherence to the quality and performance objectives (Table 4-11, practices 1.2 and 1.4). This selective monitoring provides you with insight into project and supplier performance so that you can predict the likelihood of achieving the project's objectives for quality and process performance. You use this information to manage the risks of the project and to initiate corrective actions in time to preserve the ability to meet the project's objectives.

4.3.5 Applying the CMMI-ACQ to Using Data in Managing Subprocesses

The CMMI-ACQ provides specific recommendations on how to quantitatively manage the project's defined subprocesses (see Table 4-12).

To support quantitative project management, you need to identify common measures that support statistical management (Table 4-12, practice 2.1). For that purpose, the measure must be an adequate performance indicator of how well the subprocess performs relative to its objectives. The measure

Table 4-12 *Quantitative Project Management Goal 2: Practices and Tips*

CMMI-ACQ Process Area: Quantitative Project Management	
2. Goal: The performance of selected subprocesses within the project's defined process is statistically managed.	
Practices	**Tips**
2.1 Select the measures and analytic techniques to be used in statistically managing the selected subprocesses. 2.2 Use the selected measures and analytic techniques to establish and maintain an understanding of the variation of the selected subprocesses. 2.3 Monitor the performance of the selected subprocesses to determine their capability to satisfy their quality and process performance objectives, and identify corrective action as necessary. 2.4 Record statistical and quality management data in the organization's measurement repository.	• Thoroughly define how supplier measures, as a key source of data, fit with acquirer measures. • Insist on a size measure.

must be controllable in that you can change its values by changing how the subprocess is implemented.

To detect the cause of a particular variation, such as an unexpected change in process performance, you typically need to understand variations in process performance and have insight into potential sources of anomalous patterns (Table 4-12, practice 2.2). You monitor process performance by comparing quality and process performance objectives to the established target limits of the measure (Table 4-12, practices 2.3 and 2.4). This comparison provides an appraisal of the process capability for each measured attribute of a subprocess.

4.3.6 Monitor and Control Projects

You are responsible for monitoring the progress and output of the project. Monitoring and control functions are instituted early in the project during project planning and definition of the acquisition strategy. As the acquisition unfolds, monitoring and controlling are essential to ensure that appropriate resources are being applied and that activities are progressing according to plan.

> **TIP**   Set the precedent for decisive corrective actions early in the project.

> **Matt:**   We continually face the challenge of determining how to invest in our business. There are always a variety of options you can choose from, depending on your particular strategy—from cost reduction to capacity additions to new business initiatives. Usually, there are more projects and ideas than available funds. We have to continue, redirect, or stop projects in the light of other opportunities.
>
> We accomplish this by staying focused on our strategic goals, which are based on an understanding of what we can be best at. This improves our decision making and allows us to outperform our competitors. Without properly designed measures and reliable monitoring and control of our projects and project portfolio, we wouldn't be able to demonstrate tangible progress or quickly terminate projects before they consume substantial resources.

After a supplier is selected and a supplier agreement is established, monitoring and control assume a twofold role. You are concerned with (1) continuing to monitor and control acquirer activities and work products while also (2) monitoring and controlling the progress and performance of the supplier's execution under the supplier agreement and the supplier's project plans.

> **TIP**   Use frequent project reviews to diligently monitor both your own and the supplier's performance.

Steve: In the supplier agreement, we agree to milestones and deliverables with the supplier. And then we ask for a detailed, resource-loaded WBS that gets the supplier to each of those milestones and deliverables. But we don't track that detailed plan; instead, we have the supplier track it for us. We track the milestones for deliverables in most cases. However, we conduct detailed weekly and sometimes daily review meetings, where we jointly review progress to plan.

Matt: Can you walk us through that, Steve?

Steve: Sure. I'll stand up in front of the group. Most of the time, this is a virtual group because the team is distributed all over the globe. So there I am on screen, with a bunch of stickers—red, yellow, and green—and we go through the critical chain of the schedule. "You said these critical activities would be completed today. Did you end today?" "The plan says you're not supposed to be more than halfway through your resource buffer. What happened? What corrective actions are you taking?" Then based on the standard project measures, we put a sticker on each critical task. So at any given time anybody can walk up to the project schedule or retrieve it from our repository and see at one glance where there are trouble areas. So we don't take ownership of the supplier's detailed plan, but we make sure they execute to it and that the project is successful overall.

You use the supplier's measurement data, reflecting its progress and output, to monitor the supplier's progress and ensure that it achieves service levels established in the supplier agreement. This task also includes monitoring the availability of resources and the skills and knowledge possessed by the personnel provided by the supplier. In addition to monitoring the status of your own work products, you monitor the fitness of supplier deliverables by establishing and exercising stringent acceptance criteria. You can obtain additional information by analyzing the supplier's industry research results.

> **TIP**   Use contractually defined measures and acceptance criteria to monitor suppliers.

> **TIP**   Consistently manage the trend of critical project parameters through output and progress measures.

Steve: For effective project monitoring and control, you have to have your House of Measures in order. This way, you can see the whole picture and yet focus on which measure—which project parameter—is critical at a given point. So when a project team comes to see me for a review of their progress, I typically pick one measure that I focus in on.

Kristin agrees.

> **Kristin:**   It's like what Matt and his team have done with their House of Measures: "What do you need on the acquirer's side? What do you need on the supplier's side? Let's both figure it out." To avoid all confusion, we figure out what a normal weekly status chart looks like. Does it only show cost? Does it show cost and effort? Does it show risks? Does it show risk mitigation? Does it show risk trending? That's one of the things we did together with Matt. A lot of acquirers don't do this.

Steve confirms Kristin's ideas.

> **Steve:**   It's not just where you are this week, but it's the trend. If you want to look at status reports, a lot of them are what I call "stream of consciousness." This week, we did blah blah blah. That's great, but were you supposed to do that during week 10 of the project? Or is that what you should have done five weeks ago or three weeks in the future? You have to have some trend to say that there's a problem and it's getting worse, or there's a problem and it's getting better.
>
> I know I'm preaching to the choir, but a lot of suppliers don't see that overall picture. Somebody might ask, "Are you on schedule?" Well, I don't know. How are we tracking schedules? Have I gotten the number of deliverables done that I was supposed to get done? I could be six months into a project before I have a real deliverable. That's a bad time to find out that we thought we were on schedule for five months and three weeks, and now we're not.

It's critical for any acquirer to stay focused and yet consider all relevant measures when monitoring and controlling a program or a portfolio of projects. Based on George's experience, this isn't always the case.

> **TIP**   Always keep an eye on all project parameters, and collectively use them to support your decision making.

> **George:**   I tend to see more acquirers requesting and looking at percent of project on time, on budget, and sometimes customer satisfaction. Unfortunately, acquirers generally aren't asking about quality and productivity even though these are the numbers we should be focused on. Acquirers think about a limited set of requirements: "You said it's going to cost this amount of money. It's going to take that much time. Just tell me that you're on track and you're spending my money as planned to deliver, and I'll be happy." If an acquirer can find a way to include quality and productivity, rework becomes visible and can be driven out of the process. Then the measures you ask about naturally improve, cus-

tomer satisfaction goes up, cycle time goes down, and you can deliver within budget.

Kristin: On some medium- and longer-term contracts, I've seen acquirers monitor a simple form of productivity. They tend to add a cost-focused continuous improvement clause. "I want you to do fixed-price maintenance," or, "I want you to manage my 100-person organization from an enhancement and new development and maintenance point of view." "I want you to reduce the number of people required by 6 percent next year, 10 percent the year after, and 10 percent the year after that." "I want you to give me a 30, 40, or 50 percent savings over a 5-year period."

George prompts Kristin for more information.

George: Okay then, how do they monitor productivity?

Kristin: It's based on a simple formula that considers something like the number of service requests and the number of workers: "Okay, we gave you 100 service requests this year and you completed them with 100 full-time workers. We'll give you 100 service requests next year, and you finish them with 90 full-time workers."

This is a start, but it doesn't take into account the size and stability of these service requests. Most acquirers are not trying to drive size. They don't understand the size measure. Unfortunately, this gives them a distorted view of productivity and quality.

In any event, the effective use of measures to monitor and control a project is strongly influenced by the acquirer-supplier relationship.

> **TIP**   Continuously communicate the intent and consequences of project monitoring to acquirer and supplier teams.

Steve: The supplier has to be actively involved in monitoring and controlling the project. If not, you tend to have only limited visibility when making decisions. You run the risk of misinterpreting measures.

George: If you don't have a good partnership in place with your suppliers, measures can even become destructive. In this situation, as a supplier we're confronted with behaviors ranging from micro-management to the measures being ignored. It boils down to having the right relationship, the right partnership, and the level of awareness or knowledge that people have of measures.

People think that metrics are just primitives, and you should be able to provide them with data on whatever question comes to their mind. Let's measure this, and let's check that, and you end up with 40, 50, 60 measures that are being calculated and controlled. Realistically, you're still not managing the relationship the right way. If a true partnership exists, excessive measuring should not be occurring. In a partnership, we set joint expectations about monitoring and controlling projects. We define an agreement showing the different measures we have to collect and how they'll be interpreted.

> **TIP**   Don't let corrective action cause measurement proliferation.

If a corrective action is required to resolve a deviation from project plans, this action should be defined and tracked to closure. You take corrective action for acquirer deviations and also when supplier execution does not satisfy the supplier agreement or align with project. You may assign some corrective actions to a supplier. When you identify, for example, through your monitoring of measurement data, that supplier progress does not appear to be sufficient to meet a service level defined in the supplier agreement, then you initiate and manage corrective action for the supplier.

> **TIP**   Use corrective action to manage the project overall, never to punish individuals or suppliers.

Steve: In a productive relationship with a supplier, you share thorny issues that happen throughout the project life cycle. You, as well as the supplier, can be perfectly open about all this, in the altruistic sense, and be able to work with the supplier and say, "Look, we've gotten to this stage in the life cycle and we're having trouble. We're not going to let you down. We'll do these things to resolve it and go forward that way." This doesn't mean you go soft. If the supplier doesn't comply appropriately with your corrective actions, then you'll have to escalate and handle this as a supplier agreement issue or dispute.

4.3.7 Applying the CMMI-ACQ to Monitoring Performance and Progress

The CMMI-ACQ provides specific recommendations about how to monitor the actual performance and progress of the project against the project plan (see Table 4-13). This monitoring begins as soon as a project plan is established. You are also responsible for monitoring the progress and output of the project as a whole, that is, your activities as well as the supplier's project execution. You monitor the progress of the supplier, including achievement of service levels established in the supplier agreement, by using the supplier's measurement data about its progress and output.

Table 4-13 *Project Monitoring and Control Goal 1: Practices and Tips*

CMMI-ACQ Process Area: Project Monitoring and Control	
1. Goal: Actual performance and progress of the project are monitored against the project plan.	
Practices	**Tips**
1.1 Monitor the actual values of the project planning parameters against the project plan. 1.2 Monitor commitments against those identified in the project plan. 1.3 Monitor risks against those identified in the project plan. 1.4 Monitor the management of project data against the project plan.	• Using output and progress measures, consistently manage the trend of critical project parameters. • Always keep an eye on all project parameters, and collectively use them to support your decision making.
1.5 Monitor stakeholder involvement against the project plan. 1.6 Periodically review the project's progress, performance, and issues. 1.7 Review the accomplishments and results of the project at selected project milestones. 1.8 Monitor the transition to operations and support.	• Continuously communicate the intent and consequences of project monitoring to acquirer and supplier teams. • Use frequent project reviews to diligently monitor both acquirer and supplier performance. • Use contractually defined measures and acceptance criteria to monitor suppliers.

A project's documented plan is the basis for monitoring activities, communicating project status, and taking corrective action. You determine progress primarily by comparing project planning parameters to the estimates in the plan at prescribed milestones or control levels within the project schedule or WBS, and identifying significant deviations (Table 4-13, practice 1.1). Project planning parameters include work products and tasks; cost, effort, and schedule; and the knowledge, skills, and experience of project personnel. Attributes of the work products and tasks include size, complexity, weight, form, fit, or function. You document significant deviations that apply either to your project execution or to the supplier's deviations from the project plan.

You also monitor overall project risk and the commitments made by relevant stakeholders to the plan (Table 4-13, practices 1.2 and 1.3). Many risks are your sole responsibility and may include sensitive information that should not be shared with the supplier (e.g., source selection, competition, internal staffing, or other risks). There can also be risks that require careful coordination with suppliers and appropriate escalation of risks and risk status (e.g., the feasibility of the technology to meet end user performance requirements). Shared risks may affect the mitigation approaches and result in jointly planned mitigations. Moreover, every acquirer needs to ensure that project data is managed against the project plan and that the level of stakeholder involvement aligns with the project plan (Table 4-13, practices 1.4 and 1.5).

It is crucial to monitor the technology solution during the operations and support phases (Table 4-13, practice 1.8). You make adequate provisions through the supplier agreement or in-house organizations to support the acquired technology solution. Typically, you use verification best practices to confirm that the organization, the physical environment, and the operations and support personnel are equipped to execute the operations and support activities.

You review operations and support organizations that have been designated to take responsibility for operation of the technology solution. You need to ensure that the workers have been identified and budgeted and are available when needed. This needs to happen very early and monitored throughout the project. The designated operations and support organizations demonstrate their readiness (capability and capacity) to accept responsibility for the product and to ensure uninterrupted support. In a typical readiness demonstration, the candidate organization executes all the activities of operations. Acquirers tend to use transition readiness criteria and verification and validation practices to determine whether the support organization meets the specified requirements. The criteria also address the readiness of the product for maintenance during the planned product life cycle.

A smooth transition to maintenance also requires monitoring to ensure that those who receive, store, use, and maintain the technology solution are trained. Typically, the supplier develops training materials for the solution it has developed. The training materials and resources to be provided by the supplier are specified in the supplier agreement and should meet the needs of various audiences (e.g., operations staff, support staff, end users). You verify that the training is provided at the appropriate times to the appropriate audiences and determine whether the training is adequate.

To monitor project performance, it is invaluable to conduct periodic progress and milestone reviews to keep stakeholders informed (Table 4-13, practices

1.6 and 1.7). These project reviews can be informal and need not be specified explicitly in the project plans. Reviews cover the results of collected and analyzed measures used for controlling the project.

You and the supplier may coordinate and conduct project reviews jointly. These reviews tend to fall into two categories: management and technical. Management reviews typically include acquirer and supplier measures, critical dependencies, and project risks and issues. Technical reviews are an important oversight tool that you can use to review and evaluate the state of the product and of the project, redirecting activity after the review if necessary.

Technical reviews typically include the following activities:

- Reviewing the supplier's technical activities and verifying that the supplier's interpretation and implementation of the requirements are consistent with the customer's interpretation
- Ensuring that technical commitments are being met and that technical issues are being communicated and resolved in a timely manner
- Obtaining technical information about the supplier's products
- Providing appropriate technical information (e.g., design constraints) and support to the supplier

As a result of project reviews, you identify and document significant issues and deviations from the plan. This includes identifying and documenting both acquirer and supplier issues and deviations. In addition to seeking ways of improving your own performance, use the results of reviews to improve the supplier's performance and to establish and nurture long-term relationships with preferred suppliers.

Appropriate visibility enables you to take timely corrective action when performance deviates significantly from the plan (see Table 4-14, practice 2.1). A deviation is significant if, when left unresolved, it prevents the project from meeting its objectives. Managing issues and corrective actions is your sole responsibility. The documentation of this effort can include sensitive information that should not be shared with the supplier (e.g., source selection, competition, and internal staffing).

You take decisive corrective action by determining and documenting the appropriate actions needed to address the identified issues (Table 4-14, practice 2.2). If a corrective action is required to resolve variances from project plans, this action should be defined and tracked to closure (Table 4-14, practice 2.3). You also analyze results of corrective actions to determine their

Table 4-14 *Project Monitoring and Control Goal 2: Practices and Tips*

CMMI-ACQ Process Area: Project Monitoring and Control	
2. Goal: Corrective actions are managed to closure when the project's performance or results deviate significantly from the plan.	
Practices	**Tips**
2.1 Collect and analyze the issues, and determine the corrective actions necessary to address the issues. 2.2 Take corrective action on identified issues. 2.3 Manage corrective actions to closure.	• Set the precedent for decisive corrective actions early in the project. • Don't let corrective action cause measurement proliferation. • Use corrective action to manage the project overall, never to punish individuals or suppliers.

effectiveness. In addition, lessons learned as a result of taking corrective action can be used as inputs to planning and risk management processes.

In addition to the project team's monitoring and control activities, your quality assurance processes provide staff and management with objective insight into processes and associated work products (see Table 4-15). The tips for project monitoring and control apply equally to quality assurance.

You evaluate how the project team executes your processes, including interactions with suppliers. In addition, you review evaluation reports provided by suppliers to determine whether the supplier follows its processes. A popular means of doing this is to review recent CMMI maturity or capability ratings. Sufficient process quality assurance will help detect noncompliance issues, which may affect your or the supplier's ability to successfully deliver the products to the customer as early as possible.

In the supplier agreement, you should retain the right to audit supplier processes if there is an indication that the suppliers are not following acceptable processes. You can review the results of the supplier's quality assurance activities for selected supplier processes to ensure that the supplier is following its own processes. Typically, some supplier processes are considered critical, such as engineering or verification processes, where the supplier is required (through the supplier agreement) to follow project- or program-specified standards. In exceptional cases, you may directly perform product and process quality assurance for selected supplier processes. You and the

Table 4-15 *Product and Process Quality Assurance Goal 1 and 2:*
Practices and Tips

CMMI-ACQ Process Area: Product and Process Quality Assurance	
1. Goal: Adherence of the performed process and associated work products and services to applicable process descriptions, standards, and procedures is objectively evaluated.	
Practices	**Tips**
1.1 Objectively evaluate the designated performed processes against the applicable process descriptions, standards, and procedures. 1.2 Objectively evaluate the designated work products and services against the applicable process descriptions, standards, and procedures.	• Always keep an eye on all project parameters, and collectively use them to support your decision making. • Continuously communicate the intent and consequences of quality assurance to acquirer and supplier personnel.
2. Goal: Noncompliance issues are objectively tracked and communicated, and resolution is ensured.	
2.1 Communicate quality issues, and ensure resolution of noncompliance issues with the staff and managers. 2.2 Establish and maintain records of the quality assurance activities.	• Set the precedent for decisive corrective actions early in the project. • Don't let corrective action cause measurement proliferation. • Use corrective action to manage the project overall, never to punish individuals or suppliers.

supplier periodically share quality assurance issues and findings of mutual interest.

The practices in the Process and Product Quality Assurance process area ensure that planned processes are implemented, and the practices in the Acquisition Verification process area ensure that the specified requirements are satisfied. These two process areas may sometimes address the same work product, but from different perspectives. Projects should take advantage of this overlap to minimize duplicate efforts while taking care to maintain separate perspectives.

4.4 Let's Go Live (and Live to Tell About It)

The technology solution is shaping up, and the supplier is getting ready to deliver the product. The customers and users are eagerly anticipating the new capability and are ready to use it. With all this anticipation in the air and the significant expenditure of resources by both you and the supplier, no project can afford to fumble this late in the game.

Successful deployment of a technology solution requires all participants to perform their defined roles. The critical components and the important aspects of your management practices must be closely scrutinized to ensure flawless execution. It is paramount to adopt a balanced approach that covers the technical readiness of the solution, its integration into the intended environment, and continued validation that the solution meets customer requirements and user expectations.

4.4.1 Technology Solution Readiness

When it comes down to it, every acquisition project must be able to answer one question: How can you insert these changes—this technology solution—into its intended environment?

> **Steve:** If you're very change tolerant or if you're not working with a mission-critical system, that's one thing. When you talk about an environment where you're going twenty-four-seven and you can never take your systems completely down, or maybe the organization just went through a traumatic reorganization, that's another thing. At the beginning stages of planning, you really need to think through what needs to be done when you deploy your solution. If you do, you can come up with a pretty good process. You can say, "Oh, I'm going to put effort and thought into this and see how this go-live approach works for my organization. Then I can apply that approach for subsequent changes in subsequent systems." You really want to build on the knowledge you've gained. You don't throw everything out. You want to reuse the successful approaches.

A key ingredient for the successful deployment of technology solutions is its technical readiness. You want to make sure—to verify—that the supplier's product meets the contractual requirements and is ready to be installed in the intended environment for further integration and user acceptance testing (UAT). Verification is inherently an incremental process, because it occurs throughout the acquisition. You begin by verifying the requirements and plans, and then you verify the evolving work products such as design and test results, and in the end you verify the completed product.

> **TIP**   Verify the technical solution throughout the project.

Kristin: Finding and fixing bugs isn't the most glamorous part of this business, but it sure is one of the most important, if not the most important, factor that separates successful projects from failures. As personal experience and a vast literature tells us, verification—quality control— is the largest cost for many technology projects. And it takes more time than any other activity—40 percent or more of the developers' time. We carefully balance defect prevention (such as proven design methods) and defect detection (such as testing) to get the best quality for the acquirer of our products.

> **TIP**   Contractually require a cost-effective blend of defect prevention and defect detection.

It is critical that you insist contractually that your suppliers apply proven best practices for verification (e.g., structured coding techniques, peer code reviews) to increase the likelihood that the product will meet the contractual requirements.

> **TIP**   Conduct detailed inspections, such as peer reviews, only on the most important acquirer work products.

It is equally important to find a cost-effective way to consistently and comprehensively verify your own work products and the supplier's deliverables. Select your work products to verify based on the products' relative importance to meeting project objectives and requirements and to addressing project risks.

Steve: Initially, we got excited about the potential savings and improved quality we could get from peer reviews. Somebody wrote something. Done. Bingo—you just earned yourself the right to a peer review. As you can imagine, this attitude slowed down the process and bloated our costs. So we took a careful look at what really matters and deserves the extra attention of a structured inspection such as a peer review. Now we only conduct peer reviews on a handful of our work products: requirements, design constraints, project plan, supplier agreement, and user acceptance test plans.

At the same time, Steve was part of an effort to select supplier deliverables for which the supplier must provide verification records such as peer review results.

> **TIP** Use predefined acceptance criteria as an open-book test for supplier deliverables.

As with other supplier deliverables, peer review results must meet predefined acceptance criteria. Supplier deliverables are considered delivered only when the acceptance criteria are satisfied. There is no partial credit.

Note that a product can be released in increments. In that case, it's a good idea to timebox each release. A *timebox* is essentially a fixed unit of development capacity. The capability to be implemented for a release of the technology solution must fit (be delivered) within a given time frame (e.g., within six weeks) and often within a given cost to the acquirer. The work to be performed in each timebox consists of both a *functionality* and a *quality* component. Verification falls into the quality component. By predefining (fixing) the duration of a release, you can better plan for adequate verification of the delivered functionality.

> **TIP** Optimize verification costs through time-boxed releases of technology solutions.

Matt: We run this as an open-book test. All suppliers and our staff know what the acceptance criteria are. There is no mystery. They also know that their payment is tied to meeting those criteria. So if a deliverable has, let's say, ten acceptance criteria, the supplier must meet all of them within a certain threshold to receive payment for this deliverable.

Testing the supplier's product is a big part of verification.

Kristin: You need to calculate the risks you're going to take during testing, because you can't test everything. So having a good test plan or at least an achievable one that mitigates risk is critical. Due to the complexity and cost involved in testing, we're always looking at how much change is feasible for us and the acquirer we work with. So you're trying to group the change, because that minimizes or at least consolidates the areas of the solution that you need to test again.

We've made rules, together with acquisition organizations, about what products or product enhancements we would deploy on a monthly basis rather than on a six-month schedule. A key rule is the dependency of a product on all the other products being used by the acquirer. If a product drives many other products—let's say, hundreds of applications—if the driver product changes, we would have to test the hundreds of applications. We don't want to do that every month.

Does an acquirer need to test every permutation or combination of every application in the system?

TIP	Let domain experts determine the focus of testing.

Steve: We need intelligent testing, and we need an understanding of how the product will be used. Let me give you an example from a couple years back. We were doing a major upgrade. It was the biggest system in this division. And we tested the new system in parallel with the system in use for two months, and everything was perfect. We compared all the reports, everything, okay, interfaces, the whole deal. So the first night the new system went live, nothing happened.

Kristin: Nothing happened?

Steve smiles.

Steve: I mean, nothing *bad* happened.

Kristin: Oh, okay. Whew.

Steve: But wait—there's more. The second night, I got a call at ten. The system had crashed. I worked all night, and we finally found out what happened. The supplier had populated the test system with data projecting only the next 24 hours of financials. As soon as we exceeded this 24-hour window in the production environment, all kinds of things started to happen—none of them pretty. In this case, a programming phenom from Russia coded for 36 hours straight to alleviate the worst of the problems.

So now we have testing standards that our suppliers must adhere to. These fairly detailed standards give, for instance, very clear direction about what length of time the testing data must cover, depending on the process a product supports.

Because the supplier deliverables go through different stages of testing, it is critical that you clearly designate which testing environment is expected for each type of testing.

TIP	Contractually define the required testing environments and the stages of testing they must be used for.

Matt: When we first sat down with our various acquisition teams to discuss testing, we got into a heated debate. Some groups argued for the right to buy equipment to stand up to their own test environments that they and the suppliers would have to use. Other people wanted us to hire an independent testing outfit to eliminate bias, and yet others wanted the suppliers to be responsible for all testing environments since they're responsible for providing the product. I favor the last option, simply because it ensures clear accountability of the suppliers.

Matt pauses before describing how this works.

Matt: For instance, in the IT area we make the hosting supplier responsible for operating the preproduction environment that the development supplier uses for user acceptance testing. The preproduction environment is a mirror of the intended environment that we use to verify and validate the product prior to deployment.

For hardware we have a certification process. For example, any generic hardware we get, the suppliers know that they can expect to run such and such software, at a minimum. So we try to push onto them a lot of the testing responsibility for the integration of their product with other suppliers' products and services in our environment. It's their product. They're driving it. Suppliers play a critical role in ensuring that the technology solution is ready for deployment.

> **TIP** Frequently communicate technology solution readiness.

Steve: We involve suppliers very heavily when we're making decisions about the readiness of technical solutions and how we measure it. For example, with software, you can count on a few things for sure: The code always has defects. Our suppliers use agreed-upon categories to group these defects. They group them in terms of when they're going to be fixed and realigned with our deployment dates. We have regular calls with our developer suppliers and with the deployment people as well as all the other relevant stakeholders.

Steve pauses to consult his notes.

Steve: So besides our standard measures, we use readiness dashboards to give everybody a consistent view of whether the solution is ready for prime time.

Matt: I like the dashboard format.

Steve: They're really useful. They display a collection of metrics and key performance indicators that show the status of the project and where it's headed. They give people actionable data in an intuitive and insightful format.

So we review those dashboards at all levels of the organization. Say we have a specific site where the acquired product will be used. One critical area might be, "Do you have your change controls approved?" We even ask if they have their change controls submitted. "Have you communicated the timing to your suppliers? Do you have your user acceptance tests and events defined?" We try to have yes/no questions, or questions that call for numbers.

For the high-performing suppliers, it's basically just a formality. They know what they need to do. For them, it's more of a last chance to offer up information or concerns. We want to make sure we agree on the code and what we're getting in the code, make sure it gives us the functionality we need.

TIP Compile technology readiness dashboards in close collaboration with suppliers.

4.4.2 Applying the CMMI-ACQ to Verifying the Acquired Product

The CMMI-ACQ provides specific recommendations about how to ensure that an acquired product, intermediate acquirer work products, and supplier deliverables meet their contractual requirements (see Table 4-16). The Acquisition Verification process area includes selection, inspection, testing, analysis, and demonstration of acquirer work products and supplier deliverables.

Up-front preparation ensures that verification provisions are embedded in the contractual requirements, constraints, plans, budgets, and schedules. Preparation also entails defining support tools, test equipment and software, simulations, prototypes, and facilities.

You select work products to verify based on the products' relative importance to meeting project objectives and requirements, and to addressing project risks (Table 4-16, practice 1.1). You also select supplier deliverables for which the supplier must provide verification records. The required methods and criteria are described in the supplier agreement. Typical acquirer verification activities include reviewing the solicitation package, supplier agreements, plans, requirements, documents, and design constraints.

In addition to selecting work products for verification, you select the verification methods. This typically begins with the definition of contractual requirements to ensure that the requirements are verifiable. The methods should address reverification to ensure that rework does not cause defects. Sup-

Table 4-16 *Acquisition Verification Goal 1: Practices and Tips*

CMMI-ACQ Process Area: Acquisition Verification	
1. Goal: Preparation for verification is conducted.	
Practices	**Tips**
1.1 Select the work products to be verified and the verification methods that will be used for each. 1.2 Establish and maintain the environment needed to support verification. 1.3 Establish and maintain verification procedures and criteria for the selected work products.	• Let domain experts determine the focus of testing. • Contractually require a cost-effective blend of defect prevention and defect detection. • Conduct detailed inspections, such as peer reviews, only on the most important acquirer work products. • Contractually define the required testing environments and the stages of testing they must be used for.

pliers should be involved in your selection process to ensure that the project's methods are appropriate for the supplier's environment. To set clear expectations, you establish in the supplier agreement requirements for verification of supplier deliverables. The supplier agreement typically includes the following:

1. A list of deliverables and other work products that must be verified by the supplier
2. Applicable standards, procedures, methods, and tools
3. Criteria for verification of supplier work products
4. Measurements to be collected and provided by the supplier with regard to verification activities
5. Reviews of supplier verification results and corrective actions

You must establish an environment to enable verification (Table 4-16, practice 1.2). This environment can be acquired, developed, reused, modified, or a combination of these, depending on the needs of the project. The type of environment depends on the work products selected for verification and the methods applied. The requirements for the environment can vary greatly. For instance, a peer review might require little more than a package of materials, some reviewers, and a room. In contrast, a product verification test might require simulators, emulators, scenario generators, data reduction tools, environmental controls, and interfaces with other systems.

Verification criteria are defined in the supplier agreement to ensure that the work products meet their requirements (Table 4-16, practice 1.3). You generate a set of comprehensive, integrated verification procedures for work products and any COTS products as necessary.

You use the verification methods, procedures, and criteria in the appropriate verification environment to verify the selected work products and any associated maintenance, training, and support services. It's good to verify acquired products and work products incrementally, because it promotes early detection of problems and can result in the early removal of defects (see Table 4-17, practice 2.1). Incorporating the results of verification into a repair process can save considerable cost for fault isolation and rework.

You must compare actual verification results to established verification criteria to determine whether the results are acceptable (Table 4-17, practice 2.2). For each work product, all available verification results are incrementally analyzed and corrective actions are initiated to ensure that the documented requirements are met for both acquirer and supplier. Corrective actions are typically integrated into project monitoring activities. Because a peer review is one of several verification methods, you should include peer review data in this analysis to ensure that the verification results are analyzed sufficiently. Analysis reports or "as-run" method documentation can indicate that bad results are being caused by problems with the verification methods, verification criteria, or verification environment.

The CMMI-ACQ includes the process area Causal Analysis and Resolution. This process area provides recommendations for identifying the causes of defects and other problems and taking action to prevent them from occurring in the future. When determining which defects to analyze further, you should consider the impact of the defects, the frequency of occurrence, the similarity between defects, the cost of analysis, the time and resources needed to correct the defects, the safety considerations, and so on. Causal

Table 4-17 *Acquisition Verification Goal 2: Practices and Tips*

CMMI-ACQ Process Area: Acquisition Verification	
2. Goal: Selected work products are verified against their contractual requirements.	
Practices	**Tips**
2.1 Perform verification on the selected work products. 2.2 Analyze the results of all verification activities.	• Verify the technical solution throughout the project. • Optimize verification costs through timeboxed releases of technology solutions.

analysis is performed by people who have the best understanding of the selected defect or problem being studied.

4.4.3 Ready, Set, Go!

Before the technology solution goes live and is available to the users, the project team needs to make sure that all involved parties are on the same page. For this, communication throughout the project is critical.

> **TIP**   Engage users early and often. There is no substitute for real users.

Steve: All the way through a project, you want to take every opportunity you can to validate with the customer and supplier that you're on track. But with all the preparation, it still comes down to the successful launch and full deployment of the new capability. Your customer satisfaction, a large chunk of your supplier's payment, and your professional ego are wrapped up in the pivotal events around going live with your product. It's like you've gone through all the rehearsals, and now it's time to perform.

Consistently delivering a successful premiere—seamlessly inserting new or enhanced technology solutions into your environment—is not without its perils. For instance, you don't want your project to be the one in which UAT came to mean "user angry at technology" instead of "user acceptance testing."

> **TIP**   Throughout the project, frequently expose the technology solution to its intended environment.

George: Surprises during user acceptance testing aren't pretty. Let me tell you a story. It was in our validation lab for one of our largest automotive clients. We had pushbuttons, industrial controllers, and screens mounted on a table instead of being mounted on a fork truck. The pushbutton and the screen are about three meters apart—the user can walk between the two just like they would in their work environment. So my team tested the system. They'd push the button and then they'd walk over to the screen to see if, for instance, a material request would show up. Then they'd clear the material request, walk back over to the pushbutton, push it again, get another material request, walk over to the screen, and so on and so forth. No problems.

So in comes the user, a woman from one of the customer's sites. She pushes the button, walks over to the screen, sees that the message came through, clears the screen, walks back to the button, and then hammers it mercilessly—bang, bang, bang, bang, bang—just as fast as she can. The button gives. It breaks. There's nothing coming through on the screen anymore, the light starts flashing, basically "smoke" comes out of the system.

And my guy says to her, "What did you do *that* for? Who would ever do something like that?" And she says, "That's going to happen. Someone's going to get frustrated, the trucks aren't going to come, so someone is just going to start hammering this button."

My guys had never tested this situation, which was very embarrassing for me. Within ten minutes the user could come in and break the system. It's probably one of the worst UAT stories I could tell. It took us a while to live that one down.

Unfortunately, these UAT surprises are common. Steve adds his favorite one.

Steve: Before I started here, I worked for a cement factory. My team went through this elaborate, sophisticated effort to create a new system to monitor the ingredients to make the best cement there is. They were so confident that this would turn out to be a home run.

So when they had the great unveiling in the cement factory, the first worker that walked up to the system—the system had a fancy touch screen—tries to start the ingredient analysis. But he can't use the touch screen! How come? Because a safety regulation requires all workers to wear big gloves—think giant oven mitts. He couldn't manage to hit even one button on the touch screen. And of course, using the touch screen was the only way a user could steer the system.

A key ingredient for successful validation of an acquired product is to have the true customer and users involved throughout the project life cycle. This is especially challenging on projects that have long life cycles.

> **TIP**   Define skill and capability profiles of the users who will participate in user acceptance testing.

George: You need one kind of user, and that's the right kind. But what happens a lot of times in UAT, the acquisition team or their management might say, "Oh, that's seven months from now. I don't know who'll be available in seven months." So the acquirer's side doesn't plan who to send to UAT because they don't know what else they're going to do. So, the week before UAT comes around, and they look around and they say, "Hey, John. You and Susie standing by the water cooler, you're going to UAT next week."

Steve: Well, I've never done that, but I can see how it happens.

George: It never needs to happen. You write up a profile that captures the agreed-upon skills and capabilities of a potential test user. Okay? You can figure out, do they meet that profile, before folks are asked to participate in UAT. Otherwise, if you're doing UAT that requires domain knowledge—and in my experience, many products require this for successful UAT—you get inaccurate feedback without the right users, and you'll spend a lot of money before you get it right.

George pauses for a moment and then continues.

George: Let's say you're validating a technology solution for the product development group. You're building something that supports structural engineering. You couldn't just send a random person who didn't know anything about this area, or knew enough about it but didn't understand that 4,000 metric tons per square inch is a bad answer for the force it takes to open a door.

So, when you find out that the UAT users you have don't fit the profile, you're stuck. You're looking at them and you have to say, "You're the wrong person for this assignment," which of course is insulting. So they push back: "Well, I work in this group, I know how the work gets done in this group." Well, they do, but they don't know this specific piece. So how can they help us validate the proposed solution if they don't know the work it will support?

So this is the biggest lesson learned. Ultimately you have to get the right people in the room or in the field to spend the time giving you meaningful feedback.

What can you do to avoid UAT surprises and increase your chances for a smooth go-live of the technology solution? It's vital to have a time-tested, proactive set of verification procedures and criteria to ensure that the product or component will fulfill its intended use when placed in its intended environment. You need to clearly identify the applicable verification procedures and criteria and then reference these procedures in the solicitation package and supplier agreement.

> **TIP**   Insist on rigorous, time-tested validation steps. Enforce them contractually without exception.

George: What we've created is essentially a manufacturing process for deploying technology solutions. We want to make sure we go live with a solution and live to tell about it. While we want to instill creativity when designing and developing the solution, we encourage all participants to rigorously stay within the deployment script. Everybody must know their roles and perform according to procedure. So even if you find things during deployment that will make the solution a little bit better, you have to be really careful about whether you'll change the deployment process to make an adjustment. Feature creep is bad enough, but during deployment it's downright dangerous.

Paula: You're so right. I can't tell you how many times we find errors in last-minute tweaking.

George: Now we're at a point where our deployment process is getting to be almost like how some automotive companies launch a new vehicle: Engineering will evolve the design, and then finally the design is ready for production. When they bring it to a manufacturing plant, the design is done. It's been tested, and we know it works. Then, we'll take a vehicle down the manufacturing line to go through the manufacturing process one last time just to verify that the new model will build properly and that our process works. So, eventually, deployment of technology solutions is like a vehicle launch, in that we pilot the technology solution to verify that the build process works and that the deployment process works. At that point we can confidently say that we can do the deployment process over and over again. Standardizing becomes even more important, since we've got multiple teams, dispersed globally, deploying the same system.

Steve strongly supports George's ideas.

> **TIP** Maximize setup work for deploying technology solutions.

Steve: A tightly controlled deployment process is critical. We're better off doing a staging operation rather than doing an "out of the box" installation at the customer's site. What we do is, we source all the materials, we take it to an assembly site, rack all the hardware components, load the software, do some elementary testing. Then we'll wire it all up and connect it to the power and network at the site. This focuses the site team on two items. One, all they have to set up are those pieces we couldn't preassemble. Two, they can pay close attention to how to migrate from the old product to the new one.

George: That sounds like a great plan.

Steve: I think it's one of the cleverest things we've come up with in a long time. We used to see the same mistakes over and over again, but the common denominator was somebody new was doing something not in the process. So we want to try to have as much repetitive stability as possible.

The closer you get to going live with the new or enhanced product, the more important it is to train the potential users and support personnel to use it. Effective training requires assessment of needs, planning, instructional design, and appropriate training media (e.g., workbooks, software) as well as a repository of training process data. As an organizational process, training has these main components: a managed training development program, documented plans, personnel with appropriate mastery of specific disciplines and other areas of knowledge, and mechanisms for measuring the effectiveness of the training.

> **TIP**   Thoroughly test and pilot your training materials.

> **TIP**   For the most effective training, combine different types and delivery mechanisms.

Paula: At minimum, we want people to be able to do their jobs without disruption on the day the technology solution goes live. One thing about training is that our primary motto, and we're fairly rigorous on this, is that during development the supplier creates the training package. It's tested as part of development and verification of the solution.

George: It sounds like you've done a lot with training.

Paula: We've used different kinds of training, everything from one-on-one training, on-the-job training, classroom training, multimedia training, and more. We now use a lot of Web-based training. We try to have this in place a short time before go-live so that the users are ready on day one. But then again, sometimes we may supplement that with face-to-face sessions where we call the people in and walk them through the latest changes in detail. This has the advantage of allowing for a dialog between the instructor and the users. Then there are a significant number of technology solutions that we've got where the business process changes so that the user training is actually embedded in some process retraining.

When the big go-live day finally arrives, acquirers can only hope that the process plays out like the Vienna Philharmonic performing Strauss at New Year's—breathtaking, flawless, and smiles on everyone's faces when it's finished.

> **TIP**   Open mandatory communication channels for all stakeholders during go-live of the technology solution.

George: Once we start the countdown to go-live, we have a whole process detailed to carry it out. Before we go live, we collect all the information; we have very detailed cut-over plans—minute by minute—that we have done in exhaustive detail and reviewed. So a great deal of work goes into that. Part of it is to make everything very visible.

Steve: Tell us more.

George: So, we have an intense focus on the communication. It's all about communication. It really is critical—communication of the right things at the right time. Where are the key checkpoints? Where will what testing be done? All this and more, to make sure the deployment is moving as expected. One of the problems I have with people is when they say, "Well, I'm going to use the new solution for 24 hours, and then I'll find out if things are okay or not." And you just don't want to do that. You want to be able to verify and validate that things are working as you expected along the way.

Steve: So what's in place on the day itself?

George: We have all the various players, every supplier that is involved, their technical personnel, available for immediate contact—if they don't have to be on-site already—and then a senior management person who can be contacted in the middle of the night if anything is needed from their company. Then when we actually start the system, we give an update on an open phone line every hour. People can just call in and ask questions or listen to the hourly update. At a point in time in the deployment we say, "Is everything ready? Do we turn the final switch?" There is a meeting, and that's when you get a whole group of people together for that final decision to go live.

> **TIP** Contractually establish that any significant error found during warranty causes the warranty period to start over.

With the technology solution ready for use, you transfer responsibility for operations and support from the development supplier to the appropriate group. This could be the same supplier or an in-house team on your side. The development supplier, however, is still very much responsible for successfully completing the warranty period for the technology solution. Steve stresses the importance of the warranty period.

Steve: In my experience, with so many different components working together, so many pieces and parts, the warranty period is a lot more important than it used to be. There are so many things that can go wrong. It's not cost-effective for the supplier to test to the degree that you would have to in order to prevent anything from happening after the solution is installed. So I think the warranty is really important. You hopefully don't have any major errors or outages, but it's always possible. If something happens, we hold our suppliers accountable. They're contractually required to fix any errors that occur during their warranty period. We also insist that any significant error found resets the warranty period, among other penalties. So it's in our mutual interest to arrive at a high-quality product quickly.

After the warranty period is complete and the responsibility for the technology solution is transferred to the operational and support organizations, you review and analyze the results of the transition activities and determine whether any corrective actions must be completed before closing the project.

4.4.4 Applying the CMMI-ACQ to Validating the Product

The CMMI-ACQ provides specific recommendations on how to demonstrate that an acquired product or service fulfills its intended use when placed in its intended environment (see Table 4-18). Validation demonstrates that the acquired product, as provided, will fulfill its intended use. In other words, validation ensures that the product meets the stakeholders' intentions and the customer requirements.

Preparation activities include selecting products and components for validation and establishing and maintaining the validation environment,

Table 4-18 *Acquisition Validation Solution Goal 1: Practices and Tips*

CMMI-ACQ Process Area: Acquisition Validation	
1. Goal: Preparation for validation is conducted.	
Practices	**Tips**
1.1 Select products or services to be validated and the validation methods that will be used for each. 1.2 Establish and maintain the environment needed to support validation. 1.3 Establish and maintain procedures and criteria for validation.	• Throughout the project, frequently expose the technology solution to its intended environment. • Define skill and capability profiles of the users who participate in user acceptance testing. • Maximize setup work for deploying technology solutions. • For most effective training, combine different types and delivery mechanisms.

procedures, and criteria. Products or services are selected for validation on the basis of their importance to stakeholder intentions and customer requirements (Table 4-18, practice 1.1). The items selected for validation may include only the acquired product or may include appropriate levels of the product components that are used by the supplier to build the product. Any product or component—including replacement, maintenance, and training products, to name a few—may be subject to validation.

You should select validation methods early in the project life cycle so that they are clearly understood and agreed to by the relevant stakeholders. Validation methods include the following:

1. Discussions with the users, perhaps in the context of a formal review
2. Prototype demonstrations
3. Functional demonstrations (e.g., system, hardware units, software, service documentation, user interfaces)
4. Pilots of training materials
5. Acceptance tests of products and components by end users and other relevant stakeholders

The supplier agreement should capture your expectations of suppliers for participation in validation of the product and components. The requirements for the validation environment are driven by the product or service selected, by the kind of work products being tested (e.g., design, prototype, final version), and by the methods of validation being used (Table 4-18, practice 1.2). The environment may be purchased or may be specified, designed, and built. The environments used for verification and for validation may be considered concurrently to reduce cost and improve efficiency or productivity.

You define validation procedures and criteria to ensure that the product or component fulfills its intended use when used in its intended environment (Table 4-18, practice 1.3). The validation procedures and criteria include validation of maintenance, training, and support services. They also address validation of requirements and the acquired product or service throughout the project life cycle. Typically, you establish formal user acceptance testing procedures and criteria to ensure that the delivered product meets stakeholder intentions before it is deployed in the intended environment. The validation procedures and criteria applicable to the supplier are typically referenced in the solicitation package and supplier agreement.

Validation activities are performed early and incrementally throughout the project life cycle (see Table 4-19, practice 2.1). They can be applied to all

Table 4-19 *Acquisition Validation Solution Goal 2: Practices and Tips*

CMMI-ACQ Process Area: Acquisition Validation	
2. Goal: The products or services are validated to ensure that they are suitable for use in their intended environment.	
Practices	**Tips**
2.1 Perform validation on the selected products or services. 2.2 Analyze the results of the validation activities.	• Engage users early and often. There is no substitute for real users. • Thoroughly test and pilot training materials. • Open mandatory communication channels for all stakeholders during go-live of the technology solution.

aspects of the product in any of its intended environments, such as operation, training, manufacturing, maintenance, and support.

The data resulting from validation tests, inspections, demonstrations, or evaluations are analyzed against the defined validation criteria (Table 4-19, practice 2.2). Analysis reports should indicate whether the stakeholders' intentions were met; if there are deficiencies, these reports document the degree of success or failure and categorize probable causes of failures. You compare the collected test, inspection, or review results with established acceptance criteria to determine whether to proceed or to address requirements or design issues in the requirements development or technical solution processes. Analysis reports or "as-run" method documentation can indicate that bad validation results are being caused by validation method problems, validation criteria problems, or validation environment problems.

Often, acceptance of supplier deliverables is tied to supplier payments. You must ensure that payment terms defined in the supplier agreement are met and that supplier compensation is linked to supplier progress, as defined in the supplier agreement (see Table 4-20, practice 2.1). You should not make final payment to the supplier until you have certified that all the supplier deliverables meet the contractual requirements and that all acceptance criteria are satisfied. When you encounter nonperformance, exercise the contract provisions for withholding or reducing payments to the supplier to the appropriate degree.

You ensure that all acceptance criteria are satisfied and that all discrepancies are corrected before final acceptance of the acquired technology solution (Table 4-20, practice 2.2).

Table 4-20 *Acquisition Management Solution Goal 2: Practices and Tips*

CMMI-ACQ Process Area: Acquisition Management	
2. Goal: Establish a productive and cooperative environment to meet the goals of the project.	
Practices	**Tips**
2.1 Receive, review, approve, and remit invoices provided by the supplier. 2.2 Ensure that the supplier agreement is satisfied before accepting the acquired product. 2.3 Transition the acquired product from the supplier to the acquirer.	• Insist on rigorous, time-tested validation steps. Enforce them contractually without exception. • Contractually establish that any significant error found during warranty causes the warranty period to start over.

Your authorized representative assumes ownership of existing identified supplier products or deliverables tendered, or approves specific services rendered, as partial or complete performance of the supplier agreement by the supplier. You, usually through your authorized supplier agreement or contract administrator, provide the supplier with formal written notice that the supplier deliverables have been accepted or rejected.

Typically, the supplier integrates and packages the products and prepares for the transition to operations and support, including support for business user acceptance, and you oversee the supplier's activities (Table 4-20, practice 2.3). These expectations and the acceptance criteria for transition to operations and support are included in the solicitation package and the supplier agreement.

After appropriate reviews of the transition activities, you make the product available for use according to the plans for pilot and transition. During this pilot, or initial period of production, you validate that the product is capable and ready for full operational use. During this defined transition or warranty period—for example, 30 days or 90 days for certain information systems— you oversee activities to make sure that the product is operating as planned and identify any corrective actions required. Although the product is in the operational environment, full responsibility for operations and support is not transitioned until this pilot period is complete and any identified corrective actions have been successfully completed. During this defined transition period, you ensure support of the product (for example, you may assign the supplier the responsibility to maintain support during transition).

Responsibility for operations and support of the technology solution is transferred by you to the operations and support organizations, which may be suppliers, only after these organizations demonstrate their capability and capacity to support the product and accept the responsibilities to perform their assigned operations and support processes. You ensure that these organizations understand post-transition service requirements from the supplier.

You maintain oversight responsibilities until the transition activities are complete and the transfer of responsibility for operations and support of the product has been accepted. This includes oversight of any supplier activities, based on the supplier agreement, for the execution of the transition of the product to operations and support.

After the transition is complete and the responsibility is transferred to the operational and support organizations (e.g., at the end of the warranty period for a software product), you review and analyze the results of the transition activities and determine whether any corrective actions (such as process improvement) must be completed before close.

4.5 Summary

One of the biggest challenges that acquirers face is to successfully collaborate with suppliers throughout the entire acquisition, including the development of design constraints for the project or program. There is a tendency to develop these constraints in a vacuum and make critical assumptions about the availability of certain technologies, COTS or otherwise, or about the suppliers' processes; the result is a disjointed, slow delivery process that wastes valuable time and resources in rework.

If you haven't included suppliers in the development process, then having design constraints that are set in stone and enforced by an ironclad supplier agreement isn't a step toward success. On the contrary, the gap between the acquirer's and the supplier's plans and processes becomes a chasm. There's a saying: "Work smarter, not harder." If you don't integrate and manage processes with suppliers, you're working hard but not working smart.

Achieving integrated project management requires bringing your design choices into conformance with the supplier's delivery capabilities. After all, one of the main benefits of outsourcing is to leverage the capabilities of the supplier; if you don't align supplier capabilities with the project, you can never realize this benefit. Integrated project management also focuses on bringing the supplier's process capabilities into conformance with your design constraints early in the system delivery process, so that the two can influence and shape one another in a timely fashion.

Note, however, that neither acquirers nor suppliers need to develop their processes from scratch in order to achieve alignment. Each organization can tailor existing, standard processes to meet the needs of the specific project. This collaboration effort also goes a long way toward establishing in-depth, long-term relationships with suppliers.

Aligning processes is a good start, but even more is required of acquirers and suppliers that want to integrate their work. Each must walk a mile in the other's shoes. You must understand the supplier's perspective on issues such as manufacturability, and suppliers need to comprehend your point of view on performance, total cost of ownership, and the environment in which the product is to be deployed.

Depending on the scope and potential risk of the project, the collaboration effort can be significant. Integration across functions and with suppliers requires that you execute specific activities to support cross-functional work. For example, suppliers build very early system prototypes and test and evaluate them in order to support your desire to develop deeper customer insight early in the process. Similarly, you and your suppliers interact with customers to strengthen and deepen their understanding of the capabilities the product will deliver. The supplier aligns its system delivery processes early in the project and tailors and develops its processes in collaboration with you. In the midst of all this activity, the integrated plan and supplier agreement keeps everyone on the same page and establishes clear roles and accountability for executing the project.

In addition to important documents like the supplier agreement, you need to track, update, and manage other significant artifacts during the acquisition life cycle in order to maintain the integrity of work products and the resulting solution. The act of planning for configuration management requires both you and the supplier to focus on separating the wheat from the chaff. In other words, acquirers and suppliers together must clearly identify the important artifacts to keep and those that are disposable. Not only that, but planning for configuration management includes defining who is responsible for controlling relevant project artifacts and the means by which they will be stored and made accessible for reuse.

Another important consideration is ensuring that the artifacts are formatted using a lowest common denominator so that they are accessible and usable by the acquiring and supplying organizations and any other third parties. Obviously, it is critical to preserve artifacts such as requirements specifications, release plans, detailed designs, acceptance tests, and test results, but if you don't maintain a tight focus on what's important the list of items to be managed could grow exponentially, especially if the project is large and complex. Another goal of planning for configuration management, therefore, is to designate only the minimum number of configuration items necessary to sustain a technical solution in the intended environment. This results, hopefully, in a well-defined list of acquirer work products and supplier deliverables to be managed. Minimizing configuration items is a crucial task, because the cost of maintenance and the number of handoffs between organizations can result in spending a large, unexpected chunk of the program budget.

Planning for configuration management head-on is essential, as is facing the risks inherent in every project. Successful acquirers take a rational approach toward managing risk. The biggest business and technical risk is that the solution will not meet the needs of stakeholders. You also assume the risks generated by the relationships that you establish with suppliers. For example, if a supplier is not financially stable or if it does not have strong processes in place to resolve issues, then issues that arise can be detrimental to the acquisition.

When it comes to managing risk, you have a difficult job because most of your risks are business-oriented, not technical. Technical risk is largely governed by science, whereas business risk can be driven by a myriad of internal and external forces, many of which are outside your control. This doesn't mean, however, that technical risks should be assigned lower criticality. It is important for all risks to be clearly identified, documented, prioritized, and made visible to the appropriate decision makers and stakeholders.

This is often easier said than done, especially in organizational cultures that do not emphasize the reporting of risks or the routing of information to relevant personnel. A stagnant risk management database is a telltale sign that an organization is not attempting to reconcile conflicting risks or to mitigate risks. Risk scorecards and periodic risk assessments are only some of the tools that you can use to ensure that you are staying the course toward risk mitigation.

When it comes to metrics, counting the right things is always better than counting the wrong things or counting just for the sake of counting. Having too many metrics obscures the truly important information and drains both acquirer and supplier teams, who are left to try to generate and interpret the results. To determine which measures are the right ones, you must be able to trace the measurement back to a business or program goal. If the metric doesn't show progress within the project, program, or organization or reveal the outcome of a specific action, then it lacks value and is raising costs and cutting into the profits offered by outsourcing.

Without metrics or a baseline, an acquisition cannot be managed. Taking no measurements or not having a baseline is akin to people who say, "I'm watching my weight, but I'm not keeping track of how much food I eat or how many calories I burn by exercising." These dieters will never know whether their efforts were successful until they step on the scale—if indeed they even know what their weight was before they started "watching." To manage projects, you use supplier-reported measures in addition to your own measures of progress and output. Supplier measures give you the information you need to meet measurement objectives and to assess the project's progress and output. The supplier agreement defines the measures the supplier must report on, including definitions and sample reports. The task of gathering data from a supplier can be coupled with regular interim reviews of supplier work.

After you have defined the measures, selected a supplier, and let the supplier agreement, you focus on monitoring and controlling the progress of the acquisition on both your side and the supplier's. It is essential to ensure that resources are applied effectively and that the project moves forward according to plan. In addition to tracking the supplier's progress, you ensure that the deliverables align with the acceptance criteria you have established. When a project plan goes awry or when a deliverable isn't up to snuff, sometimes corrective action is required. As with any deviation or changes from the original plan, changes in course must be clearly defined and tracked to closure. Again, the onus is on you to initiate corrective actions for deviations from both your and the supplier's plans, as is ensuring that issues are resolved.

Both you and the supplier verify deliverables produced by the supplier. The supplier must verify that the product will function in the intended environment, that it is of the specified quality, and that it meets the criteria set forth in the supplier agreement; you must also verify these things. Because you seldom have insight into the low-level technical details of how a system is built or how software code is written, it is important that you find a cost-effective, intelligent way to test supplier deliverables before deployment. This is especially important with mission-critical systems or those that fill a safety or defense purpose where human lives are on the line. It is vital that you have a tested set of processes and criteria to ensure that the deliverable fulfills its specification when deployed in its intended environment. These verification procedures and criteria should be identified and referenced in the solicitation package and supplier agreement.

The processes are in place, the technology developed, and now it's time to again focus on the people in this equation. It's vital to ensure that personnel are trained to operate the new product. A system that isn't used as intended diminishes in value proportionately to the time and effort that were put into development of the unused or unusable features. Or perhaps new, timesaving features are not known to users, who continue to do things the old way. Training is especially important for those systems that involve the safety and security of human life.

In this chapter, we focused primarily on how acquirers and suppliers must work as integrated teams, handling important project assets under configuration management, managing and mitigating risk, measuring for success, and deploying a technical solution. In Chapter 5, we discuss how you can foster and build a culture in which personnel strive to accelerate process improvement efforts.

Chapter 5

Accelerating Acquisition Improvement

The art of progress is to preserve order amid change and to preserve change amid order.
Alfred North Whitehead (1929)

Organizations that stand still can neither prosper nor survive. Many of us find ourselves in organizations that want to do things "better, cheaper, and faster" but are not sure how to get there. And, in many cases, an organization's culture can't support its aspirations to reach world-class status as the best of the best. We find that leadership isn't there, we don't have effective teams, functional groups are more focused on preserving their territory than producing results, problem-solving processes are superficial, and attempts to implant best practices here and there with good initial results often seem to be rejected shortly thereafter—especially when we must focus on averting the next crisis.

Welcome to the world where most of us live. The scenario just related describes symptoms of an underlying inability to sustain change. And sustaining change is hard work. But examples from many industry and government projects have shown that this hard work pays off over time. The most successful organizations adapt to and sustain change to remain ahead of the competition. So where should you put your energy to accelerate becoming and staying the best acquirer of technology solutions?

To do so, you must ensure that you continue to progress in implementing the activities required not only to meet the best practices set forth in the CMMI-ACQ, but also to meet the underlying challenges of leading and sustaining change. If you can successfully recognize and manage this duality, you will be well on the way to achieving and sustaining progress within your organization.

What is crucial in accelerating acquisition improvement is to gain insight and understanding about how your organization works in practice. Letting imitation or adherence to the status quo guide your improvement won't result in a better, more efficient, more accurate way of delivering technology solutions. Organizations tend to imitate those organizations they admire. However, replicating the behaviors of these role models without a clear understanding of how it affects performance in your own context is a certain recipe for disaster. Solving the problems that limit performance requires a detailed understanding of the root causes of those problems as they play out in the specific circumstances of your organization's acquisition processes.

A key ingredient is to learn from experience, not only to introduce change but also to sustain significant improvements in the acquisition of technology solutions over long periods. This applies equally whether you're in a commercial firm outsourcing help desk services to an IT service supplier, or you're managing a large-scale Department of Defense program, buying control system software developed by a defense contractor.

Another key to accelerating improvement is to avoid management-induced oscillations that result from adopting the management approach "de jour"—a practice that seems to govern some organizations. Often, managers read articles about good management practices and adopt these practices simply because they have been labeled "good," without knowing how these practices affect their economics as acquirers. This is a sure way to get tangled up in the web of management fads, while the organization treads water. Instead, if you are to succeed you must adopt an approach and maintain focus and purpose, and you must do so as efficiently as possible. Following a model-based approach such as the CMMI-ACQ is an effective way to maintain focus and dampen the effect of management-induced oscillations.

Critics of the process improvement approach for acquirers of technology solutions argue that the process takes too long and incurs too high an overhead cost, so why not just adopt the suppliers' processes? If you have done a good job of picking a supplier, what's the problem? You can rely on their process maturity—after all, that's what you're paying for, isn't it?

Not so fast! You have a legal and fiduciary responsibility to oversee the acquisition process and the quality of the product or service being purchased. As discussed in the previous chapters of this book, some of these processes necessarily differ between supplier and acquirer. However, many processes can be shared, and among these, there is a need for harmony. It's not uncommon for suppliers to have a higher process maturity than you have. If there is a mismatch between supplier and acquirer processes, the equation is pretty simple:

Process degradation = inefficiency and rework = increased acquisition costs

So one very important reason that acquisition organizations should be interested in improving their process maturity is to reduce acquisition costs by avoiding inefficiency and rework. It's ironic that many outsourcing efforts or acquisitions are critical to the success of an enterprise, and yet few resources are allocated to ensuring that the acquisition is staffed adequately and that personnel have the proper tools and training to manage the job successfully. Because you'll most likely be given a minimal amount of resources to accomplish the outsourcing project, this means that you need to do so as efficiently as possible.

But cost avoidance is not the only reason to adopt an improvement philosophy. Applying best practices and disciplined processes improves risk management and mitigation activities, generates better early warnings about budget and schedule trends, fosters improved planning and forecasting based on historical evidence, and improves the overall ability to leverage lessons learned (some of which an organization may pay for dearly).

Some organizations begin process improvement to "check a box"—that is, to comply with a regulation or requirement imposed on them, such as a mandate by the executive leader of the organization. However, once begun and properly supported, process improvement is like a snowball rolling downhill. If it is done right, acquirers that embrace process improvement and properly support it realize improved efficiency and a better ability to perform core acquisition functions, such as solicitation and contract monitoring, systems engineering, requirements management, and insight and oversight into the supplier's development activity. Also, they realize the benefit of the overall maturity improvement of the acquisition project, as described earlier.

So what do you do? You have to start somewhere. Let's discuss some approaches to assist your acceleration of process improvement to realize business bottom-line returns quickly and efficiently.

5.1 The Need for Process Stability

Getting off to a good start is critical to any project or program, but especially in an acquisition. Acquirer and supplier processes, particularly where they interact or intersect, need to be stabilized as quickly as possible. In this way, you avoid costly rework and potential negative impacts on the supplier agreement and schedule, not to mention legal ramifications.

When you first start to think about adopting a model-based improvement approach for an acquisition, it is difficult to know where to begin. Looking at the CMMI-ACQ, you quickly realize that the model is comprehensive and complex, with many interrelated best practices. Few acquisition offices have the luxury of dedicated staff to devote to process improvement. The reality is that you can't work on all the process areas at one time, especially if your project has a limited budget for improvement activity. In most cases, improvement must be done incrementally over time.

Let's look at some suggestions for understanding the business goals of the project and seeing how they interrelate with CMMI-ACQ goals and practices. This will help you prioritize your improvement efforts and follow a measured, incremental approach to improvement that begins to return business value quickly.

5.1.1 A Good Hard Look in the Mirror

Working with Paula Ressel, the internal customer of our fictitious acquirer, is an experienced project manager named Steve Reiter. In a meeting with Paula, Steve has identified some important milestones in the acquisition process and has begun to relate them to the CMMI-ACQ. They're pondering a question: What are examples of important, stable processes that we share with our supplier?

After discussing it for a while, they both realize the importance of the contracts area. It's especially crucial in managing the relationship with the supplier as the supplier agreement is put in place and the supplier begins work. So they decide to start there, with acquisition management as an example of a process that must be stable.

Paula: I reread a section of the CMMI-ACQ last night. One key process that we need to stabilize is acquisition management. Let me read the list of what's involved: maintaining ongoing communications and mutual understanding with the supplier, resolving issues and disputes, devising and closing the supplier agreements, accepting delivery of acquired products, transitioning acquired products to the project, and managing the payment to the supplier.

　　After I read this, it really hit me. If we don't get this stuff right early on, we'll have a lot of problems later. Especially since legal issues are involved with contract compliance and performance.

Steve:　And when problems occur later, they're more expensive to fix, since they usually involve schedule or budget slips.

Steve agrees with Paula because he knows the story well from firsthand experience. He worked on several projects earlier in his career that required contract termination actions. He wants to avoid these kinds of situations on this project. For one thing, they're potential career killers. What's more, when contracts get to the point that they require remedies involving potential legal action, no one really benefits. Both the supplier and acquirer stand to lose a lot, so Steve emphasizes with Paula the importance of having the best people for the job in the contracts area.

Steve:　We're interviewing a really sharp contracts person this week to come on board with the project. I want to make sure we're rock solid with the contracts aspects of this project.

Steve and Paula discuss the importance of eliminating redundancy and waste from the contracts process. Paula recalls that on another project, they saved significant amounts of time by streamlining the post-award acceptance of supplier deliverables. Working together, the acquirer and the supplier were able to collaborate on a process that enabled parallel reviews of specifications and deliverables, cut cycle time, and improved teaming between the two parties.

Paula:　We eliminated the "over the wall" approach to contract specification and acceptance, which traditionally is a serial process. You know, that's where we complete a task, throw it over the wall to the supplier, and then wait. The supplier does their analysis, which may include many of the same elements, throws it back over the wall and waits, and so on. The only way we could break this vicious cycle was through constant communication.

Steve:　We had the same issues on another project I worked on. But we never got over the issues created by that wall!

Paula and Steve agree that it's important to maintain appropriate ethical behavior. They know that certain legal and fiduciary functions can't be shared with the supplier, but most functions can and should be subject to open sharing through routine communication.

> **TIP**   Share as much information as possible as often as possible between acquirer and supplier.

Steve recalls another example of shared process—risk management—that paid benefits on a previous project. He relates his opinion that a shared risk management database for the current acquisition project would be key to its success.

Both Steve and Paula agree that contract administration and risk management are examples of processes that can be shared initially and can offer big paybacks in improved communications and reduced overall project cycle time. The key is to stabilize these shared processes early on.

Steve tells Paula about a speech given by their boss, Matt Vauban, to the other company executives. In the presentation, Matt talked about the "hidden truths" of successful acquisition processes. One of the hidden truths was, "Strategic partnering is essential." Steve quotes from his notes of the briefing:

> Coordination costs for outsourcing are incurred by both the acquirer and the supplier in this relationship; the acquirer largely assumes the risks of the supplier. Acquirers and suppliers must acknowledge these costs and risks and mitigate them through ongoing collaboration.

> **TIP**   Shared processes support strategic partnering.

Steve points out to Paula that one of the most important ways that this strategic partnering can occur is through shared processes. He's pleased that they're beginning to define and implement the high-level strategies to which Matt and the other executives had agreed.

Steve: This process improvement approach just might work after all.

Paula: When you came in here today, you mentioned process stability, Steve. We've talked around this concept. I think I know what you mean, but could you explain a bit more how we can implement it?

Steve: Sure, Paula. Question 1, which we've talked about, is what can we collaborate on and share between us and our suppliers? That's important, but the "what" isn't the whole story. You also have to define the "how"— how can we work together? A crucial part of this is process stability up front. In a manufacturing setting, you have all kinds of measurement and analysis to define things like upper and lower control limits for a process. But we're not ready for that. What are the alternatives?

I've been discussing this project with Rosa Gonzales. Do you know Rosa? She's our resident process improvement expert. Matt loaned her out to another division to help them get a project started, but now she's back and we'll have her as a key adviser.

Steve explains that Rosa has given him a chart that shows activities that occur at maturity and capability level 4 in the CMMI framework. He shares his impressions of it with Paula. He believes strongly that using measurement to manage process performance at the organizational level is an important goal. The issue is that they just aren't ready to do that.

Steve: No way will we have "statistically managed subprocesses" any time soon! These are important concepts, and this is what many people mean by stable process performance. I think we should keep them in mind as we move forward, but we're nowhere near ready to implement them at this level of detail yet.

Paula: Well, then, what do you mean by process stability for our project? How will we know it when we see it?

Steve: Good question. Here's my thought. If we and our supplier collaborate on managing and measuring the performance of our common processes and reduce process churn as much as possible, we'll go a long way toward establishing stable processes. In other words, start small, measure how we're doing, and base corrective actions on performance, not management whim. Later we can get more sophisticated in our methods.

> **TIP** Be mindful of higher-level maturity processes even at the beginning, but don't try to do too much too soon.

Paula agrees with this approach. She notes that "touch points" between acquirer and supplier are a good place to start to think about collaboration opportunities. But other topics are pressing, so they agree to talk about touch points at a later time.

Paula: Steve, I think you just answered another question for me. I'm thinking about applying the CMMI-ACQ to another project I'm already working with. That project started about six months ago, and I think we can do a better job of stabilizing our processes. It seems that what you're saying can apply equally well to a project that's just starting up as a project that has already established a relationship with suppliers. What do you think?

Steve: I don't see why not, although it's probably a good idea to talk to our contracts people first. You need to avoid asking for a change that will incur additional cost without realizing that you're committing us to that change. It definitely needs to be done with the help of our contracts people.

> **TIP** Acquisition process improvement can start at any time in the acquisition life cycle, not just at project start-up.

How do you begin to accelerate improvement? You need to establish where you are before you can determine where you want to go. What are the strengths on which you can build, and what are the weaknesses that need to be addressed?

Steve decides to consult with Rosa Gonzales again. They meet in a small conference room and close the door so that they can discuss the challenges of process improvement in private.

> **Steve:** Something that has been troubling me, Rosa, is that five process areas in the CMMI-ACQ have the word "organization" in the title.

Steve is concerned that in terms of what the CMMI-ACQ requires, his project doesn't necessarily have a robust organization structure supporting it. How can he implement the model without one?

> **Rosa:** Well, without a solid organizational structure, you may not be able to comply with all aspects of the model. But that doesn't mean you can't begin a process improvement effort. It depends on what your process improvement goals are. You should identify these in the project's process improvement plan.

So far, this sounds good to Steve.

> **TIP** Process improvement efforts can start at the project level even without an organizational-level support structure.

Rosa continues.

> **Rosa:** The CMMI-ACQ permits projects to get a maturity or capability rating by going through a formal appraisal process. Some organizations undergo an appraisal to not only help guide and plan improvement efforts, but also for other business reasons. For instance, some contracts require suppliers to demonstrate a certain level of maturity or capability before they're allowed to bid. If your goal is to quickly get a level rating for the project, you may have some issues. You don't have the organizational process areas in place that you can tailor for this project. That means your project can't meet all the model requirements, and your appraisal would expose some areas that aren't fully covered by your implementation.

Steve: That doesn't sound good.

Rosa: Well, it depends on your goal. If your goal is to begin a process improvement program to take advantage of best practices, there's nothing keeping you from getting started! In fact, the CMMI-ACQ is structured to support best practices at the project level.

Steve: It's really about improving the business for us, making it more efficient and improving the quality of products we deliver to our customers. I think that's more important to us than a rating.

Rosa smiles knowingly.

Rosa: In some cases, the project becomes the prototype or flagship for the organization, which then takes what the project has done and builds on that to expand it to the larger organization. Using the materials you develop can help me expand process improvement throughout our entire organization.

Now Steve starts to get nervous all over again. He must complete this outsourcing effort with minimum resources, and the process improvement manager is telling him that along with all the other things he has to be concerned about, he has to help the entire organization, too. This isn't scoped in his project plan, and he doesn't see how he can sell this to Matt and the leadership team. The impacts on cost and schedule will be too great. Steve makes this point emphatically to Rosa.

Rosa: Whoa, slow down! I think you misunderstood my meaning, Steve. Many of the things that can contribute to building an organizational capability are really just good project management practices. They really shouldn't be an "over and above" burden to the project. For instance, collecting metrics about project performance and generating ideas for improving performance are good practices for any project.

> **TIP**   Project improvement efforts can be harvested for successful practices that can be used across the organization.

Steve feels a little better, but he's still skeptical.

Steve: I wonder how we know where to start, Rosa. The CMMI-ACQ is very comprehensive, and many of the process areas seem interrelated. Dropping this entire effort onto our project team right now is a nonstarter. We can't possibly do everything we need to do if we're spending all our time on process improvement. If we try to do it all at once, we'll frustrate our people and miss our deadlines.

Rosa: What you need is a place to start building an understanding of where you are. I think you should start with the Organizational Process Focus process area.

Your first step is to get with the stakeholders—Paula, Matt, and the others. Find out what they think your potential problem areas are, and what your strengths and weaknesses are. To help with this, you might want to try a tool called the Strengths, Weaknesses, Opportunities, and Threats analysis. It's a pretty simple exercise, and it helps you identify the project's weaknesses and threats and understand how to turn them into strengths and opportunities. And identifying strengths and opportunities may give you ideas about how to build on these and maybe pick some low-hanging fruit.

Steve: Wait a minute. I thought we just said we didn't necessarily have the organizational process areas in place around here. So how can we use them in this project?

> **TIP** You can't do everything at once. Understand what your business objectives are. Then start small with focused improvement efforts that return business value quickly.

Rosa: Well, in an ideal world, you'd have them in place. Your project could draw them from a process asset library, and you could tailor them to your needs. But you don't have that. So your best bet is to take a bottom-up approach and get started at the project level. As we move forward, we can start to build up our organizational assets.

Steve: I like the idea of picking low-hanging fruit, Rosa. That will help us demonstrate early wins and help build and sustain momentum for the project and our organization.

Rosa: Steve, I think one of the most important things about getting started is to understand where you are. Watts Humphrey, the founder of the SEI Software Process Program, once said, "If you don't know where you are, a map won't help!"

There's a lot of wisdom in this. One thing that distinguishes high-performing organizations from the rest of the pack is that they're brutally honest about themselves, and they do their best to get an objective view of where they are. Sometimes a third-party assessment or appraisal can help.

Our process group does informal assessments, and in the past we've contracted with some companies for formal appraisals. What this does is set a baseline for where you are. Then you can decide where you want to go.

> **TIP**   Baseline where your project is in terms of the CMMI-ACQ. Inexpensive, informal assessments that target a few process areas are a good way to get started.

Steve: I don't mind being self-critical, but I'm afraid we wouldn't learn much from an appraisal. We don't have any processes documented, and we don't have time to do that now. Remember the schedule we have!

Rosa: I don't agree, Steve. You have a lot of processes in place already and many artifacts that show you're following them. Maybe these processes aren't documented, but they sure are in our organizational DNA. You just don't realize it. We've had success in the past with doing an informal assessment and then identifying one or two areas to focus on. Then build from there.

Steve: Okay. Maybe an in-house assessment would help us baseline where we are. But we need to talk some more about how many resources it will take.

> **TIP**   Prioritize process improvement. Address high-risk areas first.

Rosa: We've done quite a few of these, Steve. They take very little time and have very little impact on your people. Let me work up a notional schedule for us to discuss next week.

Steve: All right, Rosa, I'm about half convinced. I hear what you're saying. If we do an assessment, we can use it to flag our problem areas and focus on them to get started. But I really want to see your plan before I sign up for it. I'm still concerned about the time commitment from my project team. What else do you have in your bag of tricks that can help?

Rosa: Well, how about risk identification and metrics? Risk identification is one of the first steps in a risk management approach, and it engages the relevant stakeholders. Let your customer help you decide where your high-risk areas are, and use the CMMI-ACQ to help identify process areas or practices that can address those risks.

You use metrics to baseline where you are. This lets you set goals and then measure your progress as you move forward with the improvement effort.

Rosa and Steve agree to get together again soon to continue discussing an internal assessment to baseline Steve's project. They also plan to create an outline for an improvement approach that makes sense given where the project is in its life cycle.

5.1.2 Applying the CMMI-ACQ to Planning Process Improvement

The CMMI-ACQ provides specific recommendations on how to plan and implement organizational process improvement based on a thorough understanding of the current strengths and weaknesses of the organization's processes and process assets (see Table 5-1). The organization's processes include all the processes used by the organization and its projects.

The organization's processes operate in a business context that must be understood (Table 5-1, practice 1.1). The organization's business objectives, needs, and constraints determine the needs and objectives of the organiza-

Table 5-1 *Organizational Process Focus Goal 1: Practices and Tips*

CMMI-ACQ Process Area: Organizational Process Focus	
1. Goal: Strengths, weaknesses, and improvement opportunities for the organization's processes are identified periodically and as needed.	
Practices	**Tips**
1.1 Establish and maintain the description of the process needs and objectives for the organization.	• Process improvement efforts can start at the project level, even without an organizational-level support structure. • You can't do everything at once. Understand what your business objectives are. Then start small with focused improvement efforts that return business value quickly.
1.2 Appraise the organization's processes periodically and as needed to maintain an understanding of its strengths and weaknesses. 1.3 Identify improvements to the organization's processes and process assets.	• Baseline where your project is in terms of the CMMI-ACQ. Inexpensive, informal assessments that target a few process areas are a good way to get started. • Prioritize process improvement. Address high-risk areas first. • Project improvement efforts can be harvested for successful practices that can be used across the organization.

tion's processes. You obtain candidate improvements to the organization's processes from various sources, including measurement of the processes, lessons learned in implementing the processes, results of process appraisals, results of product evaluation activities, results of benchmarking against other organizations' processes, and recommendations from other improvement initiatives in the organization.

The organization's process needs and objectives cover aspects that include the following:

- Characteristics of the processes
- Process performance objectives, such as time to market and delivered quality
- Process effectiveness

Before you evaluate processes against the CMMI-ACQ or other industry standards such as ISO 9001, it is critical to obtain sponsorship of the process assessment or appraisal from senior management. Assessments can be informal efforts (even done by an in-house team) that result in a quick snapshot of process performance. Standard CMMI appraisals are more rigorous; they follow Software Engineering Institute (SEI) guidelines and must be led by SEI-trained and approved team leaders.

Senior management sponsorship includes the commitment to have the organization's managers and staff members participate in the assessment or appraisal and to provide the resources and funding to analyze and communicate the findings. Process assessments can be performed on the entire organization or on a smaller part, such as a single project or business area. The scope of the assessment depends on the following:

- Definition of the parts of the organization (e.g., sites or business areas) that will be covered by the assessment
- Identification of the project and support functions that will represent the organization in the assessment
- Processes that will be evaluated

It's critical to identify opportunities for true improvement to the project's and the organization's performance (Table 5-1, practice 1.3). You have a myriad of ways available to identify improvements:

- Measure the processes, and analyze the measurement results.
- Review the processes for effectiveness and suitability.
- Review the lessons learned from tailoring the organization's set of standard processes.

- Review the lessons learned from implementing the processes.
- Review process improvement proposals submitted by managers and staff as well as other relevant stakeholders. A relevant stakeholder is one who is identified for involvement in specified activities and is included in a plan.
- Solicit inputs on process improvements from senior management and other leaders.
- Examine the results of process appraisals and other process-related reviews.
- Review results of other organization improvement initiatives.
- Review process improvement proposals submitted by your suppliers.
- Obtain feedback from suppliers on your processes and supplier-acquirer interface points.

To focus energy on those improvement opportunities with the highest impact, you must prioritize them. To do so, you consider the estimated cost and effort to implement the improvements, evaluate the expected improvement against your improvement objectives and priorities, and determine the potential barriers to the improvements and develop strategies for overcoming these barriers.

5.1.3 Back to Basics

Many organizations make the mistake of trying to document all processes simultaneously, or they attempt to create highly detailed process descriptions. Organizations that attempt these approaches soon realize that they are not effective. Steve consults with Rosa to get some guidance about starting the process.

> **TIP** Adopt CMMI-ACQ practices incrementally, and prioritize them according to the value they add to the organization.

Steve: Okay, Rosa, so the CMMI-ACQ gives us some pointers on how to prioritize our efforts. But once we decide on what to focus on, what do we do next? We can't afford the time to run around documenting all our processes at once! How do we communicate what's important?

Rosa smiles.

Rosa: You're right! Remember, I've been down this road before. I know your driving force is the need to meet your project schedule, come hell or high water. So we have to demonstrate how adopting the model is going to help you get predictable on your schedule.

What you need is a playbook approach, one that builds on what your organization knows about itself from its good hard look in the mirror. Simple, concise, objective statements that are unambiguous and communicate the improvement goals clearly are worth much more than a set of complex "shelfware" that is too cumbersome to be used in daily practice.

Rosa continues to encourage Steve.

> **TIP**   Build an improvement playbook that states goals and measures simply. Use the playbook to guide your efforts.

Rosa: In this first process improvement project, remember that you're looking for the low-hanging fruit. If you start small and demonstrate success quickly in some area of the project, even a small one, it will help build momentum. Remember how we started this conversation? You can't do it all at once!

Steve nods.

Rosa: This approach keeps your team motivated, too. If they get positive feedback more often and see progress with incremental steps, you'll have a much easier time keeping them enthused than if you attempt the "Mother of All Process Improvement Efforts" that seems to take forever and is too complex.

Steve: Okay. But it needs to be worthwhile, too, not just a showpiece.

Rosa: Absolutely. Later on, after you've gotten some stable processes in place, one of the most productive techniques for understanding where you can improve efficiency is something called value stream mapping. I've used this a lot. You use it to eliminate areas of little value-added activity that add time or effort to your process without much return.

Let me tell you a story.

I have a friend who works at the Department of Defense. Their office supports military aircraft. Okay, so the field maintenance techs would find a failed component. They'd remove it, pack it up, and ship it back through the government transportation system to begin the repair cycle. In between these guys and the repair facility was this checkpoint. At this checkpoint, they unpacked the item, compared it with the paperwork, and then packed it up again and put it back in the shipping cycle. All this took three days or more.

Well, guess what? More than 90 percent of the time, the items were already properly documented and addressed. All this checking was a holdover from an attempt to fix the process that had failed years ago.

But meantime, the world turned, and the checking process had outgrown its usefulness and was now a drag on the system. So they did value stream analysis, and it told them to cut out this non-value-added step and save a bunch of cycle time in the aircraft repair value chain.

Steve: Well, the value of that kind of thing is obvious.

Rosa: Still, making this change wasn't easy. It meant a potential loss of jobs, maybe closing facilities. That's what I mean by being brutally honest. Matt is big on driving out waste from our processes. I think he'll implement changes we might come up with, if they're well supported and make good economic sense.

Steve nods.

Rosa: These are some things to think about for later, after you get initial process stability. I feel your pain, Steve. Obviously, you can't do all this at once and still keep the project going. Let me think about how to help you get the most return for your time commitment, and which technique or combination we might use first to get started.

Let's look at your project. Can you give me an example of a strength of your process?

> **TIP**   Use sophisticated techniques such as value stream mapping appropriately, as project processes mature and stabilize.

Steve: Sure—contracts. I've been talking with Paula, and we both agree that we have to get the contract right up front. Our contracts process has been in place for a while—I think you would call it a stable process—and it's laid out pretty completely. Maybe this is a strength we can build on.

Rosa: Good idea! The CMMI-ACQ gives us a couple of relevant process areas with some best practices: Solicitation and Supplier Agreement Development, and Acquisition Management. I'll bet our contracts shop already meets many of these. This might be the quick win or low-hanging fruit we're looking for.

Steve smiles.

Steve: Well, that was easy.

His tone tells Rosa he's only kidding. But a small step is still a step.

Rosa: If you want me to, I can help you with some of the documentation. And I can use what we produce to start up our corporate knowledge repository of project process artifacts. One of these days, we'll be able to give projects like yours some templates and checklists to help get them started, but we're not quite there yet. You're going to help us get there.

Now, Steve, don't be nervous. It's true, I'm using your project work to help us get started with our improvement goals at the corporate level. So, for instance, your lessons learned will help people all over the company with their own improvement activities. For you, the beauty is that you get my full attention—and, well, I know how to do this. You'll help me, and I'll help you. This incremental implementation of processes is reflected in the structure of the CMMI framework, which supports building project-level capability before organizational capability.

Let's look at the structure of the model. Table 5-2 lists the five generic goals.

Any project that is accomplishing work, delivering products, and meeting its project goals is *performing* processes. They may not be documented processes, and they may not all be repeatable, but the project is following processes nonetheless. A key point is to understand which ones should be documented and repeated because they add business value through efficiency or effectiveness. These processes can become the foundation for describing the way a project routinely does its work and how it should continue to do its work in the future.

Once a project begins to *manage* its processes, it has begun to institutionalize specific practices at the project level. The CMMI-ACQ defines a managed process this way:

> A managed process is a performed process that is planned and executed in accordance with policy; employs skilled people who have adequate resources to produce controlled outputs; involves relevant stakeholders; is monitored, controlled, and reviewed; and is evaluated for adherence to its process description. The process may be instantiated by a project, group, or organizational function.

Table 5-2 *Generic Goals and Progression of Processes*

Generic Goal	Progression of Processes
GG 1	Performed process
GG 2	Managed process
GG 3	Defined process
GG 4	Quantitatively managed process
GG 5	Optimizing process

> **TIP** Look carefully at the processes that your organization already has in place. They may be a good place to start improvement activity.

Steve: You know what Matt was saying the other day? What we are really doing with this project is building on our foundation practices and our core competencies to come up with a strategy for what we do in-house and what we want to outsource [Prahalad and Hamel 1990]. This is getting back to basics at the organization level.

 What we're talking about here is extending our work, and getting back to basics at the project level.

Rosa: Yes! You have to start with the basics. In the CMMI-ACQ, just as in the entire CMMI framework, there are ten generic practices that satisfy the generic goal of institutionalizing a managed process. They're really pretty straightforward and follow a logical progression. And they apply to any process area in the model.

Table 5-3 shows the list of generic practices that Rosa showed Steve.

This makes sense to Steve, and he begins to see the point Rosa is making. The model requirements for generic processes address foundation practices and include most of the things that a project should do anyway: Establish goals

Table 5-3 *CMMI-ACQ Generic Practices*

GP 2.1   Establish an Organizational Policy
Establish and maintain an organizational policy for planning and performing the process.
GP 2.2   Plan the Process
Establish and maintain the plan for performing the process.
GP 2.3   Provide Resources
Provide adequate resources for performing the process, developing the work products, and providing the services of the process.
GP 2.4   Assign Responsibility
Assign responsibility and authority for performing the process, developing the work products, and providing the services of the process.

Table 5-3 *CMMI-ACQ Generic Practices (continued)*

GP 2.5   Train People
Train the people performing or supporting the process as needed. Refer to the Organizational Training process area for more information on training the people performing or supporting the process.
GP 2.6   Manage Configurations
Place designated work products of the process under appropriate levels of control.
GP 2.7   Identify and Involve Relevant Stakeholders
Identify and involve the relevant stakeholders as planned. Refer to the Project Planning process area for information on project planning for stakeholder involvement.
GP 2.8   Monitor and Control the Process
Monitor and control the process against the plan for performing the process, and take appropriate corrective action. Refer to the Project Monitoring and Control process area for more information about monitoring and controlling the project and taking corrective action. Refer to the Measurement and Analysis process area for more information about measurement.
GP 2.9   Objectively Evaluate Adherence
Objectively evaluate adherence of the process against its process description, standards, and procedures, and address noncompliance. Refer to the Process and Product Quality Assurance process area for more information about objectively evaluating adherence.
GP 2.10   Review Status with Higher-Level Management
Review the activities, status, and results of the process with higher-level management, and resolve issues.

or policy, plan how to accomplish the goals of the process area, resource it and assign people to it, make sure the people are adequately trained, configuration-manage your work products (whether they're contractor-provided or generated by the project office), ensure that the project's stakeholders are involved, monitor and control project activity, provide quality assurance over work products and the project's adherence to its established policies and processes, and make sure that higher management is informed routinely about project status.

> **TIP** Implement CMMI-ACQ generic practices to sustain improvement.

Steve: Rosa, the project is already doing or planning to do much of what's called for in the Solicitation and Supplier Agreement Management process area.

Rosa: You're beginning to break the code! Much of what the CMMI-ACQ requires is just good management practice that you're probably doing already. What it does is raise your awareness of processes in use and ensure that they're supported, standardized, and institutionalized over time. The generic practices are a great place to start. And remember, the model doesn't tell you how to meet its requirements. It focuses on what constitutes a best practice, but it leaves the "how" up to the project.

Steve: Yes, it's making sense.

Rosa: Let me share something with you. I have a friend who works for a big government agency in Washington. Up until about a year and a half ago, they were using the Software Acquisition Capability Maturity Model [SA-CMM] as a reference model. My friend and his process guys and a couple of functional subject matter experts went off in a corner and hammered out beautiful processes and took them back to the projects.

You know what happened? They crashed and burned!

Beautiful processes that don't match reality are about the last thing projects want to see or use. I've come to realize that this simply isn't the way to do it. And this is also in the overall CMMI model, and it's something our consultants have told us, too.

Steve: I'm glad to hear that. I was afraid of trying to meet some impossible goal that would turn out not to be very helpful anyway.

Rosa: Look at the generic practices. One is to "plan the process." What we're trying to do is work with a couple of projects to plan out the activities to implement the necessary practices in their project. Then see how that goes. Based on that, those two projects will pull back and say, "Here are the eight steps you had planned for getting requirements management going. So how did that go? If you had to do it again, what would you do differently?"

Steve nods.

Rosa: At that point, we'll begin to document the process steps by looking at the planned activities that occurred in those projects. We'll be documenting the "as-is"—build on what we already have. We'll just work with the teams and say, "How have you done it? How will you do it on this particular project?" With no judgmental notion about it. Just put it on paper, write it out, plan it out, and then let's watch it and see how it goes. See where the bottlenecks are, see what really happens.

Then based on that experience, we begin to document the process descriptions. Now, of course, all along we had the CMMI model in our hip pocket and our mind, and we're looking for those practices to be planned into these efforts. We do it as we work with the project, or if not, we help them understand the reason it needs to be done. But certainly we don't go off and write a process first in some ivory tower with the intent that everybody has to use it.

> **TIP**   If you take a discovery and experimental approach, you may find that you are changing the process a little through each review cycle. Don't "lock down" the process until you are finished with the cycles.

Steve: No ivory tower. Check.

Rosa smiles.

Rosa: Ultimately, once the two projects are done, we'll let the dust settle, pull them together, and say, "What did you do? What worked?" Then document a process formally from that. That's really what "plan the process" means. That's what we're trying to get to.

It's very, very fundamental, and a lot of times it's very soft—you know, GMA.

Steve: GMA?

Rosa: "General milling around." People are sort of doing stuff, but it isn't clear exactly what they're producing and who's doing it. Is it us or them?

Steve: Now I'm a little bit lost.

> **TIP**   Often, only suppliers produce a project plan. The acquirer also needs a project plan to manage its activity and its various interfaces with the supplier.

Rosa: No problem. Let's look at Project Planning again. We go in and ask a project manager, "Do you have a project plan?" He says, "Well, yes, that's what we're getting as a deliverable from the supplier."

Uh-oh. We say, "No. Do you have a project plan for your effort?" The project manager says, "Just the one the supplier's delivering." So all of a sudden, you crack into the supplier's plan, and you see very few acquirer activities in there. It's all about what the supplier's going to do for this project and how they're going to execute the task order, and that sort of thing.

So what we're trying to do is say, "Look, the basic concept is that we have to plan, write our own project plan specifically on the acquisition side. The roles and responsibilities have to be explicitly stated in there, so it's very clear to everybody who does what."

There is a pause while Steve thinks through what Rosa has said.

Steve: Wow, you've said a mouthful, Rosa. I like your good practical advice about avoiding the ivory tower approach to document the "perfect process," and how to build on what we have in a practical way by using basic building blocks like the generic practices. I also like the points you made about making sure we exercise our responsibilities.

Rosa: Good. You understood me perfectly.

Steve: But I think some of the team, including some of our managers, thought we could just adopt contractor processes and plans without effort on our part.

Rosa smiles.

Rosa: I told you—I've been down this road before.

5.1.4 Applying the CMMI-ACQ to Planning Process Improvement

The CMMI-ACQ provides specific recommendations on how to plan and implement process improvement activities (see Table 5-4). To implement your process improvements successfully, the process owners, those who perform the process, and support organizations need to participate in the process definition and improvement activities.

The acquirer involves stakeholders such as process owners, process action teams, and the management steering committee to obtain buy in of the process improvements. This approach increases the likelihood of effective deployment (Table 5-4, practice 2.1).

Process action plans are detailed implementation plans. They typically cover the following:

- Process improvement infrastructure
- Process improvement objectives

Table 5-4 *Organizational Process Focus Goal 2: Practices and Tips*

CMMI-ACQ Process Area: Organizational Process Focus	
2. Goal: Improvements are planned and implemented, organizational process assets are deployed, and process-related experiences are incorporated into the organizational process assets.	
Practices	**Tips**
2.1 Establish and maintain action plans to address improvements to the organization's processes and process assets. 2.2 Implement process action plans across the organization. 2.3 Deploy process assets across the organization. 2.4 Incorporate process-related experiences into the organizational process assets.	• Often, only suppliers produce a project plan. The acquirer also needs a project plan to manage the project office's activity and its various interfaces with the supplier. • Build an improvement playbook that states goals and measures simply. Use the playbook to guide your efforts. • Project improvement efforts can be harvested for successful practices that can be used across the organization.

- Process improvements that will be addressed
- Procedures for planning and tracking process actions
- Strategies for piloting and implementing the process actions
- Responsibility and authority for implementing the process actions
- Resources, schedules, and assignments for implementing the process actions
- Methods for determining the effectiveness of the process actions
- Risks associated with process action plans

Process action plans differ from the organization's process improvement plan in that they target specific improvements that have been defined to address weaknesses usually not covered by appraisals. If the processes that define interfaces between acquirer and supplier are targeted for improvement, suppliers may be involved in developing the process action plans.

You should implement process action plans and deploy organizational process assets or changes to organizational process assets in an orderly manner (Table 5-4, practices 2.2 and 2.3). It may not be appropriate to implement some organizational process assets or changes to them in some parts of the organization (for example, because of customer requirements or the current life-cycle phase being implemented). It is therefore important that those personnel who are or will be executing the process, as well as other organization functions (such as training and quality assurance), are involved in deploying changed or new processes. In the supplier agreement, you define how changes to organizational process assets that affect the supplier (e.g., standard supplier deliverables, acceptance criteria) must be deployed.

You derive lessons learned from defining, piloting, implementing, and deploying the organizational process assets (Table 5-4, practice 2.4). For example, projects collect lessons learned from a project activity such as a design review or user acceptance test so that they can improve the process the next time. This requires effort on the part of projects to identify and collect useful improvement information, and on the part of the organization to designate a method and a place to store this information and make it widely available. Many firms and agencies use electronic collaborative workspaces for this purpose.

5.2 Establish Standardized Work Processes

"Standardize whenever possible" was one of the hidden truths that Matt spoke about in his briefing to the other senior managers.

> Processes, contracts, requirements, products, and product components are all viable candidates for standardization. Don't buy in to the myth that standardization stifles creativity. On the contrary, teams have more freedom to be creative and productive when they are allowed to focus on a handful of requirements that are specific to the project and can leverage predefined requirements and reuse products and product components.

TIP Standardize processes to ensure continuous flow of work and encourage creativity and initiative.

Steve believes that implementing this concept (especially with standardized processes) is critical to the start-up phase of the project. He realizes that the project is already following a standard process in the procurement area. All projects must follow the standard procurement rules, or else they don't get funded. Contracting and procurement seem to him to be a good example of a process that is already standardized across the organization.

Another is metrics. The organization requires routine earned value reports on project status and requires a standard way to present project cost and schedule data. Using these existing processes as starting points for process improvement makes sense to Steve. The existing processes are not very far out of line with the best practices called for in the CMMI-ACQ.

TIP Standardized processes already exist in many organizations. If possible, build on what is already there.

Steve mentions this observation to Rosa. She tells him that those two examples touch on several process areas in the model, such as Acquisition Management, Measurement and Analysis, and Project Monitoring and Control.

> **Rosa:** This is why I really like the model. It's not just theoretical. We can use it to translate a real-world issue and guide our thinking about how to implement best practices.

> **Steve:** Come on, Rosa, you know I'm a fan of this approach. I just wish you had a magic wand sometimes! The acquisition management suggestion is a good one, and it fits with what Paula and I were thinking. Thanks for the idea.

Even though things are starting to fall into place, Steve is still struggling with the issue of how to standardize work with the supplier. He thinks the answer may lie in touch points, a topic he and Paula have agreed to discuss further.

The buyer-seller relationship between acquirer and supplier implies that not all processes can be shared between them. But it's important to look at the entire value chain embodied in the acquirer-supplier relationship to understand the effects of collaboration (or the lack thereof). If the supplier and acquirer don't or can't completely share all processes that they have in common, they can easily find themselves in a maturity "mismatch."

A growing body of evidence suggests that just because a company, a government program office, or a supplier has a certain maturity or capability level rating, it is no guarantee of future performance. In fact, as illustrated in Figure 5-1, a high-maturity supplier paired with a low-maturity acquirer can experience degradation in their supplier processes. The cause is the acquirer tends to take actions such as encouraging shortcuts. To use a statistical analogy, both organizations can tend to "regress to the mean" of their combined maturity levels. This is why it's important to collaborate and cooperate at key points in the overall process value chain. Not only does it make the entire cycle more efficient, but also it vests both supplier and acquirer in the success of their mutual enterprise and binds them together toward the common goal.

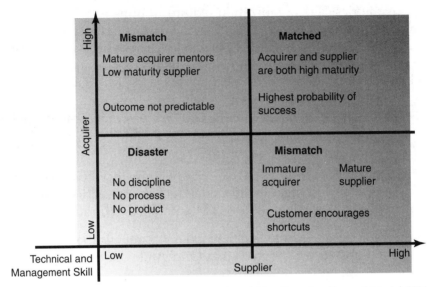

Source: Adapted from Software Engineering Institute, Acquisition Overview Course Material, 2004.

Figure 5-1 *Acquirer-Supplier mismatch*

What are the boundaries of processes in the acquisition context? In this instance, we're addressing not only the internal processes of the acquirer and the supplier, but also the fundamental and important linkages and touch points between them that are critical to the success of the acquisition.

Figure 5-2 illustrates the flow of acquiring a product or service, including the critical touch points between supplier and acquirer. Note that the acquirer and the supplier adopt different primary roles as the acquisition process progresses and also that linkages occur throughout the process. For instance, the acquirer adopts an insight and oversight role during development of the technology solution, whereas the supplier adopts a builder role. Their touch points can take the form of meetings, artifacts (such as source code and test results), and many other forms. The individual processes of the acquirer and the supplier must be in harmony to maximize efficiency and throughput of the overall acquisition.

TIP   Support standard roles and responsibilities through clearly defined acquirer-supplier touch points.

Note that throughout the development of the product, even though you are not directly producing the product you must maintain insight into and over-

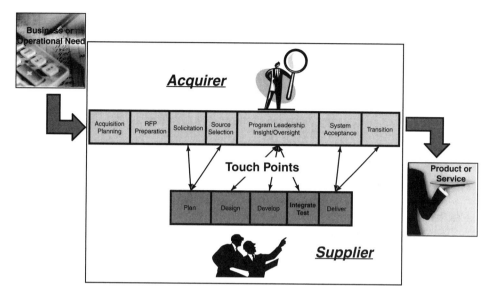

Source: Adapted from Software Engineering Institute, Acquisition Overview Course Material, 2004.

Figure 5-2   *The acquisition process context*

sight of the supplier's processes. You must do this in a disciplined manner that doesn't impede the efficiency of the process. This is an example of how the CMMI-ACQ applies to the processes of both the supplier and the acquirer.

TIP To optimize the execution of projects, align your life-cycle model with the supplier's.

When Steve and Paula get together in the morning, Paula begins the discussion.

Paula: We talked yesterday about the need for process stability. You remember that I mentioned touch points, and how we might use them to decide what our most important collaboration opportunities might be. Let's talk about touch points.

Steve: I hate to admit it, but I'm not sure what the term means exactly. Can you help me out, Paula?

Paula: I think that "touch points" originally comes from marketing and advertising. It's how a company "touches" a customer. Hold on, I think I have a good definition here.

Paula reads from her laptop screen (http://www.livework.co.uk/home/research0/glossary.html).

Service touch points are the tangibles that make up the total experience of using a service. Touch points can take many forms, from advertising to personal cards, web, mobile phone, and PC interfaces, bills, retail shops, call centers and customer representatives. When we design services, we consider all touch points in totality and craft them in order to create a clear and consistent unified customer experience. The tangible touch points of the service are one of the key factors that determine people's experience of service quality.

Steve: Oh, okay.

Paula: In our context, I think of touch points as part of the overall value chain that creates, delivers, and maintains our product. When you look at the value chain as an overall process, the interfaces where we and the supplier interact are the touch points.

Paula brings up an image on her laptop and turns the screen toward Steve (see Figure 5-3).

Paula: I originally drew this on a cocktail napkin, but I've cleaned it up a little. It may not cover all the touch points, but I think it's a good start.

Steve: Okay, so look at the solicitation and source selection phases. What touch points does the supplier have there?

Paula: We often do RFIs to try to identify whether the supplier has the capability to perform—or even to identify potential suppliers. This is

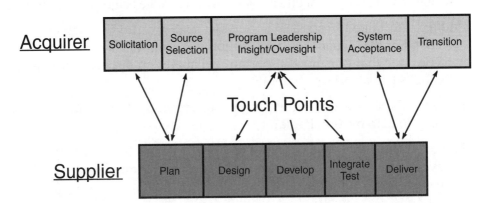

Source: Adapted from Software Engineering Institute, Acquisition Overview Course Material, 2004.

Figure 5-3   *Acquirer-Supplier touch points in the acquisition process*

before we begin formal solicitation, bidding, or source selection. So to respond to that, the suppliers need to begin to plan their potential product design early on. So the RFI is our first touch point with them.

Matt Vauban has talked to Steve and Paula about the relationship that needs to be established between the acquirer and the supplier during development. This is the phase in the life cycle when the acquirer adopts the role of monitoring and overseeing the supplier's development process. In many cases, acquirers opt out of this role and more or less wait passively for the acceptance test of the final product. Paula and Steve know that this practice often has dire consequences.

> **Paula:** You know, Steve, we talked yesterday about the formal contract relationship between us and the supplier, and how we have a legal and fiduciary responsibly over the development. I can think of many touch points along the way that we need to define.

> **Steve:** You're right. A lot of these are pretty straightforward, like specifications, system test, formal acceptance and sign-off, and so on. But some of them aren't so obvious—like shared risk management and configuration management over work products that we use to manage the project. It's really important to look at this entire process as a value chain that flows back and forth between us and the supplier.

> **Paula:** I see what you mean. We have to look at the whole supply chain, not just one segment. If we don't, we'll be suboptimizing our efforts.

> **Steve:** I think we need to get our brain trust together to develop a list of the most important touch points. Then we can evaluate the ones we already have a process for and the ones we don't. This will help us focus on the most important ones first.

Paula agrees, and they plan how to proceed by listing the key acquisition functions: contracts, systems engineering, the customer or functional representative, and others. With input from these stakeholders, they'll be able to list key touch points and use this list to guide and prioritize their process improvement activity.

Paula and Steve talk briefly about the steps that will follow this initial work: documenting and verifying existing processes and beginning to address the activities that don't have documented processes. After a supplier is identified, this effort can serve as the beginning of collaboration and standardization of the interfaces between the acquirer and the supplier.

Steve leaves Paula's office believing that they're on the right track with their decision to base collaboration opportunities on touch points. In the hallway he runs into Matt, who pulls Steve into his office.

They sit and talk about the idea of using touch points, and then Matt waxes philosophical about the difficulty of changing the way an organization functions.

Matt: What we're trying to do is adopt a life cycle that's standards-based so we have some sort of underlying framework that ties everything together. But it's hard work.

In any organization, as you go along in time, the way people do their work gets ingrained in their day-to-day activities. The longer that occurs, the more resistant they are to understanding or moving to a common framework. So that presents challenges to us.

Steve agrees. He tells Matt that he's concerned about managing change within his team. He relates Rosa's point that the ivory tower approach to improvement doesn't work and talks about his commitment to small, practical steps.

Matt: That's good. The team is more apt to engage with you if you do it that way. Coming to a functional group with a nice clean-looking process makes their eyes glaze over. You have to adopt different roles in different situations: mentor, coach, or teacher. If you work with them and show them you understand where they're coming from, you open the door. And then as you work with them, you're teaching, you're guiding. Then they begin to contribute: "Hey, how about adding this step in here?" And so they feel a part of the whole effort. They like that. And they know the big boss is really all into this. So, it all works together.

> **TIP**   Don't design "ideal" processes in a vacuum; engage practitioners to define their processes.

Matt leans back in his chair.

Matt: I have a friend who still works for a big industrial firm where I used to work—huge company, international. They've gone into outsourcing in a big way. They use what DoD calls the "alpha contracting" approach. Here, Steve, here's a write-up.

Steve reads from a Navy reference that Matt has downloaded and printed (http://acquisition.navy.mil/navyaos/content/view/full/132).

> Alpha Contracting streamlines the acquisition process and reduces cycle time for contracts. It emphasizes conducting actions concurrently, with a close relationship between an integrated Gov-

ernment team and the contractors. For example, under Alpha contracting, the Government and contractors may work together to develop a solicitation package that meets the Government's needs, while also eliminating contractor questions or concerns with it. Similarly, as the contractors complete development of portions of their technical and cost proposals, an integrated Government team, including representatives of the program office, the contracting office, the contract administration office, and the Defense Contract Audit Agency (DCAA), may review the proposal and attempt to resolve issues the team identifies. When the completed proposals are then formally submitted to the contracting officer, much of it may already be negotiated. This approach is much more likely to result in an optimized program with an achievable scope, improved performance or quality, and the avoidance of non-value added requirements, at a lower overall cost than what was originally contemplated.

TIP Encourage collaboration, not competition, between acquirer and supplier.

Matt: You get the picture. The acquisition is viewed as a collaborative effort between supplier and acquirer. Both parties participate mutually to ensure that the overall process and touch points, such as solicitation, proposal review, and so on, are collaborations and not adversarial.

Steve: It sounds kind of like what we're trying to do.

Matt: Let me tell you a story. My former company adopted this philosophy in outsourcing their IT work. They were heavy users of IT services, but IT was not their core business. So they brought in all the suppliers to develop the process and the overall operational environment they'd be living in for the next few years. They jointly defined and developed common global IT execution processes. By having the potential suppliers work together with the company, it fostered a "one-team" mentality. So they were able to identify and resolve problems early. It let them leverage the best thinking in the industry. The suppliers, even before they were suppliers, got an early, up-close look at the operability of the processes.

The bottom line is, those suppliers have a sense of joint ownership. So the company can focus on delivering innovation and business value instead of spending much of their time managing supplier interactions.

> **TIP** Use touch points between acquirer and supplier processes as guides for beginning collaboration on improving your processes.

Matt pauses and then continues his story.

Matt: The suppliers also work with each other, so the company doesn't have to mediate all the time. This frees up management to focus on being an IT "broker," which I think is the wave of the future. The company focuses on their core competencies: IT strategy, operations oversight, and supplier management, and the suppliers handle the tactical day-to-day execution and delivery. They determine "what" and "how well," and the suppliers determine "how."

Steve: This reminds me of an article I read about "swim lanes." You know—how you map ownership of all your tasks so everybody knows what lane to be in.

Matt: Yes! Swim lanes is a good way to look at it.

> **TIP** When you document process flows, clearly indicate which role is responsible for which activity.

Touch points are a key innovative element of Steve's model. Touch points are the formally defined interactions in a process, each of which typically has predefined deliverables. You define touch points not only for acquirer-to-supplier interactions but also for supplier-to-supplier interactions. The result is a clear and consistent understanding of what is expected during the execution of a process between all parties involved, including those between different suppliers. It removes you as the intermediary between multiple suppliers, improving cycle time and freeing up your resources. Reinforce touch points by including them as requirements in the contracts.

Matt: There are quite a few lessons learned there, Steve. I can put you in touch with a friend of mine who still works there, if you want to follow up. In fact, I think he's coming to town in a couple of weeks. I'll see if he can spend some time with us and share some of his insights.

Steve: That would be great. Thanks!

Steve leaves this meeting feeling that he's taking the correct approach, at least as far as Matt is concerned. Steve feels better knowing that he has an experienced resource from whom to draw lessons learned. If this is what Rosa is trying to do to help projects get started, Steve is all for it. He decides to visit Rosa again soon.

> **TIP** You are not the first to begin improvement activity. Leverage lessons learned from as many sources as possible.

You must provide a "home" for process improvement activity—a so-called process asset library. This repository can have humble beginnings and might be as simple as one person using commonly available desktop programs such as spreadsheets and presentation software to document processes. Starting simply, this effort can be initiated from the bottom up, starting project by project. However, without higher-level management support, it is difficult to sustain this activity over time and expand it across the organization (where even larger benefits can be realized).

> **TIP** Combine bottom-up and top-down approaches to begin building the process asset library as soon as possible, using early improvement projects as a starting point.

5.2.1 Applying the CMMI-ACQ to Creating a Process Asset Library

The CMMI-ACQ provides specific recommendations on how to establish and maintain a usable set of organizational process assets and work environment standards (see Table 5-5). Organizational process assets support consistent process performance across the organization and provide a basis for cumulative, long-term benefits.

An organization's set of standard processes typically includes technical, management, administrative, support, and organizational processes (Table 5-5, practice 1.1). Your set of standard processes also describes standard interactions with suppliers. Supplier interactions are typically identified in terms of deliverables expected from suppliers, the applicable acceptance criteria, standards (e.g., architecture and technology standards), and standard milestone and progress reviews.

Basing standard processes on industry standards and widely accepted models, using common terminology, enables seamless interactions between you and the supplier. In a multisupplier environment, this is most important for your standard processes that directly interface with the supplier processes. Also, you may gain cost and coordination benefits from having suppliers work together to develop or reconcile common support processes that are aligned with your processes.

Standard processes can be defined at multiple levels in an enterprise, and they may be related in a hierarchical manner. For example, an enterprise might have a set of standard processes that is tailored by a division or site to

Table 5-5 *Organizational Process Definition Goal 1: Practices and Tips*

CMMI-ACQ Process Area: Organizational Process Definition	
1. Goal: A set of organizational process assets is established and maintained.	
Practices	**Tips**
1.1 Establish and maintain the organization's set of standard processes. 1.2 Establish and maintain descriptions of the life-cycle models approved for use in the organization. 1.3 Establish and maintain the tailoring criteria and guidelines for the organization's set of standard processes. 1.4 Establish and maintain the organization's measurement repository. 1.5 Establish and maintain the organization's process asset library. 1.6 Establish and maintain work environment standards.	• You are not the first to begin improvement activity. Leverage lessons learned from as many sources as possible. • Begin building the organizational process asset library as soon as possible, using early improvement projects as a starting point. • Project improvement efforts can be harvested for successful practices that can be used across the organization. • Combine bottom-up and top-down approaches to build the process asset library. • When you document process flows, clearly indicate who is responsible for which activity.

compose its own set of standard processes. The processes may also be tailored for each business area or product line. Thus, your organization's "set of standard processes" can refer to standard processes established at more than one level, although some organizations may have only a single level of standard processes.

When you work with more than one supplier or when technology solutions must be delivered to different customers and markets, you may identify more than one life-cycle model for use (Table 5-5, practice 1.2). The life-cycle models describe acquisition life cycles, depending on the specific acquisition strategy chosen. The acquisition life cycle typically begins with the pre-award phase of a supplier agreement, continues through the phases of awarding and managing the agreement, and ends when the agreement period of performance ends. The latter is usually marked by the acceptance and completion of the warranty for the acquired product and the transition of the product to a support organization.

Tailoring is a critical activity. It allows for controlled changes to the processes to meet the specific needs of a project or a part of the organization (Table 5-5, practice 1.3). Processes and process elements that are more directly related to critical business goals and objectives should usually be defined as mandatory (allowing less variation), but those that are less critical or only indirectly affect business objectives may allow for more tailoring (and therefore more variation). The degree of tailoring can also depend on the life-cycle model of the project, the supplier, or the acquirer-supplier relationship.

To fully leverage the supplier's process capability, you may choose to minimize the tailoring of the supplier's standard processes. Depending on the interfaces between your processes and the supplier's processes, your standard processes may need to be tailored to allow the supplier to execute its standard processes.

For process improvement, it is critical that you establish and maintain a measurement repository and a process asset library (Table 5-5, practices 1.4 and 1.5). The measurement repository contains product and process measures related to your set of standard processes. It also contains or refers to the information needed to understand and interpret the measures and assess them for reasonableness and applicability. For example, the definitions of the measures can be used to compare similar measures from different processes.

It is equally important for you to establish work environment standards (Table 5-5, practice 1.6). These standards allow the organization and projects to benefit from common tools, training, and maintenance and to realize cost savings from volume purchases. Work environment standards address the needs of all stakeholders and consider productivity, cost, availability, security, and workplace health, safety, and ergonomic factors. Work environment standards can include guidelines for tailoring and the use of waivers that allow you to adapt the project's work environment to meet specific needs.

5.3 Smooth Sailing

It seems that getting started is one of the most difficult things for an organization to do in the process improvement arena. Most successful efforts start small. If the project resides in an organization that already uses defined processes, it can get a start by tailoring them. But just like trying to do things on too grand a scale, unbounded tailoring also can be a pitfall.

As he planned, Steve is meeting with Rosa in her office.

> **TIP** Identify and target bottleneck activities and processes for improvement.

Steve: Last time we talked, Rosa, you gave me some really good ideas. I need to present them to the team so we can plan our kickoff. I've been thinking about that quite a bit—the issue of how to get started in the right way and then keep momentum going. Any lessons you can share in this area?

Rosa: Well, Steve, remember what you *don't* want to do. You don't want to try to document all your processes. What we've been talking about is picking your targets for quick payback first, and then tackling the more complicated problems.

Let's get started by looking at the flow of work and the work environment to identify the bottlenecks. I'll tell you a secret. We process people love to draw boxes with arrows between them almost as much as engineers do!

My point here is that you have to get the basic things right first. Hire good people, train them, and give them the right tools. Plan the activity and measure progress. You know, the basics!

After we get started with this project, Steve, I'm going to host some of your project templates and checklists in the process asset library I've started. We have a long way to go, but you have to start somewhere, right?

> **TIP** Make it safe for the project and the organization to experiment and to make mistakes. But capture lessons learned for next time in a process asset library.

Steve nods and writes on his yellow notepad.

Rosa: Remember, one size doesn't fit all. Don't be afraid to make mistakes. If you find yourself in a box, try something else. Don't take no for an answer. You can get a good start by removing non-value-added controls—low-hanging fruit, right? Remember my story about the military package inspectors? Cutting out an activity is just one approach.

I was talking to Paula the other day. She's a big advocate of making detailed plans for small increments of projects that can be managed more easily. She claims she's been successful in starting and maintaining measurable progress because she's able to quickly manage increments to closure. This helps her keep the overall effort on track. She can make midcourse corrections before problems get too big. It also helps staff morale, since team members get quick feedback and frequent closure on tasks.

But Paula likes the small-ball game most because her customers like it.

Steve: Small ball? I didn't know you were a baseball fan.

Rosa: I'm originally from D.C.! Whenever I'm home, I try to catch a Nationals game.

Steve and Rosa briefly discuss the merits of the National League versus American League styles of play, and then Steve brings them back to the subject at hand.

Steve: You were saying that Paula likes her incremental project management style because her customers like it.

Rosa: Yes. Instead of waiting for a "big bang" delivery that might be off target, they're happy to get incremental delivery and have the chance to make corrections along the way .

Steve: Good. That makes sense. Any more ideas?

Rosa: I think one of the most fundamental issues is, you must manage the process improvement effort as a project, with all the rigor and discipline you'd apply to any other project. It's critical to get quality and process performance objectives documented and agreed to by all the key players. The worst thing you can do—and believe me, I've seen this happen—is to go in and brief your boss and Matt with a wishy-washy, touchy-feely program status review. They'll cut you off and tell you to come back when you're prepared and have your data. They *absolutely* make decisions based on facts and evidence, not intuition and feeling.

> **TIP** As with any project, use objectives and measures to manage improvement activities.

Steve: Thanks, Rosa. That's good advice. I've worked for these guys for a while now, and I know exactly what you mean! It's a great idea to manage this effort as a real project, with milestones, metrics, program reviews, decision points—the whole nine yards.

Rosa: So Steve, are you using the CMMI-ACQ to help you build your project plan for the improvement part of the project?

> **TIP** Explore correlations between factors that affect organizational performance.

Steve: Hmmm. I hadn't thought of using it like that. But now that you mention it, we could use the process areas to structure our plan. Maybe . . . Project Planning, and Measurement and Analysis, and Project Monitoring and Control.

Rosa: Exactly.

Steve: That would also give our team more practice with using the model before we get deep into the acquisition. I'm going to take this back to our team and get it started.

A fundamental aspect of managing process performance is the ability to manage multiple improvements simultaneously, whether they occur in individual projects, at the organization level, or in process areas. It's a good idea to take a portfolio approach. You manage improvement projects individually, but you manage the overall set of improvements as a portfolio.

This portfolio management approach requires that the process improvement manager as well as senior management have a view of the enterprise and a set of goals to guide their execution and improvement efforts. For example, a stock portfolio is managed to reduce risk and maximize return. In the same fashion, a process improvement portfolio is tied to business goals, with an objective such as maximizing efficiency in the overall acquirer-supplier value chain. Setting such overall objectives is critical to guiding a portfolio of improvement projects.

TIP Use quantitative analysis to understand any constraints that impede the overall performance of the organization.

To set objectives that target those areas that yield the highest impact, you can also apply the theory of constraints to the project portfolio. For instance, suppose that an overall goal of a supply-chain system is to move from a forecast model to a replenishment model. In a forecast model, acquirers forecast their demand and provide it to vendors, and then vendors plan to meet the demand accordingly. Inaccurate forecasts or data latency can often cause shortages or stock-outs or, conversely, oversupply and excess inventory handling costs. In a replenishment model, a just-in-time approach is used to ensure that vendors have an accurate view of a production line in nearly real time. This enables a vendor to replenish necessary items to the line as close as possible to the time they are needed. Applying the theory of constraints provides a methodology to evaluate the existing condition, model the desired end state, and then provide implementation steps to begin the transformation process.

One afternoon, Matt calls Paula into his office.

> **TIP** Keep the overall objective in focus, and communicate how every individual and every project contributes to the overall success of acquisition in the organization.

Matt: Paula, I've been thinking about our process improvement program. I think we have a pretty good handle on managing at the project level, but I'm not so sure we're doing as well at the overall organizational level. If we don't look at the entire flow of work between us and our suppliers as an interrelated system, I'm afraid we're missing the point.

Paula: You're right, Matt. Everything I've read indicates we need to manage this effort as a set of interrelated activities that contribute to our overall objectives.

Matt: Yes! We need to keep managing projects individually, but we also need to take a big-picture view of our entire value chain and determine the contribution of each project to it. If we don't look at the big picture as well as the individual project, I'm afraid we will be suboptimizing our scarce resources—both human and capital.

Here's my issue. If we do each acquisition as an individual procurement, our suppliers will treat our work as a one-time thing every time. We'll pay for each buy as if it's the first time, and we won't realize as much benefit as we should. Even worse, we won't have a handle on our overall performance from the standpoint of our bottom line. What we need to create is a funnel of solutions that moves smoothly through the acquirer and supplier acquisition process and gives results when the customer needs them—not too early, and certainly not too late.

After you have stable processes and process measures in place, how can you understand where to start in optimizing the overall acquirer-supplier process? First, you need to determine what the process chain looks like for your project—or, more important, for the family of projects, if you have multiple projects ongoing within the organization. Then you can refer to the Organizational Process Performance process area in the CMMI-ACQ. It provides best practices for selecting processes for improvement focus, setting goals for organizational processes, and then tracking progress toward meeting the goals.

A good place to start is with the pacesetters in the integrated process chain (i.e., the subprocesses that determine the "delivery speed" of the joint acquirer-supplier capability). You can identify the pacesetters by using a number of project management techniques, such as critical path or critical chain analyses. These techniques are based on the idea that resources and processes determine delivery capability and that you must have a good handle on available resource capacity on the critical tasks and processes.

Again, think about not only how these processes operate at the individual project level, but also how you can apply them beyond a project or program to the entire organization. This thinking should account for the context of the acquisition strategy and the organization's overall strategic and business objectives or mission. When starting out, often projects don't yet have the means or the data to quantify process improvement, because they don't have stable processes that can be repeated and measured over time.

> **TIP** Gradually expand your process performance model to encompass your entire value chain from end to end.

After you have identified these pacesetters, you baseline their performance and set their performance objectives. Here again, the CMMI-ACQ provides best practices, and again, it is important to emphasize that these practices are established at the organizational level so that projects don't reinvent the wheel.

However, because acquisition activity often occurs at the project level, remember that these objectives can be tailored for a project according to guidelines already established by the organization. Additionally, to apply portfolio management to the entire set of activities requires a means to manage according to a master plan and schedule. Note that this activity is described in the Project Planning process area. Naturally, these aggregated plans and schedules must be based on and support the overall acquisition strategy and strategic objectives of the organization.

5.3.1 Applying the CMMI-ACQ to Establishing Your Standard Processes

The CMMI-ACQ provides specific recommendations on how to establish and maintain a quantitative understanding of the performance of your organization's set of standard processes in support of quality and process performance objectives, and to provide the process performance data, baselines, and models to quantitatively manage the organization's projects (see Table 5-6).

Process performance is a measure of the actual results achieved by following a process. It is characterized by process measures (e.g., effort, cycle time, and defect removal effectiveness) and product measures (e.g., reliability, defect density, capacity, response time, and cost). Most organizations are not ready to begin rigorous quantitative organizational process improvement until stable processes exist at the project and organizational levels that can be repeated and measured over time.

Nonetheless, keeping these practices in mind can guide near-term activity in other process areas and facilitate migration to organizational process perfor-

Table 5-6 *Organizational Process Performance Goal 1: Practices and Tips*

CMMI-ACQ Process Area: Organizational Process Performance	
1. Goal: Baselines and models that characterize the expected process performance of the organization's set of standard processes are established and maintained.	
Practices	**Tips**
1.1 Select the processes or subprocesses in the organization's set of standard processes that are to be included in the organization's process performance analyses. 1.2 Establish and maintain definitions of the measures that are to be included in the organization's process performance analyses. 1.3 Establish and maintain quantitative objectives for quality and process performance for the organization. 1.4 Establish and maintain the organization's process performance baselines. 1.5 Establish and maintain the process performance models for the organization's set of standard processes.	• Gradually expand your process performance model to encompass your entire value chain from end to end. • Identify and target any bottleneck activities and processes for improvement. • Explore correlations between factors that affect organizational performance. • Use quantitative analysis to understand any constraints that impede the overall performance of the organization.

mance when the time is right. Many organizations have adopted approaches such as "lean," often supported by six sigma or other quantitative techniques. These approaches complement the improvement framework set forth in CMMI-ACQ. Organizations that have adopted these approaches have a strong foundation on which to base a robust measurement and analysis capability, organizational process performance, and quantitative project management when required to meet organizational and business needs. The CMMI-ACQ provides a means to institutionalize these approaches over time and realize long-term organizational change.

Typically, it is not possible, useful, or economically justifiable to apply statistical management techniques to all the processes or subprocesses in your set of standard processes (Table 5-6, practice 1.1). When you select the processes or subprocesses for analyses, it is critical to understand the relationships between the various processes and subprocesses and their impact on your and the supplier's performance in delivering the product specified by the customer. Such an approach helps ensure that quantitative and statistical management is applied where it has the most overall value to the organization.

Here are examples of criteria that you can use for selecting a subprocess for organizational analysis:

- The relationship of the subprocess to key business objectives
- Current availability of valid historical data relevant to the subprocess
- The current degree of variability of this data
- Subprocess stability (e.g., stable performance in comparable instances)
- The availability of corporate or commercial information that can be used to build predictive models

To measure your quality and process performance objectives, you may need to combine existing measures into additional derived measures to provide insight into the overall efficiencies and effectiveness at a project, program, and organization level (Table 5-6, practices 1.2 and 1.3). You can use the analysis at the organization level to study productivity, improve efficiencies, and increase throughput across projects.

The expected process performance can be used in establishing the project's quality and process performance objectives and can be used as a baseline for comparing actual project performance. This information is used to quantitatively manage the project. Each such project, in turn, provides actual performance results that become a part of the baseline data for your process assets.

You derive process performance baselines by analyzing the collected measures to establish a distribution and range of results that characterize the expected performance for selected processes when used on any individual project in the organization (Table 5-6, practice 1.4). You use process performance models to estimate or predict the value of a process performance measure from the values of other process, product, and service measurements. To estimate progress toward achieving objectives that cannot be measured until later in the project's life cycle, process performance models typically use process and product measurements collected throughout the life of the project (Table 5-6, practice 1.5). These measurements are also used to set performance objectives for the suppliers and to provide data that can help suppliers achieve them. The results of your process performance models are frequently shared with the suppliers so that they can ensure synchronized delivery of products and services.

5.4 Leading the Charge for Change

Changing human behavior at the individual, group or team, and organizational level is a complex subject about which volumes have been written. In this section we discuss the cultural changes that can be accomplished within the context of the CMMI-ACQ.

Most change management authors agree that for change to succeed, the organization's management must be involved at multiple levels: Top, middle, and team or group leadership must be engaged. This ensures that the effort focuses on the behavioral and cultural aspects that need to be addressed if change is to be successfully begun and sustained. Communication, training, and rewarding behavior that supports the change are key aspects of reinforcing cultural change. The CMMI-ACQ offers best practices to help in the "charge for change."

5.4.1 Nurturing Change

Successful organizations have made the internal transformation to a culture of identifying problems and solving them as quickly as possible. This transformation must be reinforced at the individual and team levels to become institutionalized as "the way we do things here."

Matt calls Steve in for a short meeting.

Matt: I just want to touch base with you on something I've been thinking about. With this process improvement, I think we need to remind ourselves how important it is to motivate people and keep them enthusiastic about the process.

Steve: Yes, I agree.

Matt: This goes along with something I've been reading about—the idea that process improvements need to deliver short-term wins that contribute to the overall project goals [Kotter 1996]. Here's a handout I picked up yesterday. This is a list of the value of short-term wins.

Matt hands the paper to Steve, who reads through it quickly.

Provide evidence that sacrifices are worth it! Wins greatly help justify the short-term costs involved.

Reward change agents with a pat on the back: After a lot of hard work, positive feedback builds morale and motivation.

Help fine-tune vision and strategies: Short-term wins give the guiding coalition concrete data on the viability of their ideas.

Undermine cynics and self-serving resistors: Clear improvements in performance make it difficult for people to block needed change.

Keep bosses on board: Provide those higher in the hierarchy with evidence that the transformation is on track.

Build momentum: Turn neutrals into supporters, and reluctant supporters into active helpers.

TIP   Identify and communicate short-term wins.

Steve: Good stuff. We all should be really aware of these issues day-to-day. If we don't walk the talk, how can we expect our people to?

Matt: Exactly.

Steve: Okay if I take this handout for reference?

Matt: Sure thing. Oh, and another great book is *1001 Ways to Reward People* [Nelson 1997]. Here, take my copy.

On his way to his team meeting, Steve stops for a cup of coffee. When he arrives at the meeting a few minutes late, his project team members are already there. He begins by giving a brief summary of his discussions over the past several days.

Steve: One of the things we need to do is to apply the model to ourselves as we plan this acquisition. And one of the things I've heard over the past few days is that it's extremely important to plan process work just as much as we expect our project managers to plan their projects. We have to take that pill ourselves, and keep ourselves from getting off track.

You know I've always been a real believer in planning, tracking to a plan, and learning from it. Maybe I'm a CMMI zealot now, because I think I get it. I see where it's so much nicer to have something on paper that you're tracking against instead of dreaming it up every time you have a meeting and rehashing the same stuff again.

The team members begin to discuss how to do this, focusing on two process areas in the CMMI-ACQ: Project Planning and Project Monitoring and Control. The first will help them build the plan, and the second will show them how to track its progress. Steve has prepared a slide show, and it guides the discussion. When he is satisfied that everyone understands the concepts, he brings up a related topic.

Steve: Another issue I've been thinking about is culture change. We have to address the human relations aspects of this. I know I can be a little too task-oriented sometimes, but maybe you can teach an old dog new tricks! I've been trying to get a handle on how we can make sure we sustain the changes we're bringing to our organization. We need to focus on two things, and in my mind they're related: process changes and short-term wins.

We need to encourage everybody to identify process changes as often and whenever they can. These are our first line of defense against "business as usual." Companies like Toyota have done this successfully, so why can't we? [Liker 2006]

Steve looks around the table.

Steve: Do we have barriers to process change? What are they?

> **TIP** Establishing a culture of change starts with employees at all levels of the organization.

Team Member 1: Shoot the messenger! People have good ideas for improving things, and they bring them up to managers. But if it's going to affect schedule or budget, it's discounted and you're told to stick to the job. It's no wonder people stop reporting problems.

Team Member 2: Right! And another thing, remember the suggestion program they introduced last year? I never hear about any feedback from it. Did you ever see anyone here get an award for a process improvement? This sends the message, "Why bother?"

Steve: Obviously, we need a new approach. I know I can get my boss and Matt Vauban to put out the word top-down that we're going to make a fresh start on employee improvement suggestions. That's a great idea.

Team Member 3: Speaking of suggestions, I have one—pizza at every team meeting.

> **Steve:** What about the pizza party we had last week?

> **Team Member 3:** So what have you done for us *lately?*

> **Steve:** Hey now, behave yourselves. Settle down.

Steve smiles.

> **Steve:** Okay, pizza every time someone brings me a serious problem on the project.

General approval is expressed.

> **TIP** Employee recognition can send a positive message that can help accelerate improvement efforts. Recognition can be formal or informal, and it need not be expensive to be very effective.

> **Steve:** Meanwhile, I have another concern. How will we identify, elevate, and track improvements? Didn't one of you work on the IT help desk a while back before you saw the light and joined our team?

One team member half-raises her hand, wincing.

> **Steve:** Please, I'm really not picking on you, Carrie. I want to see whether we could use something like a trouble ticket system to track process improvements. Doesn't have to be sophisticated, but I think it could help us get started.

> **Carrie:** Well, I think we could make that work. It could be Web-based.

> **Steve:** Yes! With a Web site, we could also give quick feedback to the person making the suggestion and publish overall project statistics that communicate what we're doing. Who knows, we could even add blog capability—let people blog our process and progress. Get everybody involved. What do you guys think?

The team members seem to agree with this.

> **Steve:** These ideas have the potential to really help us improve our efficiency in day-to-day operations. They'll also help us meet the overall goals of the acquisition project, which of course is our "real" job.

People's attitudes about change can make or break change efforts. Behavior change must be reinforced at all levels to be successful. It's important to have executive support and a clear, consistent message from top leadership that is sustained over time and equally vital to have change supported by middle management and at the team and individual levels. Sometimes the mechanisms to reinforce changes in behavior already exist in an organization, and sometimes new approaches are required.

> **Steve:**   Obviously, we should not lose sight of the overall strategy, but I'm convinced we need to focus on small steps as we move along. The short-term win approach has a lot of appeal for me. I think the internal Web site we talked about can help us do this. What we're trying to do is to say, "Stop and look around. If you see a problem or bottleneck, report it. Let's tackle it and solve it." We need to make sure this message gets out.
>
> I'll also talk to my boss and Matt Vauban about using the quarterly awards ceremony to highlight everybody's improvement suggestions. Maybe we can get some coverage in the monthly employee newsletter, too.

> **Team Member 3:**   What about us? Some of us are supervisors, and we need to set an example in our daily work as well as get the word to employees about how to use the new system.

> **Steve:**   Okay, I'll talk to corporate training and see if we can get some help from them on putting some stuff in our curriculum as part of our tactical project training. Let's see—training about the new Web site, "low-hanging fruit" for process improvement, and awareness of change management.

> **TIP**   Training is a key element of reinforcing change over time.

Organizational training is one of the process areas from the overall CMMI framework that is likely to be mature in most medium-sized to large organizations. Corporate human relations departments usually have at least a rudimentary approach to planning and managing training activities. But execution of the plans is another story, especially if training is centrally funded. There are always more requirements than resources for training, and it seems to be one of the first areas affected when budgets are cut. Isn't it ironic that most organizations claim that their people are their most important asset, and yet employee development often is one of the first things cut during a budget crisis?

Steve catches himself thinking back to the generic practices from the CMMI framework he and Rosa discussed.

- Web site = resources = generic practice 2.3
- Training = generic practice 2.5
- Involve senior management = stakeholders = generic practice 2.7

"Scary!" he thinks. "I'm starting to apply the model just like Rosa said!"

Steve shares this revelation with the team. They discuss these ideas and pledge to identify and communicate short-term wins along the way. At the end of the meeting, they parcel out actions, set target dates, and agree to review progress at next week's team meeting.

Many medium-sized and large organizations have well-established programs to manage and track training activity. As you begin an improvement program, it's important to link to these efforts to ensure that the right training is provided at the right time to the personnel who are implementing changes at the project and organizational levels. Folding improvement requirements into existing infrastructure leverages scarce resources and ensures that change training is aligned with overall organizational training.

> **TIP** Ensure that training for managing change is included in corporate training programs.

> **TIP** Ensure that specific training for groups or teams is managed over time.

In addition to strategic training needs, organizational training addresses training requirements that are common across projects and support groups. These groups have the primary responsibility for identifying and addressing their specific training needs. The organization's training staff is responsible only for addressing common cross-project and support group training needs—for example, training in work environments common to multiple projects.

In some cases, however, your organization's training staff may address the additional training needs of projects and support groups, as negotiated with them, within the context of the training resources available and your training priorities. You must manage this activity over time to ensure that employees are receiving current training when refresher classes are needed, and to ensure that you account for employee turnover by training employees who are new to the effort.

> **TIP** To sustain change over time, review training effectiveness.

Most organizations evaluate or test their training. Often, the employee receiving the training can provide feedback on its effectiveness, and the employee's manager or team leader can also assess the effectiveness of the training in aligning with and meeting organizational goals. It's important for those engaged in the management of process change to review these documents, assess the effectiveness of the training effort in meeting overall goals, and make any needed corrections.

5.4.2 Applying the CMMI-ACQ to Training Processes

The CMMI-ACQ provides specific recommendations on how to develop the skills and knowledge of people so that they can perform their roles effectively and efficiently (see Table 5-7). You identify the training required to develop the skills and the knowledge necessary to perform enterprise activities. After the needs are identified, you develop a training program to address them.

Effective training requires assessment of needs, planning, instructional design, and appropriate training media (e.g., workbooks, computer software) as well as development of a repository of training process data. As an organizational process, the main components of training include a managed training development program, documented plans, personnel who have appropriate mastery of specific disciplines and other areas of knowledge, and mechanisms for measuring the program's effectiveness.

Table 5-7 *Organizational Training Goal 1: Practices and Tips*

CMMI-ACQ Process Area: Organizational Training	
1. Goal: A training capability that supports the organization's management and technical roles is established and maintained.	
Practices	**Tips**
1.1 Establish and maintain the strategic training needs of the organization. 1.2 Determine which training needs are the responsibility of the organization and which will be left to the individual project or support group. 1.3 Establish and maintain an organizational training tactical plan. 1.4 Establish and maintain training capability to address organizational training needs.	• Establishing a culture of change starts with employees at all levels of the organization. • Training is a key element of reinforcing change over time. • Ensure that training for managing change is included in corporate training programs.

The organization identifies the needed training (Table 5-7, practice 1.1). Strategic training must address long-term objectives by filling significant knowledge gaps, introducing new technologies, or implementing major changes in behavior. Identification of training needs may also address some training needs of suppliers, especially in those process elements that define supplier interfaces and expectations.

In addition to strategic training needs, organizational training addresses training requirements that are common across projects and support groups (Table 5-7, practice 1.2). Based on the training needs, you develop a tactical plan for organizational training. The goal of this plan is to deliver the training that is the responsibility of the organization and is necessary for individuals to perform their roles effectively (Table 5-7, practices 1.3 and 1.4). This plan addresses the near-term execution of training and is adjusted periodically in response to changes (e.g., in needs or resources) and to evaluations of its effectiveness.

Many factors may affect the selection of training approaches, including audience-specific knowledge, costs and schedule, work environment, and so on. To select an approach, you must consider how to provide skills and knowledge in the most effective way possible given the constraints.

Training should be planned and scheduled (see Table 5-8, practice 2.1). You should provide training that has a direct bearing on the expectations of work performance. Therefore, optimal training occurs in a timely manner with regard to imminent job performance expectations. These expectations often include training in the use of specialized tools and in procedures that are new to the individual who will use the tools and perform the procedures.

Keep records of all personnel who successfully complete (or fail) each training course or other approved training activity (Table 5-8, practice 2.2). Training records may be part of a skills matrix developed by the training organization to provide a summary of the experience and education of staff, as well as training sponsored by the organization.

In addition, a process should exist to determine the effectiveness of training (Table 5-8, practice 2.3). You can take measurements to assess the benefit of the training against the project's and the organization's objectives. You should pay particular attention to the need for various training methods, such as training teams as integral work units. When used, performance objectives should be shared with course participants and should be unambiguous, observable, and verifiable. The results of the training effectiveness assessment should be used to improve training materials.

Table 5-8 *Organizational Training Goal 2: Practices and Tips*

CMMI-ACQ Process Area: Organizational Training	
2. Goal: Training necessary for individuals to perform their roles effectively is provided.	
Practices	**Tips**
2.1 Deliver the training following the tactical organizational training plan. 2.2 Establish and maintain records of the organizational training. 2.3 Assess the effectiveness of the organization's training program.	• Ensure that specific training for groups or teams is managed over time. • To sustain change over time, review training effectiveness.

5.4.3 Riding the Waves of Change—and Having Fun

Outsourcing creates significant organizational change. Failure to address this change is a risk factor for both you and the supplier. Organizations often do not realize the cost reduction and productivity improvements that they projected because they ignore the impacts of change on their own organization.

A key feature of organizational change activities is communication—with employees, system users, and management. Workshops are a mechanism that you can use effectively to make individuals aware of the process improvement project. Workshops are also a good way for people to work together to achieve common goals. Other effective techniques are to use early adopters as key influencers in the change and to offer incentives, such as recognition and rewards, that are tied directly to performance. Whatever approaches you use to implement organizational change, they require the same level of planning as any other program.

Any organizational change activities for the supplier should be built into the supplier agreement, and the agreement should clarify the ownership of tasks and deliverables, scope, and resources.

TIP	Actively manage organizational change at the same time as the supplier agreement, if not before.

Recent research into change management has shown consistently that a key factor in the success or failure of a change effort is executive sponsorship. Senior leadership must set a course and deliver a consistent message over time to keep an organization's change efforts on track.

Early one day, Matt Vauban's secretary calls Steve to request an urgent meeting. When Steve is shown into Matt's office, Steve's boss is already there.

Matt: Steve, please sit down. I asked your boss to join us this morning because I have some concerns about the project you're working on. You know how interested I am in your acquisition project. I've seen your draft project plan for managing the outsourcing effort, and it seems that you have that pretty well under control so far. But I'm concerned that we don't have a plan for managing the changes that adopting the CMMI-ACQ will bring to the organization as a whole.

Matt pauses to let this sink in, and then he continues.

Matt: If I look at what companies like Toyota have accomplished, it's not because they have put in place fixed-price contracts and challenging pricing targets. I've been reading the literature. It turns out that Toyota invests in their suppliers and develops those relationships over a long period of time. Their focus is on a quality product. They have a quality culture that gets everyone involved, from the employee in the front office to the supplier who develops a component for the technology solution. This quality focus gives them opportunities to eliminate waste and opportunities to innovate.

Steve: Yes, I've read something about that, too.

Matt: Steve, here's the thing. Your project has the potential to change our organizational culture in some fundamental ways. I need to be convinced that we've thought through all the implications. Can you do some research and get back to us with an approach for change management?

Steve pauses for a moment to collect his thoughts.

Steve: Sure, Matt, I'd be glad to. But as far as Toyota, keep in mind that they've been building this culture for many years, and working on their supplier relationships to make it all work.
    We've looked at the cultural alignment between us and our bidding suppliers, and we've reviewed some of the things you're referencing—trust, long-term relationships, mutual well-being, discipline, continuous improvement, learning. These things don't happen overnight, and they don't happen just because an agreement gets signed. But on the other hand, just because we're not a Toyota doesn't mean we can't begin to

demonstrate the leadership behavior to work with our suppliers more effectively.

Matt: I want to make sure we've done our homework before we get into this too deeply.

Steve: Sure, and I'll get you some research. But don't forget we have process experts in house, like Rosa Gonzales. I've been meeting with her. Plus, we're not jumping into it with both feet. We're starting with processes we already do that will be easy to document. Our team has also been looking at ways to bring in our suppliers to help us shape this from day one, and use incentives and energize employees and managers to adopt a process improvement mentality.

   I'll meet with Rosa and Paula and put something together for you. How about if we get back to you in a week or two with some ideas?

Matt: Thanks, Steve. See my secretary on your way out to schedule us for an hour on, say, Wednesday afternoon in three weeks.

As Steve leaves the office, he thinks about what has just happened. He's encouraged that Matt is engaged with the project, because everything he's read about change management and CMMI adoption concludes with the admonition that senior leadership engagement is an essential ingredient to a successful project. Matt is certainly engaged. Now Steve must make the most of the opportunity Matt has presented and meet the challenge of addressing Matt's concerns and putting together a change management plan. Steve's first stop is to see his boss. Steve wants to make sure his boss is on board with what Steve has been asked to do.

Steve's boss: Come on in, Steve! Matt must have been thinking in the shower again.

This is a shared joke among Steve's colleagues. Matt once admitted in a staff meeting that he often got his best ideas while taking his morning shower.

Steve: The way he started out talking about "concerns" brought me up short. But it turned out okay. I'm glad he's engaged!

Steve's boss: Yes, I know you told me about the need for senior leadership in this effort. But why does it always have to be first thing Monday morning? Just kidding!

   I was glad you answered the way you did. You know Matt puts a lot of stock in what Rosa says, and Paula is our internal customer. If they've bought into it, you'll have a much better chance of getting the boss's approval.

Steve: Thanks. That's what I was thinking, too.

Steve's boss: I know you don't have much time between now and our next meeting with Matt. How about showing me what you've got first thing next week?

Steve: Sounds good. See you then.

> **TIP** Understanding change management is one key to accelerating process improvement.

Steve is under the gun. He has only a very small window of opportunity to put together a change management plan. Luckily, both Paula and Rosa are available mid-morning. They all get together in a small conference room with plenty of whiteboard space. Steve tells them about the meeting with Matt. Rosa walks over to the whiteboard and draws a diagram (see Figure 5-4).

Rosa: This represents the life cycle of technology adoption. It's nothing new. It's based on research done in the 1950s by a professor at Iowa State named Everett Rogers [http://en.wikipedia.org/wiki/Everett_Rogers]. The change management experts say that you need to focus on early adopters and then build toward early majority acceptance. Paula, I think you might be classified as an early adopter of CMMI-ACQ!

Paula: Well, that's all well and good, but what does it get us?

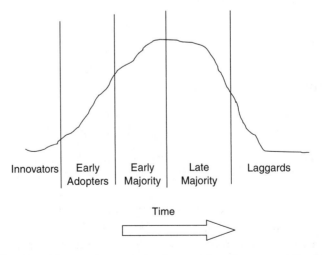

Source: Adapted from http://www.sei.cmu.edu/ttp/presentations/tcm.presentation/sld015.htm

Figure 5-4 *Technology Adoption Life Cycle*

> **TIP** Endorsement from early adopters in line or functional positions is a key to accelerating improvement efforts.

Rosa: Like Aretha Franklin said, "R-E-S-P-E-C-T." If we want to use CMMI-ACQ throughout the company, then for openers, we need two things: senior management support, which it seems we already have, and credibility from someone that people *respect*.

With your leadership, Paula, other divisions will see that we're making a difference. Sure, I'm supposedly the process improvement "guru," and Steve's the acquisition project manager, but we don't have the kind of credibility you have. You're a manager from a functional area. You do *real* work. That's why early adopters are an important part of leading the change.

Paula: I never thought of myself in that role. But I do believe that this is the way we should go, and I'll be glad to do what I can to get the word out.

Steve: This is good. We'll be including a change management approach in our project plan for the acquisition. And we'll have a communication plan supported by metrics to get the word out about what our goals are and how well we're meeting them.

Rosa: There is another piece to this puzzle. Another researcher, Geoffrey Moore, says the most difficult aspect of technology adoption is "crossing the chasm" between early adopters and early majority. Having Paula's support is really important. But we also need to support the effort through a "product perspective." It's a marketing term. It means supporting the effort with a holistic approach to meet the needs of the customer.

Rosa pulls a chart out of her briefcase and shows it to the others (see Figure 5-5).

Rosa: So Paula's division is the customer of the outsourced services. The entire effort needs to be supported like any other product. That will help bridge the gap between Paula, our early adopter, and the early majority groups in our organization.

Steve reiterates that his plan already includes many of these topics.

Steve: But I wasn't looking at this from the perspective of accelerating acceptance of the CMMI-ACQ approach. It's just common sense to try to support the product.

Paula: You're right, Steve. But letting people know that you're taking a product support approach to the acquisition project will help others feel more comfortable. In fact, that's one of the reasons we're adopting the CMMI-ACQ. It takes a life-cycle approach to acquisition.

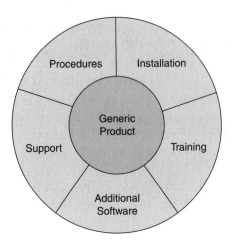

Source: http://en.wikipedia.org/wiki/Whole_product

Figure 5-5   *Whole product concept*

Steve: Taking a whole product approach also means that we can't do this alone. We need to involve our supplier and make them an integral part of continuous improvement. Let's put together a meeting with our new suppliers to talk about some of the aspects of partnering that we want to emulate, and start building that culture.

> **TIP**   Taking a whole product approach can help bridge the gap between early adopters and the next level of acceptance: the early majority.

> **TIP**   Make continuous improvement a norm for the integrated acquirer-supplier team.

Rosa and Paula nod in agreement. Paula says that George Taylor and Kristin Wells, from the supplier organization, should be a part of the meeting, and Paula agrees to ask them to host it.

The supplier meeting is convened the next day, and it quickly becomes an idea-generating session. Steve has a suggestion.

Steve: We need to work together as a learning organization. I mean we need to set up sessions where we focus on initiatives together, maybe even initiatives outside of the regular work activities, and bring in some of the other suppliers as well—sort of a think tank.

George Taylor: All of us together?

Steve: That's right. That way, we can take some specific challenges from our day-to-day work and come up with solutions. This would give everyone a chance to work together and do things that we could immediately implement. We've already begun this process in-house with my acquisition team. I think it's important to make this a collaboration among all of us.

George: Well, how much time are you thinking this would take?

Steve: That's a good question, George. We can decide that together. I want to make sure that this is not just a meeting where we bring in leadership at the end of the day and everyone goes home and forgets about what we talked about. So I've been thinking about ways that we can make this well worth everybody's time.

I hate this cliché, but it's really true: Every challenge is an opportunity. We need to proactively capture the opportunities so that we can use them and improve what we're doing. To some extent, this goes back to what Kristin was talking about earlier. If I look at a problem as a problem and don't look at it from the standpoint of continuous improvement, I just have a problem, and I handle it, and nobody learns anything. But if we start talking about issues, challenges, and problems (big, medium, and small) from an improvement point of view, then we look at the problem differently. We can try to determine why it's happening, especially if we believe there's a strong possibility it might happen again. We can begin to live and breathe continuous improvement and support it as a way of life. If we can all problem-solve, then we can all continuously improve.

Steve pauses and then continues.

Steve: Now, this means a culture shift for all of us, and we know that won't happen overnight. But let's look for some situations that we could use to demonstrate to management how this might work, and examples of how it's critical to the success of our organization and our suppliers.

The dialog continues for some time. Eventually, the team puts together the prioritized list per the original instructions for the workshop. The list looks like this:

- Set targets for specific quality improvements.
- Set up mentoring relationships between new staff and existing staff.
- Set up a simple decision matrix to evaluate the impact of any problem, including symptoms and root causes.

- Set up a process for a "Plan-Do-Check-Act" cycle, and begin to make it visible. Reward individuals for demonstrating these behaviors. Evaluate monthly and overall at the end of six months.

And the list goes on . . .

> **TIP** Use common process improvement initiatives to encourage the partnership between acquirer and supplier.

Steve and the team also decide to invite Matt for an interim "temperature check" at the end of the meeting. They want to let Matt know were they're headed before Steve formally briefs him at the scheduled change management meeting. Matt is brought into the session and listens to the report from the team. Then he takes center stage.

Matt: I want to commend you all for spending this time and working together as an integrated team to set some direction on how we can take our organization to the next level. Many of the items you're focusing on are areas that we as a management team have discussed as well.

Although we're all concerned about how we manage the business from a cost perspective, we also need to be mindful of managing from a quality perspective first. Now, don't get me wrong. Don't think you can wave the "quality" flag in my face and I'll immediately give you whatever you ask for. I'm not convinced that you have to spend big bucks to eliminate waste and improve quality. That's where the creativity and transformational opportunities lie.

I'm in full support of the output of this workshop, your priorities, and I want a team meeting scheduled in three months to determine how much progress we've made. Steve, please make sure the meeting is on my calendar.

Matt asks Steve to take the lead in putting in place activities to foster collaboration, with the goal of continuous improvement for the integrated team. Those items should become a critical part of continuous improvement going forward.

> **TIP** Maintain momentum by holding frequent progress reviews.

As continuous improvement takes hold, data becomes increasingly important for managing projects and the organization. An important characteristic of high-maturity organizations is their ability to base decision making on data. At the organizational level, data is used to select which process changes to deploy and then track their performance. Of course, this capability must be built over time. One successful method is to use pilot projects to test changes and begin to build an organizational database that supports analysis and future change deployments.

Matt and Rosa are talking about this one day while waiting for a meeting to start.

Matt: In the company I used to work for, they were big on pilot projects. One year, we picked two projects and tried them out separately. Once we were done with the piloting and those six process areas, we were able to sit down and ask, "What were the common activities they did? What seemed to work best for the so-and-so division? How did these people over there do configuration management with their suppliers?" Things like that. Then we began to nudge out, for example, a process description and templates that seemed to work best from that pilot and began to get those into other projects as they came out. These served as lessons learned and experience under our belt, in terms of what works and what doesn't work. That's kind of the way I think we're going to do it here as well.

Rosa: Who did you choose for a pilot?

Matt: The project that was the most open to new approaches. Of the two projects, one of them was particularly open to trying new things; they wanted to do the pilot as soon as they heard about it. The other project, we talked to the director of that group and there was a new project coming on-board, kind of newbies—a lot of new people—so we said, "Hey, here's a chance for us to get going in the planning part, right off the bat." So that's why that group was chosen.

     Both were major initiatives, and so they got a lot of visibility, which was good and bad. But at least with a lot of visibility, they got the resources they wanted and were in the thick of it. That's the main thing—to be in the thick of it. I think one of the most important things we learned is that the people go through a cycle of team formation with these pilots.

Rosa: You mean the good old "storm-norm-perform"?

Matt: Yes, small group dynamics, teaming stuff. When a group is first put together, it goes through stages of development as a group, just like an individual person goes through infancy, childhood, adolescence, and adulthood. With groups, it's "form, storm, norm, perform, and adjourn." They need to form up and understand their task, and then they go through a stage where they "storm"—voice and resolve contending approaches or viewpoints. Then they settle down to setting group norms, and then they perform their tasks. Then when they complete their task, they adjourn.

Rosa: Yes, I've seen that dynamic in groups I've worked with, too.

> **TIP**   Understand and manage the group dynamics of your improvement team.

Matt: We also found that it went faster if we had more face-to-face meetings. One of our teams was split across two locations. We had a videoconference every week, and we tried to meet face to face at least every month or six weeks, but we were so busy we couldn't always do it. So when we did meet, we seemed to go through these stages each time. The longer we went between face-to-face meetings, the more time we spent storming before we could get to norming and performing, even in a single, two-day meeting. Go figure.

Rosa: That's very interesting. I've been thinking about managing our pilot kick-offs with trained facilitators. This sounds like a good thing to look at. Team leaders need to understand what the pilot teams are going through, and help them through it!
     One last thing. How did you go from pilot to wider rollout?

Matt: Well, like I said, Rosa, we tried to figure out what worked and what didn't across the pilots.

After you've determined which improvements to deploy across the organization, it follows that the next step is to plan, manage, and deploy them. The CMMI-ACQ suggests that this be done in successive cycles of improvement that are managed and measured. In this way, the organization can build on what it has learned from previous improvement cycles.

This is where the real fun begins.

Steve and Rosa are chatting in the hallway after the staff meeting.

Steve: You know, Rosa, we've talked a lot about how to get things going—what to do, what not to do, and so on. I'm really looking forward to just getting started. I guess I'm at the point where I need to dig in and get my hands dirty and try a few things.

> **TIP**   Sometimes the toughest part of getting started is getting started. Don't wait too long to begin!

Rosa: Why, Steve, I didn't know you engineers got your hands dirty! I thought you left that to the mechanics. But you're right. At some point, it's just time to quit talking about it and jump into the pool. And you know what? I think the anxiety about something is usually much worse than actually going through it.

Steve: Well, I wouldn't say I was anxious exactly.

Rosa: Steve, don't go misunderstanding me again. I think we're saying the same thing. You can only plan and anticipate so much. At some point, the only way to advance to the next level is to get started. I hope you'll have fun doing it, too. I know you'll be successful. After all, you have me as your process adviser!

But seriously, after all this planning I think we'll find it very satisfying to get started and begin to see some results, some data that we can use to track progress. I know that's the real fun of it for me, to begin to see progress. And then to think about rolling out the next wave of change.

Steve: I couldn't agree more, Rosa. I think it'll be fun to really make a difference in the way we do business around here, too. And with all this talk of data and analysis, I think I'm having a positive influence on you—you sound more like an engineer every day and not just a "process geek."

They both laugh at this as they head down the hall.

5.4.4 Applying the CMMI-ACQ to Making Incremental Improvements

The CMMI-ACQ provides specific recommendations on how to select and deploy incremental and innovative improvements that measurably improve your organization's processes and technologies. The improvements support the organization's quality and process performance objectives as derived from its business objectives (see Table 5-9).

You must continuously improve your processes and your alignment with your suppliers (Table 5-9, practice 1.1). You can look for opportunities to maximize throughput based on the identification of the most limiting resource and, as a result, create a more agile supply chain (e.g., improvement proposals that promote a supply chain that responds both quickly and cost effectively). Create a proposal for process and technology improvement to document your proposed incremental and innovative improvements to specific processes and technologies. Managers and staff, as well as customers, end users, and suppliers, can submit such proposals. Process and technology improvements can be implemented at the local level before being proposed for the organization.

Table 5-9 *Organizational Innovation and Deployment Goal 1: Practices and Tips*

CMMI-ACQ Process Area: Organizational Innovation and Deployment	
1. Goal: Process and technology improvements that contribute to meeting quality and process performance objectives are selected.	
Practices	**Tips**
1.1 Collect and analyze improvement proposals. 1.2 Identify and analyze innovations. 1.3 Pilot process and technology improvements to select which ones to implement. 1.4 Select process and technology improvements for deployment across the organization.	• Identify and communicate short-term wins. • Make it safe for the project and the organization to experiment and to make mistakes. • Use projects that have successfully overcome bottlenecks as pilots for improvement across the organization. • Use common process improvement initiatives to encourage the partnership between acquirer and supplier. • Make continuous improvement a norm for the integrated acquirer-supplier team.

One way to focus initial improvement efforts is to target process bottlenecks at the project level. It follows that a successful improvement activity that removes bottlenecks and improves throughput at the project level might be a candidate for wider application across the organization.

Your customers and suppliers are vital sources of innovative ideas. Interorganizational and organizational learning are therefore critical to actively identifying and analyzing innovations (Table 5-9, practice 1.2). Together with your suppliers, you can establish an innovation review program. This program might create time-boxed innovation solicitation, which is a well-communicated formal process for analysis and guaranteed response to innovative ideas proposed by customers, employees, and suppliers.

Pilots are performed to assess new and unproven major changes before they are broadly deployed, as appropriate (Table 5-9, practice 1.3). When you plan pilots, it is critical to define quantitative criteria to be used for evaluating pilot results. Reviewing and documenting the results usually involve the following tasks:

- Deciding whether to terminate the pilot, replan and continue the pilot, or proceed with deploying the improvement
- Updating the disposition of improvement proposals associated with the pilot

- Identifying and documenting new improvement proposals as appropriate
- Identifying and documenting lessons learned and problems encountered during the pilot

You select process and technology improvements for deployment across the organization based on quantifiable criteria derived from the organization's quality and process performance objectives (Table 5-9, practice 1.4).

You and your suppliers may share the costs and benefits of improvements (Table 5-10, practices 2.1–2.3). You can increase the incentive for suppliers to participate in improvement efforts across the supply chain by allowing suppliers to appropriate all the value derived from a contributed improvement in the short term (e.g., 6 to 18 months). Over time the supplier might be expected to share a proportion of those savings with you (for example, through cost reductions). Therefore, your plan for deploying improvements might include openly sharing most process know-how with your suppliers.

Any process-related knowledge that you or one of your suppliers possesses is viewed as accessible to virtually any other supplier in your supply chain (perhaps with the exception of a direct competitor). In this case, you need to establish rules and norms that prevent suppliers from accessing your knowledge unless they first explicitly agree to openly share knowledge with other suppliers of yours. For example, you have the ability to impose economic sanctions (such as withdrawal of business) on suppliers that violate the rules.

Table 5-10 *Organizational Innovation and Deployment Goal 2: Practices and Tips*

CMMI-ACQ Process Area: Organizational Innovation and Deployment	
2. Goal: Measurable improvements to the organization's processes and technologies are continually and systematically deployed.	
Practices	**Tips**
2.1 Establish and maintain plans for deploying the selected process and technology improvements. 2.2 Manage the deployment of the selected process and technology improvements. 2.3 Measure the effects of the deployed process and technology improvements.	• Leverage previous efforts in other process areas to begin organizational innovation and improvement activity. • Maintain momentum through frequent progress reviews.

5.5 Summary

Accelerating, or even initiating, a process improvement program within an organization can seem like an overwhelming undertaking. Keeping "order amid change" while simultaneously keeping "change amid order" is a challenge that is best faced wearing the armor of proven best practices.

However, merely imitating a successful organization isn't sufficient for affecting long-term, sustainable processes. In fact, you can get into trouble if you imitate without first considering the native processes and practices that have grown within your organization out of necessity. Often, creating processes in an ivory tower and mandating from on high that they be followed only strengthens a culture's resolve to maintain the status quo. Instead, organizations should focus on maintaining process stability while gradually introducing small, incremental changes. And these incremental changes shouldn't just be "good ideas" that someone thought up in the shower that morning. Instead, they should be based on the organization's actual performance data and other metrics.

Most likely, your organization has already put in place some processes that allow it to operate within the boundaries of acquisition budgets, schedules, internal policies, and external mandates—that is, within the boundaries some of the time. By concentrating first on improving existing processes and then keeping up that momentum, you can execute acquisition projects and programs more effectively and efficiently. Process improvement can result in long-term benefits that will enhance your overall management of acquisition projects and ultimately the organization as a whole. Not to mention that you will gain the benefit of better fit and quality of deliverables after they're deployed in the user community.

For all these reasons, you must treat a process improvement initiative as you would any other project, with milestones, metrics, program reviews, decision points, and so on. It should be planned and managed rigorously and should have appropriate resources. Applying the project planning practices from the CMMI-ACQ to the improvement project helps coordinate the work while allowing people to become familiar with the model. The executive team and management must do their part to support the work by clearly and consistently communicating the goals of the effort and the progress it's making. Senior leadership should also endorse, encourage, and fund training to further develop the capabilities of their staffs.

When you begin a process improvement journey, it's critical that you determine two things: where you stand in applying existing processes, and the destination you would like to reach. Taking a good, hard look at what you do well and where you stumble is certainly a start. Performing an in-house assessment is a confidential, unobtrusive, and less expensive way to gauge your organization's current process maturity. Keep in mind, however, that people in an organization tend to rate their performance higher than an external, objective appraisal team would, especially in an organization that's somewhat unfamiliar with process improvement or maturity models. There is plenty of room to interpret the questions, and when faced with questions about an unfamiliar subject, people usually just make their best guess.

The old saying "Hindsight is 20/20" is heard often, and with good reason. Analyzing historical data—or a lack thereof—can reveal facts about a project's performance and provide clues about the level of adherence to existing processes. Tracing through past documentation reveals the paths that an organization has already traveled. The road ahead, however, can become confused, with off-ramps, roundabouts, and dead ends. Improvement efforts that start small, on a single project or program, are usually more successful in navigating, making adjustments, and then staying the course than are efforts to make big changes quickly.

After groups of process improvement scouts have found and documented the way, other projects and programs can follow that map. Leverage these artifacts to gradually build a process asset library, keeping in mind that clear, concise, objective statements that communicate improvement goals are much more usable than volumes of detailed "shelfware" that is too cumbersome to be used in daily practice.

The early adopters of process improvement efforts can pave the way for change by eliminating redundancy and waste in existing, well-known processes. Begin by focusing on foundational processes—those processes and practices that just make good project management sense. Root out the processes that don't add value, and eliminate or streamline them. Pick working processes and tailor them to work optimally. Also identify strengths and opportunities, leverage their associated processes for quick payback, and use them to build momentum.

Techniques such as S.W.O.T (strengths, weaknesses, opportunities, and threats) can provide simple ways for you to identify a project's weaknesses and threats. They also give you opportunities to pick low-hanging fruit by identifying and eliminating activities that don't add much value to the overall process.

Use a simple mechanism to track process improvements and suggestions—for example, a Web site—and then reward early adopters for their short-term innovations. These practices encourage people to offer more improvement suggestions. Rewards don't have to be formal or elaborate; they can be as simple and immediate as a gift certificate to a nearby restaurant or store. This type of approach catalyzes a new culture of collaboration and ownership, and it weakens barriers to change. Such barriers include the cynics in an organization, the chasm between early adopters and the early majority, and a "shoot the messenger" mentality. After suggestions for improvement are gathered, test them by piloting a controlled number of changes on a small project. In this way, you will gain an opportunity to polish and fine-tune the process with minimal disruption before it is widely implemented.

It may seem counterintuitive, but process improvement work can apply equally to a project that is in execution as to a new acquisition. It's not necessary to wait until the "perfect time" or "perfect project" comes along; the perfect time is now, and the perfect project is the one you're working on. Don't get rattled if things don't go smoothly at first or if there are a few false starts. It's unrealistic to expect high-maturity performance right away, but that should not stop you from laying the foundation through managing and measuring process performance.

It's vital for suppliers to participate in process improvement projects; they are stakeholders in the outcome. A shared responsibility for improving common processes curbs the "throw it over the wall" approach. Not only are the individual organizations' processes strengthened, but also the relationships themselves grow stronger.

Identifying touch points—those parts of the overall process where acquirers and suppliers interact or intersect—is the key to identifying opportunities for collaboration and improvement. For example, one touch point during the solicitation and source selection phase of the acquisition life cycle is the RFI process. You issue a request for information to determine whether the capabilities to fulfill your needs exist in the industry. Other areas, such as contracting, configuration, change, and risk management, are often ripe with shared processes that can be standardized for the mutual benefit of you and your suppliers.

Using techniques such as alpha contracting to mutually delineate the scope of the requirements and define the deliverables can foster partnering and a sense of cooperation, and it can result in more efficient processes. The contract should spell out the scope of the shared process improvement activities to avoid misunderstandings and unplanned costs that may arise after the supplier begins executing the contract. And, as always, the key to successful collaboration is close communication—early and often.

During phases of the life cycle when processes aren't shared and are instead being executed in parallel—for example, when the supplier is developing the technology—it is important for you to retain and exercise certain responsibilities, such as contract oversight. While you're focusing on strengthening touch points and monitoring and improving individual projects and programs, don't lose sight of the big picture: the health of the organization as a whole.

Along the way, don't forget to have fun. Process improvement is hard work that requires individuals, teams, and middle and senior managers to wrestle with difficult problems, such as changing the culture and behavior of people and groups. But by collecting appropriate data and sharing it across the organization to determine, deploy, and measure successive cycles of improvement, you can make a tremendous difference in employee morale, customer satisfaction, and the organization's bottom line. This should be satisfying and fun! Let's get started!

Appendix

Overview of CMMI-ACQ

The initial draft CMMI for Acquisition (CMMI-ACQ) model focuses on the activities of the acquirer. The draft CMMI-ACQ addresses those activities required for supplier sourcing, developing and awarding contracts (supplier agreements), and managing the acquisition of solutions (such as products and services) by using a set of standard measures, acceptance criteria, and supplier deliverables. Supplier activities are not addressed in this report. CMMI for Development (CMMI-DEV) can be treated as a reference model for suppliers that develop products and services for an acquirer of technology solutions.

A.1 Introduction

The CMMI-ACQ contains six process areas unique to acquirers. A *process area* is a cluster of related practices in an area that, when implemented collectively, satisfies a set of goals that are considered important for making significant improvement in that area. The six process areas unique to the CMMI-ACQ describe those practices and capabilities that differentiate acquirers from other organizations such as developers:

- Acquisition Management (AM)
- Acquisition Requirements Development (ARD)
- Acquisition Technical Solution (ATS)

- Acquisition Validation (AVAL)
- Acquisition Verification (AVER)
- Solicitation and Supplier Agreement Development (SSAD)

The CMMI-ACQ also includes 16 foundation process areas common to all CMMI models. These process areas cover project management, process management, and support processes. These 16 process areas essentially describe practices and capabilities that an acquirer must possess. Each process area amplifies the nuances that successful acquirers master to implement those commodity practices and capabilities.

- Causal Analysis and Resolution (CAR)
- Configuration Management (CM)
- Decision Analysis and Resolution (DAR)
- Integrated Project Management (IPM)
- Measurement and Analysis (MA)
- Organizational Innovation and Deployment (OID)
- Organizational Process Definition (OPD)
- Organizational Process Focus (OPF)
- Organizational Process Performance (OPP)
- Organizational Training (OT)
- Project Monitoring and Control (PMC)
- Project Planning (PP)
- Process and Product Quality Assurance (PPQA)
- Quantitative Project Management (QPM)
- Requirements Management (REQM)
- Risk Management (RSKM)

The CMMI-ACQ does not specify that you must follow a particular acquisition process flow or that you must achieve a certain number of "deliverables per day" or specific performance targets. Instead, it specifies only that you have processes in place for adequately addressing acquisition-related practices. To determine whether this is so, you map your processes to the process areas contained in this report.

This mapping of processes to a process area allows you to track your progress to the CMMI-ACQ as you successfully deploy incremental process improvements or innovations. It is not intended that every process area of the CMMI-ACQ maps one to one with a given organization's or project's processes.

A.2 Process Improvement with CMMI

Like most organizations, acquirers strive to abandon ad hoc and chaotic processes. An acquirer attempts to continually enhance its ability (as well as its suppliers' ability) to reliably meet its business objectives through incremental and innovative improvements in processes and technology. In such organizations, success no longer depends on the competence and heroics of a few individuals but on the use of proved processes applied by competent staff.

To support an acquirer to reach excellence, CMMI provides two improvement approaches. Experience has shown that organizations do their best when they focus their process improvement efforts on a manageable number of process areas at a time and that those areas require increasing sophistication as the organization improves.

In one improvement approach, you choose the focus of your process improvement efforts by choosing those process areas, or sets of interrelated process areas, that best benefit you and your business objectives. Once you select the process areas, you also select how much you would like to mature the associated processes (i.e., you select the appropriate capability level).

This selection is typically described through a target profile. A *target profile* defines all the process areas to be addressed and the targeted capability level for each. This profile then governs which goals and practices you will address in your process improvement efforts.

Target staging is a sequence of target profiles that describes the path of process improvement to be followed. When building target profiles, you should pay attention to the dependencies between generic practices and process areas. If a generic practice depends on a certain process area—either to carry out the generic practice or to provide a prerequisite product—the generic practice may be much less effective when the process area is not implemented.

In the second improvement approach, you use designated sets of process areas to follow a defined improvement path or maturity level. If you do not know where to start and which processes to choose to improve, this approach is a good choice. It gives you a specific set of processes to start improving as an acquirer of technology solutions. In other words, it provides a predetermined path of improvement from maturity level 1 to maturity level 5, each a layer in the foundation for ongoing process improvement.

As you progress and learn more about where you need targeted improvements, you can switch between the two improvement approaches.

The following sections summarize groupings of process areas that allow acquirers to get the project management and sourcing basics in place and to achieve sophisticated quantitative management. These sections also represent the predefined improvement path provided by the initial CMMI-ACQ. This path is cumulative in the sense that it requires you to continue to expand on previous process areas and capabilities to achieve the next higher plateau of excellence.

A.2.1 Managed Processes

Projects establish the foundation by institutionalizing basic project management and supplier management practices. The acquirer ensures that processes are planned and executed in accordance with policy; employs skilled people who have adequate resources to produce controlled outputs; involves relevant stakeholders; and monitors, controls, reviews, and evaluates projects for adherence to their process descriptions (see Figure A-1).

The process discipline helps to ensure that you retain existing practices during times of stress. For instance, the status of the work products and the delivery of services are visible to management at defined points (such as at major milestones and at the completion of major tasks). Commitments are established among relevant stakeholders and are revised as needed. Work products are

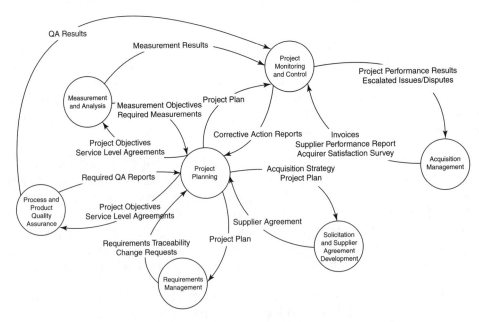

Figure A-1   *Level 2 process areas*

reviewed with stakeholders and are controlled. The work products and services satisfy their specified requirements, standards, and objectives.

The acquisition strategy and existing supplier agreements drive how much work, and what work, to give to a supplier. Depending on your acquisition strategy, there may be intermediate phases for the creation of prototypes, increments of capability, or spiral model cycles. In a complex project, you may be managing multiple supplier agreements simultaneously or in sequence. In such cases, any acquisition life cycle can end during any phase of the project life cycle.

You consider all supplier agreements within the context of the acquisition so that you develop an integrated approach rather than deal with activities individually. The characteristics of prequalified or other potential suppliers—including technical and financial capability, management and delivery processes, production capacity, and business type and size—are key elements of project success, and therefore you consider these characteristics in identifying constraints for the project.

The Solicitation and Supplier Agreement Development process area defines practices to prepare a solicitation package, select a capable supplier, and establish the supplier agreement. Acquisition Management focuses on maintaining the supplier agreement, including resolving disputes and managing your relationship with the supplier. This includes managing payments to and ongoing communications with suppliers. The Solicitation and Supplier Agreement Development and Acquisition Management process areas are described in detail in section A.3.

The purpose of the Project Planning area is to establish and maintain plans that define project activities. The amount of supplier work for a project largely determines the amount of your work that it takes to manage the project and the supplier. Estimate supplier work at a high level, and your work at a more detailed level. Your effort includes (1) effort associated with defining the scope of the project, (2) effort associated with the development and deployment of the technical solution, (3) operating and maintenance effort associated with the maintenance of the solution, and (4) disposal effort.

In addition to creating an estimation of the work products, you are encouraged to have your estimate independently reviewed by individuals outside the project to ensure that your estimates can be validated. Be sure to include the effort and cost of supporting execution of your processes as well as developing the product.

You develop a work breakdown structure (WBS) that clearly identifies which project work is performed by you and which is performed by the supplier.

The WBS includes activities performed by you as well as milestones and deliverables for the suppliers. The supplier work identified in the WBS becomes the foundation for the statement of work for suppliers. The WBS identifies the deliverables from the supplier and the work products you develop. Your understanding of suppliers' life-cycle models and processes, especially those that interact directly with your processes, enables you to plan for seamless interactions between you and your suppliers, resulting in a successful acquirer-supplier relationship.

During supplier selection and negotiation of the supplier agreement, you reconcile overall project work and resource levels based on the proposals from the supplier. Following completion of the supplier agreement, you incorporate supplier plans at an appropriate level of detail to support alignment of the plans. For example, you might incorporate major supplier milestones, deliverables, and reviews.

The project plan may include multiple plans, such as staffing plans, stakeholder involvement plans, risk mitigation plans, transition plans, quality assurance plans, and configuration management plans. Regardless of the form they take, the plans should address the acquisition strategy as well as the cradle-to-grave considerations for the project and product to be acquired. For example, you should consider what facilities and equipment must be provided by the supplier, as well as what you may need to provide for acceptance of the supplier deliverables, transition, and support of the acquired product. The supplier agreement must include any facility or equipment requirements for the supplier. You must also identify and ensure that any facilities or equipment to be provided to the supplier for its project work are accounted for in the project plan.

You must also plan for how data will be shared between you and the supplier as well as among relevant stakeholders. This planning avoids unexpected costs to procure, reformat, and deliver data. In many cases, the ideal solution is to leave your data in the physical possession of the supplier and have access to the supplier's data. In addition to data access, the data management plan should include the requirement for your use of data and for its reproduction, manipulation, altering, or transfer of possession.

The supplier agreement specifies appropriate acquirer rights to the data in addition to requirements for delivery or access. Data, whenever it is delivered to you, is formatted in accordance with accepted data standards to ensure its usability by you. Include plans for managing data within the project teams and for the infrastructure required to manage data between the supplier, operational users, and other relevant stakeholders. Decide which project data and plans require version control or more stringent configuration control, and establish mechanisms to ensure that project data is controlled. Consider the implications of controlling access to classified and sensitive data (e.g., proprietary, export-controlled, source-selection-sensitive) and other access-controlled data.

When you provide data access to the supplier, security and access control are critical. This includes creating access lists of authorized supplier personnel and nondisclosure agreements between you and the supplier. For example, when the supplier performs work for you off-site (e.g., at an offshore development center), then you need to consider additional security measures. Examples include a firewall between your network and the supplier's and restricted access to your workplace.

Ideally, the data management plan is supported by an integrated data system that meets the needs of both initial acquisition and the support community. Integrating acquisition and maintenance data systems into a total life-cycle integrated data environment lets you plan effectively for maintenance and facilitates insertion of new technology. It also ensures that acquisition planners have accurate information about total life-cycle costs.

The purpose of the Requirements Management process area is to manage the requirements of the project's products and components and to identify inconsistencies between those requirements and the project's plans and work products. Typically, you directly manage changes to customer and contractual requirements developed by you and oversee the supplier's requirements management process. You negotiate commitments with the customer and supplier before committing to any changes in requirements. Requirements changes may result in changes to the supplier agreement; these changes need to be agreed upon between the project and the supplier after appropriate negotiations. The supplier maintains comprehensive bidirectional traceability to the requirements you define in the supplier agreement, and you verify that traceability.

You are responsible for monitoring the progress and output of the project. The Project Monitoring and Control process area is concerned with monitoring and control of acquirer activities and oversight of the progress and performance of the supplier's execution according to the project plans. Project Monitoring and Control practices give you an understanding of the project's progress; in this way, you can take appropriate corrective actions when the project's performance deviates significantly from the plan.

As the acquisition unfolds, monitoring and control are essential to ensuring that appropriate resources are being applied and that your activities are progressing according to plan. For instance, you track commitments for resources that will result in expenditures (e.g., issued purchase orders and completed supplier deliverables that have been accepted) when they are incurred, even before formal payment. In this way, you can ensure that future financial and legal obligations are accounted for as soon as they are incurred.

You monitor overall project risk. Many risks are your sole responsibility and may include sensitive information that should not be shared with the supplier (e.g., source-selection-sensitive, recompetition, internal staffing, or other risks). There can also be risks (e.g., the feasibility of the technology to meet end user performance requirements) that require careful coordination with suppliers and appropriate escalation of risks and risk status. Shared risks may affect the mitigation approaches and may result in jointly planned mitigations.

After you select a supplier and establish a supplier agreement, the role of monitoring and control becomes twofold. You continue to monitor and control your activities and work products while also monitoring and controlling the progress and performance of the supplier's execution under the supplier agreement and the supplier's project plans. You monitor the progress of the supplier—including achievement of service levels established in the supplier agreement—by using the supplier's measurement data about its progress and output. This includes monitoring the availability of resources provided by the supplier and the skills and knowledge of the supplier personnel. In addition to monitoring the attributes of your work products, you monitor the attributes of supplier deliverables through acceptance criteria and through analysis of the supplier's peer review results.

If a corrective action is required to resolve variances from project plans, these actions should be defined and tracked to closure. Corrective action is taken for your deviations and when supplier execution does not satisfy the supplier agreement or align with project planning (e.g., date slippages in milestones and work products). Some corrective actions may be assigned to a supplier. When your monitoring of measurement data indicates, for example, that supplier progress does not appear to be sufficient to meet a service level defined in the supplier agreement, then you initiate and manage corrective action for the supplier. If the supplier does not comply appropriately, you escalate and handle this as a supplier agreement issue or dispute.

You use the practices in the Measurement and Analysis process area to support the information needs of the business, organization, and project. Some of this information may be needed from you, some from the supplier, and some from all parts of a project. The supplier agreement must designate all information required from the supplier. The measures you specify are designed to enable you to determine the status of your progress and output, the supplier's progress and output per contractual requirements, and the status of the evolving products.

You use measurement objectives to define specific measures and their collection, analysis, storage, and usage procedures. You establish measurement objectives for your activities and work products and for supplier deliverables. The measurement objectives are derived from information needs that come from project objectives, organizational objectives, and business needs. Measurement objectives focus on your performance as well as the supplier's performance, and on your understanding their effects on customer, operational, and financial performance. Measurement objectives for the supplier enable you to define and track service level expectations documented in the supplier agreement. You need to consider the impact of existing supplier agreements on measurement objectives.

To manage projects, you use supplier-reported measures in addition to your own measures of progress and output. The supplier measures allow you to comprehensively address the measurement objectives and determine the progress and output of the project. In some cases, these supplier measures will augment your measures. For instance, your return on investment measure can incorporate the supplier's cost performance index.

In most cases, the supplier measures are the primary source of data, especially with regard to the development of the product. For instance, for effective management of the quality, size, cost, and schedule of the project (e.g., the amount of new, modified, and reused code; the percentage of function points complete; defect removal efficiency), it is essential that you apply technical performance measures to measure and analyze the product or components provided by a supplier.

When you are acquiring multiple products to deliver a capability to the end user, or when there are relationships with other projects to acquire joint capabilities, you can identify additional measures to track and achieve interoperability objectives in terms of programmatic, technical, and operational interfaces.

Measures may be provided by the supplier as detailed measurement data or measurement reports. The measures that come from suppliers must be associated with your acceptance criteria for supplier measures. The acceptance criteria can be captured in measurement specifications or by checklists, if appropriate.

The acceptance criteria should be defined in a way that enables the intended use of the supplier measures, such as potential aggregation and analysis. They need to include any criteria associated with the collection and transfer mechanisms and procedures that must be performed by the supplier. Consider all characteristics of the supplier measures that may affect their use, such as differences in financial calendars used by different suppliers. If data is not available or data integrity checks indicate potential errors, follow up with suppliers.

Supplier measures must be defined in the supplier agreement, including the supplier's measurement collection requirements and the measurement reports to be provided to you. Data collection from a supplier can be integrated with periodic monitoring and review of supplier activities. You can conduct validity checks of supplier data by means of periodic audits of the supplier's execution of the data collection and analysis procedures for your required measures. The supplier agreement specifies which measurement data the supplier must provide to you, the required format, the means of its collection and storage (e.g., retention period of data), how and how often it will be transferred to you, and who has access to the data. The supplier may consider some supplier data proprietary, and you may need to protect it as such. Also consider that some of your measurement data (e.g., total project cost data) may be proprietary and should not be shared with suppliers. You need to plan for the collection, storage, and access control of this type of sensitive data.

The Process and Product Quality Assurance area has processes for evaluating your critical work products, your processes, and the results of the supplier's process quality assurance activities with respect to supplier deliverables and processes. You evaluate the project's execution of your processes, including interactions with suppliers and reviews of the quality assurance reports provided by suppliers, to determine whether they follow their processes. There should be sufficient process quality assurance that you can detect noncompliance issues as early as possible that may affect your or the supplier's ability to successfully deliver the technology solution to the customer. For example, process and product quality assurance ensures that the solicitation package was developed per the standard processes you agreed to and that it conforms to all applicable policies.

You can review the results of the supplier's quality assurance activities for supplier processes to ensure that the supplier is following its own processes. Typically, you select critical supplier processes, such as engineering or verification processes, where the supplier is required (through the supplier agreement) to follow project-specified standards. In exceptional cases, you can directly perform product and process quality assurance for selected supplier processes.

You and the supplier periodically share quality assurance issues and findings that are of mutual interest. For example, the supplier agreement can require the supplier to provide detailed appraisal results of mandatory, acquirer-scoped CMMI for Development appraisals of supplier processes. Through the supplier agreement, you should retain the right to audit supplier processes if there is an indication that suppliers are not following acceptable processes.

You perform product quality assurance by applying practices from the Acquisition Technical Solution and Acquisition Verification process areas. In addition to objectively evaluating your critical work products, you use objective acceptance criteria to evaluate supplier deliverables throughout the project life cycle. For that purpose, your acceptance criteria for supplier deliverables are consistent with the project objectives and sufficient to allow the supplier to satisfactorily demonstrate that the technology solution conforms to contractual requirements.

The Configuration Management process area (not depicted in Figure A-1) uses configuration identification, configuration control, configuration status accounting, and configuration audits to establish and maintain the integrity of work products such as solicitation packages. Your approach to configuration management depends on acquisition-specific factors, such as your acquisition approach, the number of suppliers, your design responsibility, your support concept, and associated costs and risks. The level of control is typically selected based on project objectives, risk, or resources (or all three).

Levels of control can range from informal control (which simply tracks changes made when you are developing the configuration items or when supplier work products are delivered or made accessible to you) to formal configuration control (using baselines that can be changed only as part of a formal configuration management process). Although the supplier may manage configuration items on your behalf, you are responsible for approval and control of changes to such configuration items.

Configuration items may vary widely in complexity, size, and type, from an aircraft to commercial off-the-shelf software to a test meter or project plan. Any item required for product support and designated for separate procurement is a configuration item. Your work products provided to suppliers, such as solicitation packages and technical standards, are typically designated as configuration items.

Consider how configuration items will be shared between you and suppliers as well as among relevant stakeholders. If you extend the use of your configuration management system to a supplier, you must exercise security and access control procedures. If a configuration management system is shared between you and suppliers, then the supplier agreement must specify clear responsibility for managing the configuration items, baselines, security aspects, access restrictions, and backup and restore processes. You must ensure that the supplier agreement specifies the configuration management requirements for the supplier (e.g., status reporting and providing configuration audit results). In many cases, you can leave acquired configuration items in the physical possession of the supplier and have access to supplier deliverables. The supplier agreement specifies appropriate acquirer rights to the supplier deliverables in addition to requirements for delivery or access. Supplier work products, whenever they are delivered to you, are formatted in accordance with accepted standards to ensure usability by you.

In any case, configuration management involves interaction between you and suppliers. You review and approve the release of the product baselines created by the supplier. You create baselines for your work products to mark the agreement regarding the description of the project, requirements, funding, schedule, and performance parameters and to make a commitment to manage the program to those baselines. For example, your baseline might be a collection of your work products such as contractual requirements and acceptance criteria that are related to the product baseline managed by the supplier.

With regard to the technical solution, you maintain configuration control of the contractual requirements, and the supplier performs configuration management for the technical solution (e.g., it establishes and maintains a product baseline). Thus, you retain the authority and responsibility for approving any design changes that affect the product's ability to meet contractual requirements. The supplier manages other design changes.

Change requests can be initiated by either you or the supplier. Changes that affect your work products and supplier deliverables as defined in the supplier agreement are handled through your configuration management process. You analyze the impact of submitted change requests to the supplier agreement. You maintain the right to access configuration data at any level required to implement planned or potential design changes and support options. Configuration management of legacy systems should be addressed on a case-by-case basis as design changes are contemplated.

A.2.2 Defined Processes

Acquirers are using defined processes for establishing and managing standard supplier agreements, and they embed tenets of project management and engineering best practices, such as requirements development and design constraints, into the standard process set. These processes are well characterized and understood and are described in standards, procedures, tools, and methods.

Your set of standard processes is established and improved over time. These standard processes are used to establish consistency across the organization. Projects establish their defined processes by tailoring the organization's set of standard processes according to tailoring guidelines.

A critical distinction between defined processes and managed processes is the scope of standards, process descriptions, and procedures. Managed processes may be quite different in each specific instance of the process (e.g., from project to project). Defined processes for a project, on the other hand, are tailored from the organization's set of standard processes to suit a particular project or unit, and therefore they are more consistent except for the differences allowed by the tailoring guidelines. Another critical distinction of defined processes is that they are typically described more rigorously than managed processes are. A defined process clearly states the purpose, inputs, entry criteria, activities, roles, measures, verification steps, outputs, and exit criteria.

Acquisition Requirements Development focuses on specifying customer and contractual requirements that express customer value (see Figure A-2). You use Acquisition Validation processes to ensure that the products received from the supplier will fulfill the stakeholders' intentions. You provide design constraints to the supplier, and the product is designed and implemented by the supplier consistent with your design constraints.

Acquisition Technical Solution covers developing design constraints and verifying the supplier's technical solution. You apply Acquisition Verification processes to address whether the acquired product, intermediate acquirer work products, and supplier deliverables meet their contractual requirements. Acquisition Requirements Development, Acquisition Valida-

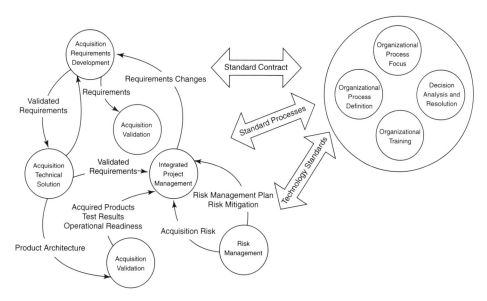

Figure A-2   *Level 3 process areas*

tion, Acquisition Technical Solution, and Acquisition Verification process areas are described in detail in section A.3.

You apply Integrated Project Management practices to establish and manage the project and the involvement of the relevant stakeholders according to an integrated and defined process that is tailored from the organization's set of standard processes. The project's defined process logically sequences acquirer activities and supplier deliverables (as identified in the supplier agreement) to deliver a product that meets the requirements. It is driven by your acquisition strategy. For example, the acquisition strategy might be to introduce new technology to the organization, or it might focus on consolidating the acquired products or services you are using. Which strategy you've adopted affects the project's defined process.

You need to involve and integrate all the relevant acquisition, technical, support, and operational stakeholders. You ensure that stakeholder coordination and cooperation are maximized to the extent possible. Depending on the project's scope and risk, your coordination efforts with the supplier can be significant. The supplier agreement provides the basis for managing supplier involvement.

The purpose of Risk Management is to identify potential problems before they occur so that you can plan and invoke risk handling activities as needed during the life of the product to mitigate adverse impacts on achieving objectives.

Risk Management has two contexts. The first context is the identification and assessment of project risks during project planning and managing these risks throughout the project. You enter the second context after the selection of a supplier and award of the supplier agreement. The risk management processes must address the risks associated with the supplier's role in the project. Throughout the life cycle of the project, you continue to manage the risks related to the supplier as well as managing project risks overall.

Because of the acquirer-supplier relationship, the need for early and aggressive detection of risk is compounded by the complexity of acquisition projects. For example, your capabilities, the supplier's experience of working with you, the supplier's financial stability, or the availability of well-defined dispute resolution processes influence the risk of a project. You should conduct a risk assessment before solicitation to evaluate whether the project can achieve the technical, schedule, and budget constraints. You should discuss technical, schedule, and cost risks with potential suppliers before the solicitation is released. In this way, you can identify and address inherent critical risks in the solicitation.

Both you and the supplier must understand the project risks and know how to modify the risk management strategy and plans as the project progresses through its life cycle. Managing a project's risks requires a close partnership between you and the supplier. Both parties need to share appropriate risk management documentation, understand the risks, and develop and execute risk management efforts.

You initially identify and categorize risk sources and categories (e.g., schedule, cost, sourcing, contract management, supplier execution, technology readiness, human safety, reliability-related risks, and other issues outside your control) and refine them over time. You consider the risks associated with a supplier's capability (e.g., meeting schedule and cost requirements), including the potential risks to your intellectual capital or security vulnerabilities introduced by using a supplier. Your risk categories typically include sourcing, contract management, and supplier execution, in addition to project management, technology, and requirements. Thresholds for supplier risks that affect the project (e.g., schedule, quality, or risk exposure due to supplier risks) are specified in the supplier agreement along with escalation actions if the thresholds are exceeded.

A risk management strategy must be developed early in the project so that relevant risks are identified and managed aggressively. The acquisition strategy evolves based on risk identification and analysis. The early identification and assessment of critical risks allow you to formulate approaches and streamline the project definition and the solicitation around critical risks. You identify some risks by using the categories and parameters in the risk management strategy to examine the supplier's WBS, product, and processes. Risks can be identified in many areas, such as requirements, technology, design, testing, vulnerability to threats, and life-cycle costs. Examining the project in these areas can help you develop or refine the acquisition strategy and the risk-sharing structure between you and suppliers.

You share selected risks with the supplier. Risks associated specifically with the acquisition process are tracked, and then they are resolved or controlled until mitigated. This monitoring includes risks that may be escalated by the supplier. To examine risks such as potential failures in products or processes, you can use tools such as failure mode and effects analysis. These tools can be used to evaluate risk management priorities for mitigating known threat vulnerabilities.

The practices in Decision Analysis and Resolution help you analyze possible decisions by using a formal process to evaluate identified alternatives against established criteria. A repeatable criteria-based decision-making process is especially important, both while you're making the critical decisions that define and guide the acquisition process and later, when you make critical decisions with the selected supplier. Having a formal process for decision making provides you with documentation of the decision rationale. Such documentation lets you revisit the criteria for critical decisions when you consider making changes or adopting technology that will affect requirements or other critical project parameters. A formal process also supports the communication of decisions between you and suppliers. Suppliers competing to develop a technical solution can be directly evaluated in a final competition that possibly involves performance or functional demonstration of proposed solutions.

Organizational Process Definition focuses on establishing and maintaining a usable set of organizational process assets and work environment standards. Your set of standard processes also describes standard interactions with suppliers. Supplier interactions are typically identified in terms of deliverables expected from suppliers, acceptance criteria applicable to those deliverables, standards (such as architecture and technology standards), and standard milestone and progress reviews.

Basing standard processes on industry standards and widely accepted models, with common terminology, enables seamless interactions between you and suppliers. In a multisupplier environment, this is most important for your standard processes that directly interface with the supplier processes. Also, you may gain cost and coordination benefits from having suppliers work together to develop or reconcile common support processes that are aligned with your processes.

The life-cycle models may include acquisition life cycles, depending on the specific acquisition strategy chosen. The acquisition life cycle typically begins with the pre-award phase of a supplier agreement, continues through the phases of awarding and managing the supplier agreement, and ends when the supplier agreement period of performance ends, usually with the acceptance and completion of the warranty for the product and its transition to the support organization. Your review of life-cycle models typically includes the participation of suppliers for those processes and process elements that define expectations and constraints for suppliers.

Tailoring is a critical activity that allows controlled changes to the processes to meet specific needs of a project or a part of the organization. Processes and process elements that are directly related to critical business goals and objectives should usually be defined as mandatory (allowing less variation), but those that are less critical or only indirectly affect business objectives may allow for more tailoring (and therefore more variation). Tailoring might also depend on the life-cycle model of the project, the supplier, or the acquirer-supplier relationship.

The supplier agreement defines how changes to organizational process assets that affect the supplier (e.g., standard supplier deliverables, acceptance criteria) must be deployed. You should encourage participation of suppliers in process improvement activities (Organizational Process Focus). Suppliers may be involved in developing the process action plans if the processes that define interfaces between you and suppliers are targeted for improvement.

The purpose of the Organizational Training processes is to develop people's skills and knowledge so that they can perform their roles effectively and efficiently. When you identify training needs, you may also want to address some training needs of suppliers, especially in those process elements that define interfaces with and expectations for suppliers.

A.2.3 Quantitatively Managed Processes

You control variation in your results by applying quantitative management. That is, you examine the business system being used to meet the needs of the end customer, identifying constraints that significantly impede overall business performance. You use statistical and other quantitative techniques to understand these constraints so that you can make the appropriate process refinements, including adjustments to your supplier interactions to better achieve business objectives. Focusing on these critical constraints, you can use process performance models to predict how to best maximize the flow of work through the project and the organization.

Defined processes are different from quantitatively managed processes in the predictability of process performance. The performance of quantitatively managed processes is controlled using statistical and other quantitative techniques and is quantitatively predictable. Typically, defined processes are only qualitatively predictable.

The purpose of the Quantitative Project Management process area is to quantitatively manage the project's defined process to achieve the project's established quality and process performance objectives. You use quantitative methods to manage your work and to gain insight into the supplier's work and products. In addition to your own quantitative data, you use quantitative data provided by the supplier (as specified in the supplier agreement) to address the specific practices in this process area. For the successful implementation of this process area's specific practices, you need to establish effective relationships with suppliers.

You establish the project's quality and process performance objectives based on the objectives of the organization and the project. You can also establish quality performance objectives for supplier deliverables. These supplier objectives are documented in the supplier agreement. You may require the supplier to provide process performance measurements for its participation in the project's processes or subprocesses (e.g., the estimating subprocess).

When you select the processes for analysis, it is critical to understand the relationships between the various processes and their impact on your and the supplier's performance relative to delivering the product specified by the customer. Such an approach will help ensure that quantitative and statistical management is applied where it will have the most overall value to the business. Using data and measures submitted by the supplier, you analyze supplier process performance as it interfaces with your processes. Performance models are used to set performance objectives for the suppliers and to help them achieve these objectives.

You monitor the performance of selected subprocesses—including those that involve interaction with a supplier—as well as the quality performance of the supplier deliverables for adherence to the quality and performance objectives. This selective monitoring provides you with insight into project and supplier performance so that you can predict the likelihood of achieving the project's objectives for quality and process performance. You use this information to manage the risks of the project and to initiate corrective actions in time to meet the project objectives.

The purpose of Organizational Process Performance is to establish and maintain a quantitative understanding of the performance of your set of standard processes in support of quality and process performance objectives, and to give you the process performance data, baselines, and models to quantitatively manage your projects. Process performance models are used to estimate or predict when to fund, hold, cancel, migrate, reengineer, or retire a project or program. Process performance models allow you to synchronize processes with the customer's needs.

Your process performance baselines provide quantitative data on those aspects of the projects and organization that can approximate the throughput potential of its processes. Focusing on these critical constraints, process performance models allow you to predict how to best maximize the flow of work through the projects and the organization. Performance models are also used to set performance objectives for the suppliers and to provide data that can help suppliers achieve these objectives. The results of your process performance models are shared with the suppliers so that they can ensure synchronized delivery of products and services.

A.2.4 Optimizing Processes

An acquirer continually improves its processes based on a quantitative understanding of the common causes of variation inherent in processes. To optimize your processes, you select and deploy incremental and innovative improvements that measurably improve your processes and technologies (see the processes in the Organizational Innovation and Deployment process area). The improvements enhance your and your suppliers' ability to meet your quality and process performance objectives.

Your customers and suppliers are vital sources of innovative ideas. Interorganizational and organizational learning are therefore critical to actively identifying and analyzing innovations. Together with your suppliers, you can establish an innovation review program. This program can create timeboxed innovation solicitation, which is a well-communicated formal process for analysis and guaranteed response to innovative ideas proposed by customers, employees, and suppliers.

You establish quantitative process improvement objectives for the organization, and then you continually revise them to reflect changing business objectives, and you use them as criteria in managing process improvement. You must continuously improve your processes and your alignment with your suppliers. You can look for opportunities to maximize throughput based on identifying the most limiting resource and, as a result, create a more agile supply chain. Examples of such opportunities include proposals that promise to make the supply chain respond both quickly and cost-effectively.

Your plan for deploying improvements can include openly sharing most process know-how with your suppliers. Any process-related knowledge that you or one of your suppliers possesses is viewed as accessible to virtually any other supplier in your supply chain (perhaps with the exception of a direct competitor). In this case, you need to establish rules and norms that prevent suppliers from accessing your knowledge unless they first explicitly agree to openly share knowledge with your other suppliers. For example, you have the ability to impose economic sanctions (e.g., withdrawal of business) on a supplier that violates the rule.

The effects of deployed process improvements are measured and evaluated against the quantitative process improvement objectives. Both the defined processes and your set of standard processes are targets of measurable improvement activities. You and suppliers can share the costs and benefits of improvements. You can increase the incentive for suppliers to participate in improvement efforts across the supply chain by allowing suppliers to appropriate all the value derived from a contributed improvement in the short term (e.g., 6 to 18 months). Over time the supplier may be expected to share a proportion of those savings with you (e.g., through cost reductions).

You typically achieve your quality and performance objectives in partnership with your suppliers. You typically focus on differentiating your capabilities along with collaborative supplier management. Achieving these objectives also depends on your being able to effectively evaluate and deploy proposed improvements to the processes and technologies. All members of the acquirer-supplier network participate in your process improvement and technology improvement activities. This requires the supplier's willingness to open its processes for inspection to you and your other suppliers. Suppliers' process improvement proposals are systematically gathered and addressed.

A critical distinction between quantitatively managed processes and optimizing processes is the type of process variation addressed. An acquirer that uses quantitatively managed processes is concerned with addressing special causes of process variation and providing statistical predictability of the results. Although processes may produce predictable results, the results may be insufficient to achieve the established objectives. Acquirers that use optimizing processes are concerned with addressing common causes of process variation and with changing the process (to shift the mean of the process's performance or to reduce the inherent process variation experienced) and thereby improve process performance and achieve the established quantitative process improvement objectives.

A.3 The Big Six: Acquisition Process Areas

The CMMI-ACQ describes six process areas that represent core competencies of successful acquirers (see Figure A-3).

The following sections describe those process areas in detail.

A.3.1 Solicitation and Supplier Agreement Development

The purpose of Solicitation and Supplier Agreement Development (SSAD) is to prepare a solicitation package and to select one or more suppliers for delivering the product or service. The Solicitation and Supplier Agreement

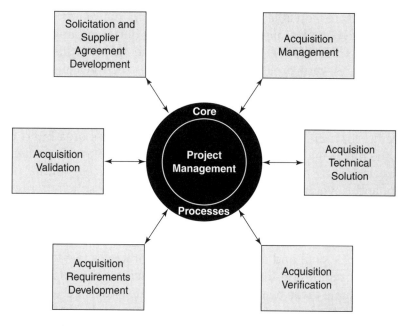

Figure A-3   *The "big six" acquisition process areas*

Development process area includes developing the acquisition strategy. The acquisition strategy is a guide to direct and control the project and a framework to integrate the activities essential to acquiring an operational product.

The Solicitation and Supplier Agreement Development process area provides a set of practices that enable the acquirer to initialize and formalize a relationship with the supplier for the successful execution of the project. A formal agreement is any legal agreement between the organization (representing the project) and the supplier. This agreement may be a contract, a license, or a memorandum of agreement. The acquired product is delivered to the project from the supplier according to this formal agreement (also known as the "supplier agreement").

The supplier agreement created using these practices enables the acquirer to execute its monitoring and control of supplier activities using other process areas, such as Project Monitoring and Control and Acquisition Management.

The practices of this process area apply equally to initial supplier agreements and to subsequent change orders, task orders, or amendments related to those agreements.

The acquirer is responsible for establishing and maintaining the ground rules for supplier communication, documenting decisions, and conflict resolution through the life of the agreement. The acquirer facilitates these activities with relevant project stakeholders. Specific roles and responsibilities of relevant project stakeholders for interaction with or direction of the suppliers are defined, coordinated, and adhered to.

The specific goals and specific practices of this process area build on each other in the following way. The Prepare for Solicitation and Supplier Agreement Development specific goal and associated practices identify potential suppliers and develop the evaluation criteria and the solicitation package. The solicitation package is developed using work products from other process areas, e.g., requirements from Acquisition Requirements Development and design constraints from Acquisition Technical Solution. The Select Suppliers specific goal and associated specific practices use the work products from the preparation for solicitation to solicit responses from potential suppliers, evaluate these responses, and negotiate and select a supplier who can best deliver to the solicitation package. Subsequently, the Establish Supplier Agreement specific goal and associated practices are used to document the approved supplier agreement. In turn, the data provided by the supplier and documented in the supplier agreement (e.g., cost, schedule, risks) is used by Project Planning practices to update the project plan.

Although this process area describes acquisition practices for a project, an acquirer would use the same practices in establishing a supplier agreement for multiple projects .The requirements included in the solicitation package and the supplier agreement would reflect the broader scope, and the evaluation and selection process would require an appropriate level of review before a selection is made.

Related Process Areas

Refer to the Acquisition Management process area for more information about managing selected suppliers' activities based upon the supplier agreement.

Refer to the Acquisition Requirements Development process area for more information about defining customer and contractual requirements.

Refer to the Acquisition Verification and Acquisition Validation process areas for more information about evaluating requirements.

Refer to the Acquisition Technical Solution process area for more information about determining the design constraints, including standards that are included in the solicitation package.

Specific Goal and Practice Summary

SG 1 Prepare for Solicitation and Supplier Agreement Development

    SP 1.1   Develop Acquisition Strategy

    SP 1.2   Identify Potential Suppliers

    SP 1.3   Develop Solicitation Package

    SP 1.4   Review the Solicitation Package

    SP 1.5   Distribute the Solicitation Package

SG 2 Select Suppliers

    SP 2.1   Evaluate Proposed Solutions

    SP 2.2   Develop Negotiation Plans

    SP 2.3   Finalize Supplier Selection

SG 3 Establish Supplier Agreement

    SP 3.1   Establish Mutual Understanding of the Agreement

    SP 3.2   Document Supplier Agreement

Specific Practices by Goal

SG 1   Prepare for Solicitation and Supplier Agreement Development

Develop the acquisition strategy, qualify potential suppliers, and develop a solicitation package that includes the requirements and proposal evaluation criteria.

SP 1.1   Develop the Acquisition Strategy

Develop and maintain the overall acquisition strategy content.

The acquisition strategy is the business and technical management framework for planning, directing, contracting for, and managing a project or program. The acquisition strategy relates to the objectives for the acquisition, the constraints, availability of resources and technologies, consideration of acquisition methods, potential supplier agreement types, terms and conditions, accommodation of business considerations, considerations of risk, and support for the acquired product over its life cycle.

The acquisition strategy results from a thorough understanding of both the specific acquisition project or program and the general acquisition environment. The acquirer accounts for the potential value or benefit of the acquisition in the light of the potential risks, considers constraints, and takes into account experiences with different types of suppliers, agreements, and terms. A well-developed strategy minimizes the time and cost required to satisfy approved capability needs, and maximizes affordability throughout the project life cycle.

The acquisition strategy for a project typically tailors a program or organizational-level acquisition strategy.

The acquisition strategy is the basis for formulating solicitation packages, supplier agreements, and project plans. The strategy evolves over time and should continuously reflect the current status and desired end point of the project.

Typical Acquirer Work Products

1. Acquisition strategy

Subpractices

1. Identify the capabilities and objectives the acquisition is intended to satisfy or provide.

   The capabilities describe what the organization intends to acquire. Typically the capability included in the acquisition strategy summary highlights product characteristics driven by interoperability and/or families of products. It also identifies any dependency on planned or existing capabilities of other projects or products.

   Refer to Acquisition Requirements Development for information about determining capabilities and customer requirements.

   At a minimum, the acquirer identifies the cost, schedule, and key performance objectives for the acquisition. Each objective consists of an objective value representing customer expectations and a threshold value representing acceptable limits that, in the customer's judgment, still provide the needed capability. While the number and specificity of performance parameters may change over the duration of an acquisition, the acquirer typically focuses on the minimum number of parameters that, if thresholds are not met, will require a re-evaluation of the project.

   The acquisition strategy establishes the milestone decision points and acquisition phases planned for the project. It prescribes the accomplishments for each phase and identifies the critical events affecting project management. Schedule parameters include, at a minimum, the projected dates for the project initiation, other major decision points, and initial operational capability.

Examples of cost parameters include the following:
- Research, development, test, and evaluation costs
- Procurement costs
- Acquisition-related operations, support, and disposal costs
- Total product quantity (to include both fully configured development and production units)

2. Identify the acquisition approach.

The acquirer defines the approach the project will use to achieve full capability: either evolutionary or single step; it should include a brief rationale to justify the choice. When a project uses an evolutionary acquisition approach, the acquisition strategy describes the initial capability and how it will be funded, developed, tested, produced, and supported. The acquisition strategy previews similar planning for subsequent increments and identifies the approach to integrate and/or retrofit earlier increments with later increments.

Examples of additional considerations for the acquisition approach include the following:
- Actions a project team can take on its own, if the acquiring organization or unit has a procurement, contracting, or purchasing department
- Who will prepare independent estimates and whether they are need as evaluation criteria
- Managing multiple suppliers
- Anticipated lead times from potential suppliers to acquire items

3. Document business considerations.

Examples of business considerations for an acquisition strategy include the following:
- Competition planned for all phases of acquisition, or explain why competition is not practicable or not in the best interests of the acquirer. This includes considerations for establishing or maintaining access to competitive suppliers for critical areas of the product or product components.
- Product and technology areas critical to satisfy or provide the desired capabilities.
- Availability and suitability of commercial items and the extent to which the interfaces for these items have broad market acceptance,

> standards-organization support, and stability. This includes considerations for both international and domestic sources that can meet the required need, as the primary sources of supply consistent with organizational policies and regulations.

4. Identify major risks and risk sharing with the supplier.

   All acquisition risks, whether primarily managed by the acquirer or by the supplier, must be assessed and managed by the acquirer. The acquisition strategy describes how risk is to be handled and identifies major risks and which risks are to be shared with the supplier and which are to be retained by acquirer.

5. Identify the supplier agreement type.

   The acquirer identifies standardized procurement documents (e.g., standard supplier agreements), if any. The acquirer also determines the type of supplier agreement planned (e.g., firm fixed-price; fixed-price incentive; firm target; cost plus incentive fee; or cost plus award fee) and the reasons it is suitable, including considerations of risk assessment and reasonable risk-sharing by the acquirer and the supplier.

   The acquisition strategy explains the planned incentive structure for the acquisition, and how it incentivizes the supplier to provide the product or services at or below the established cost objectives and satisfy the schedule and key performance objectives. If more than one incentive is planned for a supplier agreement, the acquisition strategy explains how the incentives complement each other and do not interfere with one another. The acquisition strategy identifies any unusual terms and conditions of the planned supplier agreement and all existing or contemplated deviations to an organization's terms and conditions, if any.

6. Identify the product support strategy.

   The acquirer develops a product support strategy for life-cycle sustainment and continuous improvement of product affordability, reliability, and supportability, while sustaining readiness. The support strategy addresses how the acquirer will maintain oversight of the fielded product.

   The acquirer's sustainment organization or supplier typically participates in product support strategy development.

7. Review and obtain agreement with senior management on the acquisition strategy.

   The development of the acquisition strategy for a project typically requires senior management sponsorship. The appropriate senior management needs to approve the acquisition strategy before initiating a project.

SP 1.2   Identify Potential Suppliers

Identify and qualify potential suppliers.

Consistent with the acquisition strategy and along with the scope and requirements for the project or program, the acquirer identifies potential suppliers to receive the solicitation. The acquirer can identify suppliers from a variety of sources, e.g., employees, international seminars, market analysis reports.

Acquirers need to limit the number of suppliers they solicit proposals from in order to reduce their cost and efforts for the solicitation, while at the same time making sure they have included suppliers who are capable of meeting the requirements and that enough suppliers are included to provide a competitive environment. This competition enhances the leverage of the acquirer in achieving its objectives, e.g., providing different approaches to meeting the requirements.

Depending upon the applicable regulations or characteristics of the project, the acquirer may determine to sole source the project rather than place it for competitive bid.

Typical Acquirer Work Products

1. List of potential suppliers prepared to respond to the solicitation

Subpractices

1. Develop a list of potential suppliers.

   In developing the list of potential suppliers, the acquirer considers which suppliers have had experience with similar systems or projects, what kind of performance the acquirer has experienced with suppliers on previous projects, what suppliers are likely to provide the specific capabilities needed for the project, and what is the availability of critical resources to staff and support the project. In addition to assessing the supplier's capabilities, a risk assessment is prepared on the supplier's financial capabilities, e.g., credit worthiness, financial stability and access to capital, and the impact to the supplier of a successful bid.

2. Communicate with potential suppliers concerning the forthcoming solicitation.

   The acquirer contacts the suppliers to outline the plans for the solicitation, including the projected schedule for releasing the solicitation package and the expected dates for responses from suppliers. If the supplier indicates its interest in responding to the solicitation, the appropriate confidentiality agreements are put in place.

Typical information included in communication to candidate suppliers:

- Anticipated scope of the solicitation
- Schedule for release of the solicitation package
- Overall project schedule
- Approach/procedures that will be used throughout the solicitation process
- High-level criteria for evaluating proposal responses
- Required supplier qualifications, e.g., appraisal at a specific CMMI level
- Schedule for return of proposal
- Date for supplier to indicate whether it will or will not participate in the solicitation

3. Verify the participants who will evaluate supplier proposals.
4. Verify the participants in supplier negotiations.

SP 1.3   Develop Solicitation Package

Establish and maintain a solicitation package that includes the requirements and proposal evaluation criteria.

Solicitation packages are used to seek proposals from potential suppliers. The acquirer structures the solicitation package to facilitate an accurate and complete response from each potential supplier and to allow for an effective comparison and evaluation of proposals.

The solicitation package includes a description of the desired form of the response, the relevant statement of work for the supplier, and any required contractual provisions (e.g., a copy of the standard supplier agreement, non-disclosure provisions). With government agreements, some or all of the content and structure of the solicitation package can be defined by regulation.

The solicitation package typically contains:

- The statement of work for the supplier, including supplier measures and service levels
- Guidance on how potential suppliers are to respond to the solicitation package
- Criteria that will be used to evaluate the proposals
- Documentation requirements to submit with the response (e.g., project plans)
- Schedule for completing the solicitation process
- Procedures for addressing questions, contacts

The solicitation package is rigorous enough to ensure consistent, comparable responses, but flexible enough to allow consideration of supplier suggestions for better ways to satisfy the requirements. Inviting the suppliers to submit a proposal that is wholly responsive to the request for proposal and to provide a proposed alternative solution in a separate proposal can do this.

The complexity and level of detail of the solicitation package should be consistent with the value of, and risk associated with, the planned acquisition. In some cases, the solicitation may not include detailed requirements, e.g., it may be a solicitation for development of detailed requirements, or it may include a statement of objectives to provide the supplier greater flexibility in addressing the scope of the project. Proposal and supplier evaluation criteria are identified and documented.

Typical Acquirer Work Products

1. Solicitation package
2. Supplier and proposal evaluation criteria

Subpractices

1. Develop the statement of work for the supplier.

   The statement of work for the supplier defines, for those items being acquired, only the portion of the project scope that is included within the related supplier agreement. The statement of work for a supplier is developed from the project scope, the work breakdown structure, and the task dictionary.

   The statement of work for the supplier is written to be clear, complete, and concise. It describes the acquired product or service in sufficient detail to allow prospective suppliers to determine whether they are capable of providing the product or service.

   Example content of the statement of work for the supplier includes the following:

   - Project or program objectives
   - Requirements (including period of performance, work location, legal, statutory, and regulatory requirements)
   - Design constraints
   - Deliverables and rights (e.g., work breakdown structure of the supplier's work, detailed design, test results)
   - Expectations for supplier transition of product to operations

- Measurements, service levels, and reports that provide the acquirer visibility into the supplier's process and results
- Collateral services required (e.g., study reports, development of training materials, delivering training to end users)
- Acquirer-specified standard processes for the project (e.g., configuration management, escalation, corrective action for non-conformances, conflict resolution, and change management)
- The type of reviews that will be conducted with the supplier and other communication processes and procedures
- Product acceptance criteria
- Post-project support

The statement of work for the supplier can be revised and refined as required as it moves through the solicitation and supplier agreement development process until incorporated into a signed supplier agreement. For example, a prospective supplier can suggest a more efficient approach or a less costly product than that originally specified.

2. Specify the measures, the acceptance criteria, and the associated service levels for the supplier.

Service levels are designed to support the acquisition strategy. Typically the service levels are a limited set with a precise definition, including the assessment and calculation of incentives and penalties.

Examples of considerations for service levels include the following:
- Specific methodology to be followed in measuring supplier performance, including goals, objectives, credits, earnbacks, and measurement calculations.
- On-going level of performance of the service acquired, the minimum allowed performance level, and the amount of credit allocated to each performance measurement
- One-time deliverables, with monthly credits to the acquirer for non-performance by the supplier

A service level for a project, for example, may refer to an output from the supplier, such as providing a specific deliverable at an agreed-upon time, and to the quality of that output. Service levels also (directly or indirectly) relate to the performance targets or thresholds of progress measures. For example, if a service level requires on-time completion of deliverables from a supplier and the supplier doesn't appear to be on schedule based on the progress measure "percent completion of deliverables," then the acquirer and supplier will trigger corrective actions to bring the supplier's delivery back on target.

3. Develop supplier evaluation and proposal evaluation criteria.

Evaluation criteria are developed and used to rate or score proposals. Evaluation criteria are included as a part of the solicitation package. Evaluation criteria can be limited to purchase price if the procurement item is readily available from a number of acceptable suppliers. Purchase price in this context includes both the cost of the item and ancillary expenses such as delivery. Other selection criteria can be identified and documented to support an assessment for a more complex product or service. For example:

The individuals identified in the Project Planning resource plan develop and document the criteria for evaluating potential suppliers and for evaluating their proposals.

Examples of areas to evaluate the potential suppliers' ability and proposals include the following:

- Compliance with stated requirements contained in the solicitation package
- Experience with similar products or services (e.g., familiarity with the acquirer's processes, technical environment, and the core business)
- Total ownership and life-cycle cost
- Technical capability (e.g., expected functional and performance compliance with the requirements and criteria, given the architecture and technical solution proposed)
- Management and delivery processes and procedures
- Proposed technical methodologies, techniques, solutions, and services
- Financial capability
- Production capacity and interest (e.g., staff available to perform the effort, available facilities, and resources)
- Business size and type
- Intellectual property and proprietary rights

---

4. Document the proposal content that the suppliers must submit with their response.

The following are examples of proposal content for suppliers to submit:

- Compliance with the requirements
- References, company overview, case studies

- Evidence of the supplier's organizational processes upon which the supplier's processes for the project will be based and the commitment to execute those processes from project inception
- Plan describing how the potential supplier will carry out the scope and content of the solicitation package, including any improvement of execution capability over the duration of the supplier agreement
- Understanding of the size and complexity of the requested work based on the requirements
- Pricing and compensation which typically include:
  - Pricing and compensation methodology that provides for calculation of the charges with respect to the services being provided to the acquirer pursuant to the supplier agreement and terms & conditions, including taxes, credits, foreign currency translation, licenses, pass-through costs, and travel reimbursements
  - Pricing and compensation schedules that provide for the charges for the products and services provided, including frequency, term, and pricing type (e.g., fixed price lump sum, time and materials) as well as rate cards and skills matrix
  - Acquirer's travel reimbursement policies
- References and experience validating the capability of the potential supplier's proposed approach to meet the proposed funding, schedule, and quality targets
- Risk management plan describing how the potential supplier will identify and manage risks associated with the risks called out in the solicitation package
- Methods for early defect identification and the prevention of defects in the products delivered
- Supplier's approach to quality assurance of the product
- Approach to escalation and resolution of issues
- Description of the potential supplier's proposed use of COTS and the rationale for the supplier's confidence that the use of COTS can achieve the requirements
- Description of the potential supplier's proposed re-use of previously developed hardware and software, and the rationale for the supplier's confidence that the re-use can be achieved.
- Approach to provide visibility of the acquirer into development progress and costs at a level appropriate for the type of contract and commensurate with the degree of risk
- Retention of critical staff during the project
- Identification of any work to be performed by subcontractors

5. Incorporate acquirer's (standard) supplier agreement, terms and conditions, and additional information into the solicitation package.

Contract terms and conditions typically include:

- Recitals
- Deliverables and rights
- Compensation and payments
- Confidentiality
- Privacy statements
- Continuous improvement and best practices
- Exclusive services, key employees, supplier's personnel at acquirer's sites
- Information gathering practices and ethical representation
- Force majeure
- Term
- Termination for insolvency, breach or non-performance
- Termination for convenience
- Termination assistance
- Indemnification
- Insurance
- Right to audit
- Notices

Typical considerations for additional instructions and general information for the supplier when responding to the solicitation package include the following:

- Submission of intent to submit proposal
- Submission due date, time, and destination
- Number of proposal copies that must be submitted
- Proposal format
- Non-complying proposals
- Proposal ownership
- Bidder inquiries
- Key dates and activities
- Discretionary selection and potential modifications of solicitation process
- No implied offer

- Response constitutes an offer to do business
- Confidentiality of information
- Publicity
- Use of subcontractors
- Due diligence
- Incurred costs
- Language and statutory units
- Warranty provisions
- Licensing provisions

SP 1.4   Review the Solicitation Package

Review the solicitation package with stakeholders to make sure the approach is realistic and can reasonably lead to a usable product.

The solicitation package is reviewed with end users and other stakeholders to make sure the requirements have been accurately and sufficiently stated so that the solicitation can lead to a manageable agreement. The acquirer establishes traceability between the requirements and the solicitation package. Suppliers may be included as stakeholders in the review of the solicitation package. The acquirer wants the solicitation package to attract a variety of responses and encourage competition. The acquirer also wants to ensure that the package is legally inclusive of all qualified suppliers.

The acquirer may use standard templates and checklists to verify that the necessary components, e.g., skills, standards, verification and validation methods, measures, and acceptance criteria, are covered in the solicitation package.

The independent cost and schedule estimates for the supplier's project work developed in the practice above are also reviewed.

Typical Acquirer Work Products

1. Record of the reviews of the solicitation package

SP 1.5   Distribute and Maintain Solicitation Package

Distribute the solicitation package to potential suppliers for their response, and maintain its content throughout the solicitation.

The solicitation package is distributed to the potential suppliers identified above.

The acquirer uses the Project Planning practices and the Project Monitoring and Control practices to monitor, control, and replan acquirer activities during the solicitation process as necessary.

Typical Acquirer Work Products

1. Potential suppliers
2. Responses to supplier questions
3. Amendments to the solicitation package

Typical Supplier Deliverables

1. Supplier proposals
2. Supplier questions, requests for clarification

Subpractices

1. Finalize list of potential suppliers.
2. Distribute solicitation package to potential suppliers.
3. Document and respond to supplier questions according to the instructions in the solicitation package.

   Verify that all potential suppliers have equal access and opportunity to provide feedback on the solicitation package. Provide the opportunity for the selected potential suppliers and stakeholders to clarify points of ambiguity in the requirements as well as any disconnects or concerns with the requirements.
4. Acknowledge the receipt of supplier proposals according to the schedule identified in the solicitation package.
5. Verify the conformance with requirements and completeness of the supplier response. Contact suppliers if the response is non-conforming or incomplete so that they can take corrective action.
6. Issue amendments to the solicitation package when changes are made to the solicitation.

SG 2   Select Suppliers

Select suppliers based on an evaluation of their ability to meet the specified requirements and established criteria.

SP 2.1   Evaluate Proposed Solutions

Evaluate proposed solutions according to the documented proposal evaluation plans and criteria.

Proposals, submitted in response to solicitation packages, are evaluated in accordance with an overall established timeline, and preliminary project plans and proposal evaluation criteria. The proposal evaluation criteria are used to evaluate the potential suppliers' responses to the solicitation. Evaluation results and decision-making notes, e.g., advantages and disadvantages of potential suppliers and scoring against criteria, should be documented and maintained.

The acquirer refines the negotiation strategy based upon the evaluation of the suppliers' proposals and the evaluation of the suppliers. The proposal evaluation and the negotiations with the suppliers provide the basis for selecting a supplier best able to meet the requirements of the solicitation.

For task orders or contractual changes against an existing supplier agreement, the acquirer uses documented evaluation criteria against which to evaluate the task order responses or proposed contractual changes. In a sole source or change order environment, this practice is critical for relevant stakeholders to understand the intent of the effort or changes before placing the additional work against the supplier agreement.

Typical Acquirer Work Products

1. Clarification correspondence between the acquirer and potential suppliers
2. Evaluation results and rationale
3. Candidate suppliers

Typical Supplier Deliverables

1. Proposal revisions based upon clarifications
2. Supplier documentation of its approach to the project work, capabilities, preliminary technical solution

Subpractices

1. Distribute supplier proposals to the individuals identified by the acquirer to perform the evaluation.
2. Schedule acquirer evaluation review of supplier proposals to consolidate questions, concerns, and issues.
3. Schedule supplier presentations.
4. Verify the mutual understanding of the statement of work.

   A good practice is to compare the supplier's estimates to those developed in the project planning practices; this comparison provides a means to determine whether there is a mutual understanding of the requirements and the associated work to fulfill them.

5. Evaluate supplier proposals, and document the findings.

6. Execute due diligence.

Due diligence provides an opportunity for the acquirer to further clarify requirements, particularly those related to the acquirer's existing environment and products in use. The potential suppliers ask questions and gain understanding, which enables them to make their proposals more realistic. It also enables the acquirer to gain insight into the capability of the potential suppliers' proposed solutions to meet requirements.

Due diligence helps to eliminate assumptions and replace them with facts, to identify and document risks and their mitigation plans or their effect on the agreement, and to list issues and dependencies between the acquirer and supplier to include in the agreement.

The following are typical examples of due diligence activities:

- Reviews of requirements with current supplier or acquirer resources that are maintaining the products or providing services
- Reviews of interfaces of a system with other systems maintained by the acquirer
- Review and validation of supplier references
- Reviews of operating environment's facilities and capabilities
- Reviews of regulatory and security requirements
- Reviews of supplier capabilities

----

7. Document candidate supplier recommendations based upon proposal evaluation.

SP 2.2   Develop Negotiation Plans

Develop negotiation plans to use in completing a supplier agreement.

Develop a negotiation plan for each of the candidate suppliers based upon evaluation of the suppliers and their proposals.

The size of a negotiation team depends upon the size and complexity of the project. Typically the team is led by supplier management and also includes individuals who possess detailed knowledge of the statement of work documented in the solicitation package. The negotiation team is typically supported by legal staff, a financial analyst, purchasing, and the project manager for the project.

Examples of items included in a negotiation strategy include the following:

- Roles and responsibilities of negotiation team members
- Key issues to be negotiated from the supplier responses
- Negotiation "levers," and where and when they should be used
- Sequence of events to negotiate the issues
- Fall-back or compromise positions as necessary on given issues (possible concessions and trades)
- List of items that are non-negotiable
- External factors that could influence the negotiations (e.g., other pending deals, strategic plans, etc.)
- Prior supplier contracting experiences to discover previous positions and issues (and negotiating styles)
- Schedule and sequence for supplier negotiations meetings
- Specific objectives for each negotiating session
- Risks, consequences, and mitigation alternatives

Typical Acquirer Work Products

1. Negotiation strategy for candidate suppliers

SP 2.3   Finalize Supplier Selection

Select suppliers based on an evaluation of their ability to meet the specified requirements and established criteria.

Proposal evaluation results are used to finalize a supplier selection based on the outcome of negotiations. The negotiations enable the acquirer to select the best supplier for the project. In some cases the acquirer may take the top two proposals and use negotiations to make the final selection decision.

The evaluation results, along with the negotiation results, support the selection decision or cause the acquirer to take other action as appropriate. If the return on investment is not sufficient the acquirer may decide to defer or cancel the project.

Typical Acquirer Work Products

1. Revisions due to negotiations
2. Supplier sourcing decision

Subpractices

1. Negotiate with supplier(s) to determine best fit for the project.

   Negotiate with the selected supplier or candidate suppliers to resolve any issues identified during due diligence and to address any remaining issues with requirements, and revise the requirements to be fulfilled by the supplier.

2. Select a supplier to be awarded the supplier agreement.

3. Document the sourcing decision.

SG 3   Establish Supplier Agreements

Establish and maintain formal agreements with selected suppliers.

A formal agreement is established based on the supplier sourcing decision.

SP 3.1   Establish Mutual Understanding of the Agreement

Establish and maintain a mutual understanding of the contract with selected suppliers and end users based on the acquisition needs and the suppliers' proposed approaches.

As points of clarification and ambiguities continue to arise after contract award, ensure that the mutual understanding is revised and maintained through the life of the project. Ensure that the supplier makes a contractual commitment to execute its proposed processes.

Typical Acquirer Work Products

1. Correspondence clarifying elements of the agreement
2. Frequently asked questions (for use with end users, other suppliers)

SP 3.2   Document Supplier Agreement

Document the approved supplier agreement.

The agreement may be either a stand-alone agreement or part of a master agreement. When part of a master agreement, the project may be, for instance, an addendum, work order, or service request to the master agreement.

Typical Acquirer Work Products

1. Supplier agreement (including terms & conditions)

Subpractices

1. Document the supplier agreement for the project.

   The supplier agreement provisions typically include:

   - The statement of work, specification, terms and conditions, list of deliverables, schedule, budget, and acceptance process
   - Product acceptance criteria to be satisfied by the supplier
   - Statement of work for the supplier
   - Measurements and reports that provide the acquirer visibility into the supplier's process and results
   - Mechanisms and deliverables that provide the acquirer sufficient data to allow evaluation and analysis of acquired products
   - Names of representatives from the project and supplier who are responsible and authorized to make changes to the supplier agreement
   - Supplier's responsibility for supporting business acceptance working with the acquirer
   - How requirements changes and changes to the supplier agreement are determined, communicated, and addressed
   - Standards and procedures that will be followed (e.g., configuration management, escalation, non-conformances, conflicts, issues, etc.)
   - Requirements for the supplier to establish a corrective action system that includes a change control process for rework and reevaluation
   - Critical dependencies between the acquirer and the supplier
   - Documentation of what the acquirer will provide to the supplier such as facilities, tools, software, documentation, and services
   - Verification methods and acceptance criteria for designated supplier deliverables
   - The type and depth of project oversight of the supplier procedures and evaluation criteria to be used by the acquirer in monitoring supplier performance
   - The types of reviews that will be conducted with the supplier
   - The supplier's responsibilities to execute corrective actions when initiated by the Project Monitoring and Control practices
   - Non-hire and non-compete clauses
   - Confidentiality, non-disclosure, intellectual capital clauses pertaining to PPQA, measurement data, personnel who would perform audits or are authorized to validate measurement data

- The supplier's responsibilities for preparation of the site and training of the support and operations organizations according to acquirer-specified standards, tools, and methods
- The supplier's responsibilities for ongoing maintenance and support of the acquired products
- Requirements for the supplier to be involved in the deployment of process assets as necessary
- Warranty, ownership, and usage rights for the acquired products
- Security and legal penalty recoveries

2. Verify that all parties to the agreement understand and agree to all requirements by signing the supplier agreement.
3. Notify those suppliers not selected for the award.
4. Communicate the supplier agreement within the organization as required.

A.3.2 Acquisition Management

The purpose of Acquisition Management (AM) is to ensure that the supplier's performance meets contractual requirements and that the acquirer performs according to the terms of the supplier agreement. The Acquisition Management process area involves the following:

- Maintaining ongoing communications and mutual understanding with the supplier
- Resolving issues and disputes
- Revising and closing the supplier agreements
- Accepting delivery of acquired products
- Transitioning acquired products to the project
- Managing the payment to the supplier

The legal nature of the acquirer-supplier relationship makes it imperative that the project management team is acutely aware of the legal implications of actions taken when managing any acquisition of products or services.

The supplier agreement is the basis for managing the relationship with the supplier, including resolving issues and disputes. It defines the mechanisms to allow the acquirer to oversee the supplier's activities and evolving products, and to verify compliance with supplier agreement requirements. It also provides the vehicle for mutual understanding between the acquirer and the supplier.

Deviations from the project plan may cause changes to the supplier agreement, and significant changes to the supplier agreement may require the project plan to be modified. When the supplier's performance, processes, or products fail to satisfy established criteria as outlined in the supplier agreement, the acquirer may decide to apply legal remedies.

Related Process Areas

Refer to the Solicitation and Supplier Agreement Development process area for more information about defining steps for escalation of issues.

Refer to the Acquisition Validation process area for information about validating products.

Refer to the Acquisition Verification process area for information about verifying supplier deliverables.

Specific Goal and Practice Summary

SG 1 Manage Supplier Agreements

> SP 1.1   Manage Supplier Agreement Communications
>
> SP 1.2   Resolve Supplier Agreement Issues and Disputes
>
> SP 1.3   Revise Supplier Agreements
>
> SP 1.4   Close Supplier Agreements

SG 2 Satisfy Supplier Agreements

> SP 2.1   Accept the Acquired Product
>
> SP 2.2   Transition Products
>
> SP 2.3   Manage Payments to Suppliers

Specific Practices by Goal

SG 1   Manage Supplier Agreements

Manage changes and revise the supplier agreement if necessary, and resolve supplier agreement issues or disputes.

SP 1.1   Manage Supplier Agreement Communications

Manage supplier agreement communications between the acquirer and the supplier about the relationship, performance, results, and impact to the business.

This specific practice covers communications internally and externally as well as the use of such information by acquirer and supplier to support marketing and public relations. The acquirer manages the relationship with the supplier to maintain effective communication on key issues, for example, change in the acquirer's business, new supplier products and technologies, and changes in the organizational structure.

Typical Acquirer Work Products

1. Marketing and communications material
2. Correspondence between acquirer and supplier

SP 1.2   Resolve Supplier Agreement Issues and Disputes

Resolve issues and disputes associated with the supplier agreement, and determine corrective actions necessary to address the issues and disputes.

This specific practice represents the escalation of unresolved issues between the acquirer and supplier through multiple phases of escalation for an issue between acquirer and supplier before possible litigation.

The acquirer collects supplier agreement related issues or disputes and tracks these issues and disputes until resolution. Issues related to the supplier's performance may be escalated from progress or milestone reviews, for example. If the supplier does not comply appropriately with the acquirer's initiation of corrective action, the acquirer escalates and handles the issue as a supplier agreement dispute.

The supplier may also escalate issues related to the agreement, especially those related to the acquirer meeting specified commitments. Each issue is tracked from identification or receipt to resolution according to the escalation process or procedure defined in the supplier agreement. The resolution may require that a change be made to the supplier agreement. Relevant stakeholders, for example, senior managers, contract manager, governance bodies, legal consultants, project manager, and suppliers, may be requested to participate in resolution of an issue to prevent the issue becoming the subject of an agreement dispute.

Typical Acquirer Work Products

1. List of escalated issues and disputed issues
2. Corrective action plan
3. Corrective action results
4. Resolution of agreement issues and disputes (e.g., proposed supplier agreement language)
5. Correspondence with supplier

Typical Supplier Deliverables

1. List of escalated issues and disputed issues
2. Corrective action plans for supplier issues
3. Corrective action results for supplier issues
4. Correspondence with acquirer

Subpractices

1. Gather escalated issues associated with the supplier agreement for analysis.
2. Determine and document the appropriate actions need to address the escalated issues.

   Collect documentation and backup material relevant to the issue, and interpret supplier agreement to compile advantages and disadvantages of various positions for resolution.
3. Review escalated issues per the process or procedure in the supplier agreement, and resolve if possible.
4. Classify issues not resolved through escalation as disputed issues.
5. Build negotiations team and strategy to resolve the disputed issues.
6. Conduct dispute resolution as required by the supplier agreement.

   Communicate proposed dispute resolution to the supplier, or analyze supplier's proposed dispute resolution.
7. Monitor escalated issues and disputes for completion.
8. Analyze results of issues and dispute resolution to determine its effectiveness.
9. Document resolution of escalated issues and disputes, and communicate as needed.

SP 1.3   Revise Supplier Agreements

Revise the supplier agreement to reflect changes in conditions where appropriate.

After award of the supplier agreement, the acquirer may find requirements that are no longer optimal or applicable based on the supplier's progress or environment changes. Examples include availability of new technology, overly burdensome documentation, and reporting requirements. Changes to supplier agreements may also occur when the supplier's processes or products fail to meet agreed-to criteria and service levels.

All changes are formally documented and approved by both the acquirer and the supplier before being implemented by this specific practice.

Approved change requests can include modifications to the terms and conditions of the supplier agreement, including the statement of work, pricing, and description of products, services, or results to be acquired.

Typical Acquirer Work Products

1. Revised supplier agreement

SP 1.4   Close Supplier Agreements

Close the supplier agreement after verifying completion of all supplier requirements.

This practice addresses each supplier agreement applicable to the project or a project phase. Depending on the acquisition life cycle, the term of the supplier agreement may be applicable only to a given phase of the project. In these cases, this specific practice closes the supplier agreement(s) applicable to that phase of the project. When a supplier agreement is applicable to an entire project, this specific practice typically closes the project. Unresolved issues or disputes may be subject to litigation after supplier agreement. The terms and conditions of the supplier agreement can prescribe specific procedures for supplier agreement closure.

Early termination of a supplier agreement is a special case of supplier agreement closure, and can result from a mutual agreement of the acquirer and supplier or from the default of one of the parties. The rights and responsibilities of the acquirer and supplier in the event of an early termination are contained in the termination clause of the supplier agreement.

Typical Acquirer Work Products

1. Supplier agreement file

Subpractices

1. Verify with stakeholders that all supplier activities and supplier deliverables specified in the agreement have been received and accepted.

   The acquirer verifies, for instance, that any warranty has been completed according to the supplier agreement and that all regulatory requirements have been met. This may also include a final supplier evaluation related to the agreement.

   Refer to the Acquisition Verification process area for information about verifying supplier deliverables.

2. Ensure that all records related to the supplier agreement are stored, managed, and controlled for future use.

The acquirer documents the performance of the supplier as a basis for future relationships with the supplier. Supplier performance evaluation by the acquirer is primarily carried out to confirm the competency or lack of competency of the supplier, relative to performing similar work on the project or other projects.

3. Communicate to appropriate stakeholders that the supplier agreement has been closed.

The acquirer, usually through its authorized supplier agreement or contract administrator, provides the supplier with formal written notice that the supplier agreement has been completed.

SG 2   Satisfy Supplier Agreements

Establish a productive and cooperative environment to meet the goals of the project.

SP 2.1   Manage Payment to Supplier

Receive, review, approve, and remit invoices provided by the supplier.

This practice handles invoices for any type of charge, for example, one-time, monthly, deliverable-based, pass-through, and expenses. It handles invoice errors or disputes, changes to invoices, billing errors, and withholding of disputed charges consistent with the terms and conditions of the supplier agreement. The acquirer must adhere to regulatory requirements, for example, tax deductions, in managing payments to the supplier. The acquirer must also ensure that appropriate financial controls are in place.

The intent of this practice is to ensure that payment terms defined within the supplier agreement are met and that supplier compensation is linked to supplier progress, as defined in the supplier agreement. When accepting supplier deliverables, the acquirer should not make final payment to the supplier until it has been certified that all the supplier deliverables meet the contractual requirements and that all acceptance criteria have been satisfied. To the degree that nonperformance is encountered, exercise the contract provisions for withholding or reducing payments to the supplier.

Typical Acquirer Work Products

1. Invoices approved for payment

Typical Supplier Deliverables

1. Invoices

Subpractices

1. Review invoice and related supporting material.

> Examples of areas of review for invoices and related support material include the following:
> - Volumes for any variable charges
> - Pass-through expenses
> - Regulatory commitments related to payments
> - Purchases made by supplier on behalf of acquirer

2. Resolve errors and manage disputes with supplier as required.
3. Process invoice for payment.

SP 2.2   Accept Acquired Product

Ensure that the supplier agreement is satisfied before accepting the acquired product.

The acquirer ensures that all acceptance criteria have been satisfied and that all discrepancies have been corrected. Requirements for formal deliverable acceptance, and how to address non-conforming deliverables, are usually defined in the supplier agreement. The acquirer should be prepared to exercise all remedies in case the supplier fails to perform.

The acquirer, usually through its authorized supplier agreement or contract administrator, provides the supplier with formal written notice that the supplier deliverables have been accepted or rejected.

With this specific practice, an authorized representative of the acquirer assumes ownership of existing identified supplier products or deliverables tendered, or approves specific services rendered, as partial or complete performance of the supplier agreement on the part of the supplier.

Typical Acquirer Work Products

1. Stakeholder approval reports
2. Discrepancy reports
3. Product acceptance review report with approval signatures

Typical Supplier Deliverables

1. Work products as defined in the supplier agreement

Subpractices

1. Review the validation results, reports, logs, and issues for the acquired product.

   Refer to the Acquisition Validation process area for more information about validating products.

2. Confirm that all customer requirements and stakeholder intentions associated with the acquired product are satisfied.

3. Review the verification results, reports, logs, and issues for the acquired product.

   Refer to the Acquisition Verification process area for more information about verifying products.

4. Confirm that all contractual requirements associated with the acquired product are satisfied.

   This may include confirming that the appropriate license, warranty, ownership, usage, and support or maintenance agreements are in place and that all supporting materials are received.

5. Confirm that all discrepancies have been corrected and that all acceptance criteria have been satisfied.

6. Communicate the product's readiness for transition to operations and support and also the product's status to stakeholders.

SP 2.3   Transition Product

Transition the acquired product from the supplier to the acquirer.

Typically, the supplier integrates and packages the products and prepares for the transition to operations and support, including support for business user acceptance, and the acquirer oversees the supplier activities. These expectations and the acceptance criteria for transition to operations and support are included in the solicitation package and then supplier agreement.

Typical Acquirer Work Products

1. Transition readiness report
2. Transfer of ownership
3. Transition analysis report

Typical Supplier Deliverables

1. Transition plans

2. Training reports

3. Pilot results

Subpractices

1. Ensure the completion of installation of the product in the production environment.

2. Conduct pilot or initial implementation, as appropriate.

   The acquirer, following appropriate reviews of the transition activities, makes the product available for use according to the plans for pilot and transition. During this pilot or initial period of production, the acquirer validates that the product is capable and ready for full operational use. During this defined transition or warranty period, for example, 30 days or 90 days, the acquirer oversees activities to make sure the product is operating as planned and identifies any corrective actions required. Although the product is in the operational environment, full responsibility for operations and support is not transitioned until this pilot period is complete and any corrective actions identified have been successfully completed. During this defined transition period, the acquirer ensures support of the product, for example, the supplier may be given responsibility to maintain support during the transition.

   Ensure the viability of either dual operations or the capability to back out the product before transitioning to the production environment

3. Transfer responsibility for operations and support.

   Responsibility for operations and support of the product is transferred by the acquirer to the operations and support organizations, which may be suppliers, only after the operations and support organization demonstrates its capability and capacity to support the product and accept the responsibilities to perform its assigned operations and support processes. The acquirer ensures that the operations and support organizations understand post-transition service requirements from the supplier.

   The acquirer maintains oversight responsibilities until the transition activities are complete and the transfer of responsibility for operations and support of the product has been accepted. This includes oversight of any supplier activities, based upon the supplier agreement, for the execution of the transition of the product to operations and support.

4. Analyze the results of transition activities.

   After the transition is complete and the responsibility transferred to the operational and support organizations (e.g., at the end of the warranty period for a software product), the acquirer reviews and analyzes the results of the transition activities and determines whether any corrective actions must be completed before close.

The following typical reports and logs are used in the analysis by the acquirer:

- Results of transition activities including defects or quality-related measures collected during pilot and warranty period
- Problem tracking reports, detailing resolution time, incident response, escalation, and root cause analysis
- Change management reports
- Operation logs to determine that sufficient information is stored to support reconstruction
- Configuration management records
- Violation of security activity reports
- Actual operations costs compared to estimates
- Actual support costs compared to estimates

5. Analyze the actual operations and support cost against the estimated costs.
6. Follow warranty terms and conditions to resolve problems during the period following transition. Ensure that storing, distributing, and using the acquired products are in compliance with the terms and conditions specified in the supplier agreement or license.

A.3.3 Acquisition Requirements Development

The purpose of Acquisition Requirements Development (ARD) is to produce and analyze customer and contractual requirements. Requirements are the basis for the selection and for the design or configuration of the acquired product. The development of requirements includes the following activities:

- Elicitation, analysis, validation, and communication of customer needs, expectations, and constraints to obtain customer requirements that constitute an understanding of what will satisfy stakeholders
- Collection and coordination of stakeholder needs
- Development of the life-cycle requirements of the product
- Establishment of the customer requirements
- Establishment of contractual requirements consistent with customer requirements to a level of detail that is sufficient to be included in the solicitation package and supplier agreement

The requirements included in the solicitation package form the basis for evaluating alternative proposals by suppliers and for further negotiations with the suppliers and communication with the customer. The contractual requirements for the supplier are baselined in the supplier agreement.

Requirements are identified and refined throughout the project life cycle. Design decisions, subsequent corrective actions, and feedback during each phase of the project's life cycle are analyzed for impact on contractual requirements.

Requirements analyses aid in understanding, defining, and selecting the requirements at all levels from competing alternatives. Analyses occur recursively at successively more detailed levels until sufficient detail is available to produce contractual requirements and to further refine these, if necessary, while the supplier builds or configures the product.

Involvement of relevant stakeholders in both requirements development and analyses gives them visibility into the evolution of requirements. Participation continually assures the stakeholders that the requirements are being properly defined.

The Acquisition Requirements Development process area includes three specific goals. The Develop Customer Requirements specific goal addresses eliciting and defining a set of customer requirements. The Develop Contractual Requirements specific goal addresses defining a set of contractual requirements that are based on customer requirements and included in the solicitation package and supplier agreement. The specific practices of the Analyze and Validate Requirements specific goal support the development of the requirements in both the Develop Customer Requirements specific goal and the Develop Contractual Requirements specific goal. The specific practices associated with this specific goal cover analyzing and validating the requirements with respect to the acquirer's intended environment.

The processes associated with the Acquisition Requirements Development process area and those associated with the Acquisition Technical Solution process area may interact recursively with one another, for instance, to iteratively refine requirements.

Related Process Areas

Refer to the Acquisition Technical Solution process area for more information about how the outputs of the requirements development processes are used for defining technical constraints.

Refer to the Acquisition Verification process area for more information about verifying that the resulting product meets the contractual requirements.

Refer to the Acquisition Validation process area for more information about how the requirements will be validated against the stakeholder intentions.

Specific Goal and Practice Summary

SG 1 Develop Customer Requirements

    SP 1.1   Elicit Needs

    SP 1.2   Develop the Customer Requirements

SG 2 Develop Contractual Requirements

    SP 2.1   Establish Contractual Requirements

    SP 2.2   Allocate Contractual Requirements

SG 3 Analyze and Validate Requirements

    SP 3.1   Establish Operational Concepts and Scenarios

    SP 3.2   Analyze Requirements

    SP 3.3   Analyze Requirements to Achieve Balance

    SP 3.4   Validate Requirements with Comprehensive Methods

Specific Practices by Goal

SG 1   Develop Customer Requirements

Stakeholder needs, expectations, constraints, and interfaces are collected and translated into customer requirements.

The intentions of stakeholders (e.g., customers, end users, suppliers, supplier agreement management personnel, manufacturers, and logistics support personnel) are the basis for determining requirements. The stakeholder needs, expectations, constraints, interfaces, operational concepts, and product concepts are analyzed, harmonized, refined, and elaborated for translation into a set of customer requirements.

Frequently, the stakeholders' intentions are poorly identified or conflicting. Because the stakeholders' intentions must be clearly identified and understood throughout the project life cycle, an iterative process is used throughout the life of the project to accomplish this objective. To facilitate the required interaction, relevant stakeholders are frequently involved throughout the project life cycle to communicate their needs, expectations, and constraints and to help resolve conflicts. Environmental, legal, and other constraints should be considered when the set of requirements for acquiring products or services are created and evolved.

SP 1.1   Elicit Needs

Elicit stakeholder needs, expectations, constraints, and interfaces for all phases of the product life cycle.

Eliciting goes beyond collecting requirements; eliciting proactively identifies additional requirements not explicitly provided by the stakeholders. Relevant stakeholders representing all phases of the product's life cycle in the acquirer's intended environment should include business as well as technical functions. In this way, needs for all product-related life-cycle processes are considered concurrently with the concepts for the acquired products.

Analyses of business processes are a common source of stakeholder needs, expectations, constraints, and interfaces. Additional needs typically address the various project life-cycle activities and their impact on the product.

Examples of techniques to elicit needs for current and potential customers and other stakeholders include the following:

- Questionnaires, interviews, and operational scenarios obtained from end users
- Operational walkthroughs and end-user task analysis
- Prototypes and models
- Observation of existing products, environments, and workflow patterns
- Technology demonstrations
- Interim project reviews
- Brainstorming
- Quality function deployment
- Market surveys
- Extraction from sources such as business process documents, standards, or specifications
- Use cases
- Business case analyses
- Reverse engineering (for legacy products)

Examples of sources of requirements that might not be identified by the customer include the following:

- Government regulations
- Policies and standards
- Technology
- Legacy products or product components (for reuse)

Typical Acquirer Work Products

1. Stakeholder intentions

Subpractices

1. Engage relevant stakeholders using methods for eliciting needs, expectations, constraints, and external interfaces.

SP 1.2   Develop the Customer Requirements

Transform stakeholder needs, expectations, constraints, and interfaces into customer requirements.

The customer typically describes requirements as capabilities expressed in broad operational terms concerned with achieving a desired effect under specified standards and regulations. The various inputs from the customer and other stakeholders must be aligned to the organization's strategy, missing information must be obtained, and conflicts must be resolved as the customer requirements are documented (e.g., customer requirements that exist as an output of another project's activities such as a previous project that delivered the initial capability).

Examples of considerations for expressing customer requirements include the following:

- Key characteristics (attributes) of the desired capability with appropriate parameters and measures
- Obstacles to overcome to achieve the capability
- Competitive gap between existing and desired capability
- Supportability of desired capability
- Level of detail of customer requirements so as not to prejudice decisions in favor of a particular means of implementation, but specific enough to evaluate alternative approaches to implement the capability

Typical Acquirer Work Products

1. Prioritized customer requirements
2. Customer constraints on the conduct of verification
3. Customer constraints on the conduct of validation

Subpractices

1. Translate the stakeholder needs, expectations, constraints, and interfaces into documented customer requirements
2. Prioritize customer requirements
3. Define constraints for verification and validation

SG 2   Develop Contractual Requirements

Customer requirements are refined and elaborated to develop contractual requirements.

Customer requirements are analyzed in conjunction with the development of the operational concept to derive more detailed and precise sets of requirements called contractual requirements to be included in the solicitation package for potential suppliers and eventually in the supplier agreement. The level of detail of contractual requirements is determined based on the acquisition strategy and project characteristics.

Contractual requirements arise from constraints, consideration of issues implied but not explicitly stated in the customer requirements baseline, and factors introduced by the design constraints and the supplier's capabilities. The requirements are reexamined throughout the project life cycle.

The requirements are allocated to supplier deliverables. The traceability of requirements to supplier deliverables is documented.

SP 2.1   Establish Contractual Requirements

Establish and maintain contractual requirements, which are based on the stakeholder requirements.

The customer requirements may be expressed in the customer's terms and may be non-technical descriptions. The contractual requirements are the expression of these requirements in technical terms that can be used for design decisions. An example of this translation is found in quality functional deployment, which maps customer desires into technical parameters. For instance, "solid sounding door" might be mapped to size, weight, fit, dampening, and resonant frequencies.

In addition to technical requirements (e.g., requirements specifying interfaces with other products or applications, functional requirements and their validation, and verification requirements such as product acceptance criteria), contractual requirements also cover non-technical stakeholder needs, expectations, and constraints.

Examples of considerations for non-technical requirements include the following:

- Frequency and format of supplier reviews
- Standard measures and service levels for the technical solution
- Supplier reports and other communications

- Availability of support to meet levels of business process or product performance
- Warranty of products provided by a supplier
- Logistics support that sustains both short and long-term readiness
- Minimal total life-cycle cost to own and operate (i.e., minimal total ownership cost)
- Maintenance concepts that optimize readiness while drawing upon both acquirer and supplier sources
- Data management and configuration management that facilitate cost-effective product support throughout the product's use by the acquirer

The modification of requirements due to approved requirement changes is covered by the "maintain" function of this specific practice, whereas the administration of requirements changes is covered by the Requirements Management process area.

Refer to the Solicitation and Supplier Agreement Development process area for more information about developing solicitation packages and supplier agreements.

Refer to the Acquisition Technical Solution process area for more information about design constraints.

Typical Acquirer Work Products

1. Contractual requirements

Subpractices

1. Develop functional requirements necessary for development of alternative solutions and the product by the supplier.

   Functional requirements or definition of functionality can include actions, sequence, inputs, outputs, or other information that communicates the manner in which the product will be used. Functionality required may be prioritized as Critical/Must-Have, Good-to-Have, and Optional requirements.

2. Develop requirements of the interface between the acquired product and other products in the intended environment.

   Requirements for interfaces are defined in terms of origination, destination, stimulus, data characteristics for software, and electrical and mechanical characteristics for hardware.

3. Develop requirements for verification and validation of the product developed by the supplier.

Requirements for verification and validation typically include types and coverage of testing and review to be carried out in the supplier's and acquirer's environment. Testing requirements may include mirroring the production environment by the supplier, type of test data to be used, and simulated testing for interfaces with other products.

Review requirements may include the form of review to be used (e.g., walkthrough, prototype review) and the required participants for reviews.

4. Develop requirements and constraints in technical terms necessary for development of alternative solutions and the product developed by the supplier.

   Refer to the Acquisition Technical Solution process area for defining design constraints.

   Design constraints express the qualities and performance points that are critical to the success of the product in the acquirer's operational environment. They account for customer requirements in the context of multiple interoperable products. The project needs to identify any dependencies on planned or existing products. This must take project or program constraints into account (e.g., affordability and schedule constraints).

   Acquirers may accelerate the development of technical requirements and design constraints by reusing shared or common constraints or requirements and their associated test cases from previous acquisitions or by leveraging the supplier's previous product developments.

5. Establish and maintain relationships between requirements for consideration during change management and requirements allocation.

   Relationships between requirements can aid in evaluating the impact of changes. Expected requirements volatility is also a key factor in anticipating scope changes and supporting the acquirer's selection of the appropriate acquisition type.

SP 2.2   Allocate Contractual Requirements

Allocate the requirements for each supplier deliverable.

The requirements for each supplier deliverables are documented. In some cases, this includes allocation of technical requirements to third-party products that must be used by the supplier (e.g., commercial off-the-shelf products).

Typical Acquirer Work Products

1. Requirement allocation sheets

Subpractices

1. Allocate requirements to supplier deliverables.

2. Allocate design constraints to supplier deliverables.

3. Document relationships among allocated requirements and design constraints.

   Relationships include dependencies in which a change in one requirement may affect other requirements.

4. Allocate requirements to suppliers.

   In situations where multiple suppliers are involved in developing the technical solution, different products or product components may be allocated to different suppliers.

SG 3   Analyze and Validate Requirements

The requirements are analyzed and validated.

Analyses are performed to determine what impact the intended operational environment will have on the ability to satisfy the stakeholders' needs, expectations, constraints, and interfaces. Considerations, such as feasibility, mission needs, cost constraints, potential market size, and acquisition strategy, must all be taken into account, depending on the product context.

The objectives of the analyses are to determine candidate requirements for product concepts that will satisfy stakeholder needs, expectations, and constraints, and then to translate these concepts into requirements. In parallel with this activity, the parameters that will be used to evaluate the effectiveness of the product are determined based on customer input and the preliminary product concept.

Requirements are validated to increase the probability that the resulting product will perform as intended in the acquirer's environment.

SP 3.1   Establish Operational Concepts and Scenarios

Establish and maintain operational concepts and associated scenarios.

Operational concepts or concepts of operations give an overall description of the way in which an acquired product is intended to be used or operated, deployed, supported (including maintenance and sustainment), and disposed of. For that, the acquirer takes design constraints explicitly into account. For example, the operational concept for a satellite-based communications product is quite different from one based on landlines.

In contrast, an operational scenario is a sequence of events that might occur in the use of the acquired product and that make explicit some stakeholder intentions. Typically, operational scenarios are derived from business process descriptions and operational concepts.

The operational concepts and scenarios are refined as solution decisions are made and more detailed requirements are developed. They are evolved to facilitate the validation of the technical solutions delivered by the supplier.

Typical Acquirer Work Products

1. Operational concepts
2. Operational scenarios
3. Requirements

Subpractices

1. Develop operational concepts and scenarios that include functionality, performance, maintenance, support, and disposal as appropriate.

   Identify and develop concepts and scenarios, consistent with the level of detail in the stakeholder needs, expectations, and constraints, in which the proposed product is expected to operate.

2. Define the environment the product will operate in, including boundaries and constraints.

3. Review operational concepts and scenarios to refine and discover requirements.

   Operational concept and scenario development is an iterative process. The reviews should be held periodically to ensure that they agree with the requirements. The review may be in the form of a walkthrough.

4. Develop a detailed operational concept, as products and product components are developed by the supplier, that defines the interaction of the product, the end user, and the environment, and that satisfies the operational, maintenance, support, and disposal needs.

SP 3.2   Analyze Requirements

Analyze requirements to ensure that they are necessary and sufficient.

As contractual requirements are defined, their relationship to customer requirements must be understood. In light of the operational concept and scenarios, the contractual requirements are analyzed to determine whether they are necessary and sufficient to meet the customer requirements. The analyzed requirements then provide the basis for more detailed and precise requirements throughout the project life cycle.

One of the other actions is the determination of which key requirements will be used to track technical progress. For instance, the weight of a product or size of a software product may be monitored through development based on its risk.

Typical Acquirer Work Products

1. Requirements defects reports
2. Proposed requirements changes to resolve defects
3. Key requirements
4. Technical performance measures

Subpractices

1. Analyze stakeholder needs, expectations, constraints, and external interfaces to remove conflicts and to organize into related subjects.
2. Analyze requirements to determine whether they satisfy the objectives of higher-level requirements.
3. Analyze requirements to ensure that they are complete, feasible, realizable, and verifiable.
4. Identify key requirements that have a strong influence on cost, schedule, functionality, risk, or performance.
5. Identify technical performance measures that will be tracked during the acquisition effort.

   The total number of performance parameters should be the minimum number needed to characterize the major drivers of the product's performance. The number and specificity of performance parameters may change over time. Early in a project or program the requirements baseline should reflect broadly defined measures of technology effectiveness or measures of performance to describe needed capabilities. As a program or project matures and requirements become better defined, the acquirer can define more detailed technical performance measures, if necessary. Data for technical performance measures is provided by the supplier as specified in the supplier agreement.
6. Analyze operational concepts and scenarios to refine the customer needs, constraints, and interfaces and to discover new requirements.

   This analysis may result in more detailed operational concepts and scenarios as well as supporting the derivation of new requirements.

SP 3.3   Analyze Requirements to Achieve Balance

Analyze requirements to balance stakeholder needs and constraints.

Stakeholder needs and constraints can address cost, schedule, performance, functionality, reusable components, maintainability, or risk.

Typical Acquirer Work Products

1. Assessment of risks related to requirements

Subpractices

1. Use proven models, simulations, and prototyping to analyze the balance of stakeholder needs and constraints.

   Results of the analyses can be used to reduce the cost of the product and the risk in acquiring and using the product.

2. Perform a risk assessment on the requirements and design constraints.

3. Examine product life-cycle concepts for impacts of requirements on risks.

SP 3.4   Validate Requirements with Comprehensive Methods

Validate requirements to ensure the resulting product will perform as intended in the user's environment using multiple techniques as appropriate.

The acquirer performs requirements validation early in the acquisition effort to gain confidence that the requirements are capable of guiding a development that results in successful final validation. This activity should be integrated with risk management activities. Mature organizations will typically perform requirements validation in a more sophisticated way using multiple techniques and will broaden the basis of the validation to include other stakeholder needs and expectations. These organizations will typically perform analyses, simulations, or prototypes to ensure that requirements will satisfy stakeholder needs and expectations.

Examples of techniques used for requirements validation include the following:
- Analysis
- Simulations
- Prototyping
- Demonstrations

Typical Acquirer Work Products

1. Records of analysis methods and results

Typical Supplier Deliverables

1. Requirements and validation methods (e.g., prototypes and simulations)

Subpractices

1. Analyze the requirements to determine the risk that the resulting product will not perform appropriately in its intended-use environment.

2. Explore the adequacy and completeness of requirements by developing product representations (e.g., prototypes, simulations, models, scenarios, and storyboards) and by obtaining feedback about them from relevant stakeholders.

   Refer to the Acquisition Validation process area for information about preparing for and performing validation on products and product components.

3. Assess the product and product components as they are developed by the supplier in the context of the validation environment to identify issues and expose unstated needs and customer requirements.

A.3.4 Acquisition Technical Solution

The purpose of Acquisition Technical Solution (ATS) is to develop design constraints and to verify the technical solution of the supplier. The acquirer provides design constraints to the supplier. The product or service is designed and implemented by the supplier consistent with the acquirer's design constraints. The Acquisition Technical Solution process area focuses on the following:

- Developing design constraints for the supplier's technical solution that potentially satisfy an appropriate set of allocated requirements
- Verifying detailed designs for the selected solutions (detailed in the context of containing all the information needed to manufacture, code, or otherwise implement the design as a product or service)
- Analyzing and verifying the development and implementation of the supplier's technical solution to ensure contractual requirements are met

Typically, these activities interactively support each other. Some level of design, at times fairly detailed, may be needed for the acquirer to select solutions. Prototypes created by the supplier may be used as a means for the acquirer to gain sufficient knowledge to develop more comprehensive design constraints.

Related Process Areas

Refer to the Acquisition Requirements Development process area for more information about requirements allocations, establishing an operational concept, and interface requirements definition.

Refer to the Acquisition Verification process area for more information about conducting reviews and verifying that the product and product components meet requirements.

Specific Goal and Practice Summary

SG 1 Develop Technical Constraints

    SP 1.1   Establish a Definition of Design Constraints

    SP 1.2   Verify Design with Comprehensive Methods

SG 2 Analyze and Verify Technical Solution

    SP 2.1   Analyze Technical Solution

    SP 2.2   Analyze Interface Descriptions for Completeness

Specific Practices by Goal

SG 1   Develop Technical Constraints

Constraints for the technical solution are developed and satisfied by the supplier's design.

SP 1.1   Establish a Definition of Design Constraints

Determine the design constraints for a technical solution.

Design constraints express the qualities and performance points that are critical to the success of the product in the acquirer's operational environment. Design constraints may include standards and design rules governing development of products and their interfaces. The criteria for interfaces are often associated with safety, security, durability, and mission-critical characteristics.

To achieve high levels of reuse and interoperability, acquirers typically establish common design constraints for products or product families that can be deployed in one or more domains. Common design constraints (also reference architectures or product line architectures) provide a proven bundling of products, applications, and configurations. They provide a base for creating technical solutions that use design constraints more reliably and cost effectively.

Example tasks for identifying common design criteria may include the following:

- Establishing the structural relations of products and rules regarding interfaces between products
- Identifying external interfaces
- Identifying common products and common interfaces
- Developing reference architectures or frameworks
- Establishing design rules and authority for making decisions
- Defining criteria for physical deployment of software to hardware
- Identifying major reuse approaches and sources including legacy and COTS products

---

Design criteria can be a part of the organizational process assets.

Typical Acquirer Work Products

1. Design constraints including criteria for design and product reuse
2. Guidelines for choosing COTS products
3. Alternative solution screening criteria
4. Selection criteria for final selection

Subpractices

1. Define interface criteria between the supplier's product and the acquirer's operational environment.
2. Develop criteria for the reuse of products and other existing assets like design elements, code components, etc.

   Analyze implications for maintenance when using off-the-shelf or non-developmental items (e.g., COTS, government off the shelf, and reuse).

Examples of implications for maintenance include the following:

- The compatibility with future releases of COTS products
- Configuration management of vendor changes
- Defects in a reused or off-the-shelf product and their resolution
- Unplanned obsolescence of off-the-shelf products

---

3. Establish and maintain criteria against which the supplier's design and product can be evaluated.

   An acquirer typically specifies in the supplier agreement how the supplier has to document the design.

   Examples of attributes, in addition to expected performance, for which design criteria can be established, include the following:

   - Modular
   - Clear
   - Simple
   - Maintainable
   - Verifiable
   - Portable
   - Reliable
   - Accurate
   - Secure
   - Scalable
   - Usable

   ---

4. Identify screening criteria to select a set of alternative solutions for consideration.

5. Develop the criteria for selecting the best alternative solution.

   Criteria should be included that address design issues for the life of the product, such as provisions for more easily inserting new technologies or the ability to better exploit commercial products. Examples include criteria related to open design or open architecture concepts for the alternatives being evaluated.

6. Document the design constraints.

SP 1.2   Verify Design with Comprehensive Methods

Verify design to ensure the resulting product will perform as intended in the acquirer's environment.

The acquirer performs design verification (or technical review or architectural evaluation) throughout the project life cycle to gain confidence that the requirements are capable of guiding a development that results in a satisfactory technical solution. This activity should be integrated with risk management activities. Mature organizations will typically perform design verification in a more sophisticated way using multiple techniques and will broaden the basis of the verification to include other stakeholder needs and expectations.

> Examples of techniques used for design verification include the following:
> - Analysis
> - Simulations
> - Architectural prototyping
> - Demonstrations

Typical Acquirer Work Products

1. Record of analysis methods and results

Typical Supplier Deliverables

1. Alternative solutions
2. Product architecture
3. Product-component designs
4. Technical data package
5. Interface design specifications
6. Interface control documents
7. Interface specification criteria
8. Criteria for design and product-component reuse
9. Make-or-buy analyses
10. Documented solutions, evaluations, and rationale
11. Updated Requirements Traceability Matrix

Subpractices

1. Evaluate each alternative solution or set of solutions presented by suppliers against the selection criteria.
2. Based on the evaluation of alternatives, assess the adequacy of the selection criteria and update the criteria as necessary.
3. Select the best set of alternative solutions that satisfy the established criteria.
4. Ensure that the selected design adheres to applicable design standards and criteria.
5. Ensure that the design adheres to allocated requirements.

   For example, putting required COTS products into the product architecture might modify the requirements and the requirements allocation.

6. Analyze the supplier's design to determine the risk that the resulting product will not perform appropriately in its intended-use environment.

7. Explore the adequacy and completeness of the supplier's design by reviewing product representations (e.g., prototypes, simulations, models, scenarios, and storyboards) and by obtaining feedback about them from relevant stakeholders.

Refer to the Acquisition Verification process area for information about preparing for and performing verification on supplier deliverables.

8. Assess the design as it matures in the context of the requirements to identify issues and expose unstated needs and customer requirements.

SG 2   Analyze and Verify Technical Solution

Analyze and verify the development and implementation of the technical solution by supplier.

The supplier implements the design verified by acquirer under the Verify Design with Comprehensive Methods practice. The implementation by supplier includes development of product components, integration of the components, unit and integration testing of the product, and development of end-user documentation.

The acquirer verifies the implementation to ensure that allocated requirements have been met by the implementation and that the product is ready to be brought into the acquirer environment for further integration and user acceptance testing.

SP 2.1   Verify Technical Solution

Verify the technical solution implementation by supplier to ensure contractual requirements continue to be met.

The acquirer examines a product to determine whether it is ready for production and whether the supplier has accomplished adequate production planning. The verification also examines risk; it determines whether production or production preparations incur unacceptable risks that might breach objectives of schedule, performance, cost, or other established criteria. The acquirer evaluates the full, production-configured product to determine whether it correctly and completely implements all contractual requirements. The acquirer also determines whether the traceability of final contractual requirements to the final production-configured product is maintained.

A successful verification of the technical solution is predicated on the acquirer's determination that the requirements are fully met in the final production configuration, and that production capability forms a satisfactory basis for proceeding into pilots or full-rate production.

Examples of success criteria for the verification of the supplier's technical solution include the following:

- Established and documented product baseline that enables hardware fabrication and software coding to proceed with proper configuration management
- Adequate production processes and measures are in place for the project to succeed
- Risks are managed effectively
- The detailed design is producible within the production budget

---

The acquirer convenes verifications of the technical solution with suppliers and subcontractors, as applicable. Verifications are conducted in an iterative fashion, concurrently with other technical reviews, such as design reviews.

Examples of considerations for follow-up verifications of technical solutions include the following:

- Changes during the production stage of the project, in either materials or manufacturing processes, occur
- Production start-up or re-start occurs after a significant shutdown period
- Production start-up with a new supplier
- Relocation of a manufacturing site

Typical Acquirer Work Products

1. Record of verification methods and results

Typical Supplier Deliverables

1. Product components
2. System documentation
3. Supplier unit and integration test plans
4. Unit and integration test results
5. Updated Requirements Traceability Matrix

Subpractices

1. Ensure that the implementation adheres to applicable standards and criteria.
2. Ensure that the implementation adheres to allocated requirements.
3. Verify that the implementation has been sufficiently tested by the supplier.
4. Verify that the issues identified during testing have been resolved appropriately, with product revisions, if necessary.
5. Ensure that sufficient end-user documentation has been developed and is in alignment with the tested implementation.

SP 2.2   Analyze Interface Descriptions for Completeness

Analyze the product interface descriptions to ensure they are complete and in alignment with the intended environment.

Example criteria for interfaces that typically are the focus of the acquirer's analyses include the following:

- The interface spans organizational boundaries.
- The interface is mission critical.
- The interface is difficult or complex to manage.
- Capability, interoperability, or efficiency issues are associated with the interface.
- The interface impacts multiple acquisition projects or programs.

Typical Acquirer Work Products

1. Record of analysis methods and results

Typical Supplier Deliverables

1. Interface description documents

Subpractices

1. Ensure that the interface description adheres to applicable standards, criteria, and required interface requirements between the supplier's product and acquirer's intended environment.
2. Ensure that the interface description adheres to allocated requirements.
3. Verify that the interfaces have been sufficiently tested by the supplier.
4. Verify that the issues identified during testing have been resolved appropriately, with product revisions, if necessary.

A.3.5 Acquisition Validation

The purpose of Acquisition Validation (AVAL) is to demonstrate that an acquired product or service fulfills its intended use when placed in its intended environment. Validation demonstrates that the acquired product or service, as provided, will fulfill its intended use. In other words, validation ensures that the acquired product or service meets the stakeholders' intentions and customer requirements.

Validation activities are performed early and incrementally throughout the project life cycle. They can be applied to all aspects of the product in any of its intended environments, such as operation, training, manufacturing, maintenance, and support services. The methods employed to accomplish validation can be applied to acquirer work products (such as customer requirements) and supplier deliverables (for example, prototypes developed by the supplier) as well as to the acquired product and service. The acquirer work products and supplier deliverables should be selected on the basis of which are the best predictors of how well the acquired product or service will satisfy stakeholder intentions.

Whenever possible, validation should be accomplished using the product operating in its intended environment. The entire environment can be used or only part of it. The validation environment therefore needs to represent the intended environment for the product or service as well as represent the intended environment suitable for validation activities with acquirer work products or supplier deliverables.

When validation issues are identified, they are referred to the processes associated with the Acquisition Requirements Development or Project Monitoring and Control process areas for resolution.

The specific practices of this process area build on each other in the following way:

- The Select Products for Validation specific practice enables the identification of the product or product component to be validated and the methods to be used to perform the validation.
- The Establish the Validation Environment specific practice enables the determination of the environment that will be used to carry out the validation.
- The Establish Validation Procedures and Criteria specific practice enables the development of validation procedures and criteria that are aligned with the characteristics of selected products, customer constraints on validation, methods, and the validation environment.

- The Perform Validation specific practice enables the performance of validation according to the established methods, procedures, and criteria.

Related Process Areas

Refer to the Acquisition Requirements Development process area for more information about requirements validation.

Specific Goal and Practice Summary

SG 1 Prepare for Validation

   SP 1.1   Select Products for Validation

   SP 1.2   Establish the Validation Environment

   SP 1.3   Establish Validation Procedures and Criteria

SG 2 Validate Products or Services

   SP 2.1   Perform Validation

   SP 2.2   Analyze Validation Results

Specific Practices by Goal

SG 1   Prepare for Validation

Preparation for validation is conducted.

Preparation activities include selecting products and product components for validation and establishing and maintaining the validation environment, procedures, and criteria. The items selected for validation may include only the acquired product or may include appropriate levels of the product components that are used by the supplier to build the product. Any product or product component may be subject to validation, including replacement, maintenance, and training products, to name a few.

The environment required to validate the product or product component is prepared. The environment may be purchased or may be specified, designed, and built. The environments used for verification may be considered in collaboration with the validation environment to reduce cost and improve efficiency or productivity.

SP 1.1   Select Products for Validation

Select products or services to be validated and the validation methods that will be used for each.

Products or services are selected for validation on the basis of their relationship to stakeholder intentions and customer requirements. For each product or service, the scope of the validation (e.g., operational behavior, maintenance, training, and user interface) should be determined.

Examples of products and product components that can be validated include the following:

- Customer requirements and design constraints
- Acquired product and product components (e.g., system, hardware units, software, service documentation)
- User manuals
- Training materials
- Process documentation

Validation methods should be selected early in the life of the project so that they are clearly understood and agreed to by the relevant stakeholders.

The validation methods address the development, maintenance, support, and training for the product or product component as appropriate.

Examples of validation methods include the following:

- Discussions with the users, perhaps in the context of a formal review
- Prototype demonstrations
- Functional demonstrations (e.g., system, hardware units, software, service documentation, user interfaces)
- Pilots of training materials
- Acceptance test of products and product components by end users and other relevant stakeholders
- In the supplier agreement, expectations of suppliers for participation in validation of product and product components are captured.

Typical expectations built into the supplier agreement include the following:

- List of acquired products that need validation by the acquirer before formal acceptance
- List of products that must be validated with customer, users, or other stakeholders by the supplier, and applicable validation standards, procedures, methods, tools and criteria, if any.
- Measurements to be collected and provided by the supplier with regard to validation activities

Typical Acquirer Work Products

1. Lists of products or services selected for validation
2. Validation methods for each product or service
3. Requirements for performing validation for each product or service
4. Validation constraints for each product or service

Subpractices

1. Identify the key principles, features, and phases for product or service validation throughout the life of the project.
2. Determine which customer requirements are to be validated.

   The product or product component must be maintainable and supportable in its intended environment. This specific practice also addresses the actual maintenance, training, and support services that may be delivered along with the product.
3. Select the product or service to be validated.
4. Select the evaluation methods for product or service validation.
5. Review the validation selection, constraints, and methods with relevant stakeholders.

SP 1.2   Establish the Validation Environment

Establish and maintain the environment needed to support validation.

The requirements for the validation environment are driven by the product or service selected, by the type of the work products (e.g., design, prototype, final version), and by the methods of validation. These may yield requirements for the purchase or development of equipment, software, or other resources. The validation environment may include the reuse of existing resources. In this case, arrangements for the use of these resources must be made. Examples of the type of elements in a validation environment include the following:

- Test tools interfaced with the product being validated (e.g., scopes, electronic devices, probes)
- Temporary embedded test software
- Recording tools for dump or further analysis and replay
- Simulated subsystems or components (by software, electronics, or mechanics)
- Simulated interfaced systems (e.g., a dummy warship for testing a naval radar)

- Real interfaced systems (e.g., aircraft for testing a radar with trajectory tracking facilities)
- Facilities and customer-supplied products
- The skilled people to operate or use all the preceding elements
- Dedicated computing or network test environment (e.g., pseudo-operational telecommunications-network testbed or facility with actual trunks, switches, and systems established for realistic integration and validation trials)

Early selection of the products or service to be validated, the work products to be used in the validation, and the validation methods ensure that the validation environment will be available when necessary.

The validation environment should be carefully controlled to provide for replication, analysis of results, and revalidation of problem areas.

Typical Acquirer Work Products

1. Validation environment

Typical Supplier Deliverable

1. Validation environment

Subpractices

1. Identify validation environment requirements.
2. Identify customer-supplied products.
3. Identify reuse items.
4. Identify validation equipment and tools.
5. Identify validation resources that are available for reuse and modification.
6. Plan the availability of resources in detail.

SP 1.3   Establish Validation Procedures and Criteria

Establish and maintain procedures and criteria for validation.

Validation procedures and criteria are defined to ensure that the product or product component will fulfill its intended use when placed in its intended environment. The validation procedures and criteria include validation of maintenance, training, and support services.

They also address validation of requirements and the acquired product or service throughout the project life cycle. Typically, formal user acceptance testing procedures and criteria are established to ensure that the delivered product or service meets stakeholder intentions before it is deployed in the intended environment.

The validation procedures and criteria applicable to the supplier are typically referenced in the solicitation package and supplier agreement.

Examples of sources for validation criteria include the following:
- Business process descriptions
- Customer requirements
- Acceptance criteria
- Standards

Typical Acquirer Work Products

1. Validation procedures
2. Validation criteria
3. Test and evaluation procedures for maintenance, training, and support

Subpractices

1. Review the customer requirements to ensure that issues affecting validation of the acquired product or service are identified and resolved.
2. Document the environment, operational scenario, procedures, inputs, outputs, and criteria for the validation of the acquired product or service.
3. Assess the product or service as it matures in the context of the validation environment to identify validation issues.

SG 2   Validate Products or Services

The products or services are validated to ensure that they are suitable for use in their intended environment.

The validation methods, procedures, and criteria are used to validate the selected products and product components and any associated maintenance, training, and support services using the appropriate validation environment. Validation activities are performed throughout the project life cycle.

SP 2.1   Perform Validation

Perform validation on the selected products or services.

To be acceptable to stakeholders, a product or service must perform as expected in its intended environment.

Validation activities are performed and the resulting data are collected according to the established methods, procedures, and criteria.

The as-run validation procedures should be documented, and the deviations occurring during the execution should be noted, as appropriate.

Typical Acquirer Work Products

1. Validation reports
2. Validation results
3. Validation cross-reference matrix
4. As-run procedures log
5. Operational demonstrations

SP 2.2   Analyze Validation Results

Analyze the results of the validation activities.

The data resulting from validation tests, inspections, demonstrations, or evaluations are analyzed against the defined validation criteria. Analysis reports indicate whether the stakeholders' intentions were met; in the case of deficiencies, these reports document the degree of success or failure and categorize the probable cause of failure. The collected test, inspection, or review results are compared with established acceptance criteria to determine whether to proceed or to address requirements or design issues in the requirements development or technical solution processes.

Analysis reports or as-run validation documentation may also indicate that bad test results are due to a validation procedure problem or a validation environment problem.

Typical Acquirer Work Products

1. Validation deficiency reports
2. Validation issues
3. Procedure change request

Subpractices

1. Compare actual results to expected results.
2. Based on the established validation criteria, identify products and product components that do not perform suitably in their intended operating

environments, or identify problems with the methods, criteria, and/or environment.

3. Analyze the validation data for defects.

4. Record the results of the analysis, and identify issues.

5. Use validation results to compare actual measurements and performance to intended use or operational need.

6. Identify, document, and track action items to closure for any work products that do not pass their validation procedures and criteria.

A.3.6 Acquisition Verification

The purpose of Acquisition Verification (AVER) is to ensure that selected work products meet their contractual requirements. Acquisition verification addresses whether the acquired product, intermediate acquirer work products, and supplier deliverables properly reflect the contractual requirements.

The Acquisition Verification process area involves the following: verification preparation, verification performance, and identification of corrective action.

Verification is inherently an incremental process because it occurs throughout the acquisition of the product or service, beginning with verification of the requirements and plans, progressing through the verification of the evolving work products such as design and test results, and culminating in the verification of the completed product.

The specific practices of this process area build on each other in the following way:

- The Select Work Products for Verification specific practice enables the identification of the work products to be verified, the methods to be used to perform the verification, and the documented requirements to be satisfied by each selected work product.

- The Establish the Verification Environment specific practice enables the determination of the environment that will be used to carry out the verification.

- The Establish Verification Procedures and Criteria specific practice then enables the development of verification procedures and criteria that are aligned with the selected work products, requirements, methods, and characteristics of the verification environment.

- The Perform Verification specific practice conducts the verification according to the available methods, procedures, and criteria.

Peer reviews are an important method for verification of work products and are a proven mechanism for effective defect removal. An important corollary is to develop a better understanding of the work products and the processes that produced them so that defects can be prevented and process improvement opportunities can be identified.

Peer reviews involve a methodical examination of work products by the producers' peers to identify defects and other changes that are needed.

Examples of peer review methods include the following:

- Inspections
- Structured walkthroughs

Related Process Areas

Refer to the Acquisition Validation process area for more information about confirming that a product or product component fulfills its intended use when placed in its intended environment.

Refer to the Acquisition Requirements Development process area for more information about the generation and development of customer and contractual requirements.

Specific Goal and Practice Summary

SG 1 Prepare for Verification

    SP 1.1   Select Work Products for Verification

    SP 1.2   Establish the Verification Environment

    SP 1.3   Establish Verification Procedures and Criteria

SG 2 Verify Selected Work Products

    SP 2.1   Perform Verification

    SP 2.2   Analyze Verification Results and Identify Corrective Action

Specific Practices by Goal

SG 1   Prepare for Verification

Preparation for verification is conducted.

Up-front preparation is necessary to ensure that verification provisions are embedded in the contractual requirements, constraints, plans, and schedules. Verification includes selection, inspection, testing, analysis, and demonstration of acquirer work products and supplier deliverables.

Methods of verification include, but are not limited to, inspections, peer reviews, audits, walkthroughs, analyses, simulations, testing, and demonstrations.

Preparation also entails the definition of support tools, test equipment and software, simulations, prototypes, and facilities.

SP 1.1   Select Work Products for Verification

Select the work products to be verified and the verification methods that will be used for each.

Acquirer work products are selected based on their contribution to meeting project objectives and requirements, and to addressing project risks.

The acquirer selects supplier deliverables for which the supplier must provide verification records. The required methods and criteria for these work products are described in the supplier agreement.

Verification can be performed by the project, as contrasted to Product and Process Quality Assurance, which is performed by an individual or group independent of the project.

Typical acquirer verification activities include review of the solicitation package, supplier agreements and plans, requirements documents, and design constraints developed by the acquirer.

Selection of the verification methods typically begins with involvement in the definition of contractual requirements to ensure that these requirements are verifiable. Re-verification should be addressed by the verification methods to ensure that rework performed on work products does not cause unintended defects. Suppliers should be involved in this selection to ensure that the project's methods are appropriate for the supplier's environment.

Typical Acquirer Work Products

1. Lists of work products selected for verification
2. Verification methods for each selected work product

Typical Supplier Deliverables

1. List of supplier deliverables

Subpractices

1. Identify acquirer work products for verification.

2. Identify the requirements to be satisfied by each selected work product.

3. Identify the verification methods that are available for use.

4. Define the verification methods to be used for each selected work product.

5. Include verification activities and methods to be used in the project plan.

   Refer to the Project Planning process area for information about coordinating with project planning.

6. Establish in the supplier agreement expectations of supplier for verification of supplier deliverables.

> Typical expectations for verification addressed in or referenced by the supplier agreement include the following:
>
> - List of deliverables and other work products that must be verified by the supplier
> - Applicable standards, procedures, methods, tools
> - Criteria for verification of supplier work products, if any
> - Measurements to be collected and provided by the supplier with regard to verification activities
> - Reviews of supplier verification results and corrective actions with the acquirer

SP 1.2   Establish the Verification Environment

Establish and maintain the environment needed to support verification.

An environment must be established to enable verification to take place. The type of environment required will depend on the work products selected for verification and the verification methods used. A peer review may require little more than a package of materials, reviewers, and a room. A product test may require simulators, emulators, scenario generators, data reduction tools, environmental controls, and interfaces with other systems.

The verification environment may be acquired, developed, reused, modified, or a combination of these, depending on the needs of the project.

Typical Acquirer Work Products

1. Verification environment

Subpractices

1. Identify verification environment requirements.

2. Identify verification resources that are available for reuse and modification.

3. Identify verification equipment and tools.

4. Acquire verification support equipment and an environment, such as test equipment and software.

SP 1.3   Establish Verification Procedures and Criteria

Establish and maintain verification procedures and criteria for the selected work products.

Verification criteria are defined to ensure that the work products meet their requirements.

Examples of sources for verification criteria include the following:
- Product and product-component requirements
- Standards
- Organizational policies
- Test type
- Test parameters
- Parameters for trade-off between quality and cost of testing
- Type of work products
- Suppliers

The verification procedures and criteria are typically included in the solicitation package and supplier agreement.

Typical Acquirer Work Products

1. Verification procedures
2. Verification criteria

Subpractices

1. Generate the set of comprehensive, integrated verification procedures for work products and any commercial off-the-shelf products, as necessary.

2. Develop and refine the verification criteria when necessary.

3. Identify the expected results, any tolerances allowed in observation, and other criteria for satisfying the requirements.

4. Identify any equipment and environmental components needed to support verification.

5. Establish in the supplier agreement the verification methods such as acceptance criteria for supplier deliverables and other work products.

6. Analyze operational concepts and scenarios to refine the customer needs, constraints, and interfaces and to discover new requirements.

   These criteria may be defined by the acquirer for critical supplier work products only, as identified under the Select Work Products for Verification practice.

   The peer review is an important and effective engineering method implemented via inspections, structured walkthroughs, or a number of other collegial review methods.

SG 2   Verify Selected Work Products

Selected work products are verified against their contractual requirements.

The verification methods, procedures, and criteria are used to verify the selected work products and any associated maintenance, training, and support services using the appropriate verification environment. Verification activities should be performed throughout the project life cycle.

SP 2.1   Perform Verification

Perform verification on the selected work products.

Verifying acquired products and work products incrementally promotes early detection of problems and can result in the early removal of defects. The results of verification save considerable cost of fault isolation and rework associated with troubleshooting problems.

Typical Acquirer Work Products

1. Verification results
2. Verification reports
3. Demonstrations
4. As-run procedures log

Typical Supplier Deliverables

1. Verification results
2. Verification reports

Subpractices

1. Perform verification of selected work products against their requirements.
2. Record the results of verification activities.

3. Identify action items resulting from verification of work products.

4. Document the "as-run" verification method and the deviations from the available methods and procedures discovered during its performance.

5. Review critical verification results and data for verifications conducted by the supplier.

SP 2.2   Analyze Verification Results

Analyze the results of all verification activities.

Actual results must be compared to established verification criteria to determine acceptability.

The results of the analysis are recorded as evidence that verification was conducted.

For each work product, all available verification results are incrementally analyzed and corrective actions are initiated to ensure that the documented requirements have been met for both acquirer and supplier. Corrective actions are typically integrated into project monitoring activities. Because a peer review is one of several verification methods, peer review data should be included in this analysis activity to ensure that the verification results are analyzed sufficiently. Analysis reports or "as-run" method documentation may also indicate that bad verification results are due to method problems, criteria problems, or a verification environment problem.

Typical Acquirer Work Products

1. Analysis report (e.g., statistics on performances, causal analysis of non-conformances, comparison of the behavior between the real product and models, and trends)

2. Trouble reports

3. Change requests for the verification methods, criteria, and environment

Subpractices

1. Compare actual results to expected results.

2. Based on the established verification criteria, identify products that have not met their requirements or identify problems in the methods, procedures, criteria, and verification environment.

3. Analyze the verification data on defects.

4. Record all results of the analysis in a report.
5. Use verification results to compare actual measurements and performance to technical performance parameters.
6. Provide information on how defects can be resolved (including verification methods, criteria, and verification environment), and formalize it in a plan.

Bibliography

Akao, Yoji. *Quality Function Deployment: Integrating Customer Requirements into Product Design.* Cambridge, MA: Productivity Press, 1990.

Alexander, Christopher. *Notes on the Synthesis of Form.* Cambridge, MA: Harvard University Press, 1964.

Anderson, Robert. "Effective use of information technology: Lessons about state governance structures and processes." Santa Monica, CA: Rand, 2003.

Argyris, Chris, and David A. Schön. *Organizational Learning II: Theory, Method, and Practice.* Upper Saddle River, NJ: Prentice Hall, 1995.

Bass, Len, Paul Clements, and Rick Kazman. *Software Architecture in Practice.* 2nd edition. Boston: Addison-Wesley, 2003.

Bernstein, Peter L. *Against the Gods: The Remarkable Story of Risk.* New York: John Wiley & Sons, 1996.

Black, Rex. *Managing the Testing Process: Practical Tools and Techniques for Managing Hardware and Software Testing.* 2nd edition. New York: Wiley Publishing, 2002.

Blanchard, Benjamin S. *System Engineering Management.* 3rd edition. New York: Wiley, 2003.

Blum, Bruce. *Beyond Programming: To a New Era of Design.* New York: Oxford University Press, 1996.

Boehm, Barry W., and Richard Turner. *Balancing Agility and Discipline: A Guide for the Perplexed.* Boston: Addison-Wesley Professional, 2003.

Bond, Robert. Software contract agreements: negotiating and drafting tactics. Derby: Thorogood Press, 1998.

Bossidy, Larry, and Ram Charan. *Execution: The Discipline of Getting Things Done.* New York: Random House, 2002.

Brooks, Frederick P., Jr. *The Mythical Man-Month: Essays on Software Engineering.* 2nd edition. Reading, MA: Addison-Wesley, 1995.

Brown, Mark G. *Keeping Score: Using the Right Metrics to Drive World-Class Performance.* New York: Quality Resources, 1996.

Center for Quality Management Journal, vol. 2, no. 4, 1993.

Collins, Jim. *Good to Great: Why Some Companies Make the Leap . . . and Others Don't.* New York: HarperCollins, 2001.

Cooper, Robert G. *Winning at New Products: Accelerating the Process from Idea to Launch.* 3rd edition. London: Perseus Books Group, 2001.

Crosby, Philip B. *Quality Is Free.* New York: New American Library, 1979.

Cyert, Richard M., and James G. March. *A Behavioral Theory of the Firm.* 2nd edition. Oxford, UK: Blackwell Publishing, 1992.

Davenport, Thomas H., and Laurence Prusak. *Working Knowledge: How Organizations Manage What They Know.* Boston: Harvard Business School Press, 1997.

De Young, L. "Organizational Support for Software Design." In T. Winograd, ed., *Bringing Design to Software.* Reading, MA: Addison-Wesley, 1996, 253–267.

Dodson, Kathryn M., Hubert F. Hofmann, Gowri S. Ramani, and Deborah K. Yedlin. "Adapting CMMI for Acquisition Organizations: A Preliminary Report." SEI Special Report CMU/SEI-2005-SR-005, June 2006.

Erl, Thomas. *Service-Oriented Architecture (SOA): Concepts, Technology, and Design.* Upper Saddle River, NJ: Prentice Hall, 2005.

Gause, Donald C., and Gerald M. Weinberg. *Exploring Requirements: Quality Before Design.* New York: Dorset House, 1991.

Glass, Robert L. *Software Runaways: Lessons Learned from Massive Software Project Failures.* Upper Saddle River, NJ: Prentice-Hall, 1998.

Goldratt, Eliyahu M. *Critical Chain.* Great Barrington, MA: North River Press, 1997.

Hackman, J. Richard. *Leading Teams: Setting the Stage for Great Performances.* Boston: Harvard Business School Press, 2002.

Hackman, Michael Z., and Craig E. Johnson. *Leadership: A Communication Perspective.* 4th edition. Long Grove, IL: Waveland Press, 2002.

Hagel, John III, and John Seely Brown. *The Only Sustainable Edge: Why Business Strategy Depends on Productive Friction and Dynamic Specialization.* Boston: Harvard Business School Press, 2005.

Hofmann, Hubert F. *Requirements Engineering: A Situated Discovery Process.* Wiesbaden: Gabler, 2000.

Imai, Masaaki. *Kaizen: The Key to Japan's Competitive Success.* New York: McGraw-Hill, 1986.

Kerzner, Harold. *Project Management: A Systems Approach to Planning, Scheduling, and Controlling.* 9th edition. New York: Wiley, 2005.

Kaplan, Robert S., and David P. Norton. *The Strategy Focused Organization: How Balanced Scorecard Companies Thrive in the New Business Environment.* Boston: Harvard Business School Press, 2001.

Kotter, John, Holger Rathgeber, Peter Mueller, and Spenser Johnson. *Our Iceberg Is Melting: Changing and Succeeding Under Any Conditions.* New York: St. Martin's Press, 2006.

Kotter, John P. *Leading Change.* Boston: Harvard Business School Press, 1996.

Kouzes, James M., and Barry Z. Posner. *The Leadership Challenge.* Indianapolis: Jossey-Bass, 1987.

Kuhn, Thomas S. *The Structure of Scientific Revolutions.* 3rd edition. Chicago: University of Chicago Press, 1996.

Lakoff, George. *Women, Fire, and Dangerous Things: What Categories Reveal about the Mind.* Chicago: The University of Chicago Press, 1990.

Liker, Jeffrey, and David Meier. *The Toyota Way Fieldbook.* New York: McGraw-Hill, 2006.

March, James G. *The Pursuit of Organizational Intelligence.* London: Blackwell Publishers, 1999.

Moore, Geoffrey A. *Crossing the Chasm.* Revised Edition. New York: Collins, 2002.

Nelson, Bob, and Ken Blanchard. *1001 Ways to Reward Employees.* New York: Workman Publishing, 1997.

Overly, Michael, and James R. Kalyvas. *Software Agreements Line by Line.* Boston: Aspatore, Inc., 2004.

Pande, Peter S., Robert P. Neuman, and Roland R. Cavanagh. *The Six Sigma Way: How GE, Motorola, and Other Top Companies Are Honing Their Performance.* New York: McGraw-Hill, 2000.

Pfeffer, Jeffrey, and Robert I. Sutton. *Hard Facts, Dangerous Half-Truths and Total Nonsense: Profiting from Evidence-Based Management.* Boston: Harvard Business School Press, 2006.

Prahalad, C. K., and Gary Hamel. "The Core Competence of the Corporation." *Harvard Business Review* 68:3 (May-June 1990): 79–93.

Reinertsen, Donald G. *Managing the Design Factory: A Product Developer's Toolkit.* New York: The Free Press, 1997.

Robertson, Suzanne, and James Robertson. *Mastering the Requirements Process.* Reading, MA: Addison-Wesley, 1999.

Ross, Jeanne W., Peter Weill, and David Robertson. *Enterprise Architecture As Strategy: Creating a Foundation for Business Execution.* Boston: Harvard Business School Press, 2006.

Schein, Edgar H. *Organizational Culture and Leadership.* 3rd edition. Indianapolis: Jossey-Bass, 2004.

Schön, Donald A. *The Reflective Practitioner: How Professionals Think in Action.* Cambridge, UK: Collins, 1983.

Scott, David. *IT Wars: Managing the Business–Technology Weave in the New Millennium.* Charleston, SC: BookSurge, 2005.

Senge, Peter. *The Fifth Discipline: The Art & Practice of the Learning Organization.* New York: Currency, 2006.

Shingo, Shigeo. *A Study of the Toyota Production System.* Cambridge, MA: Productivity Press, 1989.

Treacy, Michael, and Fred Wiersema. *The Discipline of Market Leaders.* Reading, MA: Addison-Wesley, 1995.

Tuckman, B. W. "Developmental sequence in small groups." *Psychological Bulletin* 63 (1965): 384–399.

Wheelwright, Stephen C., and Kim B. Clark. *Revolutionizing Product Development: Quantum Leaps in Speed, Efficiency, and Quality.* New York: The Free Press, 1992.

Womack, James P., and Daniel T. Jones. *Lean Thinking: Banish Waste and Create Wealth in Your Corporation.* New York: Simon & Schuster, 1996.

About the Authors

Hubert F. Hofmann, PMP, and **Deborah K. Yedlin** were members of General Motors' (GM's) global systems development organization during the preparation of this book and were among the principal authors of the initial CMMI for Acquisition (CMMI-ACQ).

Hubert Hofmann, currently with Telefónica Deutschland, was a global senior manager of information systems and services for GM, responsible for standardizing and improving acquisition processes and system delivery. In that role, he led GM's worldwide adoption of the CMMI-ACQ. Dr. Hofmann was a member of the CMMI-ACQ Advisory Board and the CMMI framework architecture team. His past writing includes a highly regarded book on requirements engineering and more than 25 other publications. He holds a Ph.D. in business informatics from the University of Regensburg, Germany.

Deborah Yedlin, currently with Borland Software Corporation, was the global director of verification and validation, information systems and services, at GM. Her work at GM around process improvement and measurement was the catalyst for initiating work with the Software Engineering Institute (SEI) to develop a CMMI model designed for acquiring organizations. Ms. Yedlin was the GM representative on the CMMI Steering Group as the CMMI-ACQ was developed. Her past writings include case studies on the implementation of information systems in academic institutions. Ms. Yedlin holds an MS in information management from Wayne State University and an MBA from Oakland University.

John W. Mishler, a Visiting Scientist in the SEI's acquisition support program, helped pilot an earlier version of the CMMI-ACQ with numerous U.S.

Department of Defense (DoD) program offices. He also has led SEI-independent technical assessments for large DoD software-intensive programs and teaches SEI CMMI and software acquisition courses. As president of the Wayfinding Group, Inc., Dr. Mishler consults in software and systems engineering, aeronautical logistics, and information systems. He holds a Ph.D. in public policy from The George Washington University.

Susan Kushner is currently a senior technical writer for an industry leader in advanced network storage solutions. She was formerly a writer and editor at the SEI, where she served as the communications point of contact for the acquisition support program. In that role, she planned, organized, and edited technical reports and other materials about the acquisition of software-intensive systems. Ms. Kushner holds an MS in technical communications from Rensselaer Polytechnic Institute.

The authors all welcome your feedback on this book, which may be addressed to: hubert.hofmann@hotmail.com and debbie.yedlin@borland.com.

Index

Page numbers followed by *f* and *t* refer to figures and tables respectively.

Learn More About the Carnegie Mellon® Software Engineering Institute (SEI)

The 2006 SEI Annual Report is available at *www.sei.cmu.edu/annual-report*. It describes the accomplishments of the SEI during fiscal year 2006 (October 1, 2005 through September 30, 2006). The report profiles people at the SEI whose contributions are shaping the future of software engineering and transferring methods and techniques to the broad software community.

The SEI Guide to Products and Services is available at *www.sei.cmu.edu/publications/guide.pdf*. It is a complete catalog of all the SEI's tools and methods, services, courses, conferences, credentials, books, and opportunities to collaborate with the SEI on research.

To obtain a hard copy of these documents, contact SEI Customer Relations at 1-888-201-4479 or *customer-relations@sei.cmu.edu*.

Software Engineering Institute
Carnegie Mellon

ESSENTIAL GUIDES TO CMMI

CMMI®, Second Edition: Guidelines for Process Integration and Product Improvement

Mary Beth Chrissis, Mike Konrad, and Sandy Shrum

0-321-27967-0

The definitive guide to CMMI—now updated for CMMI v1.2! Whether you are new to CMMI or already familiar with some version of it, this book is the essential resource for managers, practitioners, and process improvement team members who to need to understand, evaluate, and/or implement a CMMI model.

CMMI® Assessments: Motivating Positive Change

Marilyn Bush and Donna Dunaway

0-321-17935-8

Written for executives, managers, technical professionals, and assessors themselves, this book illuminates every phase of the assessment process, from planning through post-assessment follow-up.

CMMI® Survival Guide: Just Enough Process Improvement

Suzanne Garcia and Richard Turner

0-321-42277-5

Practical guidance for any organization, large or small, considering or undertaking process improvement, with particular advice for implementing CMMI successfully in resource-strapped environments.

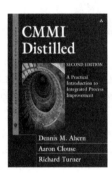

CMMI® Distilled, Second Edition: A Practical Introduction to Integrated Process Improvement

Dennis M. Ahern, Aaron Clouse, and Richard Turner

0-321-18613-3

This book is a compact, informative guide to CMMI for practitioners, executives, and managers and includes expanded coverage of how process improvement can impact business goals, and how management can support CMMI adoption.

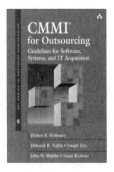

CMMI® for Outsourcing: Guidelines for Software, Systems, and IT Acquisition

Hubert F. Hofmann, Deborah K. Yedlin, Joseph Elm, John W. Mishler, and Susan Kushner

0-321-47717-0

Best practices for outsourcing and acquiring technology within the CMMI framework, reflecting initial results from a joint General Motors-Software Engineering Institute project, and written for both vendors and suppliers needing to improve their processes.

CMMI® SCAMPI Distilled: Appraisals for Process Improvement

Dennis M. Ahern, Jim Armstrong, Aaron Clouse, Jack R. Ferguson, Will Hayes, and Kenneth E. Nidiffer

0-321-22876-6

Offers concise, realistic guidance for every stage of the SCAMPI process, and demonstrates how to overcome the obstacles to a successful appraisal.

For more information on these and other books in The SEI Series in Software Engineering, please visit www.awprofessional.com/seiseries

informIT

BOOKS ONLINE
ENABLED

THIS BOOK IS SAFARI ENABLED

INCLUDES FREE 45-DAY ACCESS TO THE ONLINE EDITION

The Safari® Enabled icon on the cover of your favorite technology book means the book is available through Safari Bookshelf. When you buy this book, you get free access to the online edition for 45 days.

Safari Bookshelf is an electronic reference library that lets you easily search thousands of technical books, find code samples, download chapters, and access technical information whenever and wherever you need it.

TO GAIN 45-DAY SAFARI ENABLED ACCESS TO THIS BOOK:

- Go to **http://www.awprofessional.com/safarienabled**

- Complete the brief registration form

- Enter the coupon code found in the front of this book on the "Copyright" page

Addison
Wesley

If you have difficulty registering on Safari Bookshelf or accessing the online edition, please e-mail customer-service@safaribooksonline.com.

Register Your Book

at www.awprofessional.com/register

You may be eligible to receive:

- Advance notice of forthcoming editions of the book
- Related book recommendations
- Chapter excerpts and supplements of forthcoming titles
- Information about special contests and promotions throughout the year
- Notices and reminders about author appearances, tradeshows, and online chats with special guests

Contact us

If you are interested in writing a book or reviewing manuscripts prior to publication, please write to us at:

Editorial Department
Addison-Wesley Professional
75 Arlington Street, Suite 300
Boston, MA 02116 USA
Email: AWPro@aw.com

Addison-Wesley

Visit us on the Web: http://www.awprofessional.com

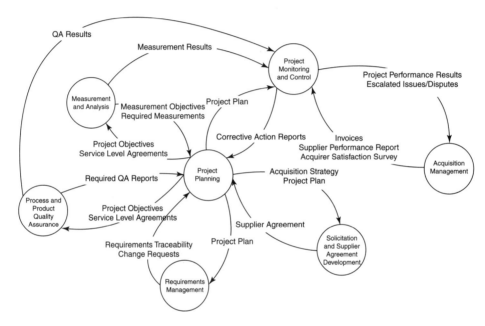

Level 2 process areas